PRODUCT PLANNING

PRODUCT PLANNING

A. EDWARD SPITZ, EDITOR
ASSOCIATE PROFESSOR
EASTERN MICHIGAN UNIVERSITY

AUERBACH® publishers

princeton
philadelphia
new york
london

To

Shirley
Bernie
Ken
Ellen

and

Suzanne

CONTENTS

LIST OF CONTRIBUTORS

Lee Adler
B. Charles Ames
Theodore L. Angelus
Warren B. Brown
C. K. Buell
Donald K. Clifford, Jr.
William J. Constandse
William E. Cox, Jr.
C. Merle Crawford
Fred Danzig
Gerald I. Eyrich
James H. Flournoy
Dennis Gensch
Lawrence D. Gibson
Lewis N. Goslin
Paul E. Green
David K. Hardin
Seymour W. Herwald
Philip Kotler

David J. Luck
Sidney Margolius
John H. Murphy
Robert N. Reitter
Barry M. Richman
Thomas S. Robertson
Richard S. Rosenbloom
Walker Sandbach
Donald A. Schon
G. E. Seavoy
Allan D. Schocker
Leonard S. Simon
Thomas H. F. Smith
William E. Souder
Dik Warren Twedt
Kenneth Van Dyck
William F. Weigel
Walter B. Wentz

PREFACE

Product Planning encompasses a diversified collection of readings designed specifically to make product planning and management more relevant to students and marketers alike. The need to understand the importance of and risk involved with innovation precedes the actual new product process of search to commercialization of new product ideas and corporate objectives. The product planning process is a step-by-step procedure that firms follow from product idea to product introduction into the marketplace. Product auditing, which should be given more importance, can be the difference between continued success or failure of a product offering or the difference between red ink or black ink on a company's books. It follows the product planning process. The legal ramifications of new products sold in the marketplace enforce corporate responsibility upon management and ethical considerations dealing with new product introductions. Even though users of new products are protected by laws and warranties, implied or express, buyers are still faced with responsibilities and dilemmas concerning their rights and corporate obligations toward them.

Since competition, costs, and legal aspects of new product offerings play roles in how and when business firms will introduce new products into the marketplace, there have been new product trends to by-pass the step-by-step process. Upon the introduction of a new-product offering, market research methods have enabled firms to better measure the performance of their new offerings so that they may proceed in new directions with their new products.

The selections were selected and arranged in such a manner as to ensure a relevant flow of information that relates one to the other and to the reader in concurrent fashion. There were countless selections available and many good ones had to be omitted for lack of space.

My sincere thanks are expressed to the authors and publications for their willingness to allow reprint privileges. Special thanks are due to Mrs. LaDona Ellis and Mrs. Joanne Yinger who assisted in preparation of the volume. I am especially appreciative of Lawrence X. Tarpey, Parker Worthing. Earl A. Roth, and Robert J. Williams for their encouragement and support.

Ann Arbor, Michigan   A. Edward Spitz
May 1, 1972

PRODUCT PLANNING

PART I
THE INNOVATING SYSTEM
OF PRODUCT DEVELOPMENT

1

THE SYSTEMS APPROACH

The annals of businesses in the United States point to the evergrowing awareness that innovation plays a crucial role in the continued growth and development of the country. As the cost of living continues to rise, many products are being priced out of reach of the average consumer. To add to their woes, American businessmen are realizing that competition is becoming increasingly keener as foreign producers begin to use cost-saving and more productive machinery and systems to compete at lower prices with them. Thus the development of new products, the design of new systems, and the introduction of new services can be the salvation for American businesses today.

To satisfy the ultimate buyer today, which in turn means more operating profits, companies have to allot more money and more time in developing newer and better products that consumers are demanding or willing to purchase. Various facets of new product development are too time-consuming and too complex for the key executive, who often is a generalist, to make decisions on his own. Too many ramifications involving financing, production, marketing, and the law, deem it undesirable for a single executive to make important decisions involving a great deal of time and money. Mistakes can be massive and costly. Division of labor into specialists and the need for diversity of opinion to reduce the cost of time and dollars warrant the need for a holistic approach to planning new products for commercial use. A systems approach utilizes the knowledge and experience of management of various functional groups, the specialists within an organization. The holistic, or systems, approach can reduce the possibility of the United States becoming a second-rate power and a debtor nation, which has long been a prevailing concern of American business and the federal government. Increased productivity, increased innovation, and the control of inflationary trends, or a combination thereof, can keep the United States on top as the largest creditor nation in the world. To reduce the reliance of decision making on one man, many American firms have adopted the systems approach. This approach underscores the need for the various members of the firm to work together as a single cohesive force to produce and market products that consumers will purchase at a price they have asked for. The following article discusses the need for such an approach and introduce the hallmarks for sound product innovations.

SYSTEMS APPROACH
TO MARKETING
BY LEE ADLER

More and more businessmen today recognize that corporate success is, in most cases, synonymous with marketing success and with the coming of age of a new breed of professional managers. They find it increasingly important not only to pay lip service to the marketing concept but to do something about it in terms of (a) customer orientation, rather than navel-gazing in the factory, (b) organizational revisions to implement the marketing concept, and (c) a more orderly approach to problem solving.

In an increasing number of companies we see more conscious and formal efforts to apply rational, fact-based methods for solving marketing problems, and greater recognition of the benefits these methods offer. While these benefits may be newly realized, there is nothing new about the underlying philosophy; in the parlance of military men and engineers, it is the systems approach. For, whether we like it or not, marketing is, by defintion, a system, if we accept Webster's definition of system as "an assemblage of objects united by some form of regular interaction or interdependence." Certainly, the interaction of such "objects" as product, pricing, promotion, sales calls, distribution, and so on fits the definition.

There is an expanding list of sophisticated applications of systems theory—and not in one but in many sectors of the marketing front. The construction of mathematical and/or logical models to describe, quantify, and evaluate alternate marketing strategies and mixes is an obvious case in

EDITOR'S NOTE: From *Harvard Business Review,* May-June 1967, pp. 346-359. Reprinted by permission of the publisher and the author. Copyright © 1967 by the President and Fellows of Harvard College.

point. So, too, is the formulation of management information systems[1] and of marketing plans with built-in performance measurements of predetermined goals. But no less vital is the role of the systems approach in the design and sale of products and services. When J. P. Stevens Company color-harmonizes linens and bedspreads, and towels and bath mats, it is creating a *product* system. And when Avco Corporation sells systems management to the space exploration field, involving the marriage of many scientific disciplines as well as adherence to budgetary constraints, on-time performance, and quality control, it is creating a *service* system.

In this article I shall discuss the utilization of the systems concept in marketing in both quantitative and qualitative ways with case histories drawn from various industries. In doing so, my focus will be more managerial and philosophical than technical, and I will seek to dissipate some of the hocus-pocus, glamor, mystery, and fear which pervade the field. The systems concept is not esoteric or "science fiction" in nature (although it sometimes *sounds* that way in promotional descriptions). Its advantages are not subtle or indirect; as we shall see, they are as real and immediate as decision making itself. The limitations are also real, and these, too, will be discussed.

(Readers interested in a brief summary of the background and the conceptual development of the systems approach may wish to turn to the Appendix at the end of this article.)

PROMISING APPLICATIONS

Now let us look at some examples of corporate application of the systems approach. Here we will deal with specific parts or "subsystems" of the total marketing system. Exhibit 1-1 is a schematic portrayal of these relationships.

Products and Services

The objective of the systems approach in product management is to provide a complete "offering" to the market rather than merely a product. If the purpose of business is to create a customer at a profit, then the needs of the customer must be carefully attended to; we must, in short, study what the customer is buying or wants to buy, rather than what we are trying to sell.

In the consumer products field we have forged ahead in understanding that the customer buys nutrition (not bread), beauty (not cosmetics), warmth (not fuel oil). But in industrial products this concept has been slower in gaining a foothold. Where it has gained a foothold, it expresses itself in two ways: the creation of a complete product system sold (1) as a

Subsystems

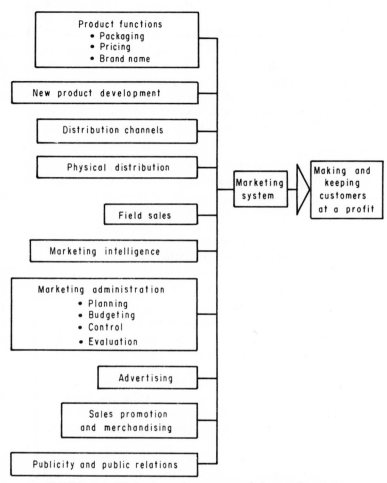

Exhibit 1-1. Marketing subsystems and the total system.

unit, or (2) as a component or components which are part of a large consumption system.

Perhaps the most eloquent testimony to the workability and value of the systems approach comes from companies that have actually used it. For a good example let us turn to the case of the Carborundum Company. This experience is especially noteworthy because it comes from industrial marketing, where, as just indicated, progress with the systems concept has generally been slow.

Birth of the Concept. Founded in 1894, the company was content for many years to sell abrasives. It offered an extremely broad line of grinding wheels, coated abrasives, and abrasive grain, with a reputed capacity for 200,000 different products of varying type, grade, and formulation. But the focus was on the product.

In the mid-1950's, Carborundum perceived that the market for abrasives could be broadened considerably if—looking at abrasives through customers' eyes—it would see the product as fitting into *metal polishing, cleaning, or removal systems*. Now Carborundum is concerned with all aspects of abrading—the machine, the contact wheel, the workpiece, the labor cost, the overhead rate, the abrasive, and, above all, the customer's objective. In the words of Carborundum's president, W. H. Wendel:

That objective is never the abrasive per se, but rather the creation of a certain dimension, a type of finish, or a required shape, always related to a minimum cost. Since there are many variables to consider, just one can be misleading. To render maximum service, Carborundum (must offer) a complete system.[2]

Organization Overhaul. To offer such a system, management had to overhaul important parts of the organization:

(1) The company needed to enhance its knowledge of the total system. As Wendel explains:

We felt we had excellent knowledge of coated abrasive products, but that we didn't have the application and machine know-how in depth. To be really successful in the business, we had to know as much about the machine tools as we did the abrasives.[3]

To fill this need, Carborundum made three acquisitions—The Tysaman Machine Company, which builds heavy-duty snagging, billet grinding and abrasive cut-off machines; Curtis Machine Company, a maker of belt sanders; and Pangborn Corporation, which supplied systems capability in abrasive blast cleaning and finishing.

(2) The company's abrasive divisions were reorganized, and the management of them was realigned to accommodate the new philosophy and its application. The company found that *centering responsibility for the full system in one profit center* proved to be the most effective method of coordinating approaches in application engineering, choice of distribution channels, brand identification, field sales operations, and so forth. This method was particularly valuable for integrating the acquisitions into the new program.

(3) An Abrasives Systems Center was established to handle development work and to solve customer problems.

(4) Technical conferences and seminars were held to educate customers on the new developments.

(5) Salesmen were trained in machine and application knowledge.

Planning. A key tool in the systems approach is planning—in particular, the use of what I like to call "total business plans." (This term emphasizes the contrast with company plans that cover only limited functions.) At Carborundum, total business plans are developed with extreme care by the operating companies and divisions. Very specific objectives are established, and then detailed action programs are outlined to achieve these objectives. The action programs extend throughout the organization, including the manufacturing and development branches of the operating unit. Management sets specific dates for the completion of action steps and defines who is responsible for them. Also, it carefully measures results against established objectives. This is done both in the financial reporting system and in various marketing committees.

Quantitative Methods. Carborundum has utilized various operations research techniques, like decision tree analysis and PERT, to aid in molding plans and strategies. For example, one analysis, which concerned itself with determining the necessity for plant expansion, was based on different possible levels of success for the marketing plan. In addition, the computer has been used for inventory management, evaluation of alternate pricing strategies for systems selling, and the measurement of marketing achievements against goals.

It should be noted, though, that these quantitative techniques are management tools only and that much of the application of systems thinking to the redeployment of Carborundum's business is qualitative in nature.

Gains Achieved. As a consequence of these developments, the company has opened up vast new markets. To quote Carborundum's president again:

Customers don't want a grinding wheel, they want metal removed. . . . The U.S. and Canadian market for abrasives amounts to $700 million a year. But what companies spend on stock removal—to bore, grind, cut, shape, and finish metal—amounts to $30 billion a year.[4]

Illustrating this market expansion in the steel industry is Carborundum's commercial success with three new developments—hot grinding, an arborless wheel to speed metal removal and cut grinding costs, and high-speed conditioning of carbon steel billets. All represent conversions from nonabrasive methods. Carborundum now also finds that the close relationship with customers gives it a competitive edge, opens top customer management doors, gains entrée for salesmen with prospects they had never been able to "crack" before. Perhaps the ultimate accolade is the company's report that customers even come to the organization itself, regarding it as a consultant as well as a supplier.

Profitable Innovation

The intense pressure to originate successful new products cannot be met without methodologies calculated to enhance the probabilities of profitable innovation. The systems approach has a bearing here, too. Exhibit 1-2 shows a model for "tracking" products through the many stages of ideation, development, and testing to ultimate full-scale commercialization. This diagram is in effect a larger version of the "New Product Development" box in Exhibit 1-1.

Observe that this is a logical (specifically, sequential), rather than numerical, model. While some elements of the total system (e.g., alternate distribution channels and various media mixes) can be analyzed by means of operations research techniques, the model has not been cast in mathematical terms. Rather, the flow diagram as a whole is used as a checklist to

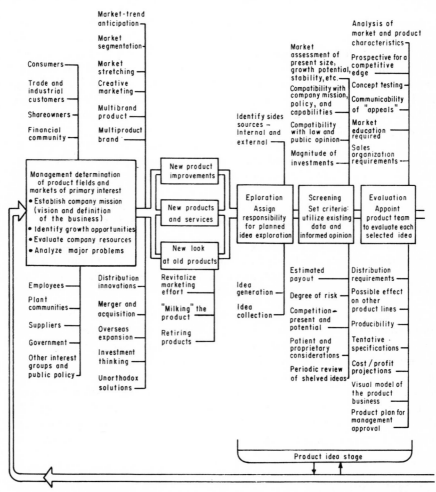

Exhibit 1-2. Work flow and systems chart for management of new products. (*Note:* This flow diagram was developed by Paul E. Funk, President, and the staff of McCann/ITSM, Inc.)

make sure "all bases are covered" and to help organize the chronological sequence of steps in new product development. It also serves as a conceptual foundation for formal PERT application, should management desire such a step, and for the gradual development of a series of equations linking together elements in the diagrams, should it seem useful to experiment with mathematical models.

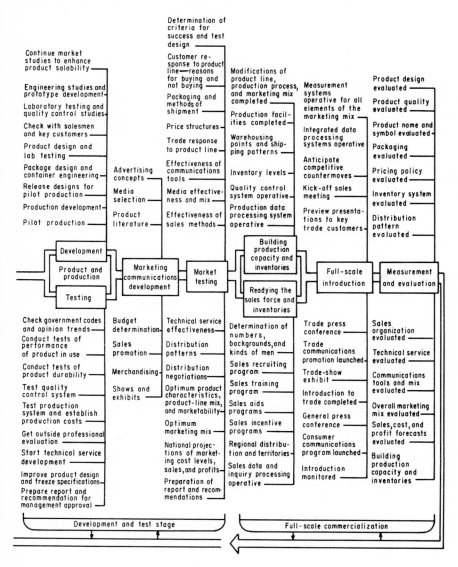

Marketing Intelligence

The traditional notion of marketing research is fast becoming antiquated. For it leads to dreary chronicles of the past rather than focusing on the present and shedding light on the future. It is particularistic, tending to concentrate on the study of tiny fractions of a marketing problem rather than on the problem as a whole. It lends itself to assuaging the curiosity of the moment, to fire-fighting, to resolving internecine disputes. It is a slave to technique. I shall not, therefore, relate the term *marketing research* to the systems approach—although I recognize, of course, that some leading businessmen and writers are breathing new life and scope into the ideas referred to by that term.

The role of the systems approach is to help evolve a *marketing intelligence* system tailored to the needs of each marketer. Such a system would serve as the ever-alert nerve center of the marketing operation. It would have these major characteristics:

1. Continuous surveillance of the market.
2. A team of research techniques used in tandem.
3. A network of data sources.
4. Integrated analysis of data from the various sources.
5. Effective utilization of automatic data-processing equipment to distill mountains of raw information speedily.
6. Strong concentration not just on reporting findings but also on practical, action-oriented recommendations.

Concept in Use. A practical instance of the use of such an intelligence system is supplied by Mead Johnson Nutritionals (division of Mead Johnson & Company), manufacturers of Metrecal, Pablum, Bib, Nutrament, and other nutritional specialties. As Exhibit 1—3 shows, the company's Marketing Intelligence Department has provided information from these sources:

—A continuing large-scale market study covering attitudinal and behavioral data dealing with weight control.

—Nielsen store audit data, on a bimonthly basis.

—A monthly sales audit conducted among a panel of 100 high-volume food stores in 20 markets to provide advance indications of brand share shifts.

—Supermarket warehouse withdrawal figures from Time, Inc.'s new service, Selling Areas-Marketing, Inc.

—Salesmen's weekly reports (which, in addition to serving the purposes of sales management control, call for reconnaissance on competitive promotions, new product launches, price changes, and so forth).

—Advertising expenditure data, by media class, from the company's accounting department.

—Figures on sales and related topics from company factories.

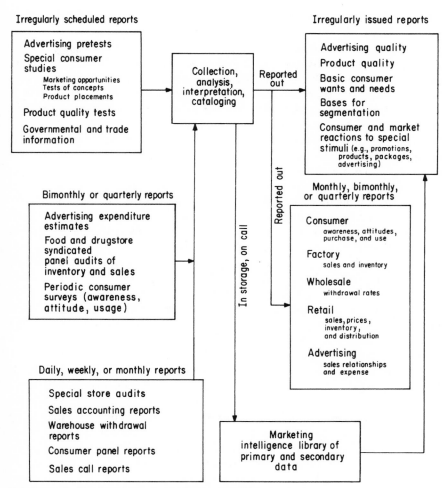

Irregularly scheduled reports

Advertising pretests
Special consumer
studies
  Marketing opportunities
  Tests of concepts
  Product placements
Product quality tests
Governmental and trade
information

Bimonthly or quarterly reports

Advertising expenditure
estimates
Food and drugstore
syndicated
panel audits of
inventory and sales
Periodic consumer
surveys (awareness,
attitude, usage)

Daily, weekly, or monthly reports

Special store audits
Sales accounting reports
Warehouse withdrawal
reports
Consumer panel reports
Sales call reports

Collection,
analysis,
interpretation,
cataloging

Reported
out

In storage, on call

Reported out

Irregularly issued reports

Advertising quality
Product quality
Basic consumer
wants and needs
Bases for
segmentation
Consumer and market
reactions to special
stimuli (e.g., promotions,
  products, packages,
  advertising)

Monthly, bimonthly,
or quarterly reports

Consumer
  awareness, attitudes,
  purchase, and use
Factory
  sales and inventory
Wholesale
  withdrawal rates
Retail
  sales, prices,
  inventory,
  and distribution
Advertising
  sales relationships
  and expense

Marketing
intelligence library of
primary and secondary
data

Exhibit 1-3. Mead Johnson's marketing intelligence system.

—Competitive advertising expenditure and exposure data, supplied by
the division's advertising agencies at periodic intervals.

—A panel of weight-conscious women.

To exemplify the type of outputs possible from this system, Mead
Johnson will be able, with the help of analyses of factory sales data,
warehouse withdrawal information, and consumer purchases from Nielsen
to monitor transactions at each stage of the flow of goods through the
distribution channel and to detect accumulations or developing shortages.
Management will also be able to spot sources of potential problems in time
to deal with them effectively. For example, if factory sales exceed consumer
purchases, more promotional pressure is required. By contrast, if factory

sales lag behind consumer purchases, sales effort must be further stimulated.

Similarly, the company has been able to devise a practical measurement of advertising's effectiveness in stimulating sales—a measurement that is particularly appropriate to fast-moving packaged goods. By relating advertising outlays and exposure data to the number of prospects trying out a product during a campaign (the number is obtained from the continuing consumer survey), it is possible to calculate the advertising cost of recruiting such a prospect. By persisting in such analyses during several campaigns, the relative value of alternative advertising appoaches can be weighed. Since measurement of the sales, as opposed to the communications, effects of promotion is a horrendously difficult, costly, and chancy process, the full significance of this achievement is difficult to exaggerate.

Benefits Realized. Mead Johnson's marketing intelligence system has been helpful to management in a number of ways. In addition to giving executives early warning of new trends and problems, and valuable insights into future conditions, it is leading to a systematic *body* of knowledge about company markets rather than to isolated scraps of information. This knowledge in turn should lead ultimately to a theory of marketing in each field that will explain the mysteries that baffle marketers today. What is more, the company expects that the system will help to free its marketing intelligence people from fire-fighting projects so that they can concentrate on long-term factors and eventually be more consistently creative.

Despite these gains, it is important to note that Mead Johnson feels it has a long road still to travel. More work is needed in linking individual data banks. Conceptual schemes must be proved out in practice; ways must still be found to reduce an awesome volume of data, swelled periodically by new information from improved sources, so as to make intelligence more immediately accessible to decision makers. And perhaps the biggest problem of the moment, one underlying some of the others, is the difficulty in finding qualified marketing-oriented programmers.

Physical Distribution

A veritable revolution is now taking place in physical distribution. Total systems are being evolved out of the former hodgepodge of separate responsibilities, which were typically scattered among different departments of the same company. These systems include traffic and transportation, warehousing, materials handling, protective packaging, order processing, production planning, inventory control, customer service, market forecasting, and plant and warehouse site selection. Motivating this revolution are the computer, company drives to reduce distribution costs, and innovations in transportation, such as jet air freight, container ships, the interstate highway network, and larger and more versatile freight cars.

Distribution is one area of marketing where the "bread-and-butter" uses of the computer are relatively easily deployed for such functions as order processing, real-time inventory level reports, and tracking the movements of goods. Further into the future lie mathematical models which will include every factor bearing on distribution. Not only will packaging materials handling, transportation and warehouse, order processing, and related costs be considered in such models; also included will be sales forecasts by product, production rates by factory, warehouse locations and capacities, speeds of different carriers, etc. In short, a complete picture will be developed for management.

Program in Action. The experiences of the Norge Division of Borg-Warner Corporation point up the values of the systems approach in physical distribution. The firm was confronted externally with complaints from its dealers and distributors, who were trying to cope with swollen inventories and the pressures of "loading deals." Internally, because coordination of effort between the six departments involved in distribution was at a minimum, distribution costs and accounts receivable were mounting persistently.

To grapple with this situation, Norge undertook a comprehensive analysis of its distribution system. Out of this grew a new philosophy. A company executive has described the philosophy to me as follows:

An effective system of physical distribution cannot begin at the end of the production line, It must also apply at the very beginning of the production process—at the planning, scheduling, and forecasting stages. Logistics, in short is part of a larger marketing system, not just an evaluation of freight rates. We must worry not only about finished refrigerators, but also about the motors coming from another manufacturer, and even about where the copper that goes into those motors will come from. We must be concerned with *total flow.*

To implement this philosophy, the appliance manufacturer took the following steps:

(1) It reorganized the forecasting, production scheduling, warehousing, order processing, and shipping functions into *one* department headed by a director of physical distribution.

(2) The management information system was improved with the help of EDP equipment tied into the communications network. This step made it possible to process and report data more speedily on orders received, inventory levels, and the actual movement of goods.

(3) Management used a combination of computer and manual techniques to weigh trade-offs among increased costs of multiple warehousing, reduced long-haul freight and local drayage costs, reduced inventory pipeline, and the sales value of an improved 'total"product offering. Also assessed were trade-offs between shorter production runs and higher

inventory levels, thereby challenging the traditional "wisdom" of production-oriented managers that the longer the run, the better.

(4) The company is setting up new regional warehouses.

As a result of these moves, Norge has been able to lower inventories throughout its sales channels and to reduce accounts receivable. These gains have led, in turn, to a reduction of the company's overall investment and a concomitant increase in profitability.

It is essential to note that even though Norge has used operations research as part of its systems approach, many aspects of the program are qualitative. Thus far, the company has found that the development of an all-encompassing model is not warranted because of (a) the time and cost involved, (b) the probability that the situation will change before the model is completed, (c) a concern that such a model would be so complex as to be unworkable, and (d) the difficulty of testing many of the assumptions used. In addition, management has not tried to quantify the impact of its actions on distributor and retailer attitudes and behavior, possible competitive countermoves, and numerous other factors contributing to results.

Toward Total Integration

The integration of systems developed for product management, product innovation, marketing intelligence, physical distribution, and the other functions or "subsystems" embraced by the term *marketing* creates a total marketing system. Thus, marketing plans composed according to a step-by-step outline, ranging from enunciation of objectives and implementational steps to audit and adjustment to environmental changes, constitute a complete application of systems theory. Further, as the various subsystems of the overall system are linked quantitatively, so that the effect of modifications in one element can be detected in other elements, and as the influences of competitive moves on each element are analyzed numerically, then the total scheme becomes truly sophisticated.

PLUSES AND MINUSES

Two elements underlie the use and benefits of systems theory—order and knowledge. The first is a homely virtue, the second a lofty goal. Marketing is obviously not alone among all human pursuits in needing them; but, compared with its business neighbors, production and finance, marketing's need is acute indeed. The application of the systems concept can bring considerable advantages. It offers:

1. A methodical problem-solving orientation—with a broader frame of reference so that all aspects of a problem are examined.

2. Coordinated deployment of all appropriate tools of marketing.
3. Greater efficiency and economy of marketing operations.
4. Quicker recognition of impending problems, made possible by better understanding of the complex interplay of many trends and forces.
5. A stimulus to innovation.
6. A means of quantitatively verifying results.

These functional benefits in turn yield rich rewards in the marketplace. The most important gains are:

¶*A deeper penetration of existing markets*—As an illustration, the Advanced Data Division of Litton Industries has become a leader in the automatic revenue control business by designing systems meshing together "hardware" and "software."

¶*A broadening of markets*—For example, the tourist industry has attracted millions of additional travelers by creating packaged tours that are product-service systems. These systems are far more convenient and economical than anything the consumer could assemble himself.

¶*An extension of product lines*—Systems management makes it more feasible to seek out compatibilities among independently developed systems. Evidence of this idea is the work of automatic control system specialists since the early 1950's.[5] Now similar signs are apparent in marketing. For example, Acme Visible Records is currently dovetailing the design and sale of its record keeping systems with data-processing machines and forms.

¶*A lessening of competition or a strengthened capacity to cope with competition*—The systems approach tends to make a company's product line more unique and attractive. Carborundum's innovation in metal-removal systems is a perfect illustration of this.

Problems in Practice

Having just enumerated in glowing terms the benefits of the systems approach, realism demands that I give "equal time" to the awesome difficulties its utilization presents. There is no better evidence of this than the gulf between the elegant and sophisticated models with which recent marketing literature abounds and the actual number of situations in which those models really work. For the truth of the matter is that we are still in the foothills of this development, despite the advances of a few leaders. Let us consider some of the obstacles.

Time and Manpower Costs. First of all, the systems approach requires considerable time to implement; it took one company over a year to portray its physical distribution system in a mathematical model before it could even begin to solve its problems. RCA's Electronic Data Processing

Division reports models taking three to five years to build, after which holes in the data network have to be filled and the model tested against history. Add to this the need for manpower of exceptional intellectual ability, conceptual skills, and specialized education—manpower that is in exceedingly short supply. Because the problems are complex and involve all elements of the business, one man alone cannot solve them. He lacks the knowledge, tools, and controls. And so many people must be involved. It follows that the activation of systems theory can be very costly.

Absence of "Canned" Solutions. Unlike other business functions where standardized approaches to problem solving are available, systems must be tailored to the individual situation of each firm. Even the same problem in different companies in the same industry will frequently lead to different solutions because of the impact of other inputs, unique perceptions of the environment, and varying corporate missions. These factors, too, compound time and expense demands.

"Net Uncertainties." Even after exhaustive analysis, full optimization of a total problem cannot be obtained. Some uncertainty will always remain and must be dealt with on the basis of judgment and experience.

Lack of Hard Data. In the world of engineering, the systems evolved to date have consisted all or mostly of machines. Systems engineers have been wise enough to avoid the irrationalities of man until they master control of machines. Marketing model-builders, however, have not been able to choose, for the distributor, salesman, customer, and competitor are central to marketing. We must, therefore, incorporate not only quantitative measures of the dimensions of things and processes (e.g., market potential, media outlays, and shipping rates), but also psychological measures of comprehension, attitudes, motivations, intentions, needs—yes, even psychological measures of physical behavior. What is needed is a marriage of the physical and behavioral sciences—and we are about as advanced in this blending of disciplines as astronomy was in the Middle Ages.

Consider the advertising media fields as an instance of the problem:

¶A number of advertising agencies have evolved linear programming or simulation techniques to assess alternate media schedules. One of the key sets of data used covers the probabilities of exposure to all or part of the audience of a TV program, magazine, or radio station. But what is exposure, and how do you measure it? What is optimum frequency of exposure, and how do you measure it? How does advertising prevail on the predispositions and perceptions of a potential customer? Is it better to judge advertising effects on the basis of exposure opportunity, "impact" (whatever that is), messages retained, message comprehension, or attitude shifts or uptrends in purchase intentions? We do not have these answers yet.

Even assuming precise knowledge of market dimensions, product performance, competitive standing, weights of marketing pressure exerted by direct selling, advertising and promotion, and so on, most marketers do not yet know, except in isolated cases, how one force will affect another. For instance, how does a company "image" affect the setting in which its salesmen work? How does a company's reputation for service affect customer buying behavior?

Nature of Marketing Men. Man is an actor on this stage in another role. A good many marketing executives, in the deepest recesses of their psyches, are artists, not analysts. For them, marketing is an art form, and, in my opinion, they really do not want it to be any other way. Their temperament is antipathetic to system, order, knowledge. They enjoy flying by the seat of their pants—though you will never get them to admit it. They revel in chaos, abhor facts, and fear research. They hate to be trammeled by written plans. And they love to spend, but are loathe to assess the results of their spending.

Obviously, such men cannot be sold readily on the value and practicality of the systems approach! It takes time, experience, and many facts to influence their thinking.

Surmounting the Barriers

All is not gloom, however. The barriers described are being overcome in various ways. While operations research techniques have not yet made much headway in evolving total marketing systems and in areas where man is emotionally engaged, their accomplishments in solving inventory control problems, in sales analysis, in site selection, and in other areas have made many businessmen more sympathetic and open-minded to them.

Also, mathematical models—even the ones that do not work well yet—serve to bolster comprehension of the need for system as well as to clarify the intricacies among subsystems. Many models are in this sense learning models; they teach us how to ask more insightful questions. Moreover, they pinpoint data gaps and invite a more systematized method for reaching judgments where complete information does not exist. Because the computer abhors vague generalities, it forces managers to analyze their roles, objectives, and criteria more concretely. Paradoxically, it demands more, not less, of its human masters.

Of course, resistance to mathematical models by no means makes resistance to the systems approach necessary. There are many cases where no need may ever arise to use mathematics or computers. For the essence of the systems approach is not its techniques, but the enumeration of options and their implications. A simple checklist may be the only tool needed. I would even argue that some hard thinking in a quiet room may be enough. This being the case, the whole trend to more analysis and logic in management thinking, as reflected in business periodicals, business schools, and the practices of many companies, will work in favor of the development of the systems approach.

It is important to note at this juncture that not all marketers need the systems approach in its formal, elaborate sense. The success of some companies is rooted in other than marketing talents; their expertise may lie in finance, technology, administration, or even in personnel—as in the case of holding companies having an almost uncanny ability to hire brilliant operating managers and the self-control to leave them alone. In addition, a very simple marketing operation—for example, a company marketing one product through one distribution channel—may have no use for the systems concept.

APPLYING THE APPROACH

Not illogically, there is a system for applying the systems approach. It may be outlined as a sequence of steps:

1. *Define the problem and clarify objectives.* Care must be exercised not to accept the view of the propounder of the problem lest the analyst be defeated at the outset.

2. *Test the definition of the problem.* Expand its parameters to the limit. For example, to solve physical distribution problems, it is necessary to study the marketplace (customer preferences, usage rates, market size, and so forth), as well as the production process (which plants produce which items most efficiently, what the interplant movements of raw materials are, and so forth). Delineate the extremes of these factors, their changeability, and the limitations on management's ability to work with them.

3. *Build a model.* Portray all factors graphically, indicating logical and chronological sequences—the dynamic flow of information, decisions, and events. "Closed circuits" should be used where there is information feedback or go, no-go and recycle signals (see Exhibit 1-2).

4. *Set concrete objectives.* For example, if a firm wants to make daily deliveries to every customer, prohibitive as the cost may be, manipulation of the model will yield one set of answers. But if the desire is to optimize service at lowest cost, then another set of answers will be needed. The more crisply and precisely targets are stated, the more specific the results will be.

5. *Develop alternative solutions.* It is crucial to be as open-minded as possible at this stage. The analyst must seek to expand the list of options rather than merely assess those given to him, then reduce the list to a smaller number of practical or relevant ones.

6. *Set up criteria or tests of relative value.*

7. *Quantify some or all of the factors or "variables."* The extent to which this is done depends, of course, on management's inclinations and the "state of the art."

8. *Manipulate the model.* That is, weigh the costs, effectiveness, profitability, and risks of each alternative.

9. *Interpret the results, and choose one or more courses of action.*

10. *Verify the results.* Do they make sense when viewed against the world as executives know it? Can their validity be tested by experiments and investigations?

Forethought and Perspective

Successful systems do not blossom overnight. From primitive beginnings they evolve over a period of time as managers and systems specialists learn to understand each other better, and learn how to structure problems and how to push out the frontiers of the "universe" with which they are dealing. Companies must be prepared to invest time, money, and energy in making systems management feasible. This entails a solid foundation of historical data even before the conceptual framework for the system can be constructed. Accordingly, considerable time should be invested at the outset in *thinking* about the problem, its appropriate scope, operations, and criteria of choice before plunging into analysis.

Not only technicians, but most of us have a way of falling in love with techniques. We hail each one that comes along—*deus ex machina.* Historically, commercial research has wallowed in several such passions (e.g., probability sampling, motivation research, and semantic scaling), and now operations research appears to be doing the same thing. Significantly, each technique has come, in the fullness of time, to take its place as one, but only one, instrument in the research tool chest. We must therefore have a broad and dispassionate perspective on the systems approach at this juncture. We must recognize that the computer does not possess greater magical properties than the abacus. It, too, is a tool, albeit a brilliant one.

Put another way, executives must continue to exercise their judgment and experience. Systems analysis is no substitute for common sense. The computer must adapt itself to their styles, personalities, and modes of problem solving. It is an aid to management, not a surrogate. Businessmen may be slow, but the good ones are bright: the electronic monster, by contrast, is a speedy idiot. It demands great acuity of wit from its human managers lest they be deluged in an avalanche of useless paper. (The story is told of a sales manager who had just found out about the impressive capabilities of his company's computer and called for a detailed sales analysis of all products. The report was duly prepared and wheeled into his office on a dolly).

Systems users must be prepared to revise continually. There two reasons for this. First, the boundaries of systems keep changing; constraints are modified; competition makes fresh incursions; variables, being what they are, vary, and new ones crop up. Second, the analytical process is iterative. Usually, one "pass" at problem formulation and searches for solutions will not suffice, and it will be necessary to "recycle" as early hypotheses are challenged and new, more fruitful insights are stimulated by the inquiry. Moreover, it is impossible to select objectives without knowledge of their effects and costs. That knowledge can come only from analysis, and it frequently requires review and revision.

Despite all the efforts at quantification, systems analysis is still largely an art. It relies frequently on inputs based on human judgment; even when the inputs are numerical, they are determined, at least in part, by judgment. Similarly, the outputs must pass through the sieve of human interpretation. Hence, there is a positive correlation between the pay-off from a system and the managerial level involved in its design. The higher the level, the more rewarding the results.

Finally, let me observe that marketing people merit their own access to computers as well as programmers who understand marketing. Left in the hands of accountants, the timing, content, and format of output are often out of phase with marketing needs.

CONCLUSION

Over 800 years ago a monk wrote the following about St. Godric, a merchant later turned hermit:

He laboured not only as a merchant but also as a shipman . . . to Denmark, Flanders, and Scotland; in which lands he found certain rare, and therefore more precious, wares, which he carried to other parts wherein he knew them to be least familiar, and coveted by the inhabitants beyond the price of gold itself, wherefore he exchanged these wares for others coveted by men of other lands. . . . [6].

How St. Godric "knew" about his markets we are not told, marketing having been in a primitive state in 1170. How some of us marketers today "know" is, in my opinion, sometimes no less mysterious than it was eight centuries ago. But we are trying to change that, and I will hazard the not very venturesome forecast that the era of "by guess and by gosh" marketing is drawing to a close. One evidence of this trend is marketers' intensified search for knowledge that will improve their command over their destinies. This search is being spurred on by a number of powerful developments. To describe them briefly:

— The growing complexity of technology and the accelerating pace of technological innovation.

— The advent of the computer, inspiring and making possible analysis of the relationships between systems components.

— The intensification of competition, lent impetus by the extraordinary velocity of new product development and the tendency of diversification to thrust everybody into everybody else's business.

— The preference of buyers for purchasing from as few sources as possible, thereby avoiding the problems of assembling bits and pieces themselves and achieving greater reliability, economy, and administrative convenience. (Mrs. Jones would rather buy a complete vacuum cleaner from one source than the housing from one manufacturer, the hose from another, and the attachments from still another. And industrial buyers are not much different from Mrs. Jones. They would rather buy an automated machine tool from one manufacturer than design and assemble the components themselves. Not to be overlooked, in this connection, is the tremendous influence of the U.S. government in buying systems for its military and aerospace programs.)

The further development and application of the systems approach to marketing represents, in my judgment, the leading edge in both marketing theory and practice. At the moment, we are still much closer to St. Godric than to the millennium, and the road will be rocky and tortuous. But if we are ever to convert marketing into a more scientific pursuit, this is the road we must travel. The systems concept can teach us how our businesses really behave in the marketing arena, thereby extending managerial leverage and control. It can help us to confront more intelligently the awesome complexity of marketing, to deal with the hazards and opportunities of technological change, and to cope with the intensification of competition. And in the process, the concept will help us to feed the hungry maws of our expensive computers with more satisfying fare.

APPENDIX: WHAT IS THE SYSTEMS APPROACH?

There seems to be agreement that the systems approach sprang to life as a semantically identifiable term sometime during World War II. It was associated with the problem of how to bomb targets deep in Germany more effectively from British bases, with the Manahattan Project, and with studies of optimum search patterns for destroyers to use in locating U-boats during the Battle of the North Atlantic. Subsequently, it was utilized in the defeat of the Berlin blockade. It has reached its present culmination in the success of great military systems such as Polaris and Minuteman.

Not surprisingly, the parallels between military and marketing strategies being what they are, the definition of the systems approach propounded by The RAND Corporation for the U.S. Air Force is perfectly apt for marketers:

An inquiry to aid a decision-maker choose a course of actions by systematically investigating his proper objectives, comparing quantitatively where possible the costs, effectiveness, and risks associated with the alternative policies or strategies for achieving them, and *formulating additional alternatives if those examined are found wanting.*[8]

The systems approach is thus an orderly, "architectural" discipline for dealing with complex problems of choice under uncertainty.

Typically, in such problems, multiple and possibly conflicting objectives exist. The task of the systems analyst is to specify a closed operating network in which the components will work together so as to yield the optimum balance of economy, efficiency, and risk minimization. Put more broadly, the systems approach attempts to apply the "scientific method" to complex marketing problems studied *as a whole;* it seeks to discipline marketing.

But disciplining marketing is no easy matter. Marketing must be perceived as a *process* rather than as a series of isolated, discrete actions; competitors must be viewed as components of each marketer's own system. The process must also be comprehended as involving a flow and counter-flow of information and behavior between marketers and customers. Some years ago, Marion Harper, Jr., now chairman of the Interpublic Group of Companies, Inc., referred to the flow of information in marketing communications as the cycle of "listen (i.e., marketing research), publish (messages, media), listen (more marketing research), revise, publish, listen. ... " More recently, Raymond A. Bauer referred to the "transactional" nature of communications as a factor in the motivations, frames of reference, needs, and so forth of recipients of messages. The desires of the communicator alone are but part of the picture.[9]

Pushing this new awareness of the intricacies of marketing communications still further, Theodore Levitt identified the interactions between five different forces—source effect (i.e., the reputation or credibility of the sponsor of the message), sleeper effect (the declining influence of source credibility with the passage of time), message effect (the character and quality of the message), communicator effect (the impact of the transmitter—e.g., a salesman), and audience effect (the competence and responsibility of the audience).[10] Casting a still broader net are efforts to model the entire purchasing process, and perhaps the ultimate application of the systems concept is attempts to make mathematical models of the entire marketing process.

Mounting recognition of the almost countless elements involved in marketing and of the mind-boggling complexity of their interactions is a wholesome (though painful) experience. Nevertheless, I believe we must not ignore other ramifications of the systems approach which are qualitative in nature. For the world of marketing offers a vast panorama of non- or part-mathematical systems and opportunities to apply systems thinking. We must not become so bedazzled by the brouhaha of the operations research experts as to lose sight of the larger picture.

NOTES

1. See, for example, Donald F. Cox and Robert E. Good, "How To Build a Marketing Information System," *Harvard Business Review.* Volume 45, Number 3, May-June, 1967, p. 145.

2. "Abrasive Maker's Systems Approach Opens New Markets," *Steel,* December 27, 1965, p. 38.

3. *Ibid.*

4. "Carborundum Grinds at Faster Clip," *Business Week,* July 23, 1966, pp. 58, 60.

5. See *Automatic and Manual Control: Papers Contributed to the Conference at Cranford, 1951,* edited by A. Tustin (London, Butterworth's Scientific Publications, 1952).

6. *Life of St. Godric,* by Reginald, a monk of Durham, c. 1170.

7. See Glen McDaniel, "The Meaning of The Systems Movement to the Acceleration and Direction of the American Economy," in *Proceedings of the 1964 Systems Engineering Conference* (New York, Clapp & Poliak, Inc., 1964), p. 1; see also E. S. Quade, editor, *Analysis for Military Decisions* (Santa Monica, California, The RAND Corporation, 1964), p.6.

8. Quade, op. cit., p. 4.

9. "Communications as a Transaction," *Public Opinion Quarterly,* Spring 1963, p. 83.

10. See Theodore Levitt, *Industrial Purchasing Behavior* (Boston, Division of Research, Harvard Business School, 1965), pp. 25ff.

ADDITIONAL SELECTED BIBLIOGRAPHY

The Systems Approach

Boulding, K. E., "General Systems Theory — The Skeleton of Science," *Management Science,* Vol. 2, No. 3 (April, 1956), 197-208.

Hannan, Mack, "Corporate Growth Through Venture Management," *Harvard Business Review,* Vol. 47, No. 1 January-February, 1969), 43-61.

Kelley, E. J. and Lazer, W., "The Systems Approach to Marketing," in *Managerial Marketing: Perspectives and Viewpoints,* ed. E. J. Kelley and W. Lazer, Third Edition, Richard D. Irwin, Inc. (1967), 19-27.

Kunstler, D. A., "Corporate Venture Groups: The Need, the Responsibility, the Organization, the Leadership," *Marketing and the New Science of Planning,* Robert L. King, ed., AMA Fall Conference Proceedings, Series No. 28, American Marketing Association (August, 1968), 449-454.

Pessemier, E. A., "New Product Ventures,' *Business Horizons,* Vol. 11, No. 4 (August, 1968), 5-19.

Wortzel, L. H., "Product Policy and the United States Multinational Corporation: Some Emerging Generalizations," *Marketing and the New Science of Planning,* Robert L. King, ed., AMA Fall conference Proceedings, Series No. 28, American Marketing Association (August, 1968), 474-477.

QUESTIONS FOR DISCUSSION AND REVIEW

1. Why is it important to you, as an employee of a firm, to recognize the systems approach?

2. What traps can a firm or department become ensnared in if a holistic approach to marketing is not developed?

3. What measures can be generated to instill a systems approach philosophy within the firm?

4. Do charismatic employees of a firm indicate eventual trouble for a firm?

5. Develop a flow chart indicating an input/output system that can solidify a holistic approach.

6. Can you discuss the relevance of showing various organization charts?

2

THE SIGNIFICANCE OF INNOVATION

What effect does introducing brand new products or design change of older products have on a business firm? Suppose a firm developed or "discovered" a new market for its on-going products. What is the outlook for success or failure of commercializaing this new product? Do new products guarantee the success of a business firm or can they enhance the success if properly marketed? The answer is YES, if all endogenous factors and most exogenous factors affirm the utility value of the product. The internal organization must believe in the product and work toward its commercial success in a holistic manner. The exogenous factors — the customer, the law, the business cycle — and competition as a grouping must accept the new product in the long run.

Most corporations are multiproduct corporations, for experience divulges to them that a single-product company could be shortlived. Why? Inventors, promoters, and competition are always seeking means and methods to increase their own material wealth. Wealth maximizers will enter a market when product success has been proven by other products. The only way for a firm to progress successfully during its life cycle is to introduce innovations at strategic time periods so that energies, time, and money are synergistically linked together for wealth maximization.

The following articles explain and depict the need for innovation and the factors taken into consideration which influence optimum profit, or for further growth in sales and profit.

PRODUCT INNOVATION
IN A SCIENTIFIC AGE
BY RICHARD S. ROSENBLOOM

INTRODUCTION

We live in an age of science. The long and steady growth of science and the cumulative nature of its work have produced a remarkably rich and fruitful understanding of nature. In the U.S.A. alone, a half-million scientists are busily engaged in research which deepens and broadens that understanding and education which enlarges the supply of trained professionals. We have married science to technology, producing changes in our ways of doing things at rates which challenge the society's ability to adapt. And more will come. Some 350,000 engineers and scientists, spending more than $13 billion annually, are now at work in industrial R&D laboratories, helping to shape our future.

Not all of this is new. The nature of the activity, its rate of growth, probably even the rate of change in technology, all can be traced back at least a century. As Whitehead said more than forty years ago, "The greatest invention of the nineteenth century was the invention of the method of invention. ... One element ... (was) ... the discovery of how to set about bridging the gap between the scientific idea and the ultimate product."[1]

What is new, if anything is, is the scale of modern science. Big science and big industry have produced new technology that challenges the imagination. Although a few firms had research laboratories 50 years ago,

EDITOR'S NOTE: From *New Ideas for Successful Marketing,* J. S. Wright and J. L. Goldstucker, eds., 1966, pp. 247-259. Reprinted by permission of the American Marketing Association and the author.

at present most large firms and many others support significant R&D activities. Research has become an important instrument of corporate strategy, and a factor in management thought.

Management, then, is learning to live with science. This paper is concerned with one aspect of that great adventure, its impact on product innovation in the firm. The discussion is limited to technologically new products and thus excludes refinements and improvements in existing products or changes in manufacturing methods, despite the great economic significance of the latter two.

The discussion stresses an organic view of the process of innovation within the firm. Successful innovation in products, it is argued, flows from an articulated system of specialized competences working in an integrated way. Innovation cannot be a sometime thing; it must be a continuing goal and constant occupation for some parts of the firm. The process of innovation draws together both technological and marketing activities; the ongoing linkage between those activities must be maintained by a continuing dialogue, that is, by the free flow of information in both directions.

This theme reappears through discussion of three topics. First, we examine the nature of the process of innovation, as illuminated by recent studies of industrial practice. Next, we consider the formulation of strategies for innovation, and the impact of technical and market factors in shaping such strategies. Third, we examine the role of research itself, as an instrument of strategy and an element in the process of innovation.

With this background, the final section discusses some organizational considerations in promoting the requisite dialogue and stimulating entrepreneurial action within the large enterprise. Although firm answers are elusive, we shall try to pose some of the right questions, and to confront them with some recent research results.

THE PROCESS OF INNOVATION

Successful product innovation implies the matching of technical possibilities with latent or manifest market needs. Although innovation begins with an idea, invention, or discovery, that is only a beginning; a complex and risky process of development, testing, and revision is necessary before an invention becomes a product which can be produced for a market. Furthermore, the introduction of an innovative product requires changes in facilities, organizations, and individual practices—changes which the entrepreneur must bring about in order to reap the gains of his innovation. Hence product innovation is the result of a process which includes both technological—i.e., R&D—and entrepreneurial—organizational, financial, strategic—activities.

The entrepreneurial role in innovation is quite distinct from the technical role. The difference is important. Technical excellence is not a sufficient basis for success in product innovation. Innovation requires a mix of activities as the new technology is reshaped, and capital and facilities and perhaps new personnel are brought to bear. Market considerations are extremely important in entrepreneurship. Hence quite different personal skills distinguish the successful entrepreneur from the successful inventor, skills which rarely are combined in a single individual or small group in an organization. The large firm must find organizational means for bridging that difference.

The electronics industry is a prime example of a field where a myriad of inventions have led to dynamic changes in products. In a recent study of innovation in electronic capital goods, Christopher Freeman found that enthusiastic individual inventors had achieved impressive results with limited means in the early stages of most developments.[2] Yet the firms successful in the difficult transition from laboratory to market were those which were "capable of integrating a well-organized research, development, and test program with good production planning and engineering and efficient marketing, maintenance, and technical service organizations." Despite the common impression of breathtaking rates of change in electronics, he found that the conception of a new product commonly preceded its real use by a long time. Invention itself, that is the first realization of a product, accounted for a relatively small part of the total cost of innovation. The reshaping of an invention to suit the realities of manufacturing operations and market needs—in other words, the process of development—proved to be an extremely important and costly step in innovation in that field.

Freeman concludes that an innovative firm does not need to invent everything. What is necessary is to have "a strong development and engineering capacity so that inventions made elsewhere may be rapidly assimilated, utilized, and improved upon." These lessons are borne out also by the history of a leading firm in another important science-based industry. The Du Pont Corporation has achieved growth and great profit from innovation in many aspects of chemical technology. Yet Mueller's study of the twenty-five important product and process innovations introduced by Du Pont between 1920 and 1949 shows that of eighteen new products Du Pont was the source of the basic invention underlying only five, and shared in the discovery of one other.[3] Put another way, two-thirds of these products were based on inventions made elsewhere, and this includes such mainstays as cellophane and dacron.

The story of successful innovation, then, has commonly been one of integration, of partnership between marketing and R&D, of a blending of insight into underlying market needs with the technical competence to create products responsive to those needs. For this reason the marketing function in innovation cannot follow R&D, it must be integrated with it. In the small innovative firm these functions often are identified as aspects of the behavior of an individual. Their balance and synthesis depend on him.

The realities of growth in the firm lead to increased differentiation. Large and highly specialized organizations emerge to deal with these functions independently, thus creating a need for systematic coordination.

Hence we are concerned with finding means to create an articulated organizational process for research, development, and innovation. These activities, taken as a whole, are aimed at both learning relevant new scientific and technical knowledge and applying it by innovation in operations. The duality of motives expressed by the terms "learning" and "applying" is necessarily present in all these activities in industrial settings, although their relative emphasis varies considerably. It implies that the process be an integrated combination not only of what we call "R&D" but also of elements of the established marketing, finance, and manufacturing operations.

STRATEGIES FOR INNOVATION

If we think of innovation as an ongoing purposeful process in the firm, as the integration of a complex of related technical and entrepreneurial activities, it is clear that some guiding orientation, some strategy for innovation, should shape the nature of those activities in each instance. I would like to discuss, briefly, two orientations which might characterize innovation strategies.

One possibility is a "marketing" orientation toward innovation. This strategy places emphasis on the search for improved means of satisfying needs in an established market. Innovation flows from the development of new technological approaches to meeting continuing marketing requirements. The contrary orientation toward innovation, which we might term "technological," proceeds not from the needs of the market but from the possibilities created by new science and technology. This approach to innovation seeks to generate and exploit new technologies in whatever markets they appear to be relevant.

A steel firm, for example, taking a technological orientation to innovation, might seek to find and exploit technological possibilities in a promising field, for example, special alloys. A breakthrough in this technology might open entirely new markets and customers to the steel manufacturer, give it a firmer position in established markets, and strengthen its competitive position not only with respect to other steel firms but also in competition with other materials such as plastics and aluminum. A different strategy for innovation would lead the firm to look in quite different technological directions. A marketing orientation might have led to emphasis on the needs of a given market, for example, containers. This might lead the firm in turn to seek to exploit technologies—for example, plastics—other than steel itself.

Both the shortcomings and strengths of these strategies as well as their implications for both R&D and marketing operations should be clear from this brief characterization. The firm which takes a technological approach to innovation can anticipate problems in exploiting the inventions which are produced by its laboratories. The possibilities created by radical improvements in technology are basically unpredictable. The firm seeking to follow those possibilities will be led often to unfamiliar markets and new customer requirements. Not only may the existing marketing organization be inadequate for these new purposes, but the invention itself may turn out to be less appropriate to the new market once the real needs of the latter can be ascertained.

The firm with a marketing orientation toward innovation necessarily puts more emphasis on design and development and the adaptation to well-known markets of whatever new technology appears to be relevant. Such a firm is likely to place much greater reliance on technologies developed elsewhere and to exploit its familiarity with market needs as a means of overcoming the common occurrence that it is not the first to develop a given new technology. The potential weakness of this strategy, of course, lies in the risk of failure to be responsive to what proves to be an important new invention and the entry to the market of another firm which is equipped to serve it effectively and has a technological lead. The demise of the steam locomotive manufacturers in the face of GM's diesel innovation is a classic example.

Excessive attachment to a given means for fulfilling a market need, as embodied in a specific product, seems inevitably to lead to an unhappy experience like that of the steam locomotive manufacturers. An eloquent warning against such shortsightedness, and a provocative argument for marketing strategies tied to customers' functional needs rather than specific product embodiments, appeared several years ago in a discussion of "Management Myopia" by Theodore Levitt.[4] The corporation, he argues, should be thought of as a "customer-creating" and "customer-satisfying" organism, not as a "goods-producer." Neglect of market realities or inadequate comprehension of the marketing process has led "growth" industries to decay and threatens the future of even some dynamic firms of today.

The cure for this peculiar defect of vision, if we may stretch the metaphor, requires bi-focals. Marketing, broadly defined, enters into both kinds of innovation strategies, but in different roles. If the strategy is technologically oriented, the marketing staff may be led to explore and exploit new types of customers and needs, while what we have termed a "marketing" orientation would fix on needs of given customers and require broadly exploratory technological activities.

A technological orientation to innovation, for example, seems best suited to firms which are in materials and components—serving a heterogeneous set of customers on the basis of a relatively homogeneous technological foundation. The manufacturer of electronic components, synthetic plastics, or non-ferrous metals falls into this category. A marketing orientation, on the other hand, seems more appropriate to the "systems" operation, in which heterogeneous technologies are combined in a functional system which is sold to a limited set of users and markets. Manufacturers of computers, machine tools, or aircraft would fall into this category.

In the components or materials business it is relatively easy to mount a significant technical effort because the area of relevant technology tends to be pretty well defined. The plastics manufacturer will employ chemists and chemical engineers, and the electronic components manufacturer will be employing electrical engineers and, increasingly, physicists. A new invention in this sort of business may require that the firm move into a wholly different market or radically change its marketing techniques. As an oversimplification, one could say that this sort of firm is more likely to have trouble innovating than inventing.

The successful systems operation, in contrast, will have much greater difficulty covering the potentially relevant technologies. In order for the manufacturer of machine tools, for example, to maintain a competence in the underlying fields which are relevant, he would have to support work in such diverse fields as metallurgy, electronics and control systems, and power transmission and generation. What he does instead is to concentrate on the systems engineering problems, although they are not yet called that in the more traditional industries, and on keeping in good touch with his customers' requirements. Such a strategy puts him in a better position to capitalize on a relevant invention when it is made, without requiring him to try to anticipate the particular field where an invention is likely to occur. If he does his job well, he can make entry into the field extremely tough for the entrepreneur who starts with a component invention, or even a new system concept, but lacks the depth of experience in customer service and systems engineering. Although this sort of firm can be very innovative, it probably will originate few inventions.

It is very easy, it seems to me, to misunderstand this distinction and draw quite misleading implications from the behavior of certain kinds of firms. It is sometimes argued, for example, that mature industries like machine tools or construction should be more aggressive in the initiation of new technology and should support research and speculative technological activities. The business problem in these industries, however, is in the adaptation of new technology rather than its initiation. It is extremely difficult and risky to start from a definition of a problem and anticipate the kind of technological solution which will finally emerge. The next major advance in machine tools may come in cutting materials, electronic control systems, metallurgy, electric motors, or something which we cannot yet anticipate The vertical disintegration which has been a strength in the American economy and the source of its rapid industrial growth makes it possible for a lower tier of suppliers to concentrate on those technologies and pursue their inventions wherever they lead. The distinctive contribution of the systems manufacturers lies in their ability to integrate diverse technologies in ways which meet users' needs effectively—a capability derived from intimate knowledge of the market, rather than the underlying technology.

Increasingly, the large enterprise which has a position in many businesses, from toasters to steam turbines, is able to pursue both of these strategies. Central R&D organizations, relatively independent of the needs and pressures of the established markets, can pursue basic technologies with some confidence that useful inventions can be exploited by the company either through the growth of new businesses or through the established positions of the operating units. At the same time, the operating divisions can enhance a natural marketing orientation toward their established fields and, aided by the presence of central R&D activities, also have the asset of good channels of communication to the fundamental developments in technology.

The attempt to do this in the large firm implies three things. First, the existence of central research activities free to explore the possibilities of new technologies. Second, the entrepreneurial capacity, somewhere in the firm, to take the more promising technical developments, reshape them, and exploit them in a market. Finally, the existence of open channels of communication which can tie R&D, "new product," and operating organizations together effectively in a single purposeful effort. We want to consider some of the implications of the last two points, but first let us examine the nature of the research activity itself.

THE ROLE OF RESEARCH

Although we often speak of "R&D" as if it were just one thing, there is a real difference between "research" and "development." Research, in this usage, means systematic investigation in science or technology oriented toward understanding of natural phenomena. Thus the "R" in industrial R&D is broader and more applied than so-called "fundamental science," as practiced, for example, in universities, but different from the design and development of specified products or processes.

Research, in this sense, must now be writ large when we deal with research, development, and innovation. The examples of its impact on innovation are legion; the transistor, nylon, penicillin, etc. More recently, scientific research—in quantum physics—pointed the way to the maser and laser. Speculative investigation of laser technology is expanding the range of possibilities for this important new field. Obviously, not all product innovations have their initial impetus in the research lab. Yet industrial research is, I believe, becoming increasingly important, not only as the birthplace of inventions, but also as the source of important knowledge for the rest of the process of development and innovation. What is the nature of this activity?

Research, basically, is a mode of searching. A familiar story about searching is the one about the good samaritan who stopped to help a somewhat inebriated gentleman who was crawling around the base of a lamp post "looking for his watch." After a period of rather fruitless searching, he learned that the loss had apparently taken place down toward the middle of the block, a hundred feet away. Asked why he was concentrating his search on the street corner, the man replied "because the light is so much better here."

Although a more sober strategy is certainly called for when searching for lost objects, something very much akin to "looking where the light is best" has proven to be a very productive technique in the systematic search for new knowledge, that is, in scientific research. The freedom to follow the unknowable paths generated in the course of research, unhampered by the restrictions of narrow practical purposes, is taken as an important characteristic of the role of the researcher. This seems a most unbusinesslike basis for spending the resources of a firm. In fact, it is paradoxical that an activity conducted on a basis which seems so impractical can produce practical benefits justifying its support in an industrial setting.

Two points help resolve the paradox. First, an industrial research lab performs several functions for the firm, of which discovery is only one. Second, the relevance of the lab's work to the firm's needs can be influenced; in other words, research is "manageable."

The primary mission of laboratories working on research or advanced technology is to give the firm access to relevant new technical knowledge. It is a mistake, however, to concentrate on the origination of relevant knowledge as the primary means of accomplishing this. Any one research organization can originate only a small fraction of the relevant new knowledge of interest to a firm. Hence, it is important for the lab to give the firm membership in the world of science, using the products of its own research as the "ticket of admission" and being alert to relevant developments elsewhere in the scientific community. Similarly, the laboratory is a repository of skills which give the firm competence in appraising potential advances throughout the world of science and technology. Through interaction with development personnel within the firm—by consultation services on particular problems, and through programs of continuing education—the research laboratory can upgrade the technical sophistication of the firm as a whole, reduce empiricism, and infuse a scientific method throughout the technical organization. Furthermore, the research organization more and more becomes a principal input gate for technically trained personnel joining the firm and a source of excellent development engineers at the proper stage in individual careers. The research laboratory, in sum, provides a mix of services for the firm which can be far more productive than the individual "products" (in the form of papers, etc.) which are its apparent output.

It is well known, and perhaps over-emphasized, that the people one hires to do this sort of job are likely to place high value on autonomy to follow the intellectual challenges intrinsic in the work. Despite this, the problem of maintaining relevance is not quite as severe as it might appear on first sight. The firm supporting research has taken a very important step in the management of research by selecting the specific fields of science and technology in which to recruit staff. Having done this, the research manager can leave the researcher relatively free to determine the best opportunities and most productive avenues of approach. The manager's task then is to create a research environment where there is good communication, reward for the right sort of effort, and a mechanism to translate relevant results into innovation.

This conception of the direction of research underscores the importance of "two-way" models of the requisite communication process. Knowledge does not flow only from research to application; knowledge about needs as well as possibilities must be exchanged in a freely flowing stream. Jack Morton of the Bell Laboratories asserts that the unifying element in the diverse R&D activities of that enterprise is a "commonness of goals which are challenging to all."[5] To sustain this it is important to maintain a dialogue on goals and possibilities up and down the line, and through this means to influence the choices which are made by the technical staff and not for them. The practicability of this view is supported by the work of two social psychologists, Pelz and Andrews.[6] They find that the most productive Ph.D.s seem to be those who are given reasonable freedom to set their own goals, but also permit themselves to be influenced by others. A concept of "shared autonomy" seems to be a practical approach to maintaining relevance in research and advanced technology work while meeting the requisites of the people and activities involved.

Hence both research and development can share in the over-all mission of learning relevant new knowledge and applying it. The problem common to both activities is one of maintaining the linkage between awareness of the possiblities of new technology on the one hand, awareness of the needs of operations and the marketplace on the other. In research the major problem is avoiding irrelevance, while in design and development the problem is one of avoiding obsolescence. In research laboratories, which tend to be well coupled to the world of science, the problem is made manifest as one of maintaining contact with the real needs of the organization. In design and development the influence of day-to-day operating requirements is great; the characteristics of a competing product introduced in the market have a much greater impact than a publication in the *Physical Review* and empirical success in making something work can seem more important than understanding why it works. The problem in that environment is one of ensuring access to knowledge of the best techniques.

These two problems, maintaining the relevance of research work and avoiding obsolescence in engineering work, are aspects of the single central continuing issue in R&D management, maintaining fruitful linkages between the sources of knowledge in the disciplines and the needs for the application of knowledge in operations, i.e., the problem of communication or the exchange of information. The effectiveness of the process by which scientists and engineers acquire and exchange information—about both needs and possibilities—is profoundly influenced by the aspects of policy in the firm dealing with organizational roles and missions, systems of evaluation and control, and methods of recruiting, assignment and promotion.

MAINTAINING THE DIALOGUE

Research, development, and innovation, viewed as an organic process in the firm, are nourished by the free flow of information, embodied in the dialogue of which we have spoken. Knowledge of market opportunities and needs, arising from groups in regular contact with the market, interacts with knowledge of the moving frontiers of science and states of the technical arts, as it arises from groups engaged in R&D work. Innovation thus has its start in the identification of a fruitful match between a need and a possibility. Its fulfillment comes, however, when the firm translates the idea into the reality of a marketable product and creates the system of manufacturing, distribution, and consumer acceptance necessary to establish the product on a working basis.

To do this, the firm must be organized in a way which permits informed entrepreneurship, since both knowledge and action appear as important components of the process of innovation. Knowledge of technical possibilities and market requirements creates the potential energy for an innovation, but positive efforts to actualize that potential are needed to overcome the recurrent inertia of organizations and society.

How does the large enterprise create a structure and an environment which promotes informed entrepreneurship, which sustains knowledgeable action for innovation? We specify large firms because the answer clearly depends upon the size of firm. Dialogue, for example, is likely to be far easier to sustain when the principals meet daily under one small roof—if not under one hat—than it is when they are spread across the countryside. The largest firms, it should be noted, account for an overwhelming share of the technical effort—five-sixths of industrial R&D takes place in firms employing more than 5000 people—even though they may not account for a proportionate share in innovation. Hence the question is an important one.

Unfortunately, it is far easier to identify what is needed than to prescribe means for meeting those needs. Within the context of a given strategy for innovation, the firm must be able to:

1. stimulate an appropriate flow of new technology from its own research laboratories;

2. identify, evaluate, and adapt new science and technology originating outside the firm;

3. maintain the technological skills required to reshape technology in its formative stages to meet emergent needs;

4. maintain the entrepreneurial ability to create new businesses on the basis of new technology;

5. fit these distinctive competences together in an articulated system.

These different functions necessarily are performed by specialized organizational units. Lorsch and Lawrence have clarified some of the factors differentiating the organizational units involved and have shown that such groups differ in respect to organization structure, orientations toward time horizons, subsidiary goals, the content of work, and elements of what they term "the interpersonal style" of participating individuals.[7] Their empirical work supports the argument that the most innovative work will be done, at least in science-based industries, where there is a high degree of differentiation between these subunits. This, in turn, implies a need for highly effective integrative devices at the operating level.

Communication depends on language, motivation, and proximity—both spatial and organizational. My own investigations of the flow of information in industrial R&D organizations suggest that these groups maintain ties to the outside world of science through a relatively small group of cosmopolitan, professionally-oriented engineers and scientists. Most industrial scientists and engineers, however, seem to be locally-oriented as far as information sources are concerned. They rely on discussion with colleagues and company documents to answer their questions. Local flows of information tend to follow the flow of work, and to be sensitive to organizational boundaries, geographic separation, and the emphasis placed by management on the kinds of information sources which should be sustained. Hence keeping the R&D professional informed is far more than a mechanical "information-retrieval" task and is very sensitive to organizational policies.

What of the action component in this process? In the setting of the operating division, committed to the daily pressures of ongoing business, radical innovation seems to emerge most commonly when there is a determined individual committed to seeing it through. Although the usual organization environment does not encourage the emergence of many "champions" for change, the firm of the future may have to learn how to nurture and sustain such men. An alternative strategy is to separate innovative responsibilities from routine operations by establishing central R&D groups whose sole function is to search out attractive product ideas and develop them into the basis for new enterprises. This approach is subject to the countervailing risk that such a group may become isolated from the realities of markets and production. To grow new businesses outside its established interests, the firm must create an organizational surrogate to provide marketing and manufacturing know-how in support of the entrepreneur.

As large firms experiment with new means for meeting the requirements of innovation in the modern environment, new modes of organization are likely to occur. Put another way, it is not surprising that, as the business environment changes and as firms adapt strategies and techniques to match the new environment, the structure of the firm should also change. Tough questions are posed by the search for organizational forms which will sustain and even encourage continuing change. Large organizations, rightly or wrongly, are better known for their resistance to innovation than for their espousal of it. Yet the rewards are there, and the chances seem good that the requisite social inventions can be called forth to help business fulfill the promise of our scientific age.

B

SIX WAYS TO
STRANGLE INNOVATION
BY DONALD A. SCHON

In most U.S. industrial firms today, there are strong, yet mixed feelings about innovation, about bringing out a new product, developing a new process.

On the one hand, management badly wants new products and processes. The company goal is to "make money for its stockholders," and the way to do this is to grow. "A company that does not go forward falls behind." In many companies, therefore, technical innovation is seen as the route to growth, and research activity is the accepted way to innovate.

On the other hand, there is also strong resistance to change, which is quite understandable, given the risks involved in new product development—risks that are sometimes overwhelming. (One large consumer products company spent close to $10 million in the development of a new product which failed because of mistaken judgments about market trends.)

Typically, in new product development, the early expense of invention is the smallest. The cost curve rises sharply in the later stages of engineering, market research and pilot plant work. Technical difficulties, which have not been anticipated, arise at a time when large amounts of money may have already been committed. It is necessary, then, to spend even more. And all of this takes place in a context in which predictions as to market response must always be in the nature of guesses. Radical new product development is much more like swimming in a fog than like running a race.

EDITOR'S NOTE: Reprint by permission from *Think* Magazine, copyright 1963 by International Business Machines Corporation.

Many consulting firms have grappled with this problem, and it has become increasingly clear that in many, if not most, companies the key problems surrounding technology have to do, not with the need for new ideas and more "creativity," but with a company's skill in using its own resources.

The primary problem is not to find new ideas and new people, but to overcome obstacles to the use of ideas and people already available. An idea of these problems comes out of the following examples, drawn from my own experience at Arthur D. Little, Inc.

A major chemical company appointed a man to take charge of the company's efforts to develop new products away from the current line of business, to diversify into new areas and markets. He was a man in his 50's who had an excellent record in product development work related to the company's present business. I asked him whether there had been any instances in the past where the company had succeeded in diversifying into a related area. Fifteen years ago, he said, they had developed a new chemical additive. It had been a product the company used itself so that it was in part its own customer.

We went on to discuss the product areas of interest to him now; none resembled the chemical additive he had described. I asked if he was planning to go into the laboratory, find ideas, carry them out and push them forward. He said he was not. It developed, then, that this man did not have the faintest notion of doing the job he had been assigned. He felt that the company was not about to let him do it; it was too risky.

It was this man's notion that the company knew this when they put him into this role and that they did not really want the job done. Here was a mission with considerable organization around it to perform no function at all.

HOW TO DIVERSIFY?

A small company had been making foundry products since the turn of the century. It had established a reputation for high quality, built for the most part on old technology. Now, however, it was being beleaguered by competition—larger companies, foreign companies, plastics. For the last two years, the company's managers had been exploring possible new products. What should they make in order to diversify?

I talked to their new-product director, who pulled out a file drawer containing 25 instances of new products he had been working on for two years. Several seemed to be very promising ideas. When I asked what had happened to them, the new-product man said, "See this sheet of paper? Here are the criteria for new products in the company. A product has to promise a gross of $3,000,000 within five years, has to have a profit margin of so much, and it cannot be the sort of business where you need a line of products to get in. It can't be too far away from our present line of business. We want to use present production facilities, and it's to be sold through our present sales force." Not one of the ideas in the last two years had passed these tests. It was the product idea, and not the criteria, which was forced to give.

We worked some years ago for a major producer of a natural product whose people were beginning to be concerned with the threat of synthetics. Our task was to find new markets and uses for the natural product, and we discovered clues to an interesting process in which the natural product was reconstituted and adapted to a number of new uses. We found, moreover, a local company also interested in the process from the point of view of process machinery rather than that of raw material.

We went back to the company producing the raw material, told them about it, and found that they were excited by the possibility. The two companies got together in a joint venture. In the course of this work, the research director of the first company mentioned one day that there was someone in the laboratory, a chemist, who had been working on the material, and who might know something about the process.

When we went to talk to him we discovered that he was as familiar with the literature as we, that he had had this same process idea, and that he had made a number of highly promising prototype products.

In short, then, if the company in question had searched the whole country, they could not have found anyone more appropriate to carry the project forward—but they hadn't known that they had him. What we had done was to reinvent something already potentially available to the company.

THE GREATEST EFFORT

By far, the greatest part of technical effort in American industry goes into minor change—a more stable formula for toothpaste, a cake that will rise higher, a lubricating material which will permit faster drawing of wire— so that costs can be reduced by a percentage point or two. These are the kinds of innovation on which development money is largely spent. The more radical innovations—the ones usually mentioned in connection with growth and progress—are rarely undertaken. The more radical the innovation, the more changes its acceptance would require, the more risk it entails, the less likelihood of its being undertaken.

As a result, companies become trapped in a conflict of policy and practice. It is company policy to seek innovation, and company practice (often for the best of reasons) to resist it. Technical and marketing people— those who are expected to develop new products and processes—become confused and discouraged over these inconsistencies. Their enthusiasm and their effectiveness suffer when they see the results of their labors unused.

Management, in turn, is able to see this lack of productivity as the failure of those below. The resulting situation is one in which resources for technical innovation are ineffectively used.

The family of problems described above suggested the need for a kind of work with client companies which would go beyond reports outlining problems—or even recommendations for change—and would focus instead on issues underlying resistance to change.

From these reflections came the formation of joint client-ADL teams which have worked together for two or three days at a time, at intervals of about six weeks, over periods ranging from six months to two years. These groups have had from six to 10 members. On the client's part they have included representatives of management, sales, technology and new products (typically, the president, the head of marketing and the head of technology). It has become something of a pattern to begin with a group at this level, then to form other groups with representatives of the same functions at divisional levels with the company.

These groups have been attempts at filling parallel functions: (1) to work at the development of new product areas or new product policy and to follow this development over time, and (2) to uncover problems within the company in product or process innovation and to work to remedy them. These have been, in effect, task forces aimed at product innovation.

IN-COMPANY PROBLEMS

In the course of this work, a number of in-company problems with innovation have come to light—all related in various ways to the central problem of ambivalence over innovation described above.

Problems of Sustained Work On Vague Problems

Within the large company, those who must work together to solve problems of innovation are frequently made to spend long periods of time doing it. When individuals from marketing, technology and management are brought together, there is a typical cycle of energetic work on the problem; depression over the failure of the obvious solutions; and, if work persists long enough, and with somebody's striving energy, recovery to new ways of looking at the problem. In ordinary company situations, the work group frequently never gets beyond the second stage and finds ways to avoid getting together again for fear of coming face-to-face with the same unsolved problem.

IDEAS, SOFT AND HARD

Within the company the process of discovery requires considerable time spent in directions of search which are at first vague and indefensible. The first intriguing ideas ("There ought to be something about solvent cleaning we could do." "A rechargeable battery should have some potential in portable tools") are not hard and defensible in the way that is usually required when ideas move from group to group or from lower to higher levels of management. The need to move from group to group or from one level of management to another in order to get work done tends to force ideas into the first hard defensible shape they can take, and frequently commits the worker prematurely to a hard idea when he is far from sure that it is the best he can draw out of the vague area he is interested in or even that it is worth pursuing at all.

In both of these instances there is a need for group support to press for sustained work on problems and for maintaining a speculative, diffuse approach where this is still appropriate.

Problems of Commitment

A man with a new product or process idea to pursue frequently comes to ask, "Is my contribution really wanted? Where in the company is the commitment for it?"

Past history plays a role in this. Projects have been started and then dropped or have been allowed to dribble off. Perhaps the company backed down when confronted with the real risks, or the R&D director couldn't be relied on to stick his neck out in support of a project, so that the man who proposed the idea originally was left holding the bag. Or it was doubted that the president was really serious about new products.

From the point of view of the rest of the company, the president's involvement in a work group aimed at product or process innovation may provide new evidence of his commitment and cause product ideas to come out of the woodwork. It is possible, too, to work out shared tests in which the initiator of a project and his boss work together to evaluate the project and determine whether the company will commit itself.

The General Problem of Taboo Issues

Sometimes the group which should be working on technical innovation with the company shows a surprising lack of energy. This can be traced in many cases to issues that "cannot be discussed." They may have to do with doubts about company commitment, with attitudes toward individuals within the company, with questions about the basis on which an outside group has been brought in. They are suppressed and, with this, energy for the task at hand declines. It is always risky to explore such issues. But when they are raised in a way that permits test of the assumptions made, or possibility of change, there is a release of vitality for the task to be done.

FLOATING BALLOONS

Proposing and Disposing

In terms of the social system for innovation within the large firm, management is apt to assign the task of innovation to those down below. Management waits for ideas, for proposals, of which it may dispose positively or negatively. Criteria are laid down ("high volume, high profit margin, the use of present manufacturing and distribution systems, etc.") which may be simply virtuous and empty. This makes of new product activity within the firm a kind of guessing game in which product ideas are floated like balloons toward the top of the company, where they may burst or are allowed to pass.

A RISKY GAME

On the basis of this performance, those down below try to guess the type of product which will be acceptable to the firm and with each guess use up a certain amount of company "capital." The game is a risky one and it tends to produce conservative, anxious play.

Within a small group, this picture can be seen clearly and challenged directly. A different approach can be substituted in which management works jointly with other functions on the problem and the solution. Here management shares some of the risk of proposal and those below share some of the task of disposal.

"Nothing Can Be Said Lightly "

This phrase reflects a two-sided problem. From below, nothing can be proposed lightly; that is, every idea is seen as a test of competence, position and prestige. From above, from top management, no comment can be lightly made; every offhand remark is given greater weight than the president intends—hence his feeling that he *cannot* enter into work on the problem. His remarks are too powerful for that. He is afraid of being drawn into commitments he does not know whether he wants to make. The result of both of these tendencies is to make exploratory *public* thinking impossible.

Testing and Challenge

How does the man at the top judge the worth of an idea under development? If the president is not technically trained he has a special problem with technical ideas. He has no way of judging the worth of a project on the basis of the content alone. His answer frequently is to challenge the man. Here, if the mores of the company do not permit active fighting response to challenge, management is cut off from information that would enable it to tell whether the idea from below is sound and tough. A vicious circle then forms in which each side is convinced of the weakness and/or destructiveness of the other.

There is the possibility of breaking such circles; the group must develop a way of meeting challenge, a way of uncovering the real reason for the challenge.

THE ROLE OF SCIENCE

Special Problems Over The Role of "Science" in The Process of Innovation

The presence in the business community of technically trained people with scientific values sets up a series of conflicts and responses, with problems on both sides. Demands on scientifically trained men to contribute to profit-based activities sometimes produce responses of withdrawal, "hack" work, or angry revolt. Management can respond to the presence of the scientists by overtrust or, again, overdemand. There are problems of defensiveness, the most common of which involves setting up barriers of technical expertise to make the problem of common work insuperable except on a manipulative or heroic basis.

If the man involved in scientific research is the best, or the only one capable of making decisions as to direction of future effort, then management must develop a basis for trusting him, and he in turn must develop a way of presenting himself so as to earn trust from management.

The Lack of Models of Innovation.

In certain companies (in the area of textiles, paper, food, for example) it may have been true that through several generations innovations were virtually unnecessary. Caretaking with respect to the day-to-day operations was what was required. The sudden shift over the last 20 or 30 years to a situation in which innovation is the order of the day takes such companies by surprise. They need exposure to models of entrepreneurial activity, including marketing and merchandising. How is it possible to sense consumer reaction more promptly, to make tests, to get in quickly and effectively? And how is it possible to move from a view of the business in which everything is centered on machines and processes and capital commitment, to one in which these are merely devices for meeting the special demands of the market?

These are some of the specific varieties of problems and certain of the directions of change which have been explored in our joint group work with client companies.

There is a general statement underlying all these problems. The demands for innovation put new stresses on the workings of a company, and expose the vulnerability of both boss and subordinate. The social system of the firm, from top management down through layers of settled operation, may be inappropriate to the new demands. This shows up within the working group itself—in symptoms of tension, lack of energy, conflicts, divergence from the task. Feelings, particularly about "undiscussable issues," are clued to the problems and ways to deal with them.

FOUR WAYS OF CHANGE

Change can occur in the small working group in the following ways:

(1) through the group's support in raising issues previously considered undiscussable, tracing them to sources and analyzing their effect on work;

(2) modeling new kinds of activities and relationships, e.g., between boss and subordinate, between technology and marketing;

(3) providing group support for *experiment* in ways of working never before tried within the company;

(4) building values that stress process, e.g., "the need to get on with the job," as the primary value in the company, the importance and legitimacy of expressing feelings about work, or digging up taboos when they affect the work at hand.

These represent directions of progress in experimental work designed to help companies make more effective use of the resources of innovation already at hand.

NOTES

1. Alfred North Whitehead, *Science and The Modern World,* New York, The Macmillan Company, 1946, p. 141.

2. Christopher Freeman, "Research and Development in Electronic Capital Goods," *National Institute Economic Review,* London, November, 1965.

3. Willard F. Mueller, "The Origins of The Basic Inventions Underlying Du Pont's Major Product and Process Innovations, 1920 to 1950," pp 323-346 in National Bureau of Economic Research, *The Rate and Direction of Inventive Activity,* Princeton, N.J., Princeton University Press, 1962.

4. Theodore Levitt, *Innovation in Marketing,* New York, McGraw-Hill, 1962, Chapter 3, "Management Myopia," pp 39-75.

5. Jack Morton, "From Research to Technology," *International Science and Technology,* May, 1964, pp 82-92.

6. Donald C. Pelz and Frank M. Andrews, "Autonomy, Coordination, and Stimulation in Relation to Scientific Achievement," *Behavorial Science,* Vol. 11, 1966, pp 89-97.

7. Jay W. Lorsch and Paul R. Lawrence, "Organizing for Product Innovation," *Harvard Business Review,* January-February, 1965, pp 109-120.

ADDITIONAL SELECTED BIBLIOGRAPHY

The Significance of Innovations

Collins, G., "Management of New Product Development," *New Ideas for Successful Marketing,* J. S. Wright and J. L. Goldstucker, eds., AMA Proceedings of the 1966 World Congress, American Marketing Association (June, 1966), 260-271.

Lorsch, J. W. and Lawrence, P. R., "Organizing for Product Innovation," *Harvard Business Review,* Vol. 43, No. 1 (January-February, 1965), 109-122.

Muse, W. V. and Kegerreis, R. J., "Technological Innovation and Marketing Management," *Journal of Marketing,* Vol. 33, No. 4 (October, 1969), 3-9.

QUESTIONS FOR DISCUSSION AND REVIEW

1. Why can't a firm continue to grow and expand without product innovations? Or, can they?

2. What does an innovation mean to a single-product firm? A multiproduct firm?

3. Why is innovation necessary for U.S. firms? Do we have too much material wealth?

4. Can you predict continued U.S. leadership in world affairs if other nations double or triple their manufacturing facilities?

5. What can be said about the Gross National Product (GNP) should net domestic investment grow at a negative rate, assuming stabilization of consumer expenditures and government expenditures?

3

CORPORATE RISK OF
INNOVATIONS

The introduction of a new product by a corporation does not guarantee success, immediately or in the long run. Some of the obstacles in the path of successful commercialization of a new product are:

1. Sales response to certain marketing inputs (advertising, quality, packaging, price, or service)
2. Insufficient marketing efforts
3. Government regulations
4. Higher production and marketing costs than anticipated
5. The competitive challenge by industry
6. Inaccurate timing and technical obsolescence of the product

The above variables show that corporate risk plays a prime role in product innovations. Corporate managers can devise a risk spectrum or an array of new product ideas and examine each idea from the standpoint of return on invested capital, cost/benefit analysis, and the probable length of time it will take from inception of new product idea to final commercialization (it is important to be aware of technical obsolescence and changes in consumer demand for a product). The decision to market new product ideas from an array of ideas presented to top management will depend not only upon timing, costs, and returns in the form of profits but also on the ability of management to integrate the new products into the existing product line or to be in a position to create and set up a subsidiary type of production-marketing organization to commercialize new products.

The following articles explain the risk of marketing new products.

A

DECISIONS INVOLVING
HIGH RISK
BY PAUL E. GREEN

Concomitant with the growing complexity of business operations, the faster obsolescence of products and processes, and the increasing costs of technological development, the function of business planning is growing in stature. As the costs of wrong decisions continue to mount, as well as the costs of delaying even the right ones, it is not surprising that more attention is being devoted to the problem-search and problem-solving activity which business planning should embody.

If, however, the need for this function is becoming more apparent, might the traditional techniques of business planning be insufficient to deal adequately with the need? And if so, what other procedures might be used advantageously?

As a basis for examining these questions, let's start with the term *business planning*. This term refers to activities associated with making high-level, high-risk decisions, taking into account the relationship of the firm to its environment and involving deployment of significant amounts of the firm's resources to reach its longer term business goals.

Peter Drucker, in *Long-range Planning, Challenge to Management Science,*[1] has cogently expressed the decision aspects of business planning by first describing some things which planning is not. He says, for example:

1. "(Long-range planning) is not forecasting. . . . Any attempt to do so is foolish. Human beings can neither predict nor control the future. . . .

EDITOR'S NOTE: From *Advanced Management—Office Executive,* October 1962, pp. 18-21, 23, 34. Reprinted by permission of the publisher and the author.

2. " . . . it does not deal with future decisions. It deals with the futurity of present decisions. . . .

3. " . . . (it) is not an attempt to eliminate risk. It is not an attempt to minimize risk."

(Drucker defines (long-range) planning as "risk-taking decision-making.")

The business planner and decision-maker are thus properly viewed as persons dealing with present decisions (which carry future implications) or what Drucker calls the "futurity of present decisions."

Moreover, the planner must also deal with a complementary concept—namely, the immediacy of future decisions. That is, the planner must also consider how the decision-maker's ability to act in the future is affected by the present decision. Actions (including maintenance of status quo) can be taken only in the present.

Our conception of business planning is, thus, decision- and problem-oriented rather then merely a consideration of some general future setting for the firm. With this view in mind, note a few of the characteristics of traditional planning techniques for dealing with the risk decisions of business planning.

1. Conventional planning procedures tend to emphasize end-of-planning period, or snap-shot, views of payoffs rather than flows of sales and costs through time which are related to the courses of action under evaluation. In some planning studies no attempt is even made to provide a simple *accumulation* of profit experience through the period required to reach the firm's expected position in the terminal year of the planning period.

2. Associated with the preceding characteristic is that little formal use is made of discounting longer term revenues and cost to present value to reduce *different patterns* of these flows to a common denominator basis.

3. The complexity of real business problems tends to force the use of polling procedures of one sort or another where persons knowledgeable of particular facets of the firm's activity—such as experts on end use markets or competitive activity—are asked to supply data estimates for their particular sphere of expertise, sometimes subject to a set of over-all ground rules. Planning activity, at least in large corporations, thus tends to involve the activities of many persons in the organization even though coordination may be restricted to a relatively small study group.

4. Estimates obtained by this polling procedure, however, are usually stated in "certainty equivalent" terms. That is, rather than being asked to state their estimates in terms of a range of responsibilities or to attach numerical probabilities to the occurrence of alternative future events, data contributors are usually asked to supply simply a single, or "most probable," estimate for those subject areas which fall within their purview.

5. The selection of alternative courses of action for evaluation tends to be narrow. Emphasis is placed on reducing some feasible set to a "representative" subset of courses of action. Emphasis is also placed on the search

for dominant courses of action—such as those acts which are expected to yield at least as large a payoff as some other act under all states of nature (environmental factors affecting the decision) being considered (and yield a larger payoff under at least one of those states of nature).

6. Little or no attempt is made to consider even low-order interactions of the courses of action being evaluated.

7. The problem of formally considering the corporate multiple goal structure is usually avoided at the outset of the study—that is, in the screening process used for obtaining candidate courses of action. Some type of formal check list may be used in this screening process.

A portmanteau variable like total profits or return on investment is then usually selected as the payoff criterion to be applied to those candidate courses of action which have survived the screening test. Risk attitudes are not explicitly analyzed by means of utility functions or similar conceptual devices for dealing formally with risk.

8. Little or no attempt is made to test the sensitivity of the outcomes of the study to departures in the basic assumptions.

9. Few formal devices are used to incorporate feedback data from the field, such as market surveys or early sales results. Insofar as the use of informal means, such as salesmen's reports, is concerned, the typically unreliable aspects of early feedback data tend to be neglected in the sense that highly generalized inferences may be made on the basis of a very small sample, particularly if there exists some "spectacular event" in this sample, such as, "Company ABC definitely does not think that the new product has sales potential!"

CONTAIN SEVERAL INADEQUACIES

Apparently traditional planning techniques contain several inadequacies for coping with planning problems. For example, although uncertainty abounds in business planning problems, few attempts have been made to incorporate a probabilistic framework in planning analyses. Although the futurity aspects of present courses of action are important, relatively little use is made of the discounting function and similar capital budgeting tools.

The deficiencies of traditional techniques might be grouped conveniently under two classes: (a) lack of a suitable conceptual framework within which the characteristics of planning problems can be viewed; and (b) lack of a means to implement this conceptual framework from a computational standpoint.

It is hardly surprising that relatively little use (at least by business planners) has been made of the procedures developed under the general heading of decision theory.

First, these techniques are, for the most part, of recent origin. Moreover, many of the contributions to this subject have had rather specialized distribution, and they have been associated with areas of interest (such as the foundations of statistics) that are typically outside the purview of business planning personnel.

A notable exception, however, is the recent book by Robert Schlaifer, *Probability and Statistics for Business Decisions*.[2] This particular wotk offers one of the most provocative and complete procedures for dealing with decisions under uncertainty, namely the Bayesian approach[3] available to the business planner.

The Bayesian approach to decision-making under uncertainty provides a framework for explicitly working with the economic costs of alternative courses of action, the prior knowledge or judgments of the planner, and formal modification of these judgments as additional data are introduced into the problem.

DESCRIBING IT IN TERMS OF QUESTIONS

While the full richness of this set of techniques cannot be explored here, at least the principal aspects of Bayesian decision theory might be described in terms of a series of questions with which this approach is designed to cope. These questions are:

1. Given specific alternative courses of action (such as different plant sizes or introductory price levels) whose effectiveness is dependent upon the occurrence of alternative "states of nature" (such as consumer demand or competitive retaliation), how should a decision-maker choose the "best" course of action, if he is not certain as to which state of nature will in fact prevail?

2. Given the opportunity to conduct, at a cost, some type of data-gathering activity (such as a consumer survey), should the decision-maker "purchase" more data bearing on the chances that alternative states of nature will occur and then take terminal action, or should he choose some "best" act now and forego the collection of additional data? Moreover, how should the data collection be designed?

3. Given the additional data (frequently subject to both sampling error and systematic error or bias), how can the decision-maker use the additional data to modify his initially held judgments about the occurrence of the alternative states of nature deemed relevant to the problem and then take optimal action?

FEATURES OF THE BAYESIAN APPROACH

An oversimplified planning example may illustrate some of the features of Bayesian approach.

Assume a decision-maker is faced with the problem of choosing an appropriate plant addition for the commercialization of a modified textile yarn product (called, say Texcel) under an uncertain future demand for the modification.

Building a plant too large, relative to demand, would result in costs associated with idle capacity. Building a plant too small, relative to demand, would result in costs associated with both profits foregone and the opportunity for competitors to increase their share of the market at the firm's expense.

If we assume the decision-maker is considering four alternative plant sizes—A, B, C, and D—ranging from large to small, then if the demand were high, payoffs would tend to favor the A plant addition, while if the demand were low, payoffs would tend to favor the D plant addition.

Assume that the firm's marketing personnel have attempted to forecast alternative levels of potential sales for the product (states of nature in Bayesian parlance) and they believe that some levels are more likely to occur than others. These alternative levels appear in Figure 3-1. Subjective probabilities of occurrence have been assigned to each forecast, 1 through 4.

The planner must then consider the payoffs over the whole planning period which would be associated with the combination of each plant size and sales forecast. These calculations would typically take into account the flows of revenues and costs after certain assumptions have been made on competitive behavior, pricing, and similar considerations.

In this example, assume that the payoff (say, in discounted cash flow)

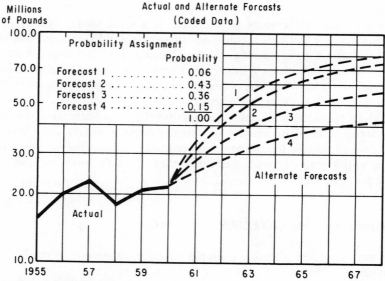

Figure 3-1. Texcel fiber forecasts.

associated with the conjunction of each alternative course of action and each alternative state of nature (potential sales) has been summarized as shown in Figure 3-2, Table 1. If the high sales forecast (Forecast 1 in the chart) were to occur, then strategy A (large plant) would provide the highest payoff.

APPLYING SUBJECTIVE PROBABILITIES

Under forecast 2, strategy B would provide the highest payoff, and so on. However, by applying the subjective probabilities associated with the occurrence of each forecast, as noted in Figure 3-2, Table 2, strategy B provides the highest expected monetary value, EMV, and would then be selected under the Bayesian approach.

Moreover, to test the sensitivity of the best choice to changes in the forecast probabilities, it is noted in Figure 3-2, Table 3, that assignment of an equiprobable measure (0.25 probability to each forecast) would not change the decision to select the strategy listed as B.

Table 1 Payoff Matrix—Unweighted (Entries-MM $)

Capacity Addition Strategy	Sales Forecast 1	2	3	4
A	30.8	21.7	(−) 2.2	(−)29.3
B	28.3	23.6	8.3	(−)17.8
C	14.8	14.2	10.9	(−) 9.8
D	7.3	6.5	5.1	(−) 7.2

Table 2 Originally Weighted Payoff Matrix (Entries-MM $)

Capacity Addition Strategy	1 (P = .06)	2 (P = .43)	3 (P = .36)	4 (P = .15)	EMV
A	1.85	9.33	(−)0.79	(−)4.40	5.99
B	1.70	10.15	2.99	(−)2.67	12.17
C	.89	6.11	3.92	(−)1.47	9.45
D	.44	2.80	1.82	(−)1.08	4.00

Table 3 Equally Likely Weighted Payoff Matrix

Capacity Addition Strategy	1 (P = .25)	2 (P = .25)	3 (P = .25)	4 (P = .25)	EMV
A	7.70	5.43	(−)0.55	(−)7.33	5.25
B	7.08	5.90	2.08	(−)4.45	10.61
C	3.70	3.55	2.73	(−)2.45	7.53
D	1.83	1.63	1.28	(−)1.80	2.94

Figure 3-2. Texcel problem.

In this example, many other features of the Bayesian approach have been omitted.[4]. Still, the illustration, though brief, does demonstrate the planner's need to consider alternative environments and their associated probabilities of occurrence, flows of revenues and costs, and the use of sensitivity analyses to indicate how the profitability of the "best" strategy might behave with changes in the assumptions underlying the analysis.

However, as can readily be imagined, the calculational burden associated in dealing with the complexities of actual problems goes considerably beyond what is illustrated here.

IMPLEMENTING BAYESIAN APPROACH

It is hardly surprising that the use of an electronic computer can assist materially in implementing the Bayesian approach as well as in other areas of business planning activity. For instance:

1. The computer can be used in screening possible courses of action. In diversification planning, for example, the usual procedure is to set up a list of criteria, against which candidate products and/or companies are matched. In large-scale programs of this sort, the computer can provide a ready means to perform this screening function.

2. The computer can be used to explore relevant states of nature via various types of forecasting models. Not only may the usual techniques of regression analysis and related statistical procedures be employed, but also forecasting models incorporating various dynamic features can be devised and tested retrospectively on the computer.

3. After various courses of action or states of nature are screened, the computer also provides an effective way to implement the Bayesian model. For example:

a. The computer provides the capacity for expeditiously evaluating a greater number of courses of action, if relevant to the problem.

b. The computer may be used to establish the initial payoff functions—a not easy calculational task if the planning period is long.

c. The computer provides a means to perform the desired sensitivity calculations after initial outcomes have been determined.

d. The computer can be used to provide a flexible model in which field data can be entered for the calculation of *revised* probabilities via the Bayesian approach. In other words, this model (for example, the computer program) can be established and maintained on a reasonably current basis, for incorporating new estimates as needed and then determining the implications stemming from these revisions.

It would thus seem that the computer can provide a useful (and frequently necessary) device to develop the payoffs associated with the complex course of action-state of nature combinations found in actual planning problems.[5] In the two years during which this approach has been used experimentally at Du Pont, computer assistance has been decidedly useful.

In summary, the decision theory-computer approach offers provocative possibilities for dealing with the uncertainty aspects and ill-structured nature of business planning problems. Continued development of this approach might well provide the business planner with a set of techniques powerful enough to be commensurate with the complexity and importance of his functional area.

AN ART, A SCIENCE OR A GAMBLE
BY G. E. SEAVOY

New-product marketing is an art; new-product marketing is a science; new-product marketing is a gamble. Take your pick. At any given time in a new-product program, one or all of the above are true. The marketing man, therefore, must be an artist, scientist, and gambler to cope with the problems peculiar to new-product marketing. He must bring all these talents to bear in an effort to define, analyze and reduce the risks inherent in the new-product market. He doesn't damn the torpedoes; he dodges them.

It is necessary to approach a new-product venture with a planned program that pre-determines the risks and moves to reduce them. These risks can generally be categorized into five different areas: risks in the product, risks in production, risks in the market, risks in distribution, and risks in commercialization.

RISKS IN THE PRODUCT

The Need for a Need

There is no such item as a successful product that nobody needs. This may appear to be an obvious snare and one that is avoided as a matter of course. The truth is that it is often overlooked in the wave of enthusiasm

EDITOR'S NOTE: From *Printers' Ink,* May 29, 1964, pp. 236-237. Reprinted by permission of Decker Communications Inc. and the author.

that sweeps a company when a truly ingenious product idea is suggested. The end result is a marvelously engineered, beautifully fabricated white elephant that enjoys a few days in the sun at one or two trade shows, then quietly and unobtrusively disappears in a pool of red ink. Whiting Corp., like most companies, has had both successes and failures in new products. One product that failed was a sophisticated system for handling commercial aircraft once they had landed at an airport. The system brought the passenger airplane to the passengers, which was a distinct improvement over the then-current practice of requiring passengers to walk through snow or rain to the aircraft. Without going into great detail, it can be said that the need was "over-service" by our product and as a result the product didn't sell. We were "warm", as they say (as witnessed by the popularity of the telescoping passenger ramps now in use at most major airports), but not exact.

The Performance Factor

Buyers are historically prejudiced in favor of products that work, whether it is a transistorized radio or an overhead traveling crane. It is much too late—and embarrassing—to pull a product off the market after its weaknesses have been broadcast to the world. This not only means that sales are lost, that the competitive edge is lost, that prestige and reputation are lost; it also means that when that product reappears or another product bearing the same company name emerges, it will immediately be suspect. To avoid this trap, the risk-reducer will see to it that the new product is thoroughly pre-tested not only for engineering characteristics but also for customer appeal, including packaging if that applies. There may be resistance to this testing on the grounds that it will take too much time or that a competitor is almost ready to make the jump. Where possible, override the resistance! When flaws are found in pre-testing, as they inevitably are, the delay will have proved itself worthwhile.

The Price is Right

One of the most important considerations about price is profit. Be certain that your profit margin is estimated as accurately as possible. Determine whether you wish to follow a large-volume small-profit policy, or a small-volume large-profit policy. Be certain you have considered such costs as packaging and packing, as well as transportation and handling. Determine if your over-all price policy is consistent with the buying habits of the market you wish to penetrate, and determine as well if your price is competitive with products already on the market. If it is higher, the product must have superior performance features or some other appeal to justify the premium.

RISKS IN PRODUCTION

Capacity and Capability

Honest appraisals rather then wishful thinking are required to find the answers here. How skilled is the engineering department? How skilled are the production people? How modern is the plant machinery? What volume of production can be maintained? Either these questions are answered honestly or the new product has problems. If the necessary skills aren't available, that means they will have to be bought on the outside, gobbling profit out of the price; if the plant machinery is out of date, that means longer manufacturing hours and perhaps overtime, which is another bite out of the profit: if volume can't be maintained that means poor delivery and causes subsequent customer resistance if not outright rejection. Reduce this risk by getting the answers before they are painfully brought to light on shop job tickets or engineering change orders.

The Special Situation

The new product that calls for special engineering for each application requires the existence of an engineering staff. If a company has no engineering department it must locate a dependable source of supply and acquaint the supplier with the product before the first engineering order is entered. Similarly, if a captive engineering department exists, the personnel should be thoroughly familiar with the product to prevent costly engineering delays.

RISKS IN THE MARKET

The Importance of Being Timely

There is something quite final about being late for a departing airline flight and watching the plane roar down the runway without you. That same finality applies to new-product timing; if you're late or early, the market will pass you by like a speeding jet. This is a risk that is best reduced by asking questions. Ask prospects. Find out what attitudes are current in the market. Test the product, if possible, and study reactions for clues. When all the evidence is tabulated the answer will probably not be clear-cut, but it will provide some basis for a decision.

Are You Out There, Customers?

A ship without a sail is no more becalmed than a product without a market. This consideration is so vital that market studies must follow immediately upon management acceptance of an idea as the basis of a new product. The information gathered through market analyses and surveys will answer numerous questions and in some cases be so revealing that new-product ideas are scrapped. Valuable data on the size of the market, its geographic location and its attitude will help answer questions on timing, on production, on pricing and on distribution. At the same time, evidence can be collected on the competitor's products, on the market's attitude toward the competition, and on product refinements that would allow an edge over the competition. If the risk-reducer doesn't look to his market with care, he is courting failure.

RISKS IN SELLING

Direct or Indirect Approach

The potential risk in establishing a sales organization for a new product is fairly obvious: don't sell a product that should be handled by distributors through company district offices, and vice-versa. In deciding on an approach, the risk-reducer considers such factors as the value of the product and the nature, size and location of the market. If the product blends nicely with the rest of the company's line, the direct sales approach through company offices should be workable. If the product is unique, or if geography is a consideration, a distributor network may be advisable. In this case, every effort should be made to line up organizations currently selling related items, i.e., a material-handling product to material-handling people, or a machine-tool product to machine-tool people. Price discounts to distributors should be in relation to the product's market, a limited market meaning a liberal discount and vice versa.

Service Factor

A new product may be rejected after initial use for lack of service. In establishing the sales organization, the service factor must be considered. Can factory service be provided or should distributor servicemen be used? A good distributor sales network, capable of providing service, offers a ready solution to this often unappreciated problem. If factory service must be supplied, are there skilled personnel available? Is there a plan to train them—and, for that matter, distributor servicemen as well—in servicing the new product?

RISKS IN COMMERCIALIZATION

The Successful Introduction

The National Industrial Conference Board lists the poorly planned or inadequate introductory campaign as a major cause of new-product failure. The potential risks in an introductory campaign are numerous but can be effectivly minimized by thoughtful pre-planning of a four-point program:

A precise statement of the objectives of the campaign.

Selection of a campaign theme.

Selection of advertising media to be used.

Coordination of promotion, publicity and collateral material.

The importance of specifying campaign objectives is threefold: it gives the entire program direction and meaning, it simplifies the selection of media to carry promotional messages and it provides a benchmark against which evaluations and measurements can later be made. The same truths apply to the second phase of communication tasks, namely, the establishment of a product theme. Whatever the theme, all promotional efforts should somehow be related to it so that the general impression conveyed to the advertising audience is consistent and forceful.

The third point to consider is the selection of media. To some extent this job has already been accomplished since the advertising message is known. Therefore, the risk-reducer will choose the channels that pertain to the market and provide editorial support of the new product as well as those general business magazines that can enhance the objectives of the campaign.

Promotion, publicity and product literature are not details that can take care of themselves. To be effective, each project should be planned and timed to support the fledging product as it takes its first steps on the market. If product literature, for example, is not immediately available when advertising inquiries first come in, the momentum, which is a natural attribute of almost any new product, is checked. Planning is the answer.

"Announcing for the First Time ... "

Enthusiasm for a new product can be generated by an exciting announcement or introduction; conversely, excitement can be stifled by a dull announcement or by no announcement at all. The dangers are more potent in this regard than they might seem because excitement and enthusiasm are either generated or squelched among two groups, namely, the prospects for the product and the salesmen of the product. An intensive advertising program may later spark the interest of the prospects, but the enthusiasm of the sales force, which is essential for the product's success, may be lost forever. Give the new product a flying start; the advertising and publicity plans previously outlined will provide the additional support necessary.

If you have concluded that new-product marketing is a risky business, you are absolutely correct. It is also correct to conclude, however, that for almost every risk, there is a safeguard. The safeguards aren't foolproof but they do exist and they can go a long way toward minimizing the inherent dangers. There are two indispensable elements for reducing risk—investigation and planning. There isn't a risk in the book that can be effectively minimized without employing these elements. Their use is the difference between success and failure.

NOTES

1. *Management Science,* April 1959, pp. 238-40.
2. McGraw-Hill Book Co., 1959.
3. The so-called Bayesian approach owes its name to a central feature of the procedure, Bayes' theorem, named after its developer, Thomas Bayes.
4. For instance, "indifference probabilities" could have been computed. These are probabilities which would have to be associated with the occurrence of some state of nature more favorable to an inferior strategy before that strategy would break even with strategy B. Also, calculation of the costs of uncertainty ($2.63 million in this case) could have been illustrated to show the stake involved in a decision to collect more information before taking terminal action. Moreover, the modification of initial probabilities by using additional data has been omitted as well.
5. As an illustration dealing with the complex characteristics of industrial market planning, the writer's: "An Application of Bayesian Decision Theory to a Problem in Long Range Pricing Strategy," Annual Meeting of American Statistical Assn. (New York, December 1961), might be of interest.

ADDITIONAL SELECTED BIBLIOGRAPHY

Corporate Risk of Innovations

Greene, M. R., "Market Risk—An Analytical Framework," *Journal of Marketing,* Vol. 32, No. 2 (April, 1968), 49-56.

Hertz, D. B., "Risk Analysis on Capital Investment," *Harvard Business Review,* Vol. 42, No. 1 (January-February, 1964), 95-106.

Marvin, P. "Products and Profits: Some Basis Concepts Underlying Company Strategy," *Developing a Product Strategy,* Elizabeth Marting, editor, AMA Management Report No. 39, American Management Association (1959), pp. 11-24.

O'Connor, M. J., "Basic Patterns of New Product Strategy," *Marketing Precision and Executive Action,* Charles H. Hendersman, ed., AMA Proceedings, American Marketing Association (June, 1962), 387-396.

"Putting A New Product on the Market Is Costly, Complicated and Risky," *The Wall Street Journal* (February 18, 1971), 1, 21.

Swalm, R. O., "Utility Theory—Insights Into Risk Taking," *Harvard Business Review,* Vol. 44, No. 6 (November-December, 1966), 123-136.

QUESTIONS FOR DISCUSSION AND REVIEW

1. Why does so much time and money go into product planning?

2. What risks do corporate planners underwrite with new products?

3. Can you suggest methods to reduce corporate risk of innovations?

4. Explain whether or not there is a correlation between risk and profit.

5. Are there risks in purchasing new successful products from other firms?

6. Give examples of individual risks linked with product innovations.

PART II
ORGANIZATIONAL APPROACHES TO PRODUCT PLANNING

4

ESTABLISHING CORPORATE OBJECTIVES

Every on-going corporation must plan for today, tomorrow, next year, and for the next five or ten years. Planning will allow a company to stride forward toward the achievement of its objectives. Objectives are not reached by hit-or-miss fashion. There is deliberate planning in reaching corporate goals. However, there must be enough flexibility to allow for changes if they are needed. It has been suggested that objectives which are to be met within a fiscal year should be reviewed quarterly; those objectives that are to be reached during an intermediate time period, such as two to three years, should be reviewed semi-annually, and those long-range goals should be reviewed annually.

Corporate objectives for product planning are established either at the vice-presidential level or higher in small to medium-size corporations or by a committee approach in larger corporations. The trend in the late 1960's and early 1970's is toward the committee approach by various-sized corporations. Apparently, this shared responsibility bears out the need for a holistic approach to minimize mistakes that could turn out to be massive and costly.

Management philosphy concerning product planning is instrumental in determining company objectives. Documented objectives can reduce waste in time, effort, and in finances. A philosophy can either be narrow in the sense that all new product ideas must not create additional expenditures for plant, equipment, or new marketing personnel, or broad in the sense of diversification to new product ideas which are radically different from the present line of products and which may require new productive facilities, extensive financing, and new marketing criteria. These criteria concern new channel management, a new sales force, and an entirely new market segment. Naturally, financial risks are involved, and firms must weigh these risks against future success of new products before a decision is made to expend the money and effort in the direction of commercializing new products. Therefore, it is necessary to determine the objectives of a firm and plan ahead with the objectives in mind. The following articles deal with the establishment of corporate objectives based on a corporate philosophy to plan ahead so as to achieve the goals set for the firm.

NEW PRODUCTS NEED
SPECIAL MANAGEMENT
BY JOHN H. MURPHY

Almost all managements are keenly attuned to the need for new products. But many are the trouble situations. Here is a list of the more common situations symptomatic of new-products troubles:

1. Management has virtually no idea of what new products it might introduce more than a year or two in the future.

2. New products are developed because of needs to meet competition or fill a current field demand, resulting in crash programs because of lack of time.

3. The R&D Department does not know what to develop, or has so many projects that almost nothing is ever completed.

4. The product manager goes to the R&D Director and persuades him to work on his pet project, with the result that a product comes into being without management's knowledge or approval.

5. A bookkeeper or draftsman has a product idea but cannot find anyone to listen to it, because no channels have been set up through which a product idea can proceed.

6. Members of management become enamored of a pet product idea and push it past all opposition, creating a "sacred cow" to be brought to market without adequate evaluation.

7. The Vice President for Marketing or the Plant Manager gives the President his case for or against a product idea at lunch or on an airplane

EDITOR'S NOTE: From the *Journal of Marketing*, October 1962, pp. 46-49. Reprinted by permission of the American Marketing Association and the author.

trip, resulting in a product decision based on incomplete or biased information.

8. The President thinks "there's a product we should look into one of these days." a symptom of an understaffed new-products effort.

9. No one man is in touch with all aspects of each program.

10. A product comes out differently from what management believes were the original objectives.

Such situations can be found in many companies today. They are a result of poor new-products management, or of not enough of the necessary elements of the new-products job.

THREE ELEMENTS FOR SUCCESS

Three elements for success most often missing are (1) forward planning, (2) coordination, and (3) communications. Other necessary elements are engineering, product development, cost estimating, facilities analysis, etc., but are usually present within the existing organization.

Forward Planning

Product plans cannot be allowed to result from chance product "finds" or the demands of competition. Someone must have the responsibility for constantly planning for the future products.

Also, product plans and product decisions must be based on more than seat-of-the-pants thinking. They must be based on facts—often facts that management does not know that it does not have.

Of course, implied here is a need for marketing research. Whether marketing research is done by an internal department, or whether it is done by external research agencies, there must be manpower available to do the necessary fact collecting, in order to supply answers to the many questions about the market and its requirements.

Forward planning, however, is more than fact gathering. Facts about the market alone cannot plan the product line. For one thing, all the completely accurate information that will be necessary will not be obtainable. Some inferences will have to be made and some "facts" will have to be assumptions based on other facts. Marketing research people, for example, cannot go out and determine the potential market of a product that has never been offered before, or how much the user will pay for a feature he has never seen. Judgment must come into the picture.

As complex as modern markets are, it will be an unusual individual who could offer the necessary creativity or make all the necessary judgments by himself. Also, several men have a stake in what the product should be; and there will be more than one man who will have a background that will permit a worthwhile contribution to forward planning. Therefore, several men should be brought together to draw conclusions from the facts and to spur each other's thinking.

This may be a job for a standing committee, a full department, or varying project teams. An approach must be taken that will assure that it is done and that will in many cases break loose the thought processes of appropriate people from their day-to-day jobs, even if only for a few hours a month.

Forward planning should cover four things:

1. Analysis of trends relating to a specific industry or any growth industry, if diversification is the objective.

2. Determination of what products or product features are suggested by these trends.

3. Consideration and screening of random product ideas that may be presented by anyone.

4. Review of the facts established as the programs progress; and a final review prior to presentation to management.

The prime consideration is that product plans should be based on the requirements of the market—not just on what a company happens to be able to make or what R&D happens to "stumble across," or on what the Industrial Relations Director happens to think would be just what the market needs.

Coordination

A company will not realize new products unless the forward planning is done and unless product ideas are evaluated and pushed through to commercialization. This involves coordination of all the people involved first in forward planning and then in R&D, facilities planning, costing, pricing, distribution planning, and decision making for a new product—in effect, taking a job that is scattered among many departments and welding it into a single unified effort. There are nine specific things that some one person or department must do:

1. Plan the product or stimulate the planning process; bring creative minds together, and insure that an organized, comprehensive, forward planning job takes place.

2. Establish long-range and immediate timetables and priorities for new-product work, and supply constant pressure to insure that the timetables will be met.

3. Evaluate product ideas and plans, and present this information to management for decision on a complete and objective basis.

4. Keep pressure on lower priority but potentially profitable projects.

5. Act as a single point for collection of all product ideas, without organizational barriers.

6. Serve as a system of checks and balances for the information and opinions developed in the course of product programs.

7. Be the guiding hand to make certain that product programs proceed according to sound practice.

8. Supply a single point of contact for outside consultants working on product programs.

9. Be a central communications center that is fully informed on all activities relating to new-products work, that can disseminate information to all interested departments and bring to appropriate people's attention the information that might alter the course of a product program.

Communications

This last point bears discussion by itself and suggests a deficiency that can cause what is probably the greatest potential source of trouble in product programs—insufficient communications. Conclusions of a planning group, decisions by management, directions to Engineering, Engineering's comments on these directions, and each basic assumption and change in any of these assumptions *should be put in writing and circulated to those directly concerned* (with copies to other interested persons, including top management).

There are two reasons for this. For one thing, memories are short. As programs proceed, there should be a clear point of reference, so that the direction in which the program should proceed can be checked. Lack of understanding of the product objectives being pursued can cause great waste of expensive R&D manpower. Also, many departments must be informed about what is going on on a continuing basis. A good coordination system can get a great deal done at all levels, while cutting down the necessity of time-consuming meetings involving high-priced people, many of whom have little or nothing to contribute.

For example, circulating the agreed-upon volume potential figure for a new product early in a program will prevent someone from commenting later, "If I had known that was all we planned to sell of these, I would have tried to stop this whole program!"; or, "We went at this all wrong; we should have done so-and-so if we planned to sell that many."

The earlier such disagreements can be registered, the less money will be spent on projects that will eventually be thrown out; and everyone who should comment is not likely to be present when all of them are discussed. Management should be kept informed about what is being tried and what the results of these efforts are, so that programs can be stopped that will not pay off.

There must be a central information clearing house. See Figure 4-1.

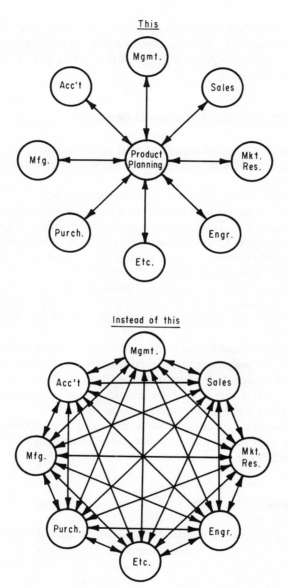

Figure 4-1. A central clearing house for program information planning is essential.

Putting the Pieces Together

These three elements have been dealt with separately, but for timely product decisions to be soundly based on the necessary market facts and other information, the new product process must be a continuing, selective one. Therefore, forward planning, coordination, and communications become intertwined to the point they become a single job. This job can be called "Product Planning."

BASICS OF NEW-PRODUCTS MANAGEMENT

Two basics of managing the job should be considered.

1. *Planning, coordination, and communications must be assigned to some one person or department.*

2. *Product planning is a top management responsibility.*

The idea that product planning represents a job that must be definitely assigned and that it is a top management responsibility suggests that the President (or Division General Manager) should do the forward planning, coordination, and communication directly. Most would prefer to do so; and if they can, all well and good. However, this is usually easier said than done. As a company becomes larger and the business more complex, specialization forces more and more people into the process. Top management loses the ability to do product planning successfully. This happens for any or all of three reasons:

1. The chief executive becomes insulated against the requirements of the market because of simple organizational expediency. He can no longer keep in close enough touch with his markets to know what they need.

2. He never seems able to find the time to devote to new products—there are always more pressing day-to-day jobs to be done.

3. He has trouble coordinating the second- and third-echelon people, and the ideas that must be considered between the time an idea is born and until a product reaches the market place.

What Happens?

When top management cannot exercise direct control over new-products work, one of two things usually happens. The responsibility for product planning becomes one of no one in particular and everyone in general, and nothing is done, or the job goes to a line function.

The former case will certainly cause trouble, but the practice of giving the job to a line function will also. It may cause a little less trouble; but it fools management into feeling that the job is well covered when it is not. Assignment of the job to a line activity is often the path of least resistance and a loose assignment of convenience, rather than a careful delegation of management responsibility and authority. The reasons why a line function has trouble doing product planning should be carefully considered.

The most common situation is that the job falls to the Marketing

Department. This is because Marketing will be the first to feel the pinch of an inadequate product line and will make the initial move for new products. There are several reasons why this usually does *not* work well:

1. Embroiled in the current job of moving goods, the Marketing man, particularly the Product Manager, is not likely to have the time to do much more than postpone thinking about tomorrow's products, too—until the time comes when it is no longer a forward planning job and becomes a request for a new product that is needed right now.

2. The job of forward planning is not always compatible with the current job of moving goods, which is marketing management's responsibility.

3. Marketing tends to be too easily affected by the influence of current market needs and is not likely to project thinking far enough into the future.

4. Marketing men may view the world through a kind of special salesman's glasses which tend to hide negative considerations in product programs.

5. Marketing does not always think in terms of diversification.

It may seem that the job of planning for future products could be done in Marketing if someone in a staff position in the Marketing organization were assigned to do that and nothing else. This is true, of course.

However, product planning does not stop with the creation of an idea. The idea must be impartially evaluated in the light of overall corporate objectives and limitations. The final recommendation to top management should not be too heavily flavored by the views and requirements of Marketing.

Some companies put the responsibility for product planning in other line functions, such as R&D, but they have some of the same problems in doing the job as Marketing. There is not enough time for them to do the job, and there may be insufficient objectivity. They have an additional problem: that they are too far from the marketplace to permit new product thinking to be sufficiently market oriented.

Also, the coordination part of the job is often better done under the aegis of the President than the Manager of Marketing or other line function.

ONE MORE POINT

Product planning, even when reporting to the President, will not be a panacea for solving all problems of new products. Supporting functions such as marketing research, product development, financial analysis, and appearance design must be available to the Product Planning Manager.

Also, management cannot expect to divest itself of the responsibility of making the program operate effectively. Product planning can take a tremendous load off the top man, and it can mean that a job will be done which otherwise might be pushed aside indefinitely. But top management must still be the force behind a successful product-planning program.

Much of what is stated here has had to be stated in general terms. People and circumstances in different companies will suggest applying these precepts differently, and product planning and emphasis on the product planner's job will vary in different companies; but observation of these operating principles is a "must" if a company is to rely on new products for growth and future profits.

HOW TO LAUNCH
NEW PRODUCTS
BY WILLIAM J. CONSTANDSE

Most business enterprises have long recognized the need for the development and marketing of new products and new uses of old products in order to broaden their market base and sustain a profitable, healthy growth in tomorrow's dynamic environment. Many companies have established line and staff departments to meet this challenge, and often they have experienced difficulty in their product planning efforts to provide a reasonable return on investment. This article reviews the experience of a group of large industrial corporations in product planning. Although this informal survey is not necessarily representative of the experience of all such firms, it is possible to pinpoint the major pitfalls encountered in product planning and to identify steps being taken by many to avoid their past mistakes.

Product planning takes place under many different names which often appear to reflect a corporation's thinking on the subject. If the higher echelons in management have made their initial career in sales, the department responsible for broadening the company's product and market base is often labeled *marketing planning*. The same function is usually called *product planning* in organizations which are highly technically oriented. Other names for the same responsibility include *corporate planning, new product management,* or simply *planning*. This article deals with a company's activity which is aimed at developing new products, new uses of the existing product line, and new markets.

EDITOR'S NOTE: From *MSU Business Topics,* Winter 1971, pp. 29-34. Reprinted by permission of the Division of Research, Graduate School of Business Administration of the Michigan State University, and the author.

Most organizations in this survey agreed that establishment of a corporate strategy was an essential prerequisite for a successful product planning effort. The development of a strategy is always a time-consuming and often highly frustrating assignment. Top management must begin this arduous job by defining what business the company is in. Theodore Levitt in his book *Marketing Innovation* has illustrated the type of thinking involved in answering the question: "What is the company"s business?" For example, a computer manufacturing company may decide that it is in the information handling business. This in turn raises several unanswered questions. Should the company restrict its activity to industrial sales or expand into consumer products and services? Does the definition of the company's business include the sale of information and the maintenance of data banks where such information is stored for subsequent retrieval by computer? Does *information* mean digital data only which can be processed by computers, or does it also include analog data represented by images which can be copied, transmitted over telephone lines, or stored on microfilm?

What are the corporate objectives? After management has defined the business the corporation is in, it has to specify the organization's objectives. These goals have to be specific and quantifiable. They may be stated as primary and secondary corporate objectives. A common primary objective of enterprises in a growth industry is an annual sales increase of 15 percent while maintaining a pre-tax profit of 30 percent. A return on investment of 15 percent is often a primary objective of companies which internally finance their growth. A secondary objective could be maintenance of market share or leadership in the industry. The objectives of publicly held corporations and family controlled businesses can vary widely. The latter's goals were often reported as the maintenance of a 15 percent annual dividend on the par value of its closely held shares.

The *corporate strategy* defines the ways in which the organization will use its resources to achieve its objectives. An airline may have defined its business as transportation and set as its goals specific growth and profitability rate. Its strategy may be to expand the passenger business by offering packaged tours supported by company-owned car rental services and hotels. It also could establish an air freight division. A hotel organization, on the other hand, could decide to branch out with motels, camping grounds, and the rental of camper trucks and trailers. Manufacturers of trailers might redefine their business of mobile homes to that of factory-produced homes and expand into the vacation and second-home market. A magazine publisher in the education business may also apply its resources to the distribution of books, records, films, and video tapes. A corporate strategy may state that its goals are to be achieved through internal growth only or by acquisitions. A technology-based enterprise could emphasize the development of a strong patent position as a springboard for meeting its corporate objectives. Supermarkets could think of their enterprises as an impulse buying business in which they set a goal of 15 percent return on investment to be achieved by a low profit margin and high turnover. Within the framework of this corporate strategy their original product line of foods could be expanded, as indeed it has, to many non-food items and services.

ORGANIZATION

How product planning should be organized appears to depend a great deal on the size of the corporation and the style of its management. A small enterprise could afford only a single marketing planning group reporting direct to the president. A large corporation would have a staff to formulate corporate strategy and planning departments by subsidiary, division, and product line. Some companies experiment with venture management in which an independent organizational entity headed by an entrepreneur is given the opportunity to launch a new product from conception to delivery. This approach aims at solving two major problems inherent in most product planning activities: NIH (Not Invented Here) and motivation. A planning group is more often than not a staff function which has to convince a line manager that his department ought to develop a new product X. As can be expected, the line manager has his own ideas about the subject and favors his proposal for new product Y. Unless he is really convinced by product planning that X is better than Y, he is not motivated to develop the former. Procrastination may be followed by the decision to develop Y, much to the frustration of the product planning group.

Many successful new products have one thing in common: the product champion. This is an individual with boundless enthusiasm and a high degree of corporate stamina who has proposed a new product, is responsible for its development, and is able to keep all levels of management sold on the value of his idea through the entire development cycle. He has staked his career in the company on the commercial success of his venture and, therefore, is highly motivated to launch a profitable product. A close cousin of the product champion is the bootleg project manager. Invariably a bootleg project is an effort which secretly develops a new product idea previously rejected by management. The project manager, thoroughly convinced that the company made the wrong decision, is out to prove he was right after all. Fueled by this type of motivation, many bootleg projects have been responsbile for the introduction of highly successful products.

Product planning can be organized along two basically different lines. The classical approach is the establishment of a staff group which researches the market needs, within the framework of the corporate strategy, to formulate the specifications of a new product. The product planner then has to convince the appropriate division or department to develop the product. In the second approach, top management and the research, development, or engineering department are the sources of a new product idea. The assistance of the project planning group is requested only to justify, from a marketing and profitability viewpoint, the budget for the development of the proposed product. Most companies have come to rely on both approaches since either one of them has proven to lead to profitable new products.

STAFFING

Most companies staff their product planning groups with former sales representatives. The arguments advanced for this position are: (1) salesmen know what their customers want and are therefore in the best position to define the market requirements, and (2) the abilities of a top flight salesman are required to sell the new ideas proposed by product planning to management.

These arguments are valid with the following reservations. A successful salesman is quite often a poor product planner because he lacks the vision and imagination to look beyond tomorrow. He has been selected and trained to sell the present product line in today's market. His sales experience may have taught him the shortcomings of this company's products and the advantages of competitive offerings. It does not necessarily follow that he has the ability to innovate, to think of entirely new products, to develop new uses for existing products, or to discover and develop new markets. Technical personnel, who have been exposed to the customer environment, have proven as capable in product planning activities as former salesmen. Several companies have also supplemented their product planning departments with professional familiar with operations research, mathematical modeling, decision analysis, and similar advanced techniques. These individuals, although fully capable of making a contribution to planning, are often handicapped by their inability to communicate the results of their work in terms which can be understood by management.

Although a good product planning department should have more than one discipline represented on its staff, the most important requirement is creative and innovative thinking. Most product planning efforts suffer from a lack of men who have good ideas and can convince management of the value of these ideas.

PROPOSAL FOR NEW PRODUCTS

There is rarely a dearth of good ideas. The problem is to convince management that it should appropriate resources to the development and marketing of a new idea. The failure to successfully resolve this problem has invariably produced frustration among many product planners and often caused management to appraise the product planning effort as ineffective. Failure of the product planning group to successfully communicate with management can usually be traced to poor preparation and ignorance of sound business decision criteria. Acceptance of a product planning proposal requires the ability to know and sense what is considered important to the group of men who control the purse strings. The timing of the proposal is important: an idea may be too advanced for the market or the technology required. Approval for such a high risk development effort is often difficult to obtain. Many times a new product was rejected because the planner did not do his homework. He made errors of commission and omission with the following outcomes: total development cost estimated too low, five-year forecast too optimistic, product cost not competitive, profitability or return on investment not in line with the corporate strategy, excessive cost to recruit or train the sales force, unfavorable cash flow, ignorance of competitive activities and plans, untenable patent position and so forth.

Each company traditionally favors techniques which greatly improve the odds for funding of a new product idea. Some of these are highly pragmatic, others are questionable from a business ethics viewpoint. An effective approach in some corporations is to discover a gap in the product line. A simple example of this would be the need for a low priced car, a mini-computer, or a medium priced ball-point pen. Another way to gain quick acceptance for new product ideas is to cater to the vanity of management, although investments in managerial egos do not always produce an adequate return. If an enterprise avoids a pioneering role, a competitive success invariably invites imitators; this avenue is most likely to produce quick acceptance of a new product proposal. The product planning department of one large corporation added a cynical twist to this latter approach. Whenever these people wanted to get funding for the development of their ideas, they wrote an article alleging that competition was moving in to capitalize on the same business opportunity. The article was placed in a magazine that was known to be scanned by the management who would decide on the proposed project. Within one week after publication, management invariably raised the question: "What are we doing about this?" and the product planning department would move in quickly to find a very receptive audience for their ideas.

NEW PRODUCT DESIGN

Once a new product proposal has been accepted, the difficult task of delivering the promise begins. The most common mistake, besides underestimating the budget and the time to produce an acceptable product, is the failure to adequately evaluate a reasonable number of alternate designs. The project manager in charge of the development project is understandably guided by his own professional training and experience in directing the product design. It is not unusual that he favors a highly sophisticated approach which appeals to his professional pride. He searches out a solution he believes is worthy of a technical paper to be read at some future international congress; one which would elevate his standing and reputation in his professional fraternity. The result is often a technological breakthrough but a commercial flop. Another example of the same expensive mistake in product design is the case of the mechanical engineer who came up with a marvelous solution which looked like a Rube Goldberg contraption if compared to the electronic alternative announced by the competition at one-half the price. A data processing company once proposed a teleprocessing solution which excited the imagination of its management, until competition marketed a simple batch system with a much better price/performance ratio. In the field of programmed instruction, the early solutions marketed were expensive and involved with use of television and microfilm systems until someone discovered that these devices were basically electronic and mechanical page-turners. Since this task could be best performed manually by the student, the programmed instruction in the traditional textbook form became a viable product. Product design failures of this nature abound in many companies. It would be quite useful to establish a new product morgue, which each project manager must visit prior to accepting a new assignment.

MARKET FORECASTING

There are are numerous textbooks and scholarly articles published on the subject of marketing forecasting. In the real world of business, very little of the theory is applied. In many cases the market forecasting tools are too sophisticated for the quantity and quality of the available data. The situation could be compared to using a computer when an adding machine would do. A forecast is only as good as the assumptions it is based on, and that is exactly one of the major problems in a reliable forecast. The market forecast assumptions consist almost entirely of subjective factors such as: the state of the economy over the next five years, the impact of potential competition, customer acceptance rate, and price sensitivity. This judgment has to be made before the computer (or abacus) can turn out the numbers. The quality of the forecast is directly dependent on this judgment. The majority of companies surveyed preferred a market forecast made by an independent organizational entity, since new product development teams tend to bias the estimated profitability of their effort by being overly optimistic. Many forecasters, who have highly scientific tools at their disposal, lack imagination. Several companies which were given the opportunity to evaluate the xerography patents of Carlson, simply extrapolated the then-existing trend in the use of copying machines without realizing that this new technology would revolutionize the copying market. Some forecasters play it safe. In one corporation, the forecasting department knew that nobody would question a market estimate of 10 percent of the total market potential. One product, which was confidently estimated to capture 8 percent of the market, turned out to have no market at all. Test marketing is not a panacea either; the test market itself may not be representative of the total market while the promotional campaign supporting the product could have used the wrong media. Also, there is always the risk of tipping off the competition.

REVENUE AND PROFITABILITY ANALYSIS

Many promising products have been inadvertently killed and an equal number of losers marketed by lack of a rigorous analysis of anticipated revenue and profit. A common pitfall is the failure to evaluate price sensitivity. Surprisingly, many forecasts estimate the market for a product only at a price, which produces a normal profit. A market forecast for three or five different sales prices produces a much better insight into the viability of a new product. The early Toni hair products, for example, were initially priced too low to capture the projected market. Variable costs, which depend on quantity manufactured, always have a significant impact. The revenue analysis should demonstrate to management at which price it can maximize revenue, return on investment, profit in dollars, or profit as a percentage of sales. Without this exercise, intelligent decision cannot be made in pricing the new product.

Another rather common pitfall in product planning is the failure to insist on periodic checkpoints during the development cycle, especially if the time span from conception to announcement is more than one year. In time, conditions change and the original assumptions that were used to justify the funding of a project may no longer be valid. Competition may have jumped the gun with a surprise announcement, government legislation can have a negative impact, a new labor contract might increase manufacturing cost more than anticipated, or an increase in interest rates could depress customer acceptance. The development of a product, which looked promising initially, may have to be terminated to prevent throwing good money after bad. That is a tough decision which only an astute and courageous management can make.

ANNOUNCEMENT

A new product, which has survived the obstacle course of funding, forecasting, pricing and profitability analysis, may still fail in the marketplace. Business is still an art, not a science. Only the customer will determine if the collective business judgment of the enterprise properly appraised the risks and benefits of announcing the new product. Failures at this late stage can be caused by several factors. The most common reason is improper timing. Market conditions change after a project has been initiated; if management does not kill the development effort a product can reach the marketplace too late. The Edsel is a case in point. The opposite is also true. Bank credit cards were introduced as early as 1956 but could not be considered a commercial success until ten years later. Poor market support planning was cited as another cause for product failure. In these cases, inadequate training of the field organization, lack of proper motivation for the salesman to push the new product, or incompatibility with the existing product line were the main culprits causing failure. Many of these factors are interrelated and it is difficult to determine which contributed most to a product's lack of commercial success. Disappointing customer acceptance could be the result of an overly optimistic forecast, a product which does not meet the market requirements, wrong pricing or distribution channels, poor timing, or insufficient promotional effort.

Many of the smaller enterprises do not have an effective system set up to monitor the performance of a new product after announcement. The first six months in a product's life are very important to the organization which fathered it. Timely feedback from the sales organization is required to determine if the product is meeting its forecast. If it is not, the why and where must be pinpointed in order to take corrective action. If remedial steps are not taken in time, the product may turn sour and be beyond recovery. The image of the company which launched the product could be adversely impacted, affecting sales of other items in the product line. Monitoring of a product should not cease after it has turned out to be a winner but is to continue during its projected life. If it does not meet the specific objectives of the corporate strategy, it should be withdrawn from the market unless new uses can be developed or improvements justified to extend its profitable life.

The intent of this article has been to review some of the most important pitfalls which many of the companies, successful in product planning, have learned to avoid. Industrial corporations would be able to learn much from an exchange of experience in this area. Unfortunately, very few enterprises are willing to discuss their failures in public.

ADDITIONAL SELECTED BIBLIOGRAPHY

Establishing Corporate Objectives

Ames, B. C., "Keys to Successful Product Planning," *Business Horizons,* Vol. 9, No. 2 (Summer, 1966), 49-58.

Karger, D. W. and Murdick, R. G., "Product Design, Marketing, and Manufacturing Innovation," *California Management Review,* Vol. 9, No. 2 (Winter, 1966), 33-42.

Taylor, S. H., "Keys Success in Product Introduction," *New Ideas for Successful Marketing,* J. S. Wright and J. L. Goldstucker, eds., AMA Proceedings of the 1966 World Congress, American Marketing Association (June, 1966), 229-237.

Weigand, R. R., "How Extensive the Planning and Development Program?" *Journal of Marketing,* Vol. 26, No. 3 (July, 1962), 55-57.

QUESTIONS FOR DISCUSSION AND REVIEW

1. Why is it necessary to establish corporate objectives?

2. What bases do firms use when they explore for new product ideas?

3. How important is planning with product innovation?

4. Do new products need special management? If so, why?

5. What are the keys to successful product planning?

5

ORGANIZATIONAL APPROACHES TO
NEW PRODUCT DEVELOPMENT

Primary responsibility for product planning can be assigned either to a product manager or to a committee. You will find that in numerous companies product planning activities bisect various major functional areas. Of course, the role that a product manager or committee plays depends upon the industry, the company, and the products in the product line. The product manager of an industrial company may, in fact, have responsibilities in areas which are considered mundane when compared with those of a product manager in a soft goods company. Organizational patterns and subdivisions also differ from industry to industry. It will prove interesting to note that though long-range goals are similar, the methods by which companies attempt to reach these goals differ in human resources, in capital application, and in a time dimension. If a product manager is given the responsibility for the success of new products, what qualifications do firms look for in product managers? What is the extent of his authority or functional authority which transcends departments? There are firms that believe that long-range company success depends upon product development and that a product planning committee holds the key to progress and success in future operations of the firm. However, keeping the committee simple and flexible, responsible, and under some control system to spur new product development are just several guidelines to consider. Organizational charts of a new products division vary from corporation to corporation. Duties of a product planner or committee also vary from firm to firm. The importance of a separate new products department (a single manager or committee) and the responsibilities and duties of separate departments are discussed in the following articles.

INTERFACES OF
A PRODUCT MANAGER
BY DAVID J. LUCK

The position of product manager was established over 40 years ago in a prominent marketing organization, that of Procter and Gamble. Despite this long history, scholarly research and writing have seemingly ignored the product management organization. Literature specifically treating product management organization is confined to perhaps three or four monographs or thin volumes which are largely descriptive.[1]

Does this obscurity imply that the product manager is a rare or unimportant functionary in modern business? Evidence points to the contrary. This writer's experience and that of other observers indicates that most large multiproduct companies have initiated the product management plan of organization.

Product managers operate on a horizontal plane, in contrast to the primarily vertical orientation of most marketing personnel. Their specialization is cross functional with primary focus on a specific product line or brand. They have numerous titles such as brand manager, product planning manager, or product marketing manager. These titles frequently denote varying emphases, but do not alter their basic responsibilities. The position of "product manager" is a radical departure in management that is not easily slotted into and absorbed by the existing organization. Consequently, it is not readily defined, staffed, and implemented.

EDITOR'S NOTE: From the *Journal of Marketing,* October 1969, pp. 32-36. Reprinted by permission of the American Marketing Association and the author.

OBJECTIVES OF THE PRODUCT MANAGER

Enthusiasts for product management have envisioned this position to be the answer to the needs of large enterprises to create true profit centers within the organization. This vision has proved generally impracticable.[2] Product managers are seriously hampered by ambiguity of authority in the execution of their plans and decisions, in addition to the problems of a new type of position asserting its intended role. Undefined authority precludes clear-cut, enforceable responsibility. Despite such problems, the main purposes of product managers are seemingly being accomplished. They are:

1. Creation and conceptualization of strategies for improving and marketing the assigned product line or brands.
2. Projection and determination of financial and operating plans for such products.
3. Monitoring execution and results of plans, with possible adaptation of tactics to evolving conditions.

An underlying role of the product manager is that of becoming the information center on the assigned products.

Product management provides integrated planning which is intimately related to the market needs and opportunities of specific products. This contrasts with decisions that formerly were diffused among functional specialists who could not bring to bear comprehensive knowledge and analysis of factors peculiar to a product. The establishment of interfaces between product manager and these functional specialists is necessary in order to insure acquisition of the variety of information which these specialists can contribute. Simultaneously, the product manager needs to maintain interfaces with the functional personnel who execute the strategies and plans that he originates.

This leads us to the product managers as vital organizational loci for the focus of marketing interfaces. The subject of these interfaces and the means whereby they may be efficiently realized thus merits our serious concern.

INTERFACES VITAL TO PRODUCT MANAGERS

Research information obtained during studies of 17 product managers in the course of an advertising decision study[3] and during a current study of eight product managers for pharmaceutical manufacturers indicates that the interfaces which are important to a product manager's work are perhaps the most numerous and varied of any in middle management. They may be placed in the following six categories.

The Buying Public

In ultimate significance to marketing strategy and planning, the buyers and users of the particular product line overshadow all other interfaces. The man who is to conceive product and promotion strategies and prepare competitively viable plans can hardly be too well apprised of how, when, and for what purposes the product is bought and used. Market segments with unique needs may be identified and are often the clue to very effective strategies. Brand images, brand loyalties, consumer profiles, and the reception of advertising and sales promotion campaigns are further examples of the vast information the experienced product manager acquires and studies as he appraises the past and explores future possibilities.

Distributors

Wholesalers and retailers play major roles in the market success of products which they distribute. Relatively small shifts in shelf facings, out-of-stocks, displays, and other dealer support may produce favorable or dangerous trends. A significant portion of the product distribution strategy may be aimed at the distributors themselves to stimulate and maintain their interests through special programs, sales aids, and other trade promotion. Often the product manager's concern includes monitoring the inventories in the pipelines in order to control production rates.

Sales Force

The salesman is a necessary ally of the product manager, although often a very independent one. For most industrial products and for some consumer products, personal selling is the principal force in promoting the product. Since the salesman is frequently selling many products of the firm, product managers often compete with one another in seeking the salesman's support. Product managers are most concerned with the development of selling methods, sales aids, and applications literature. For industrial products, the product manager often makes sales calls with the salesman, particularly where technical expertise is needed.

Advertising Agencies

The degree of involvement with advertising agencies varies widely among product managers. For most industrial products it is of less concern than the sales force. In some consumer goods organizations, product managers are limited by policy to working with the agencies only to the extent of developing advertising strategies, with all other liaison conducted through advertising departments. At the other extreme, there are companies which place virtually all collaborations with the agencies in the hands of product managers. Typically a consumer goods product manager works intimately and continuously with his counterparts in the agency—a relationship that has received some criticism where inexperienced product managers have been troublesome to agencies.[4] Regardless of such views, agency account men tend to work as a team with product managers of major advertisers in developing advertising campaigns and in providing market information and merchandising ideas to the client.

Product Development

The product manager's involvement with new product development is dependent on the firm's organizational structure, the nature of the product itself, and the background of the manager. Where there is a separately designated manager for new products, the managers of current products are usually confined to planning modifications in existing products and packaging. With new products that can be designed relatively quickly, the product manager may maintain a close relationship with all stages of their development; in cases requiring prolonged research and development, product managers tend to have little contact with the emerging products until a market testing stage approaches. Another factor is that, typically, industrial products managers are technically trained and oriented, while the contrary is true in consumer goods. The former naturally have more frequent interface with research and development.

Marketing Research

In their roles of originating and formulating marketing plans and of monitoring the progress and obstacles of products, product managers require substantial marketing research information. Typically, they depend heavily on marketing research personnel to obtain and process this information. Within the enterprise, a marketing researcher may be the closest collaborator with a product manager.

Other Marketing and Corporate Personnel

The product manager's superior within the organization represents the interface most critical to the manager's personal career. Regardless of the superior's title, which will vary from firm to firm, this superior will usually bear the responsibility for marketing planning of a division or corporation. Very commonly these men are themselves former product managers and a high level of empathy tends to exist between these men, as the superior strives to develop the analytical and decision powers of his product managers.

When a product manager interprets his position broadly, he may have many intra-firm interfaces. For example, Scott Paper Company's diagram of its product manager relationships depicts up to 17 interfaces with other departments in the company and its advertising agency, not including the higher management line of responsibility.

SIGNIFICANCE OF PRODUCT MANAGEMENT INTERFACES

One may assert that product managers' interfaces are exceedingly important to effective marketing, at the same time acknowledging the value of involving other corporate personnel. The much more numerous confrontations of salesmen with buyers might be considered of primary importance; yet these are relatively routine and remote from marketing strategy and policy. High echelon marketing executives' interfaces, both internal and external, are quite important since the more comprehensive and far-reaching decisions on goals, allocations, and programs are reached at that level. Regardless, product managers' interfaces are of high importance from each of three viewpoints.

Product Manager Viewpoint

Position descriptions for product managers are aptly couched in terms of "formulating" or "originating" product plans and strategies, or "centralizing" information about assigned products. A man placed in a conceptual and informational hub of the organization must personally be an intelligence headquarters. To maintain competitive position and profit of his products, with his performance starkly exposed to higher management, he must strive to be the best informed man about any aspect substantially affecting their future. He must arrange and nurture a number of information interfaces to achieve his functions.

The verb "coordinate" is often and aptly used to describe how a product manager should execute his "responsibilities." His interfaces are used to enthuse others about his plans and to obtain their concurrence and action. To a substantial degree, his success depends upon his effectiveness in motivating others to implement his plans with direct organizational authority.

The Firm's Viewpoint

The properly functioning product manager is the firm's main intelligence center for its product lines. Much more than a repository, he is an action center at which all strategy and plans for his product lines converge. A large company cannot rely on higher executives, functional middle managers, or committees to become sufficiently informed about the situation and opportunities facing an individual product line. Higher executives and committees should be well briefed in order to integrate various product managers' recommendations and make allocations fairly to each program; however, they cannot possess the depth of understanding and analysis of each product manager.

A General Marketing Viewpoint

The marketing institution viewpoint and the consumer or user viewpoint, taken broadly, should coincide in seeking what Paul Mazur considered marketing's goal—to deliver a standard of living. This can be accomplished only when marketing interfaces with its buying publics as fully and intelligently as possible. The potential for effectively realizing this goal is enhanced when the information focus and the marketing strategy focus are centered within one position in the firm. This position ideally is that of a product manager who can devote all his powers and attention to his assigned product area. The man who serves as a gatekeeper in the firm at the spot where market needs and opportunities meet the firm's capabilities, objectives, and strategies, is most critical from a socially-aware marketing viewpoint.

OBSTACLES

While the number of interfaces realized by product managers may be adequate, the quality of these relationships tends to fall seriously short of the ideal. Product managers should be of gregarious nature, ready and anxious to meet others, and typically they are. Establishing a wide network of contacts is thus not overly difficult. The deficiency tends to arise from the failure of the product manager to develop the most productive associations in depth. Causes underlying this failure might include the following:

1. Preoccupation with trivial and distracting tasks. Many product managers find their time burdened with correspondence with salesmen and customers about minor problems and adjustments. Many allow themselves to become expediters of deliveries, and of the production and distribution of promotional literature.

2. Lack of assistance. This tends to prevent a product manager from

allocating time to the interfaces which are most important. Most product managers have no help beyond a secretary (and some share secretaries). Some have trainees who are only temporary help before being elevated into full production managerships. More companies are providing assistant product managers, but there has not been general recognition of the need.

3. Lack of cooperation with functional departments. This may result in the functional department either passing along to the product manager tasks that the functional department should assume, or conversely, encroaching on the decision sphere of a product manager by making decisions that are rightly his. At the extreme, a functional department may actually balk at cooperating in carrying out product plans.

4. Lack of well-conceived formal position descriptions. Where they exist, such descriptions either tend to assign the product manager too broad a responsibility, or list his duties in unrealistic detail. The interfaces implied for the manager may be too many and too unsystematic to be efficient. Sometimes the number of products and brands assigned a manager are excessive. In one case, for example, the author found a product manager responsible for 17 distinct nationally advertised products.

5. Restriction of the product manager to a single brand or type of a product with no supplemental participation regarding new products serving the same needs. While specific brand managers are needed where a single brand sells in enormous volume, product managers should not be excluded from the dynamics of product improvement and innovation.

6. Inadequate scheduling of available time. A specific set of priorities should be established and periodically reviewed, particularly for the novice product manager.

7. Inadequate training of product managers. Because the demands of the position are more varied than those of most other middle management jobs, training of product managers is relatively more important. Unfortunately many product managers learn under loose supervision or by trial and error. If each product manager kept explicit records of his planning and decision analyses and of the ensuing results, others could profit from this store of experience. This training technique, however, is often overlooked.

8. Short job tenure. The median in consumer products is about two years. The period is usually somewhat longer for industrial products managers. One product line, aggregating over $20,000,000 annual sales, was observed to have had three product managers in four years. In addition, new product managers appear to have little communication with their predecessors, although they are still working in the company.

9. Last, but very important, is the excessive number of interfaces that most product managers attempt, particularly intra-company. The product manager should be selective in the interfaces he establishes. This positions him to concentrate on decoding and analyzing the inputs he receives from these especially strategic linkages, and where necessary, to direct his communications skills toward them.

SOME RECOMMENDATIONS

There appears to be a gradual shift in the positioning, functioning, and training of product managers as firms which utilize this approach gain experience. The writer has identified four dimensions of development which may promote effective interfacing by product managers.

1. Realignment of product managers' assignments toward a market orientation. The typical assignment is in terms of a particular product or products, and the concentration is on promoting their sales. The result can be a myopic vision of the market in terms of the given product. A more balanced and progressive view is likely when this manager is assigned a specific market or product-use area, in which he works to improve market penetration through innovation while simultaneously formulating the optimal strategy and marketing mix to increase the profitability of his existing products. This should result in a systematic market/product development while also accentuating the entirety of the market interface. Further, involvement with a homogeneous market may be less confusing for the product manager than a strict product alignment which often involves dealing with the heterogeneous uses and markets that a single product may serve.

2. Provision of an improved atmosphere for the serious study by product managers of markets and alternative strategies in product, pricing, promotion, and distribution. Some companies do provide sufficient privacy and, on a smaller scale, some seek to limit the many tasks and other distractions in order to provide product management with adequate time for marketing planning.

3. Restrictions of the interfaces attempted by product managers to the few that are most productive. This avoids the superficial contacts and fragmentary communications that are much too common. It is suggested that a consumer goods product manager restrict himself within the interfaces shown in Figure 5-1 and concentrate on those itemized below.

Marketing research
Advertising agency
The market (dealers and buyers)
Sales management
Advertising management
Product development

His relationships should be conducted primarily through one liaison in the four named departments and the advertising agency. This is increasingly common with the market research interface, the chief and constant aid of many product managers. It is further suggested that the time saved by reducing intracompany communication be devoted to more personal interface with markets.

4. Development of complete and realistic job descriptions accompanied by more specific performance evaluation criteria. In addition to removing

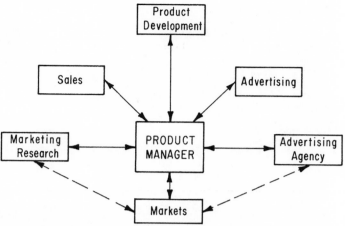

Figure 5-1. Interfaces of a product manager.

much of the vagueness that contributes to inefficient product manager work, this would relieve personal frustration and direct the manager's efforts, including those related to interfacing within and outside the firm. In providing a solid basis for extensive job training and manpower development, this procedure can make a long-range contribution to the product manager concept.

CONCLUSION

Product managers are surely here to stay, for it appears that no other organizational arrangement so well promotes efficient marketing planning in the spirit of the marketing concept. Clear recognition of the fundamental role that effective interfaces play, both within the firm and with the external publics who shape the firm's destiny, will be a long first step to realization of the profit potential of the product manager system.

DILEMMA OF
PRODUCT/MARKET MANAGEMENT
BY B. CHARLES AMES

FOREWORD

Is there any industrial marketing executive in business today who has not had to wrestle with the problem of whether to opt for product managers or market managers for a particular situation? Traditional ground rules for deciding which managerial approach is the most appropriate no longer apply when product lines expand and the markets for them proliferate. Under these conditions of multiple products flowing into multiple markets, the industrial marketing executive faces a real dilemma. The solution, says this author, is to use a dual management concept of having both product managers and market managers to meet the changing needs of the marketplace.

Mr. Ames is a Director of McKinsey & Company, Inc. and Managing Partner in the firm's Cleveland office.

As companies have expanded into new product and market areas, they have changed their organizations to deal with the new complexities that have arisen in these areas. Over the past decade companies have responded to product/market growth by adding either product managers or market managers to their staffs.

Both positions were developed—and have been used successfully throughout industry—to provide the necessary market orientation and to

EDITOR'S NOTE: From *Harvard Business Review,* March-April 1971, pp. 66-74. Reprinted by permission of the publisher and the author. Copyright © 1971 by the President and Fellows of Harvard College.

ensure sound planning for various product/market segments. And the purpose of both has always been the same—namely, to safeguard the commercial health of the product/market business by ensuring that the necessary plans, decisions, and commitments made throughout the company effectively meet the changing needs of the marketplace.[5]

Nevertheless, the emphasis and appropriateness of each position differs with each company. Product managers have been used when a company has multiple products flowing into a common market through the same channels and to the same customer groups.

Market managers have been used in the reverse situation—when the company needs to develop different markets for a single product line. In this case, focus on developing the market rather than on taking the product to market has been the chief objective, and market managers have been used to provide this focus.

Both of these positions were designed to ensure that a single person had the full-time responsibility for planning the growth and development of each significant product/market segment. As long as a company has either a series of products that funnel into one market or a single product line that flows out into several markets, a single product manager or market manager can handle this responsibility. For, as shown in Exhibit 5-1A and 5-1B, it is relatively easy to carve out a discrete area of responsibility for such a manager under these fairly simple product/market conditions.

But because product/market proliferation has increased greatly in a large and growing number of industrial companies, many find themselves selling multiple products in multiple markets. When this happens, as Exhibit 5-1C shows, there is not a neat product/market match in most cases, but rather a crisscross of products and markets that dramatically increases the complexity of the planning and management job to be done.

At this point, planning from only one perspective—product or market—tends to be self-defeating. Neither one nor the other can be downgraded or disregarded in the planning process without severe penalty.

THE DILEMMA

Let us consider the consequences of choosing one kind of manager over the other to do the planning in this crisscross product/market situation.

If product managers are chosen, each man is likely to have responsibility for one product line or area that is sold in several different markets, and, quite possibly through different channels. In most cases, it is simply impossible for one man to know enough about the characteristics and requirements of the different markets to plan for profitable participation and growth.

Thus the product manager is more than likely to concentrate on selling his existing products, rather than on determining what it takes to serve his

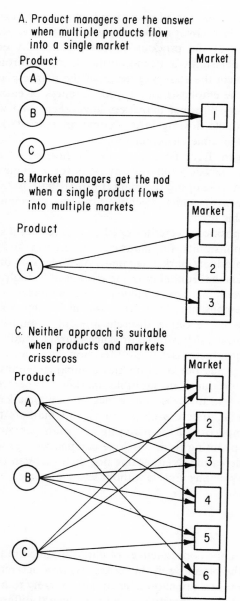

A. Product managers are the answer
when multiple products flow
into a single market

B. Market managers get the nod
when a single product flows
into multiple markets

C. Neither approach is suitable
when products and markets
crisscross

Exhibit 5-1. Three product/market business situations.

markets more effectively. In so doing, he will probably miss important
opportunities in related products and services. Even more important,
without sufficient focus on the market, the chances are good that his
product line will lag behind competitive offerings, or even become obsolete,

as he finds himself unable to keep up with ever-changing user needs.

Alternatively, if market managers are selected, each manager will tend to focus on meeting the requirements of his assigned market without regard for the impact that his actions or recommendations may have on the company's ability to properly meet the needs of other market areas with the same product line. Thus, if a company has exceptionally strong or persuasive managers covering one or two market areas, it can very easily end up with product plans or actions in these markets that seriously jeopardize the company's positions in other market areas.

For these reasons, it becomes readily apparent that neither of these solutions is adequate in the crisscross situation. As I see it, meeting the requirements of this situation represents one of the most serious and complex organizational challenges that industrial management has had to deal with in a long time. It is serious because, unless an intelligent solution is found, the marketing planning effort is almost certain to be ineffective, causing both market position and profit growth to suffer. And it is complex because the only solution I know adds to overhead costs and sets up the potential for debilitating organizational conflict unless it is implemented properly.

Solution Is Difficult . . .

How, then, can this challenge be faced? How does one ensure the right planning emphasis and balance in this kind of situation? A small but growing number of industrial companies have found that the only solution to this dilemma is to stop trying to decide between product or market managers and, instead, to use them both.

Under this dual arrangement, market managers have an external focus toward the market. They have the primary responsibility for developing a deep understanding of market needs and determining what the company could and should do to be more responsive to these needs.

Product managers, on the other hand, watch over their product areas in the same way any intelligent general manager would if his operation consisted of a single product flowing into several markets.[6] The product manager's job is to seek a balanced response to the needs and opportunities in certain markets without jeopardizing the company's position in others and without placing an unfair burden on manufacturing and engineering.

This dual approach positions the center of gravity for a particular product/market business between these two managers. In so doing, it provides the basis for achieving (a) the market orientation that is so essential to competitive success in any business and (b) a system of checks and balances to ensure that unbridled enthusiasm for market response does not wreak havoc within the business.

Admittedly, setting up two managers with joint responsibilities for product/market development is an organizational anomaly, and one could logically ask: Who is responsible for what?

While this is a good question for academic discussion, it does not represent a significant problem in practice. Product managers can be held accountable for all aspects of product line management, including long-term profitability. Similarly, market managers can be held accountable for long-term growth and profitability of their assigned markets.

Although neither manager would have line authority for decisions and actions that affect his areas of concern, both should be given full responsibility for using their superior knowledge and ideas about what is right and what is wrong for their areas to get the appropriate actions and decisions taken. If they assess and plan correctly, they will be successful in their roles; if they do not, they will not be successful. Thus both should be held accountable in this fashion to ensure the best planning and management job for each product/market segment.

Inevitable conflict: It is clear that a dual management approach conceived this way offers a means of coping with the complex product/market situation that exists in many large-scale companies. However, it is important to bear in mind that when product and market managers are set up to work parallel with each other, a conflict situation is automatically created.

After all, the fundamental purpose of either of these two men is to fight for time and attention from engineering, manufacturing, and sales for their assigned products or markets. The potential for conflict is sharply brought out when both product managers and market managers are present in an organization. Let us look at the inner workings of this conflict more closely:

■The market manager's primary responsibility, on the one hand, is to identify his market's needs and to seek modifications in the existing product/service package or additions to it that will better enable him to meet the needs of the market. He has no interest in any other market or in the functional difficulties he may create.

■The product manager, on the other hand, has the basic responsibility for maintaining the integrity of his product line so that costs, design or performance characteristics, pricing policy, service and warranty arrangements, and so on, are broadly responsive to the needs of all the company's markets.

(Given this charge, it is clear that he cannot bend indiscriminately to the requirements any one market manager perceives. So, in addition to the conflict which he encounters in vying with his colleagues for functional time and attention, his major concerns often conflict with those of the market managers.)

Although it is inevitable, the conflict arising from the interaction of product managers and market managers should not be viewed as a negative factor. In fact, this kind of conflict is specifically what the dual management concept is designed to produce. It should be regarded as a positive force.

Moreover, if it is properly managed, the conflict should help uncover a multiplicity of market opportunities that would otherwise go unnoticed, and, at the same time, provide a mechanism for sorting through these opportunities so that the company's overall interests are best served. However, the key phrase is "properly managed." If not properly managed, the whole idea can turn into a two-headed monster.

Providing proper management places a heavy burden on the marketing head, since both product and market managers typically report to him. Thus he has the primary responsibility for ensuring that the conflict which develops is constructive and that it leads to better and more productive ideas. This means that he must ensure that these men work together as a team to blend their different points of view into better ideas for building the product/market business as a whole.

At times, of course, this means that the marketing head will have to decide between strongly contested alternatives. And he must do it in a way that avoids ruffling too many feathers or discouraging his managers from coming up with ideas and taking strong stands in the future.

. . . But Success Is Possible

The reward has been well worth the effort for those companies that have built this concept into their organizations and made it work. Here are two actual examples of companies that adopted the dual management approach successfully and very profitably:

■An engine manufacturer found that his three product lines were losing ground in terms of both market and profit growth after a period of rapid expansion.

The company president and his vice president of marketing agreed that they were missing the boat on too many sales opportunities because they were not getting the right kind of management attention on key products and markets. But they were not able to agree on how to organize to provide this management attention.

The president thought that setting up a product management group would be the answer. The vice president argued that market managers would be a better choice since the products were sold in three separate markets, and each had its own distinct characteristics and requirements.

Although the president saw the need for a market focus, he feared that using market managers would lead to product problems and pricing conflicts as each market manager sought to meet the needs of his particular market without regard for the others.

After a lot of give-and-take discussion, the president wisely concluded that both product and market managers were necessary to provide the proper attention to both products and markets. Within a few months, the market managers had developed a host of ideas for modifications in the existing product/service packages as well as several promising ideas for new product entries. The product managers then screened these ideas, and the two groups working together were able to help the company develop a stronger product/market strategy that significantly accelerated profit growth; volume gains and earnings per share were nearly doubled.

■A textile fibers company, confronted with a similar situation, actually made the shift from product managers to market managers as the key planning unit. This company sold three basic fibers in several end-use markets. Because the characteristics and requirements for these markets were significantly different, management reasoned that a market focus on planning was more appropriate than a product focus.

A chaotic situation arose, however, when plant and development managers discovered that they could not possibly respond to all of the requests coming to them from the market managers. As one plant manager put it: "Our production costs on Product 'X' have gone up by 12% because of all the short-run requests for additional stocking requirements. Also, we are running out of capacity for one of our most profitable products, and no plans are being formulated to add new capacity. It is a fine thing to be responsive to market needs. But someone had better watch out for product costs and capacity, or we will have a plant full of unprofitable business and will lose the chance to sell more of our profitable items."

Management then correctly decided to reinstate a product management group to work parallel with the market managers. The product managers quickly took hold of the product planning problems that had led to the chaotic situation in plant and development operations. And, at the same time, the market managers provided the end-user orientation so essential to success in the marketplace.

As a result of product and market manager cooperation, the company struck a better balance between control of its manufacturing process and market response and achieved a short-term profit pickup of several hundred thousand dollars and a much stronger market share position.

THE REQUIREMENTS

While the dual management concept unquestionably requires careful thought and attention to implement successfully, it does not require esoteric or ultrasophisticated management know-how. Rather, it simply demands attention to six management fundamentals.

Determine the Need

First, management must make sure that there really is a need for this concept. In this already complicated world, it does not make sense to add complication unnecessarily, especially when it is costly and difficult to do so. Before deciding that an organization built around product and market managers is the best basis for planning and managing future growth, management should satisfy itself on these points:

■It should be certain that the crisscross flow of multiple products to multiple markets actually exists and that it is too complex for traditional approaches to the planning job.

■Even more important, management should assure itself that more concentrated or comprehensive planning for a larger number of discrete product/market segments will, in fact, provide the basis for accelerating profit growth.

Define the Roles

Second, if management agrees that this dual management approach is appropriate, the next step is to decide how the roles of the two types of managers should be defined and structured. Of course, the specific responsibilities of either the market or the product managers will depend on the particular situation, but, by and large, their basic roles should be defined to include certain activities.

Thus *market* managers should concentrate their efforts on:

■Developing a comprehensive understanding of customer and end-user operations and economics and specifying ways that the existing product/service package can be improved to provide a competitive edge.

■Identifying related products and/or services that represent attractive opportunities for profitably enlarging the company's participation in the market through either internal development or acquisition.

■Drawing together at regular intervals an organized summary of the most attractive opportunities in the marketplace, specifying what must be done internally to capitalize on them, and recommending a first-cut strategy for the business.

■Developing a reputation for industry expertise among key customer and end-user groups and bringing this know-how to bear on the negotiation of major orders and on the training and development of field sales personnel.

In a similar vein, *product* managers should focus their efforts on:

■Protecting the pricing integrity of their product—that is, seeing to it that the pricing policies and practices in one market do not jeopardize the company's position or profit structure in another.

■Maintaining product leadership by making certain that product design, cost, and performance characteristics not only are broadly responsive to customer needs in all markets but also are not inadvertently altered to meet the needs of one market at the expense of the company's position in another.

■Ensuring that their product is responsive to market needs while at the same time protecting the engineering and production process from getting cluttered with a proliferation of small-lot, custom, or special orders; in effect, they temper market managers' enthusiastic customer orientation with sober judgments on operating capability and economics.

■Ensuring that production scheduling and capacity are intelligently planned to profitably meet current and anticipated aggregate demand of various markets.

■Providing the in-depth technical and/or product knowledge required to support selling efforts on major and complex applications.

The broad activities just cited are always the core of the job for both market and product managers. However, the makeup and importance of the company's various products and markets should determine exactly how their jobs are structured. Product managers invariably function on a full-time basis but may, of course, be given responsibility for more than one product. There is little latitude in structuring this position.

The market manager's job, however, is quite a different matter. It may be structured in three different ways, depending on the number, importance, and geographic spread of the markets involved. Thus his role may be set up so he functions as (a) a full-time staff planner, (b) a full-time staff planner with line sales responsibility, or (c) a part-time staff planner. Consider:

■Most companies assign the market manager a full-time staff role, dividing the product/market planning job into two parts and setting up the two groups—product managers and market managers—in parallel, as shown in Exhibit 5-2A. This first approach is popular because it is a natural evolution from either product or market managers and is the easiest to introduce.

Moreover, this setup is the right one to follow when all the markets are about equally important to the company and the number to be covered is relatively small, say, four to eight. Under these circumstances, it is economically practical to have a full-time staff planner for each one.

■Some companies have developed the market manager's job into a stronger full-time position, giving him line sales responsibility as well as the staff planning assignment, as shown in Exhibit 5-2B. This means that the market manager has direct responsibility for a group of salesmen that specialize in selling to the accounts that make up his market.

Theoretically, this second approach is best, since it gives one man a combined responsibility for both planning and execution within each market area and thus makes it possible to hold him fairly accountable for results. It also ensures that he has a firsthand feel for customer and market requirements and helps him avoid ivory-tower planning.

But, practically, its application is limited because it is often difficult to justify the degree of sales specialization inherent in this kind of arrangement. Although most companies can point to a cluster of accounts in certain geographic areas for which they could economically justify a specialist salesman, to get national coverage they must inevitably turn to the general salesman who sells all products to all markets. Accordingly, in most cases, it simply is not feasible to work out an arrangement where the sales force can be divided neatly under several market managers.

■Still other companies have adopted the third approach—that of a part-time planner—which gives them the market focus they are seeking without the added cost of full-time market managers. As we have noted, these companies add market planning assignments to the responsibility of senior salesmen, sales managers, or application engineers who have some expertise in a given end-use market. This compromise approach is normally followed by companies which deal in such a large number of markets that they simply cannot afford to provide full-time market manager coverage for each one.

For example, one company identified over 30 markets that needed to be brought into focus. Even after considering various ways these markets might be combined into planning assignments, the number of full-time market managers required could not be justified. Consequently, the company gave market planning assignments to selected salesmen who had special experience or a concentration of accounts in key markets.

Although I have described these approaches to the market manager's job separately, they can be combined as necessary to meet the needs and structure of the marketplace. Thus, for example, one company was able to give two of its market managers line sales responsibility because there were groups of specialist salesmen that could logically be assigned to them. The company could also justify the appointment of two additional full-time market managers in a staff planning capacity. To complete its market coverage, the company gave half a dozen key salesmen part-time market manager assignments with the thought in mind that these positions could be upgraded to full-time assignments if the markets developed to any great extent.

Change the Systems

Third, management must change the information and planning systems to reflect the existence and needs of both managers. On the information side, product managers need detailed operating infomation (e.g., engineering standards, production schedules, and cost breakdowns) to perform their jobs effectively. Market managers must have access to cost information for all products sold in their markets and to detailed market and customer information. And, ultimately, both managers should have profit and loss statements for their respective areas as a bench mark for evaluating their performance.

In many cases, the kind of cost, operating, and market information

A. Market manager in staff capacity only

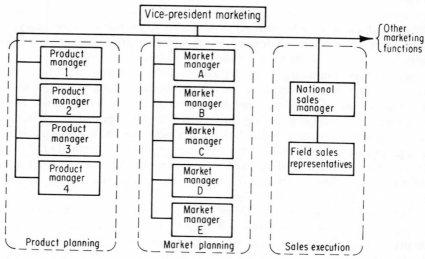

B. ...and with combined line and staff responsibility

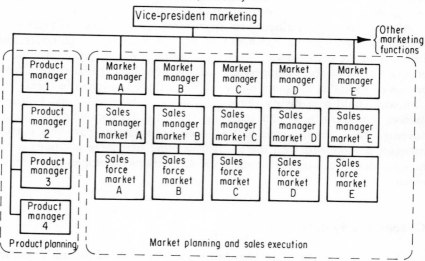

Exhibit 5-2. Two approaches to meet the needs of the marketplace.

required for intelligent product and market planning either is not available or is in a form that is unusable. Correcting this situation may require a major effort (e.g., special research projects, restructuring of accounting information).

Moreover, modifying the information system also requires providing a close working relationship with engineering, manufacturing, and finance, so that managers can secure the assistance necessary to interpret much of this information in the correct manner. Regardless of the effort involved, the information and assistance must be provided or the concept does not stand a chance of getting off the ground.

On the planning side, two changes are necessary. One is a change in the way strategic plans are developed. Here market managers should be given the responsibility for developing an overview of their market and a no-holds-barred set of recommendations for capitalizing on the opportunities they see. They should then review their ideas with the product managers concerned with their markets to determine what is feasible and what is not—as well as to gain agreement on a going-in point of view that can be presented to other functional managers. From this point on, the process follows a normal planning pattern with all the functional managers collaborating to come up with a final recommendation for top management.[7]

The other change in planning affects the way top management reviews and responds to strategic recommendations. Basically, the planning system must be adjusted to cope with an increased amount of planning inputs. As discussed previously, if the dual management approach is successful, it should generate a vastly increased number of options and recommendations for building the business in various product/market segments.

For example, one company adapted this approach in a way that freed certain managers to focus full time on uncovering market opportunities. This, in turn, led to the generation of some 20 different strategic options for building just one product/market business and involved different levels of resource commitment and payoff expectations. To cope with this avalanche of ideas, the top managers had to draw extensively on their central planning staff and had to set aside substantial blocks of their own time to decide which options to accept and which to reject.

Admittedly this may be a unique situation, but bear in mind that the fundamental purpose of this dual management approach is to generate more ideas and recommendations for accelerating growth and profits. Top management must properly evaluate and respond to this flow of ideas to avoid frustration and discouragement in the product and market groups that could cripple the concept.

Choose the Managers

Fourth, management must select the right candidates for both product and market manager positions. High-talent manpower is essential in these positions, for these men will be more responsible than anyone else for the fate of their assigned product or market areas.

Since the product manager has an internal focus, candidates should be selected on the basis of their product and technical know-how as well as on their understanding of the company's operating economics. In choosing market managers, emphasis should be placed on a strong commercial orientation and business judgment. Naturally, the men in both positions must have the necessary personal skills to work effectively in a situation where conflict is certain to occur and where good working relationships with a wide range of functional executives are crucial to their success.

My experience suggests that this fourth management fundamental is one that everyone will quickly agree with but few will take seriously enough, particularly when it comes to selecting market managers. There is a natural tendency to choose men for this position on the strength of their sales experience, without regard for their analytical ability or overall business judgment. This is not to say that market managers should not be drawn from the sales force, but rather that the sales force should not be regarded as the exclusive source of candidates for this position.

Explain the Concept

Fifth, management has to do a thorough job of explaining to key managers in all functional areas of the company exactly how the product/market manager organization concept will work and what the underlying rationale is for moving to it. This can, of course, be done in many ways.

For example, one company that had success with this approach took the time to develop appropriate explanatory material in writing and then used it at a series of group meetings to explain the concept and respond to questions. In doing so, the company emphasized the distinctions between the roles that product and market managers would play in the management process and outlined the contributions expected from each type of manager.

Top management also went into some detail to explain how product and market managers would interact with other functional managers and executives and stressed the cooperative working relationships that were expected. And management made it clear that although the two types of managers would have totally different areas of responsibility, their importance to the company's planning effort was to be equal and their contributions to the total management process on a par.

Monitor the Activities

Sixth, once the product/market concept has been installed, management must monitor and coach the activities of both product and market managers to make sure that they stay on the track. This is essential, because the nature of their jobs is such that these men can easily lose the focus the dual concept is intended to provide.

My experience indicates that the product manager seems to get bogged down in administrative matters that naturally develop when he is involved in multiple markets. Although this work must be done, it cannot be done at the expense of the product line planning and developing efforts—his core responsibilities. Thus provision must be made to give him administrative assistance as required.

The market manager can easily fall into the trap of looking for new fields to conquer before he has mastered his present business. If this occurs, the result could be a plan that places far too much emphasis on getting into new fields and not enough on preserving the business that is already on hand.

This monitoring responsibility rests basically with the head of marketing. And to carry out this job effectively, he must be prepared to spend a great deal of time in face-to-face discussions with each manager. The need for this effort cannot be emphasized too strongly. For no matter how well the responsibilities of these managers are documented or explained, on-the-job coaching is essential to ensure the understanding and to make the necessary adjustments.

It should be clear from this discussion of management fundamentals that using both product and market managers requires close and thorough attention to the kind of detail that frequently drops between the chairs in the pressure-jammed environment where most top executives operate. But unless this attention is given, the company will end up with a costly and cumbersome superstructure—and nothing else. However, if the dual management concept is implemented properly, with rigorous adherence to the requirements just discussed, it can be a powerful vehicle for accelerating profit growth in many companies.

CONCLUSION

As I see it, using both product managers and market managers provides a basis for achieving the kind of product and market planning necessary in most multibusiness companies. The concept unquestionably means added manpower, added expense, and greater complexity in the management process. And making the concept work will probably add problems for most companies.

But if a company with a crisscross of products and markets balks at attempting this organization approach simply because it sounds too complex or because it will add to marketing overhead, I strongly believe it is missing a real bet. For it has been the experience of those who have tried it that this concept can provide a significant payoff in increased market opportunities, stronger competitive actions, and ultimately greater profits that far outweigh either the added costs involved or the difficulties of making it work.

NOTES

1. The more thorough analyses of product manager's work are in: Gordon H. Evans, *The Product Manager's Job* (New York: American Management Association, 1964) and Gordon Medcalf, *Marketing and the Brand Manager* (London, England: Pergamon Press, Ltd., 1967).
2. David J. Luck and Theodore Nowak, "Product Management: Vision Unfilled," *Harvard Business Review*, Volume 43 (May, 1965), pp. 143-150.
3. This study under sponsorship of the Marketing Science Insitute contributed to the volume: P. J. Robinson and D. J. Luck, *Promotional Decision Making* (New York: McGraw-Hill Book Company, 1964).
4. In *Management and Advertising Problems* (New York: Association of National Advertisers, 1965) this problem is discussed on page 53. The study reported in this volume, however, later affirmed the continuous growth of product management, but in more effective relationships with advertising agencies. (p. 92.)
5. See my article, "Payoff from Product Management," HBR November-December 1963, p. 141.
6. Ibid.
7. See my article, "Marketing Planning for Industrial Products," HBR September-October 1968, p. 100.

ADDITIONAL SELECTED BIBLIOGRAPHY

Organizational Approaches to New Product Development

Callander, W. S., "Product Management and Its Challenge to General Organization Concepts," *Marketing Precision and Executive Action*, C. H. Hindersman, ed., AMA Proceedings, American Marketing Association (June, 1962), 369-375.

Evans, E. H., "The Product Manager's Duties," *The Product Manager's Job*, AMA Research Study No. 69, American Management Association (1964), 23-48.

Fulmer, R. M., "Practice and Philosophy of Product Management," *Marketing in a Changing World*, B. A. Morin, ed., AMA Proceedings, Series No. 29, American Marketing Association (June, 1969), 104-107.

Grayson, R. A. "If You Want New Products You Better Organize to Get Them," *Marketing in a Changing World*, B. A. Morin, ed., AMA Proceedings, Series No. 29, American Marketing Association (June, 1969), 75-79.

Lear, R. W., "The Product Planning Committee: Its Opportunities and Responsibilities," *Establishing a New-Product Program*, Albert Newgarden, ed., AMA Management Report No. 8, American Management Association (1958), 57-66.

QUESTIONS FOR DISCUSSION AND REVIEW

1. Draw an organization chart depicting a new product development department.

2. What are the primary responsibilities of a product-planning committee?

3. List the differences in responsibilities of a product-planning committee and of a product manager.

4. Describe the duties of a product manager in a soft-goods industry and a hard-goods industry.

5. What is the trend in organization of a new product department? Do you agree with this trend?

6

THE RESEARCH PROGRAM

A research organization is established in order to improve existing products in a product line, to develop new uses or determine new markets for the existing product line, and to develop new products to add either to the present product line or to a new line of products. Research is the innovating aspect of a progressive firm which should lead to greater sales and additional profits.

There are certain inherent dangers of research and development that marketing students should recognize. At times, many firms organize their research efforts and budget toward research and development without the necessary controls needed to prevent the flow of red ink. There are firms that also favor research and development and the innovators to such a degree that they neglect a holistic approach, much to the consternation of the marketing department.

Research ought to be divided into two parts: industrial or commercial research and consumer research. Before the utilization of an industrial designer or director of packaging and graphics is contemplated, what is sorely needed is an understanding of the use of and users for the new or improved product. That is, research is needed to improve upon an inefficient marketing system that results in a high rate of mortality of new products. To reduce this time-consuming and wasteful mortality rate, products that are being "groomed" for commercialization should be tested before and during development and after their introduction into the marketplace. Industrial research means, in this text, research performed on the product either by controlled conditions in the laboratory or by outside testing performed by independent agencies. New product research can create some unique problems or further accentuate problems that already exist within the confines of business firms that allocate a budget for research and have a separate research department. In other words, research problems do exist or can be cultivated by research-oriented firms.

The following articles expound on the question of the values of research and development, the possible dangers incurred by management by research and development, the problem of budgeting for R&D, the problem of when to terminate R&D, and the problems encountered by the firm from the scientists and innovators working in R&D.

A

BUDGETING FOR R & D: A CASE FOR
MANAGEMENT SCIENCE METHODS
BY WILLIAM E. SOUDER

Today, research and development is truly "big business." And it becomes even bigger business with each passing year. In 1950, total domestic R&D expenditures amounted to $4.2 billion; ten years later, this figure had tripled to $12.8 billion, and by 1965 the figure was $18.2 billion.

R&D exerts considerable influence on our lives through the variety of new products produced, and has a vital role in our economy in supplying new employment opportunities. In addition, this effort often determines the success of an enterprise; how much a firm spends on what kind of R&D in today's world can determine whether it is a proprietary giant or a struggling commodity dwarf in tomorrow's world. R&D budgetary decisions are therefore vital to both the individual company and the total economy. Yet few industrial firms appear to give the R&D budgeting decision adequate attention. This article reviews and criticizes some of the budgetary practices in R&D today, and proposes some improvements.

R&D BUDGETARY FUNCTIONS

Figure 6-1 distinguishes two basic types of budgetary functions in R&D. Policy functions involve the nature, scope, and direction of the total effort. Operational functions involve the optimal planning and control of the project efforts over their life cycles.

EDITOR'S NOTE: From *Business Horizons,* June 1970, pp. 31-38. Reprinted by permission of the publisher and the author.

Figure 6-1. The functional budgetary view of R&D.

As the figure indicates, effective policy planning for R&D begins as a long-range corporate planning function. Deciding where the company wants to go and how it will get there must be done in the corporate planning function, because this is the only point in the organization that completely overlooks both the performance and the financial aspects of the R&D program. An effective program requires considerable financial support in the form of both the initial cash outlays and continuing "patient money" or "venture money." Frequently, a diversified combination of R&D investments is developed in the hope of generating the proper flows of profits to achieve both long- and short-range corporate goals. In this way, a well-planned R&D program can ultimately be self-financing; profits from shorter-range successes can cover the costs of longer-range efforts.

Closely related to the policy functions are the operational functions of planning the R&D efforts, as shown in Figure 6-1. Specific projects must be tailored around the policies. To do this, some companies have set up special departments to search for, evaluate, and select proposals on a continuing basis. The objective is a storehouse of suitable projects that can be quickly phased in as soon as other efforts are terminated. Once a set of projects is selected, funds must be allocated to them in such a way that the effectiveness per dollar spent is maximized. This problem of how much to spend on which individual projects is often a critical one. A misallocation of funds at this stage of the planning process can result in overemphasis on some projects and too little emphasis on others.

Scheduling, the problem of deciding when to pursue which project, can be equally critical. This is especially true with certain consumer products where the first company to introduce a new product often captures the largest market share. Finally, the quality of the project planning and the amount of coordination of interdepartmental efforts on the project is often a critical factor in determining the timely success of an R&D project.

Control is another important operational budgetary function. R&D efforts frequently tend to diverge from the planned efforts more often than nonresearch activities. Researchers continually discover side problems that are temporarily more academically interesting than the central problem of the project; to investigate them, however, would delay obtainment of the primary goal. In addition, R&D efforts must be replanned frequently to reflect rapidly changing technologies or competitive situations. Timely and effective replanning depends on the existence of close control and good feedbacks from the market place.

PERFORMING BUDGETARY FUNCTIONS

Few R&D managers would argue that the policy and operational functions that have been described are not necessary. However, they are likely to disagree on the methods for performing them. In some organizations, R&D tends to be highly exploratory and long range; in others it tends to be short range or current market oriented. In some organizations, it is regarded as just so much "fat," trimmed when profits are low and increased when profits are high. In some organizations, the function is closely controlled and performance is closely monitored. Other organizations permit many R&D personnel to work on their own ideas.

These differences reflect the fact that there are few generally accepted principles of R&D management. Thus, the budgetary functions tend to be carried out in the fashion the executives feel are best. Personal philosophies are used in place of guiding principles or hypotheses that can be statistically supported or discredited. Without a framework to guide the conduct of the policy and operational functions, they tend to be performed through dynamic interplays of conflicts, negotiations, and compromises within the framework of informal organizational groups and power structures.

The process of deciding on the scope and nature of the R&D program is likely to be one of conflict and negotiation among competing departments. Pure bargaining is often the means for setting satisfactory corporate budgets. At the department level, conflicts may arise over vested interests on various projects, over the funding levels, or over budgetary allocations. But even when satisfactory policies are established, the policies may not be feasible at the operational level, and new policies may be sought at the corporate level. This cycle of trying out various policies may repeat until an over-all satisfactory policy and its operational plan are found.

Four unique forces within the R&D process and its interaction with the organizational environment naturally operate against the optimal performance of the planning and control functions. *First,* top organizational R&D decisions are seldom self-contained. Few top corporate executives feel exclusively competent to formulate policies in this area; they rely on feedbacks from the lower levels. This subjects top policy decisions to bias and distortion from power groups or cliques, and to biases from the lower levels. *Second,* there are always competing alternative uses for R&D funds, such as advertising or plant improvements. The inherent difficulties of accurately forecasting the costs and returns from R&D projects make many executives reluctant to accept an R&D proposal when competing alternatives seem more certain to pay off. *Third,* experience has shown that most R&D programs eventually require vastly more funds than are originally budgeted. *Finally,* management has erroneously attempted to apply traditional planning and control techniques to an area that requires more powerful approaches. The whole R&D area is a dynamic one; plans and estimates that are made today are usually outdated by tomorrow. Data flows in the area are extremely complex and subjective, and budgetary estimates are tentative and often include considerable error.

Because of the operation of these four forces, handicraft methods must give way to newer management science techniques. More sophisticated budgetary techniques must be used in the planning and control functions— techniques that can combine and digest more data, collate estimates from various organizational levels, and simultaneously evaluate multiple and competing alternatives. These are necessary for optimal budgeting.

Many formal techniques for R&D budgeting have been developed. Mathematical methods and quantitative approaches have been devised for selecting projects, allocating funds among projects, scheduling, planning project efforts, and controlling ongoing efforts. The various classes of techniques that have been developed to date will be reviewed and evaluated. The evaluation is based on a review of more than one-hundred articles from the current literature.[1]

PROJECT SELECTION TECHNIQUES

Several types of techniques have been proposed for R&D project selection. They are: capital budgeting formulas, cost prediction formulas, scoring and ranking methods, and resource allocation methods.

Capital Budgeting Formulas

The capital budgeting approaches that have been used are modifications of the standard return on investment and discounted rate of return methods. The major modification is the inclusion of risk parameters such as the probability of commercial and technical success. In general, for each project a "value" is computed, which is some variation of the ratio of anticipated profits to the project's estimated cost. This value is then discounted for the risk of the project, usually by multiplying the value figure by the probability of success of that project. The projects are then ranked on the basis of the resulting value, with the higher rank going to the project with the higher value. Projects are then selected from the top of the ranked list down until the budget is exhausted. Considerable use of this approach has been reported for the chemical industry. An example of such a capital budgeting formula is equation (1) in Figure 6-2.

(1) $\text{Value} = \dfrac{\text{Anticipated Profit}}{\text{Anticipated Costs}} \times \text{Probability of Success}$

(2)   Cost = Predicted cost $\times$ Certainty factor
(Predicted cost = Ratio $\times$ Anticipated sales)

(3) $\text{Score} = \dfrac{\text{Patent rating + Sales rating + Technology rating}}{\text{Expected project cost}}$

Figure 6-2. Planning models.

The deficiencies of the capital budgeting formulas lie in their often incorrect assumptions that the same rate of return exists over the life of the project, that the earnings can be reinvested at this same rate, and that the same level of risk exists throughout the life of the investment. These defects become critical for R&D projects. A project is an ever-changing bundle of information and technology; its chances for failure and its rate of return are constantly changing throughout its life cycle. Furthermore, because competitive R&D activities are often unknown and rapidly changing markets may quickly make new products obsolete, one never knows if earnings can be reinvested in the project at acceptable rates. Therefore, capital budgeting methods should *not* be used for R&D project selection, despite the fact that such approaches appear to have won much favor among many R&D managers, particularly within the chemical industry.

Cost Prediction Formulas

In general, these formulas estimate the amount of investment necessary to complete specific R&D projects, given certain related parameters such as the expected sales. An example is shown as equation (2) in Figure 6-2. The "certainty factor" is the probability that the cost estimate is correct. The "ratio" is the historical ratio of project costs to sales for prior successful projects.

Underlying such cost estimating approaches is the premise that historical relations exist between the cost of an R&D project and the total sales from the product of the effort. Since the variable "sales" is often easier to estimate reliably than R&D costs, it is logical to try to predict those costs from estimates of sales. However, to make accurate sales estimates, one needs to know the performance of the product from R&D, and this information is seldom known until the project is completed. Thus, there is often little basis for estimating R&D costs from sales estimates.

Scoring and Ranking Techniques

Scoring and ranking criteria are the most numerous of all of the single classes of project selection methods in the literature. In general, these methods consist of simply ranking projects according to some list of criteria, and then selecting projects from the top to the bottom of the list until some cutoff point is reached. The approach is similar to some of the capital budgeting methods in that the objective is to obtain a ranking of projects. However, the capital budgeting and the scoring methods differ in the criteria used to rank projects and the methods used to determine cutoff points in selecting projects from the ranked list. A scoring model is illustrated as equation (3) in Figure 6-2.

Uses and applications of scoring and ranking methods at several large companies are reported in the literature. The types of criteria used in developing scores were product (life, patentability, and so on), market (price, competition, and so on), and financial criteria (cost, personnel, and so on), with market considerations often predominantly influencing the scores and rating numbers developed. Some companies treated different types of R&D differently, with basic R&D being weighted more heavily in the product aspects in determining scores.

The scoring and ranking methods have been even more popular than capital budgeting formulas for R&D. On the whole, managers have preferred the scoring methods to capital budgeting techniques because of the greater uncertainty in accurately estimating the necessary data for the latter. However, like the capital budgeting formulas, these approaches are pseudo-funding methods; they do not take into account the fact that there are alternative funding levels on every project. A project does not have to be, say, "100 percent selected" this year; it can be 50 percent selected both this year and next. Thus, ranking methods are not necessarily optimal. They treat only part of the R&D budgeting problem—the "what to work on" question.

Because ranking and scoring models treat only part of the over-all R&D planning problem, they are suboptimal. Suboptimization is like starting your automobile and letting it idle in the driveway! This author is of the opinion that ranking and scoring techniques should not be used because they do not treat the entire problem. Rather, resource allocation techniques should be used.

Resource Allocation Techniques

Resource allocation techniques address themselves to the problem of "how much to spend for what projects." Only a few such models have been developed. Similarly, few applications of resource allocation models to actual R&D budgeting problems exist. However, work is known to be progressing at this time on such models at Monsanto,[2] American Cyanamid, and North American Rockwell.

In general, resource allocation models hold the best current hope for methods that can collate masses of data and analyze multiple and competing candidate projects. Alert R&D executives would do well to keep abreast of the literature on resource allocation model applications to their problems. Resource allocation techniques may well represent present-day prototypes of future techniques which smart managers will routinely use to effectively combat the organizational dynamics forces discussed above. Resource allocation techniques are flexible and dynamic, and can be used to merge feedback data at all levels of the organization.

PROJECT SCHEDULING TECHNIQUES

Scheduling treats the "when do we do it" question in R&D budgeting. The whole area of scheduling has been largely dominated by one basic technique: PERT/Critical Path. A recent bibliography cited 205 references on PERT/Critical Path techniques.

PERT/Critical Path techniques have been combined with decision tree methods, sensitivity analyses, and with minimax computations, and have been successfully applied to problems ranging from opening a Broadway play to building the St. Louis Gateway Arch visitor's center. When one basic approach can do so much, there is little reason to develop other methods.

PROJECT CONTROL TECHNIQUES

When one looks hard at the literature on project control, one gets the impression that here indeed is a situation where everyone talks about it but no one does anything about it. The control methods in use today for R&D appear to center largely around the "periodic confessional" and the "pressure" approaches. In the former, R&D management asks the project personnel from time to time to "tell us where you are." Such a treatment may lead to a destruction of creativity and to distorted reporting, as the personnel cover up undesirable results. The other approach is a sort of "beat the horse to get him to go faster" approach. Both methods are straight out of the Dark Ages! The alternative seems to be a free rein, where there is little control and little constructive communication. Perhaps this is a method straight out of modern permissiveness!

An effective R&D project control model may be defined as one which informs the manager of any achievement/cost/time deviations from the plan, indicates the corrective actions needed by management, and communicates these to the project manager. Effective techniques are simply largely nonexistent at this time. However, one can see the forerunners of effective project control techniques in the monitoring methods used by NASA, defense contractors, and other industry sectors.[3]

WHERE DO WE STAND?

The general picture that emerges is that management has been, on the whole, reluctant to adopt many of the emerging management science methods for budgeting R&D. In planning expenditures, the favored methods appear to be a combination of judgment and subjective opinion, tying the investment to the sales dollar (next year's R&D as a percentage of last year's sales), or spending whatever the competition spends. In controlling R&D, budgetary cost performance has been over-emphasized, integrated cost/progress methods have not been considered, and insidious personal involvement of the manager is more often the rule than the exception.

Why are we not using more formal techniques and budgetary procedures? To a degree, the fault lies with those who are in the business of developing formal R&D budgeting techniques: the operations research specialists and and the management scientists. Frequently, they have preferred to talk to themselves rather than to their practical-oriented management counterparts. The communications link between management and management scientists has traditionally been weak. One consequence of this is an absence of good techniques where they are perhaps needed most—in the performance of all the policy R&D budgeting functions and in the performance of the operational functions of searching for candidates and controlling ongoing projects. Surely the reader has noticed an absence of these kinds of techniques from our list.

It simply is not reasonable to believe that these areas are impregnable to attack by the management scientist or operations researcher. The fault probably lies with a simple lack of understanding between managers and management scientists. Management scientists cannot maintain an ivory tower attitude if their profession is ever to advance. They must become aware of and build their models to reflect the realism of the R&D environment, including the above organizational dynamics aspects. But managers also have a professional responsibility to maintain a patient attitude and train themselves to understand the quantitative approach. Management science techniques *are* complex. But so are managerial problems! Complex techniques are just simply necessary for complex problems.

We all must also understand that organizational dynamics naturally operates against the use of rigorous budgeting procedures. Anything that dilutes the power of the various informal cliques and factions will automatically be resisted. By substituting objectivity for subjectivity in many cases, budgeting techniques remove the informal group's authority. Anything that improves the ability of the organization to assume more risk, as formal techniques may do, will be resisted. The fear of failure is great in every one of us. And there are many small empires in every organization that fear the disruption in their comfortable existence that might result from taking a larger risk and failing to succeed. (Of course, there is also a natural resistance to success; success may result in promotions that destroy the clique.) Finally, anything that tends to cut off negotiation, conjecture, and conflict, or anything that lubricates decision making will be resisted because this is not the normal way of operating.

R&D management involves many budgetary functions: policy planning of the scope and nature of the program; investment planning of the types of projects; scheduling that will maintain the proper balance between cash flows into new projects and cash flows out of successful projects; planning and controlling projects over their life cycles; and integrating R&D into the entire company budget. Budgetary planning is the essence of good R&D management. The timing, amount, and sources of funds needed will depend upon the timing and amount of flows from R&D, the degree of long-range orientation of the R&D, and its probability of success.

However, several peculiarities of R&D make the performance of the budgetary functions difficult, and their integration into the firm's over-all financial functions even more difficult. First, a prima donna complex may surround R&D, which makes it difficult to measure results and obtain good estimates of future trends. Sometimes industry feels that R&D cannot be planned in detail. Second, R&D is highly technical and the budgetary functions are therefore often not easy to divorce from the technical aspects. Whether or not a proposal is worth financing may hinge directly on its technical probability of success, and few budgetary decisions are made without the advice of scientists and technical specialists. Furthermore, top management often promotes competent scientists into managerial positions, so that the budgetary functions are performed largely by technically trained people with little knowledge and appreciation for budgeting. Finally, the R&D budgetary functions are particularly susceptible to the perverse effects of organizational dynamics.

A number of techniques and methods have been proposed by management scientists to help management perform the operational R&D finance functions of planning and control. Beyond certain simple capital budgeting

formulas, certain project scoring methods, and PERT/Critical Path scheduling techniques, it appears that few of the proposed models have actually
been used or even tried.

There is a definite need for R&D managers to study these techniques and
use them. How else will management scientists be able to provide more
powerful, improved second- and third-generation techniques? Companies
that are foremost in using and improving such approaches will also be
foremost in profits.

WHEN TO TERMINATE A RESEARCH AND DEVELOPMENT PROJECT

BY C. K. BUELL

A survey made by the Board of Editors of *Research Management* disclosed that a substantial number of subscribers would like to see papers written on the difficult problem of deciding when to terminate a research and development project that seems to be getting nowhere. Guidelines are conspicuous by their absence. Subsequently, the writer was asked to present his views from the standpoint of an industrial corporation's research and development department.

I suspect that the reason so little information has been published on this subject is because it is most difficult to set down specific and reasonably incontestable guidelines of widespread applicability. Indeed, one might well ask how any guidelines whatsoever can be advanced when the projects in question may be so diverse, complex or of such a pioneering nature that decisions as to their fate are based upon subjective areas such as intuitive judgment, educated guesses, hunches, or even hopeful aspirations. Furthermore, at some stage almost every project involving relatively large R&D expenditures comes under not only the scrutiny and evaluation of R&D but also top management and key personnel of other corporate departments, all of whom have widely divergent technical and business backgrounds, viewpoints, and objectives. When one considers all the multitudinous risk factors that must be weighed in advancing a new process or product from test tube to commercialization, it is impossible to even approach unanimity within the company on a given project's fate.

EDITOR'S NOTE: From *Research Management,* Vol. 10, No. 4 (1967), 275-284. Reprinted by permission of the publisher and the author.

Doubtless all of us would like to base our decisions at any point in time as a project proceeds down the research and development path, on precise scientific, technological, and marketing knowledge, all translated into realistically projected, business venture economics. Ideally, we would like to wrap up everything in a neat set of quantitative mathematical expressions, the net result being some kind of a numerical rating that would indicate we should temporarily shelve, terminate, or accelerate a project. However, at our present level of sophistication, and even employing the lightning-fast computers now at our disposal, I am convinced that we are still a long way from this Utopia. I believe that most R&D administrators in decision-making positions, if they honestly look back, will conceded that they were sometimes dead wrong when they based decisions to terminate a project on a numerical rating that did not have superimposed upon it the varied and mature judgment of top management and other knowledgeable segments of the company's organization. On the other hand, corporate management can make drastic mistakes if it "over-exercises" its prerogatives (particularly at early stages of R&D work) in deciding to terminate a project. None of the foregoing comments are intended in any way to imply that the writer is not a strong advocate of judiciously using every numerical project evaluation tool, including "subjective" probability analysis, which will assist R&D and other corporate personnel in making better decisions.

Certainly, without corporate management's wholehearted support of R&D programs, along with its business skills, judgment, foresight, and courage to assume the risks inherent in commercializing many projects, no R&D department can be truly effective. However, R&D should be in a somewhat favored position to exercise the best judgment as to ultimate probability of success of most projects. The more echelons of higher management committees that must successively pass judgment on the importance and merits of R&D findings and recommendations, the greater the chance a good project might be "killed." This results from the fact that other pressing demands for the time of the men on such committees oftentimes precludes their looking into and assaying all the pertinent technical and business ramifications of the project. Further, if committees made up of other corporate departments (such as manufacturing and marketing) rather than top management exercise *dominant* control over R&D's broad planning and programming, other deleterious effects can result. The responsibilities of other corporate departments are of an entirely different type that those of R&D. They are primarily responsible for the profitable operation of the physical facilities already in existence, whereas R&D is primarily responsible for developing new technology that will help ensure the long-term profitable growth of the company. If R&D is controlled too tightly by other corporate departments, it can easily degenerate into a technical service organization of a troubleshooting nature working on day-to-day problems. Now that I have tried to explain why it is most difficult, perhaps inadvisable, and certainly presumptuous on my part to write on this subject, nevertheless, I hope the reader will forgive my temerity if I try. Certainly this subject deserves increasing attention, particularly in view of rapidly rising R&D costs and the ensuing cost-productivity squeeze. Also, I believe that terminating a research and development project is one of the most agonizing decisions that confronts R&D administrators because those working on a problem are invariably sure that success is just around the corner. However, like drilling oil wells, it is not practical to keep on drilling forever. If one does not strike oil, a decision must be made to stop drilling.

Before delving deeper into this subject, I would like to reiterate that this paper will only address itself to the question of terminating a project from an industrial (not government or university) point of view. The sole purpose for the existence of an industrial research and development organization is to increase the company's growth and earnings, even if it engages in basic research without regard to how such knowledge might specifically be used. I would also like to qualify my remarks by adding that when I use the word "terminate," it does not necessarily imply that a project should be buried forever. Situations can and do arise where it may be advisable to reinstate work on a project that has been "terminated" within a few years or even within a few months. For example, new science or technology may be developed in some unrelated areas of research and development that is applicable to the project in question and thereby the feasibility and economics are suddenly improved. Perhaps changes in a company's raw material position or marketing capabilities will have a favorable bearing on the project. Or, perhaps, the top management's goals may shift toward greater diversification and thereby have a salutary effect on a project's status. Obviously, R&D administrators should constantly keep such considerations in mind when working on project planning and programming.

Against the above background, and after careful consideration, I have decided that it would be extremely inadvisable and dogmatic on my part to set forth specific and rigorous guidelines. In my opinion, the subject matter we are dealing with is too subjective to make "hard and fast" guidelines; at some later date we can hopefully take much of the present "art" of such decision-making into the realm of science. Rather, I shall attempt to raise a number of "warning flags" having to do with the question of when to terminate a project. If one or more of the questions raised by the "warning flags" indicate that there *may be* valid reasons for terminating a project, then every project evaluation tool and technique, and every corporate channel of communication at our disposal, should be fully and rapidly used to reach a final decision. A list of such "warning flags" (along with an explanatory note, if needed, that elaborates on the underlying reasons or circumstances for raising the questions) follows:

(1) Is there any doubt that the project is related to the present general objectives or goals of the company, or is responsive to the immediate or long-term needs of the company? Most companies have certain primary appraisal

tests set by corporate management that are applied to any project to make certain that it conforms to broad company policies, spheres of activities, and economic goals. These tests, including profitability indices, may vary considerably depending on the size of the company, amount of capital currently available for expansion, its raw material position, extent to which it wishes to diversify, its particular background of skills and know-how, its patent position, and other competitive factors and considerations. As a company's resources and technical background grow, or perhaps as its management shifts its viewpoints, the company's broad policies, objectives, and lines of activities change, thus oftentimes necessitating a different set of appraisal tests. Although, for most effective results, R&D should have considerable latitude in programming its own activities, projects should continuously be scrutinized as they progress from research to commercial scale to make certain that they continue to meet the company's basic tests. (Even pure research projects may have to pass these tests depending upon management's degree of permissiveness or insistence that even basic research work be conducted in fields very closely connected with the company's present spheres of activities.)

If in doubt on this question, R&D should periodically review with corporate management the status and objectives of work on major projects. Such reviews, for maximum effectiveness, should also cover (with the assistance of other departments) the market outlook, patent position, raw material supplies, projected economics, and other related subject matter.

(2) Does the project have a practical goal? An industrial research and development department's goals are to develop new processes, products, markets or services, or improve existing ones, to ensure the company's continued progress. Industrial research and development is effective only when it succeeds in maintaining or increasing profits and assets. No matter how successful an accomplishment might be from a scientific point of view, it is worthless to the corporation unless we can find ways and means of exploiting it in the market place.

(3) Is there any doubt that management, as a major project proceeds from test tube toward commercialization, is enthusiastic enough to support the increasing research and development effort with the necessary funds, men, physical facilities, and working environment—whatever it takes to get the job done when it should be done? This question is particularly important if the project happens to involve work in a major new field of business that the company heretofore has not engaged. In this situation it is imperative that R&D frequently point out to top management both the attractve profit potential and the technical and economic hazards that exist and solicit their help and advice in evaluating and passing judgment on the opportunities for commercialization.

(4) Is there any doubt that the over-all scope of a major project is compatible with the company's ability to finance and commercialize the project when the technology is presumed to be ready?

(5) Considering the research and development department's budget and the company's over-all needs and objectives, do any projects within the R&D department raise questions as to whether or not R&D has a "balanced program" in all areas of the company's interest? Any good research and development organization has more ideas than it can possibly handle. Some of these ideas may relate to current operational problems in some phase of the company's engineering, manufacturing, or marketing business. Other ideas may anticipate radically new departures in the more distant future. Each of these ideas or prospective programs (particularly those of a break-through nature waiting in the "wings") should be carefully analyzed in light of probability of timely and successful solution and that the profitability will well exceed the cost. Since R&D funds of any company are not unlimited, we cannot afford to work on all new ideas or discoveries. To allocate our manpower and budget funds most wisely, we must be selective in choosing the "horse" we will ride, whether in basic, applied, or service areas.

(6) If the project involves a new or improved product, process, or service of immediate or near term interest to the marketing, manufacturing, or other corporate departments, does it have the support of those departments? The best research and development efforts may be doomed to failure unless we gain the confidence and support of other corporate departments. Although top management can certainly help, by and large the research and development organization itself must sell its new ideas and projects. This involves staying in close and constant communication with key personnel in other interested departments and taking maximum benefit of their comments, suggestions, and constructive criticism. Such contacts are invaluable in helping program and expedite R&D's work.

(7) Because of manpower, dollar, or other constraints, does it appear that research and development effort is being spread so thin on too many projects such that it appears likely that none of them will get "over the hump" in a reasonable time? If this situation pertains, decisions obviously should be made to concentrate on and expedite the potentially most important projects. The reason is obvious—accomplishments are the best measure of success of any research and development endeavors.

(8) Because of budgetary or other reasons, are research and development efforts spread too thin on a single project? If too few men are assigned to a given project, they can do little more than keep up with the literature, much less forge ahead of the competition.

(9) Does it appear that research and development efforts on a project are producing technology too far ahead of the time when company might reasonably expect to commercialize upon such technology? Research and development must keep abreast of new scientific discoveries, new industrial develop-ments, economic trends, and other factors with a view toward anticipating effect of such things on the company's operations, how their company may profit thereby, and instituting new research and development projects well

ahead of the time when the information will be actually needed. However, if R&D efforts too far outrace a company's ability to finance and commercialize a given project, then the manpower on that project might temporarily be better utilized elsewhere.

(10) Does the research and development administrator have a feeling that the group working on a project is "playing minor variations on the same tune," or that the men working on the project have run out of new ideas and are "grasping at straws?" There is a tendency for a group working on a project to get stale. If work were stopped for a year or so and then reinstated, new ideas or technology might be generated and major improvements achieved. This technique helps overcome the tendency to always justify "just one more experiment." Many of these experiments are in reality of minor economic importance and the manpower could be much better utilized on "breakthrough" research.

Alternatively, the project might be temporarily shelved until a new team having different disciplinary backgrounds and fresh ideas can be organized and assigned to the project.

(11) Does it appear that work on a project has little chance of the company's developing a substantial patent or know-how position, but that industry as a whole may need the kind of technology expected to come out of the project to improve its operation? Perhaps this kind of research and development should be "farmed out" to an industry-supported cooperative or "non-profit" research organization.

(12) Does the project involve service work that can be handled just as well by other segments of the company's organization or farmed out? If so, R&D should consider terminating its work and concentrating on its basic mission of producing new science and technology. As a corollary, R&D professional groups will function most effectively when they are relieved of service functions so they can be free to concentrate on their primary responsibilities. Before passing judgment on this question too hastily, however, I would like to point out that some service work is desirable to keep in contact with operating departments and thus avoid becoming an "ivory tower" type of R&D organization.

(13) Is the project staffed with the right kind of people? If there is serious question that the men on the project do not have the proper multidisciplinary technical knowledge and experience, a genuine enthusiasm for their work, will accept responsibility for their actions, and have the courage of their convictions, perhaps the project should at least be temporarily shelved until the project organization can be strengthened.

(14) After research and development has expended every effort to sell its new ideas and projects, does it still encounter a great many negative reactions to doing research in particular fields from top management, marketing, manufacturing or other corporate departments? Normally, a selling function is not associated in most people's minds with a research and development organization. This is far from the true situation. Doubtless, most all R&D

organizations can look back at some wonderful business opportunities that were missed simply because someone up or down the line in the R&D organization did not do an effective job of selling. Technical ability counts greatly in our business, but this ability will be largely wasted and the company's future progress impeded if R&D cannot sell its achievements and overcome obstacles that may force project terminations because of lack of support on the part of top management or other corporate departments.

(15) What is the longevity of the current projects? Ideally there should be a distribution of project ages with some very new, the majority of intermediate age, and only a few very old projects. If an R&D organization finds itself in the position where the distribution is skewed and a large portion of the projects are very old, it is probably slipping on creativity or its management is not sufficiently risk-minded.

(16) What is the relationship between efforts on product research and process research? This factor will vary from industry to industry. In some industries it is fatal to concentrate too much effort on improvement of products made by existing processes and ignore the possibility of improvements in the process itself.

(17) Is it necessary to continue research in a process field of great importance to the company but one which has been "thoroughly plowed?" In general, most major technological investment fields should be backed up by continuing research and development effort to effect technological improvements and improve economics. However, long-established processes probably justify little work.

(18) Has the company lost the services of a key man or men who are the "spark plugs" on a project? If this situation arises, the project might best be temporarily shelved until remedial measures can be taken.

(19) Are the men responsible for (working on) the project enthusiastic about their chances of success?

(20) Considering the time value of money, have the possibilities been explored of purchasing the desired technology from others rather than developing it ourselves?

(21) As a project advances from bench scale through pilot-planting, do continuously projected economic analyses show every reasonable expectation that the project will meet whatever minimum profitability index guidelines top management has set? R&D management must recognize good ideas and research discoveries at the earliest possible time and put the wheels into motion to aggressively pursue potentially profitable projects. On the other hand, R&D's basic drive and desire to create, develop, and commercialize new science and technology must be tempered with good economic judgment. Consequently, the research and development administrator should continuously scrutinize the economics from research to projected commercial plans to make certain that the project will contribute substantially to the company's future growth and earnings and therefore be expected to have the support of top management when it reaches a commercialization appropriation request stage.

In conclusion, I hope that I haven't posed so many questions bearing on reasons why we, as R&D adminstrators, should consider terminating current projects that we will lose our courage to initiate new ones. Doubtless, we will continue to make mistakes, but we will also continue to produce profitable achievements.

C

R&D CONFLICT:
MANAGER VS. SCIENTIST
BY WARREN B. BROWN AND LEWIS N. GOSLIN

Research and development activities have had an explosive growth in recent years and at present there is no sign that this trend will be reversed (see Figure 6-3 below). In light of the high cost and the often limited supply of highly skilled personnel, one of the resulting needs of industry is the efficient use of its R&D resources. However, R&D administration poses several types of problems usually not found in other management activities. Most of these problems typically revolve around the differing needs and values held by businessmen and scientists.

Strains between industrial management and the scientific employee have plagued their relationship for a number of decades. Management has assumed that the professional person should fit into the same concept of organization as that practiced by industry. When there is a merger of various activities under one common organizational standard, the degree of difference between these two groups is made plain. Each tries to impose upon the other its own traditional views and expectations, R&D management function can be organized to overcome these problem areas and the conflicts they generate.

The supervisor of any R&D group usually knows that professionally oriented people, such as the scientists and engineers who work in his organization, have a need for professional achievement. Kornhauser and Hagstrom have observed four criteria of professionalism: expertise in an

EDITOR'S NOTE: From *Business Topics*, Summer 1965, pp. 71-79. Reprinted by permission of the Division of Research, Graduate School of Business Administration of the Michigan State University, and the authors.

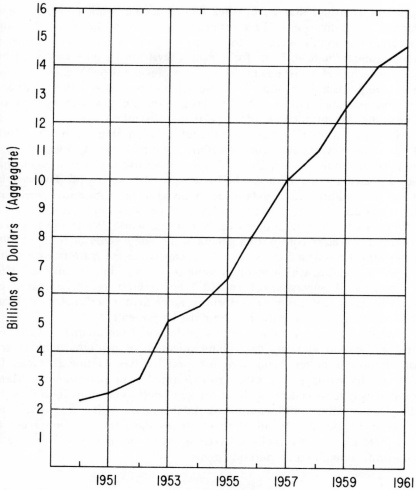

Figure 6-3. R & D expenditures in the U.S., 1950 to 1961–62.
SOURCE: Annual Reports of the National Science Foundation, 1950–51, 1962, 1963.

intellectual and educational context; autonomy; career commitment; and responsbile influence in the sue of one's competence.[4]

While all scientists and engineers may not operate under these four criteria, Shepard has noted that many scientists and engineers in industry view themselves as professionals.[5] For such a professional person to gain and maintain a sense of professional achievement, he must have free communication with his colleagues, who form the basis for an evaluation of his professional career. We know that an individual's sense of success or failure in a task is often highly dependent upon the evaluation of the task by his peer group, that is, whether they think his work is difficult and creative, or relatively easy. Free communication is essential if this dialogue concerning a man's work is to occur. Without such commentaries it becomes much more difficult for a man to evaluate his progress toward his goals of technical achievement. Thus the professional technical man must be able to publish the results of his research and related activities, to attend scientific meetings, and in general to have an open pathway to information concerning the current state of his particular discipline.

Management often believes that the information obtained by the efforts of the scientists should remain within the organization. Even if such information would not impair the firm's competitive position, it is felt that the time used for writing might be better spent "at the bench." The scientist or engineer additionally needs to be involved in the substantive decisions that affect his work. To exclude professional people from these decisions is only to invite their refusals to carry out the work. While the engineer working for a large corporation generally has some sense of responsibility to perform the assigned tasks, he also is sensitive to the maintenance of his professional status, which involves some freedom of inquiry and selection of activities. A supervisor of an R&D group must recognize that if he wants his technical group to perform in more than a perfunctory fashion, this feeling of personal participation must be present.

Awareness of the technical man's professional requirements, however, must go beyond allowing easy communication of his achievements and consultation in matters concerning his specialty. Recognition also must be regarded by management as a critical stimulus to performance. Many companies give formal recognition for good performance in several ways: titles, better offices and equipment, salary raises, extra secretarial aid, achievement awards. By all of these means the administration seeks to contribute to the individual's self-esteem and to promote his allegiance to both professional and corporation goals.

PROBLEM AREAS

One area which can create day-to-day leadership problems is that of authority relationships. The professional training of a scientist or engineer leads him to accept a system of colleague authority relationships rather than the executive authority system so prevalent in business firms. Basically, a colleague authority system presumes man's prestige is based on his abilities, and on actual evidence of his accomplishments. Decisions are made by groups and not by individual command, and the general atmosphere often involves collaboration among unequals in terms of the corporate pecking-order. Thus in the colleague authority system a person's recognized expertise is the critical factor for decision-making.

Executive authority, on the other hand, is the type more commonly practiced in business. It depends on the traditional power hierarchy where the supervisor has complete legitimate control. While a supervisor may utilize a democratic form of management, he is under no compulsion to do so. Essentially, he gives the orders and the subordinates are expected to carry them out.

Authority Conflict

The two systems typically come into conflict when management uses executive authority to control an R&D group when the persons in the group have been educated to accept only colleague authority relationships. The scientist, through years of university training in critical analysis and scientific methods, naturally gravitates to the colleague system and often has trouble living with the authority hierarchy typical of business firms. The businessman, on the other hand, often is more fully aware of the economic ramifications of R&D decisions, and is concerned with the manner in which such factors coincide with the company's objectives. These differing objectives may not only exist in day-to-day decisions, but such conflict also has larger implications for company planning in the R&D area, such as the degree to which shortrange economic considerations control long-term scientific endeavors.

In nonresearch organizations, the supervisor is at least as qualified as the man whom he directs in an administrative capacity. In research organizations, however, the subordinate often knows more about his job than does the superior. The administrator may rank high in the hierarchical structure, but low in the informal status ranking assigned to him by the researcher. This lack of uniformity may lead the scientist to resent any such control or evaluation by any other source than colleagues.

Organization Size

Another complicating factor that faces an R&D supervisor is one relating directly to the size of the technical organization. As the group expands, its management is forced to rely more and more heavily upon impersonal controls and prescribed procedures. This in turn causes a decrease in personal relationships, and the group engineer finds that instead of the expected close, professional relationship with his supervisor he is treated like just another employee. This situation can create resentment and it often leads to a lower level of performance than otherwise could be achieved. If the resentment becomes strong, it may develop into a psychological block to creativity, and thus one of the critical kinds of performance expected from R&D personnel may become sharply suppressed.

This condition is quite prevalent today in the aerospace industry. The orientation of management toward the project concept forces the rise and collapse of specialized organization and staff as the project progresses through various phases. Formal rules may accentuate the problem; certain military regulations require transfer or promotion of military administrators after a certain time period on a project. This forces a fluid relationship upon the organization—with a resulting loss in morale and efficiency.

Still other leadership problems arise from the interaction of the R&D group with other functional areas in the company, especially production and marketing. In both of these cases the problems may have two basic sources: the classic lack of good communication, and the problem that arises when people with differing values must necessarily work together. The first factor is primarily a linguistic problem, one of translating technical theory and laboratory models into actual products for manufacture and sale. Since an R&D group is constantly exploring new ground in its work, using new designs, materials, and procedures, there is a continuing problem of transmitting and receiving information of many different types while maintaining a high degree of understanding. An awareness of the critical need for clarity is essential here.

The second factor is primarily a problem of status and power. For example, some scientists may have little or no appreciation of the styling, pricing, and distribution problems faced by a marketing manager, and consequently have little regard for the man making decisions in these areas. The production manager may be downgraded in a similar fashion, and of course a reverse process of degrading may also occur.

There is still the problem of stereotyping. Scientists and production and marketing men often are viewed in terms of standard types by those persons in the company who are not directly connected with their specific departments. This tendency to oversimplification does not help to build sound departmental relationships, and certainly does not ease the difficulties inherent in bringing together diverse and sometimes conflicting group interests. The result may be bickering, reciprocal criticism, attempts to expand one group's control area at the expense of another, and mutual frustration. All of these hurt the organization's efficiency.

A CONFLICT IN GOALS

The above discussion has suggested some of the human problems in R&D. We should bear in mind that many of these arise from a difference in values between the traditional goals of the professional technical man and the businessman. In an oversimplified fashion it can be said that the scientist wants to generate knowledge and transmit it to others. To him the administrator just serves to enable him to do this more efficiently. The administrator, however, sees the R&D function as only one activity which must be integrated with many others in order to make the company viable.

Correspondingly, a serious value conflict can arise as a scientist moves up in the ranks of the corporate hierarchy. This occurs when the technical person finds that his advancement means that he must spend an increasing amount of his time on administrative and nontechnical matters. If this shift to managerial activities continues, a point is reached at which the person stops regarding himself as being primarily a scientist or engineer, and regards himself as primarily a manager. His advancement then depends on his rise on a managerial ladder rather than a technical ladder.

The scientist may prefer to look at a ladder system as a matter of choice of preference. Kornhauser and Hagstrom have noted several problems that may be raised by the use of a technical ladder. Such problems are:

1) A tendency to isolate the scientist from the rest of the organization.

2) The ceiling for scientific advancement may be below the ceiling on the supervisory ladder.

3) Scientists may become too independent of management.

4) A lower level administrator may be placed above a high level scientist who is on the professional ladder.

5) The whole ladder may be unnecessary, as other means can be found to recognize scientific achievements, such as the freedom to publish.[6]

Management, however, has given the managerial ladder more importance by associating more and higher levels of advancement on the management ladder. Those scientists who are unfit for management are associated with the technical ladder. Farr has suggested that the duality approach must satisfy the needs of the professional and it must also include some relevance to the particular activity you want to motivate.[7] This duality approach requires equally satisfying rewards to the participants, or the technical ladder may become the symbol of managerial inability.

The integration of the scientist is often bypassed by management because of lack of identification of the scientific group in the hierarchical structure. This tends to isolate him and aggravate the problem of divergency. This emergent position in administration, however, creates many new problems. No longer is the man's success dependent on his technical achievement and skills. Instead he may find that a direct transfer of his quantitative and scientific skills that served him so well in the past may lead him to misunderstand and underestimate the new administrative and more person-oriented problems. As his professional underpinning continues to diminish and disappear, the scientist placed in a managerial position may find that a corresponding foundation for his executive work is lacking. This situation, along with seemingly less exact answers to the questions he must confront, leads him to frustration and poor adjustment in the new position.

Of course one can look for an ideal technical manager, a man who has professional traits such as a good scientific background and the capability to deal in abstract ideas, an appreciation of the scientist's need to create and institutionalize knowledge, and a professional ethos that will help to stimulate his professional work force. This ideal man must also have certain business abilities: 1) a firm commitment to fulfilling the particular needs and goals of his company, 2) a broad comprehension of his company's activities and resources, 3) skill in human relations since much of his work will be with people, 4) a practical and realistic outlook in his evaluations as opposed to an idealistic frame of mind, and 5) an ability to integrate organizational subsystems and to make decisions relevant to them. Obviously it is difficult—though not impossible—to find a man who has all of these qualities.

To some extent semi-experts are available. These are persons who have at least a moderate professional background combined with a personality which fits well with managerial activities. Often they are technical persons who feel that they have little chance of achieving success if they remain in their specialties, or who, because of natural inclination of their interests and personalities, gravitate into committee work and then full-time administration. In addition, some universities make an effort to train a few of their students so that they have an appropriate background. This is often accomplished through a blend of selected undergraduate and graduate programs. Examples are programs in hospital administration, industrial management, and school supervision.

Many professional organizations have lay administrators, persons who do not share the professional values of the other group members; their abilities and interests are focused elsewhere. Since such a person can easily endanger the professional values of the group, it seems clear that an R&D administration of only this kind will be an inherent source of strain.

A POSSIBLE SOLUTION

Rather than striving to find one particular "natural leader" for each level of R&D management, one who combines all of the desired characteristics, it is reasonable to ask if the leadership function itself cannot be restructured. Such a restructuring would attempt to minimize the basic conflict in objectives that can arise between scientists and corporate managers, and also the conflict in roles between the scientist and the R&D administrator. Such a restructuring of the leadership function must take into account the needs for technical guidance and a professional atmosphere on one hand, and the demands for economic and human relations skills on the other.

The R&D organization chart shown in Figure 6-4 is suggested as one reasonable method of attacking this problem. Of course the exact structure would vary with the size and activities of a specific group.

In this arrangement the Director of the R&D organization as well as the Division Heads would be persons whose skills and interests were primarily (though not exclusively) in the management area, while the Technical Board and the Project Leaders would be selected primarily on the basis of their technical abilities. The idea is to provide consideration for

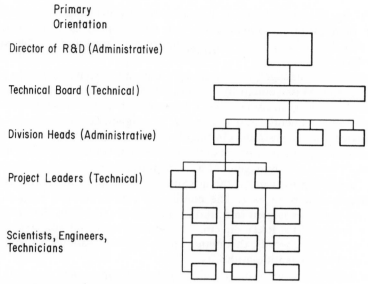

Primary
Orientation

Director of R&D (Administrative)

Technical Board (Technical)

Division Heads (Administrative)

Project Leaders (Technical)

Scientists, Engineers,
Technicians

Figure 6-4. A proposed organization chart for R&D.

both technical and managerial goals when decisions are to be made without demanding that any one person be expert in all areas. This system, however, will also give weight to individual interests and characteristics. The Technical Board is composed of professional personnel who serve as a screening and review group for new and old projects. They also should insure the existence of a professional atmosphere for their colleagues; this includes a responsibility to promote the use of colleague authority (as opposed to executive authority) in the laboratories. The Project Leaders in this plan are technical experts who supervise and guide the work on a particular project or in a specialized field.

By using managerially-oriented people on alternate levels in the organization, a means is provided for insuring that overall corporate goals will not be forgotten in the decision-making. In this manner the scientific norms will not be allowed to dominate to the point where they become detrimental in a wider corporate sense; thus a system of checks and balances begins to operate. Further, the administrative details connected with research activities and with the recognition of technical achievements should be readily accomplished assuming that those selected for their administrative expertise were well chosen.

CONCLUSION

Flexibility in managerial control is imperative. The degree of control hinges upon a realization that creativity is spontaneous. It cannot be speeded up or extracted from the scientists by exerting pressure. Some degree of tension is unavoidable, but where there is a premium on individual thinking, initiative, and ingenuity, a relaxed and flexible system is necessary.

Participative management as an approach adds some emphasis to the human aspect. Management by participation allows scientists to have some influence regarding decisions. R&D management must communicate with the scientists frequently and efficiently. Management must rely on scientists' advice and suggestions. On the other hand, scientists need advice and stimulation from their superiors. Participation involves joint response on the part of both top management and scientists.

This approach focuses on the advantages of group interaction, but it is not offered as a panacea to the conflict of control versus freedom. The argument for it is a cogent one, and in prestige in minimizes this conflict to a great extent. The R&D director must work with and not through his scientists. In other words, this management approach allows a blending of managerial and scientific authority.

The degree of control in any given research department depends upon several factors. If research is basic, a much less degree of control is required than if research involves product development and design—at the other end of the spectrum. For these reasons control and communication techniques must be flexible enough to adapt to changing conditions of the organization and yet be uniform enough to insure predictability. Needless to say, this approach, if carried too far, involves a waste of time and energy. Yet scientists need self-assertion and recognition; R&D management, through participation, can build self-control and self-motivation in the scientific groups. Scientists are highly educated individuals and highly motivated to solve problems and do not need the degree of control necessary in other areas of the firm. If any group of employees has the ability, intelligence, and knowledge to make this management approach a success, it is the creative scientists in research and development.

Since today's emphasis on science has transformed many small laboratories into large, complex organizations, it has become very important to take a hard look at what is being fostered; scientific manpower is much too valuable to be squandered away because of poor leadership.

NOTES

1. A list of the references surveyed and some supplementary material will be supplied without charge to interested users. The author asks that these persons provide reimbursement for postage.

2. William E. Souder, "Planning R&D Expenditures with the Aid of a Computer," *Budgeting*, XIV (March, 1966), pp. 25-32.

3. William E. Souder, "Cost/Progress—a Pattern for Operational Budgeting," *Managerial Planning*, XVII (January-February, 1969), pp. 1-9.

4. William Kornhauser and Warren Hagstrom, *Scientists in Industry: Conflict and Accommodation* (Berkeley and Los Angeles: University of California Press, 1962), pp. 147-48.

5. Herbert B. Shepard, "Nine Dilemmas in Industrial Research," *Administrative Science Quarterly*, December 1956, pp. 295-309.

6. Kornhauser and Hagstrom, *op. cit.*

7. James N. Farr, "A Motivational Approach to Research Management," *Research Management*, IV, 4 (Winter 1961), 277-89.

8. Tom Burns, "Research, Development and Production: Problems of Conflict and Cooperation," *IRE Transactions on Engineering Management*, EM-8 (March 1961), 15-23.

9. Amitai Etzioni, "Authority Structure and Organization Effectiveness," *Administrative Science Quarterly*, IV (June 1959), 43-67.

10. Norman Kaplan, "The Role of the Research Administrator," *Administrative Science Quarterly*, IV (June 1959), 20-42.

11. Simon Marcson, "Role Concept of Engineering Managers," *IRE Transactions on Engineering Management*, EM-7 (March 1960), 30-33.

12. Simon Marcson, *The Scientist in American Industry* (New York: Harper & Bros., 1960).

13. Eugene Raudsepp, *Managing Creative Scientists and Engineers* (New York: The Macmillan Company, 1963).

ADDITIONAL SELECTED BIBLIOGRAPHY

The Research Program

1. Berenson, C., "The R&D: Marketing Interface—A General Analogue Model for Technology Diffusion," *Journal of Marketing*, Vol. 32, No. 2 (April, 1968), 8-15.

2. Collier, D. W., "How Should Management Determine How Much Company Funds to Invest in R&D?" *Research Management*, Vol. 7, No. 6 (1964), 393-406.

3. Cook, L. G., "How to Make R&D More Productive," *Harvard Business Review*, Vol. 44, No. 4 (July-August, 1966), 145-153.

4. Cooper, A. C., "R&D Is More Efficient in Small Companies," *Harvard Business Review*, Vol. 42, No. 3 (May-June, 1964), 75-83.

5. Dessauer, John H., "How a Large Corporation Motivates Its Research and Development People," *Research Management*, Vol. 14, No. 3 (May, 1971), 51-55.

6. Galloway, E. C., "Evaluating R&D Performance — Keep It Simple," *Research Management*, Vol. 14, No. 2 (March, 1971), 50-58.

7. Hodge, M. H., Jr., *"Rate Your Company's Research Productivity,"* *Harvard Business Review*, Vol. 41, No. 6 (November-December, 1963), 109-122.

8. Pessemier, E. A., "Directing R&D for Profitable New-product Development," *Marketing and Economic Development*, P. D. Bennett, ed., AMA Fall Conference Proceedings, American Marketing Association (September, 1965), 279-287.

9. Quinn, J. B., Jr., and Cavanaugh, R. M., "Fundamental Research Can Be Planned," *Harvard Business Review*, Vol. 42, No. 1 (January-February, 1964), 111-124.

10. Roberts, E. B., "A Basic Study of Innovators: How to Keep and Capitalize on Their Talents," *Research Management*, Vol. 11, No. 4 (1968), 249-266.

11. Talley, W., "Marketing R&D: Neglect Way to Profit-Growth," *Business Horizons,* Vol. 5, No. 3 (Fall, 1962), 31-40.

QUESTIONS FOR DISCUSSION AND REVIEW

1. How can you ascertain the amount of a total research budget?

2. Determine by some rating scale how to apportion research by individual product.

3. What methods can you use to rate a company's research productivity?

4. Is R&D more important in large companies? Explain your answer.

5. How important is it to keep your scientists and engineers (innovators) satisfied?

PART III
THE PRODUCT PLANNING PROCESS

The step-by-step process of exploring for new product ideas, screening these product ideas, analyzing these ideas from a quantitative point of view, product development by model building, testing the product, and finally commercializing a new product will be espoused in some detail in this part. This step-wise process is utilized by many firms in many industries. Many top managers feel that risks of failure are reduced considerably by utilizing this process.

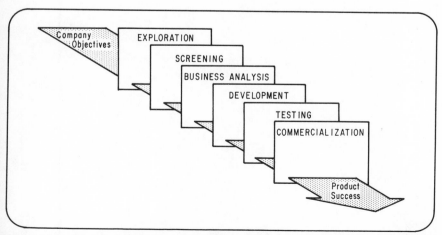

Stages of product evolution. Reproduced courtesy Booz, Allen and Hamilton, Inc.

143

7

EXPLORATION AND SCREENING

The first step toward commercializing a new product requires that the firm initially assign in writing the task and responsibility to either a product manager or a committe of executives for product development. Then the same committee or a new committee should direct and coordinate exploration of new product ideas. New product ideas could be in areas of present current interest, or the ideas could be in areas completely outside the company's domain. In other words, a company may exploit all product ideas made available to the committee, or it can accept for further study only those ideas that are deemed relevant to their present market segment, line of products, or total resources. New product ideas can be solicited internally from individual firm members working in various departments or externally from private consulting firms, individual inventors through direct contact or "invention shows," from actual or potential competition, from company's distributors or dealers, from a licensor, or by the direct purchase or purchase control of another company whose product would "fit the needs" of the controlling company. A large number of ideas must be brought to the attention of the search manager or committee to assure success of some new products.

Screening can be performed either by a single top executive or by a screening committee. Regardless of who has the responsiblity, screening must be handled with a lucid understanding of the firm's productive facilities which include the physical plant, warehousing, and human resources as well as the financial resource capabilities of the firm and the prowess of the marketing department to sell and service the product. Unless a firm has wide interests and an explicit research and development policy

145

of expanding into diverse fields, it may not wish to continue searching for new products outside of its presently manufactured products. The firm may wish only to expand its present line or to improve some of its present products. Reasons for this can be that the firm may be unwilling to acquire new capital for manufacturing the new product because of the amount needed before the factory is "on stream," and the risk involved should the product not return sufficient profits; or that the market segment is different from its present line and would require the employment and training of a new sales force; or that special knowledge is required for producing, selling, and servicing the new product.

Many of the new product ideas brought to the attention of the company will be eliminated entirely or shelved temporarily to be considered again at a future date. Without a doubt, product ideas not compatible with company objectives should be shelved or dropped. If there is indication that the new product idea "fits" company objectives, then further screening will be done on the basis of a company's plant and equipment, financial resources, human resources, primary and selective demand as well as a determination made as to whether demand for the probable new product will be of a derived nature. Firms have used checklists, matrices, rating devices, cluster analysis, and other ingenious methods to screen new product ideas. The following articles indicate how screening can be accomplished with some degree of accuracy.

ORGANIZING FOR AND GETTING
NEW PRODUCT IDEAS
BY JAMES H. FLOURNOY

Where do you get new product ideas, and how do you organize to get them? To clear up any ambiguity about whether this question refers to your company as a whole, or to you personally, the company will ordinarily reflect what the individuals in management do—at least as far as generating new product ideas is concerned. The only place that ideas come from is people. Machines, to my knowledge, can only produce if they are given something to work on. And in this instance that means the output of people.

General management's conventional role has been to manage an existing business, and this has tended to give senior executives a controller-oriented point of view. In the notable exceptions to this general state of things, growth, innovation, and risk-taking have been the manager's responsibility, and new products have happened. That should surprise no one. Isn't it clear that a man who *needs* ideas will get them? At least he will get more of them than if the need were not there—or if it were not recognized that finding ideas was part of his job.

So need is a great stimulus. Encouragement is another. Each of you has experienced a situation where you could have contributed your idea, but didn't. Why not? You might have thought that the other fellow didn't need it, or that he wouldn't appreciate it. Or maybe he wasn't one to give credit for others' ideas; so you thought, "Why let him take over this one too?" The

EDITOR'S NOTE: From *The Professionals Look at New Products,* Brand, Gruber and Co., eds., Michigan Business Papers No. 50, 1968. Reprinted by permission of the Graduate School of Business Administration, The University of Michigan, and the author.

negative experiences stick in your mind and inhibit you from contributing your ideas.

A management that wants new ideas tries to create positive experiences. If you, yourself, feel that your ideas are not only welcome but needed, and that they will be acknowledged, your imagination and insight are not hampered. If management says, "Only through ideas can growth be planned," you feel confident of a hearing. Further, if one of your ideas becomes the basis for the company's growth, and if the fact that you had contributed the idea was openly acknowledged, you would feel even more encouraged to contribute. And maybe you would give even more conscious effort toward developing ideas. If these things work with you, they will work with others.

More and more we need an environment that is conducive to creating and recognizing ideas, and more and more is being done to define the optimum environment. Successful advertising agencies are among those most clearly concerned. In these agencies, copy is developed and communication to others is forged at an increasingly rapid rate.

Not long ago, in an interview reported in the *New York Times,* Victor Bloede said that when he joined Benton and Bowles as a copywriter in 1950 he had only two accounts and had to write only four ads a month. Under those conditions a man had plenty of time to wait for ideas to come to him. But people now are working a lot harder than they did. Television takes a lot more work than print—and it takes a lot more ideas.

The agency world has therefore had to foster the environment that stimulates the contribution of ideas. And others can do the same if they will recognize the need. The conditions that make up the best climate for ideas seem to be these:

1. An expressed need for ideas as a requisite for growth.
2. Confidence among personnel that an idea won't get shot down before it is thought through.
3. A willingness by management to consider all ideas. This is a corollary to the preceding item.
4. Recognition of the person who contributes an idea.

Important as it is to create an encouraging atmosphere for developing new product ideas, these ideas have to be sought out among many different people. The most fertile sources are:

1. The market place
2. The laboratory or technical research section
3. Other places within the firm

The market place is normally one of the best sources of new product ideas. Today's opportunities are certainly more consumer-oriented because of the large array of needs. Developing awareness of solutions, making them available at a price consumers can afford—all these create both limitations and opportunities in relation to new products.

To understand the opportunities, you must understand the needs, in other words, customers' problems. You must put yourself in the consumer's place and find out more about him. We have developed many techniques to make it easier to see things from the consumer's point of view. When you can do this, the perspective begins to take shape and the consumer values in your potential market begin to be understood. *And ideas form,* but not unless you're willing to assume the role of your consumer.

One way in which consumers' attitudes can help you get new product ideas in in concept testing. You may feel that the concepts are good ones, or simply the best you can develop, but you need to know how others will react to an idea that you present to them. Consumers are like you: They can criticize a lot better and a lot easier than they can invent.

We could do this by exposing some concepts on slides and letting you vote on whether they are good concepts or bad concepts. The scores would be fun. You would enjoy seeing how you stack up with others. But the point is that you would react either positively or negatively, and these reactions give us insights. If you were a consumer in our market, they would lead to ideas. Even concepts that make a poor showing can provoke ideas also, if you go on to learn why the consumer reacts negatively and what kind of product he would rather have.

You do not need to go directly to the consumer, however, to get ideas from the market place. Salesmen and suppliers are excellent sources, both directly by perceiving consumers' needs, and indirectly by passing on customers' complaints. Consumers themselves often write letters that suggest new products or tell you what is unsatisfactory about existing products. Advertising agencies and research organizations, as we all know, represent other valuable sources of ideas. Finally, your own company's failures in the market place can be turned to good account. Many times, the farther you've carried your failing product, the more clearly the successful direction is indicated.

From the market place let's turn to the laboratory and the problem of getting technical ideas that can become the basis for research proposals. Environment is very important here, too. Because their jobs are specialized, professional technical people need all the stimulus you can give them to orient themselves to the consumer market that you want to enter. General interest consumer studies undertaken to get information about a market and to help define consumer attitudes, can provide exceptionally good stimulus to technical people. One of the more productive ways to encourage ideas in the laboratory and among other technical people is to ensure that market research evaluations of their product prototypes are presented to them so that they are vividly aware of the reaction of the consumer as well as the way the product prototype performs.

The encouragement of ideas from the laboratory and technical staff, to be effective, requires a continuing dialogue with management. Recognition of individuals is important. One way to recognize them is to initiate a research project to explore the value of an idea. The input from the consumer market here is priceless. Consumer input obviously takes somewhat different forms in different companies. It can embrace sales trends, consumer complaints, market trends, and data about attitudes and other matters from the companies' consumers.

There are formal idea-generation programs which can help develop the atmosphere and willingness to contribute ideas. Generally, in these programs a team works on the problem. Its objective is to suppress negative reactions in the working group so that idea input is encouraged and received by the group. A good example of this type of program is the synergism program offered by Synectics, Incorporated, Cambridge, Massachusetts. A typical synergism program calls for six men to work together for six consecutive half-days to better their understanding of each others' needs and develop the ability and willingness to contribute.

There are other formal programs directed more specifically toward solution of particular problems. The early brainstorming techniques are fairly well understood. Programs based on the synectics method are beginning to develop broader use. These generally involve a group of individuals, each expert in an area of the problem. The nature of the exercise is to take mental excursions beyond the limitations of the specific problem, then screen back the results to those seeming to fit the criteria of the problem solution.

Synectics, Incorporated, offers a problem-solving program which, in its present form, involves six or seven experts for a period of three days. Another group doing work in problem-solving is Behringer and Jacobson in New York City. They employ a graphical method developed from synectics principles. The benefit of this kind of effort is that it produces problem solutions that would not normally be encountered in an environment of normal business constraints.

Outside the laboratory areas, but within the firm, there is usually less dialogue on new product ideas, with the exception of the "market place people"—those directly concerned with sales, marketing, and development. We need to create an open channel for ideas from those in manufacturing, financial, and personnel work. Many times it's not easy to draw out these people, because they are likely to undervalue their contributions and to think that marketing or development people have probably long since arrived at the same ideas.

Here too an environment that encourages and recognizes the contribution such people can make is worth cultivating. I remember a product concept that an employee actually wrote up and presented to a development manager. It was turned down. A couple of years later after the employee left to build a business as a consultant, he resubmitted the idea, supported by data that he had obtained himself about consumers' reaction to the concept. This time a contract was set up and the idea was tried. The prototype product passed the trial, and the company had a success. It may have cost the company more to get the idea that way, but management saw the necessity of providing a responsive channel for new product ideas.

Some specific steps that can be taken to promote such contributions are:

1. Establish a place where ideas can normally be submitted. The development manager, the general manager, or the new products manager, depending on the company structure, are likely persons. But the person selected should be an executive with a broad understanding of opportunities and a readiness to grasp them. People should be encouraged to talk about the idea, and the originator should present it in a written statement.

2. Set up orientation sessions with representatives of other departments, so that the operation and needs of those concerned with new products are understood better.

3. Respond to the offer of an idea in some tangible way. You'd be surprised what a short letter to a man's home will do. (It's hard work to be a hero to your wife, but this helps.)

4. Credit the originator openly if the idea is successful. Many times the first page of our Turnover to Marketing document will credit the originator of an idea.

In summary, what are the important principles that I have tried to uncover here? First, you must work to create an environment that fosters the development of ideas and encourages people to propose them to management. Emphasizing the need for ideas is one means of eliciting ideas; being continually willing to listen to all kinds of ideas in a positive way is another.

Giving recognition to people who submit ideas is an evidence of appreciation that can do more than hours of talking to stimulate others to contribute. Assuming the role of the consumer opens up new avenues by which ideas can reach you. Sharing these can stimulate ideas in others. You know the old saying, "When all else fails, why not try some consumer research." There are also professional systems for idea development, like brainstorming, synectics, and sensitivity training, that may work for you.

The American Marketing Association is always ready with counsel, if you are in doubt about the best approach for you. Certainly, seminars like these are a fine way to see the impressive range of ideas that can be generated about new products if you provide a place where they can be heard.

TOWARD THE IMPROVEMENT OF NEW PRODUCT SEARCH AND SCREENING

BY ALLAN D. SHOCKER, DENNIS GENSCH, AND LEONARD S. SIMON

SEARCH AND SCREENING WITHIN THE PRODUCT DEVELOPMENT PROCESS

In any conceptualization of the new product development process, search and screening occupy primary roles. As the first stage in the process, search is concerned with identifying many ideas for new products, while the next stage, screening, involves the reduction of the number of ideas through assessment (often subjective) of the compatibility of each idea with company resources, procedures, and objectives. Screening is also often associated with economic analysis of product profitability. Screening and the subsequent stages of the development process filter the results of search. These early stages of product development are carried out in a somewhat sporadic manner since search normally does not produce a continuous stream of ideas or stockpile them for "batch" processing. In order for these procedures to function, product ideas are evaluated with respect to some previously arrived at standards (which too often reflect only a company's previous product experiences and its current capabilities) to decide whether a product idea is passed for further evaluation, immediately commercialized, or let lay. Each successive stage in the entire development process is

EDITOR'S NOTE: From *Marketing Involvement in Society and the Economy,* P. R. McDonald, ed., 1969, pp. 168-175. Reprinted by permission of the American Marketing Association and the authors.

aimed at reducing uncertainty about the future profitability of the product (idea), but normally at higher costs for the information. Of course, since product development takes place over a prolonged period of time, technological changes, competitive developments, changes in corporate personnel or in their influence, etc., may offer new information which will change the results of prior analysis and affect future evaluations.

Because of their primacy in the development process, one might suspect that search and screening would have received considerable attention in the scientific revolution which appears to be pervading management practice. After all, an idea needs to be verbalized before it can be evaluated, and thus, the whole product planning effect can be said to be tied to the quality of the search process. Similarly, since screening is thought to be relatively less expensive than succeeding stages, improved efficiency could lead to a reduction of the twin errors of (1) passing through products that will fail at some later stage or (2) screening out products that would have been successful if commercialized. Similar "errors," of course, affect each stage of the development process, including that of search. Yet, the truth is that these stages have received only scant attention in the management science literature, particularly search. Most models of the product development process already assume the existence of a tangible product.[1]

The purposes of this paper are, briefly, to review the "state of the art" in the areas of new product search and screening, to identify promising methodologies and approaches and suggest some of their potential, and to look at some of the issues and problems that limit research and its implementation in these areas.

NATURE OF SEARCH AND SCREENING ACTIVITIES

Search and screening have traditionally been viewed as separate stages. While this distinction may be useful for expository purposes, it has served to draw attention from their natural interrelation. Screening criteria can often influence the areas of search activity and even the intensity of search into a given area, while search procedures obviously determine which product ideas will be subjected to screening. Perhaps, there exists a considerable potential for improvement through identifying some means for consolidating these two phases of the product development process. The intensity of search in a given area has sometimes been a function primarily of past successes in the area. To illustrate, a company which develops a highly successful new product will thereafter devote considerable effort for extended periods to identifying more opportunities in the same area, not infrequently with little or no payoff.

Search methodology is usually quite informal, and the authors are not aware of many formalized models for actually conducting search activities and evaluating the efficienty of the process.[2] Usually, the search procedure concentrates on identifying those sources which may generate new product ideas, finding ways to motivate the source, and then routinizing the flow of new product ideas. Probably a great number of ideas are never uncovered by the search process because: (1) the person with an idea does not know how to enter it into the new product development process, (2) the person originating the idea does some sort of screening himself and decides to eliminate the idea, and (3) the mechanics of the flow are not well specified so the ideas are forwarded to the wrong person or place. In this latter instance, screening may be done by other than the new product development committee, but sometimes the idea is just lost in the course of transit. Correction of these problems requires, more than anything else, indoctrination of the personnel from entire organization (as well as those outside persons and groups who may also be sources) with respect to the importance of new product ideas and explanations of how these ideas should be handled.

Most screening models consist of checklists of important factors which the persons conducting the evaluation are to consider. The point of such lists is to be as systematic as possible in evaluating ideas on similar criteria and to reduce the likelihood that some important factor might not be considered. Significant refinements of this basic method include: (1) subjective weighting of the factors, (2) use of scales to score the potential product ideas on each factor, (3) multiplication of factor weights and product scores and summation across factors to produce a single product score, (4) establishment of one or more cut-off scores below which product ideas are dropped from further consideration, seen as requiring more information before a decision can be made, or sent on into the next stage in the total product development process, and (5) formulation of techniques for combining the judgments of several different raters. Examples of this type of screening model are reported in several places.[3]

This *"scaled-checklist" method* is probably the most widely used method for screening new product ideas but, unfortunately, it has a number of important flaws which we shall enumerate briefly.[4]

The scaled-checklist procedure assumes more knowledge on the rater's part about product and market characteristics than he may possess. Further, the aggregation of scores of different raters assumes consistent application of rating criteria, an assumption which may not be valid because of inter-rater differences. Moreover, raters may have different degrees of confidence in their ratings and the procedures do not incorporate means to reflect these. Frequently, too, the factors are not independent. For example, if one of the martketing factors has to do with the ease with which the product may be advertised, this is hardly an independent consideration from the types of distribution channel which can be utilized.

There is, in addition to the above, a class of problems with the checklist method having to do with the interpretation of the summated factor scores for given product ideas. First, the conventional procedure generally gives little guidance as to the appropriate cut-off scores in discriminating between acceptable and non-acceptable ideas. Second, attention must be given to the product score-factor weight interaction because product ideas which achieve very high scores on a set of relatively unimportant factors may obtain the same overall, or summated, score as other ideas scoring moderately on very important factors; the two cases are quite different and it should be a carefully thought out decision as to whether they should be treated in identical fashion. Third, variance in the summated score is affected by the method chosen for combining the judgments of the various raters.

However, despite the preceding flaws in the scaled-checklist approach, none is so serious as one which has recently been suggested. Checklist type screening models are extremely insensitive to changes in rating of product ideas on specific factors or changes in factor weights. As a result, given the most commonly reported relationships of relative risk of failure to expected profits gained, if successful, the decision must almost always be in favor of proceeding further in the development process.[5] Essentially, even improved checklist methods may be relatively poor screening tools except for products at the extremes on the successful-unsuccessful continuum.

NEWER APPROACHES TO SEARCH AND SCREENING

Having identified the purposes of search and screening activities and indicated some of the deficiencies in traditional approaches, let us examine some of the newer approaches that have been proposed.

Pessemier's Approach

Pessemier has developed a simulation model to provide the firm with recommendations concerning areas to search and the search effort to expend in each area.[6] This model takes cognizance of the relationship between search and screening. Management must identify areas to be considered for search, specify alternative policies for search (degrees of search intensity), specify a minimum expected rate of return required before a new product idea is moved on to further analysis, provide estimates of the nature of the universe of potential product ideas (in terms of the cash flow of investments and earnings from potential new product ideas) that might result from search activity in each area, and estimate the response to specified search policies in each search area in terms of the rate of generation of new product ideas. The model uses these inputs to generate, through simulation, a series of distributions of return on investment produced when area i is searched with search policy j and cutoff rate of return k. These distributions are then characterized by expected values and standard deviations. When these expected values for each search area, policy, and cutoff return (i,j,k) are plotted against the standard deviations, the "best" search plan can be selected. The expected value constitutes the measure of return, while the standard deviation is construed to be a measure of risk. Management can subjectively determine an acceptable risk-return balance (tradeoff), and this is also plotted. Each search area falling within the acceptable risk-return region can be searched using that search policy and cutoff return criterion providing a maximum expected rate of return. Thus, the output of this model is a specification of the areas i appropriate for search, the intensity of search j in that area, and the cutoff return k to use in preliminary screening projects.

Unfortunately for the successful implementation of this model, management is asked to supply a considerable amount of input information in the form of estimates.[7] It is not clear, particularly as concerns the profitability of product ideas resulting from specified areas of search, (even with the eventual development of a data bank) that the estimates will be good. Few companies introduce so many products as to permit the accumulation of valid and reliable data upon which to base profitability estimates. Undoubtedly in any firm's product development history, some products which would have been successful never were marketed or were abandoned too early. Others which were marketed might have failed for reasons of inadequate marketing planning (which may have had little to do with the quality of the product idea). Still others which were deemed successful might have been even more so under more nearly optimal commercialization. As the number of search areas and levels of search areas and levels of search activity proliferate, the number of possible combinations grows and the demand for data grows accordingly. A sufficiently large data bank may include product histories which are outdated in terms of the future guidance they can provide. Changed tastes and preferences, new technologies, and the like, can all affect both the identification of worthwhile areas for search and the judgments of the value of search in each area. Yet, the model induces search primarily in areas which have previously been productive and for which actual or judgmental data already exist. Moreover, the uncertainties about the validity and reliability of such data are magnified in the use of expected values as measures of probable return and (more importantly) in the use of standard deviations as measures of risk. Further, the computational burden to the model may be large. The model requires separate simulations for all possible combinations of search area, intensity, and cutoff rate of return. Thus the potentially large number of such combinations intensifies both the data problem and the computational burden.

Stefflre's Approach

Conceptually, a rather different approach to search and screening is that proposed by Stefflre. Stefflre calls his procedure "Market Structure Studies". As the name implies, his aim is to describe the structure of various product-markets in an attempt to discover gaps in the distribution of product preferences which are not adequately served by existing products. Unlike Pessemier's proposals, the procedures which Stefflre advocates have been implemented in a variety of marketing situations.[8]

Stefflre's procedures make it possible to identify product-markets in terms of product-product and brand-brand competition and evaluate the dimensions along which such competition takes place. They permit identification of gaps in this market structure, locate product descriptions to match these gaps, and predict what shares the new products (matched to the descriptions) will enjoy and from which existing products (brands) such shares will come.

The procedures of Market Structure Studies are quite general in their applicability. (1) In order to determine the boundaries of product-markets a small number of consumers (less than 50) are asked to judge whether each of the specified set of items (products and brands) is appropriate to each of a specified set of uses. Computer analysis determines (a) the judged similarity of each use to each other use in terms of whether the same products are seen as appropriate and (b) the judged similarity of products in terms of their pattern of uses. These analyses are used to determine which items constitute the market of interest. (2) This smaller set of items resulting from the analyses at stage (1) is presented to another small, heterogeneous sample of consumers who are asked to judge (through rank orderings) the similarity of each item to every other item. They are also asked to suggest features or ways in which the items so judged are similar to each other. Techniques of nonmetric multidimensional scaling (to be discussed later) can then be used to find the configuration of the products in n-dimensional space which affords the greatest consistency with the judged similarity measures. The indicated features which make items similar are used to interpret the dimensions of this space (i.e., to discover the reasons products are judged similar). From observation of the positioning of products in this dimensioned space, gaps will become obvious. The interpretation of the dimensions of the space permits one to describe products which might fit within those gaps.

(3) Stefflre goes on to construct what he calls a "pattern of preference tinkertoy." From a 200 person national sample, Stefflre obtains rank orders of products and of descriptions of features consumers previously have mentioned in describing ways products are similar and different. The tinkertoy is a physical model which positions the products and descriptions in a three dimensional spatial arrangement. Items and descriptions liked by the same individuals are placed near each other. From the tinkertoy, a possible validation of previous results can be obtained (i.e., previous estimates of which brands are where and why they are positioned as they are can be checked), In addition, potentially better information about the descriptions of brands that might occupy "holes" in the current market structure are now available. The tinkertoy may, however, offer an imperfect

overview of the structure of the market, in part because of the limitations imposed by only three dimensions. (4) The final step in the market structure study consists of testing a small number of new product descriptions using data from a large (1500 person) national probability sample to determine the number of people (for proportion of buying volume) that prefer each description to the brands they currently use, the products each description takes its choices from, and the increases (and decreases) in existing products' shares of market with the addition of a brand that performs like each description. With the discovery of description that performs as desired (*i e.,* maximizes the share of market for all of a manufacturer's brands), the market structure study is completed. A second phase of Stefflre's procedure helps the manufacturer evolve the product, packaging, advertising, etc., that fits the new product description. This is done through a series of sequential presentations of various stimuli to small samples of consumers to find out how to translate the target description into physical and symbolic terms. When this has been done, a large scale preference test is conducted to check that the product in fact performs like the description it was built to match.

Market Structure Studies can contribute to the product strategy of a manufacturer who competes by offering several brands in the same product-market. Previously, when faced with a threat from a competitive brand which had substantial appeal to the tastes of a particular market segment, his strongest competitive action was often to introduce a similar ("me-too") product. Analysis of predicted market structure, after the introduction of the competitor's brand, now may identify new product options which will do more to enhance his entire product *line* than simply copying the features of the new brand.[9] However, it should be noted that the procedures of Market Structure Studies do not enable a manufacturer to locate his optimal product response. These procedures do not measure market response for each possible combination of product qualities, and thus, cannot predict how such responses will be distributed (in terms of market share) for all possible new product additions to the previous structure. It is entirely possible that gaps in an existing product-market will be present because there is but minimal preference for products that would fill those gaps. For such products, Stefflre's procedures may discover this absence of demand only during the second phase following completion of the Market Structure Study.

Stefflre claims that his procedures are *generalizable* to poorly defined product-markets.[10] The argument for this generality rests upon several assumptions. First, it is his contention that one can infer people's product purchase behavior from their preferences for product *descriptions*. Related to this assertion is a second—that one can construct a physical "product" (in the broadest use of this word) which will match the description. The hoped for end result is that people will *behave toward this product* in a manner consistent with their *preferences for the description*. If one can deal with people's reactions to descriptions and determine their semantic content, then the procedures become generalizable to ill-defined markets, rather than situations where one is talking principally of minor variations in product quality in distinguishing new products. To the authors' knowledge, Stefflre has presented no researched data attesting to the validity of his assumptions in the marketing context.

Each step in a Market Structure Study is designed to provide some validation for the results of previous steps. Yet, the results from the earlier stages, which provide guidance and direction to later ones, are based upon extremely small samples from national markets. It is, therefore, possible that this aspect of the methodology will lead to results which are not found to be generalizable, because the small sample did not adequately represent the heterogeneity in the marketplace. While the predictive validity and reliability of market structure studies have yet to be published, Stefflre has made a substantial contribution to the methodology of new product search and screening. Market structure studies can be viewed as an implementation of the "marketing concept" in that the ideas for new products originate in the preferences and perceptions of potential customers. The promise of such market-based search lies in the greater efficiency with which the entire product development process can be conducted.

Freimer-Simon's Approach

The Freimer-Simon approach deals with the deficiencies identified earlier in discussing the checklist or rating scale approach to screening.[11] Unlike the two models already discussed, this approach does not possess direct implications for new product search. The Freimer-Simon approach starts by hypothesizing an n-dimensional space where n is equal to the number of factors upon which a product idea is evaluated. The summated score for each product idea is replaced by a vector producted by the scores on the individual factors. In this dimensional space are located two density functions, one representing scores (vectors) of successful products, the other of unsuccessful products. Linear discriminant analysis is then used to obtain the likelihood ratio of success to failure for a product idea, or point, in this space. Next, Bayesian analysis is utilized to obtain a measure of the risk of accepting the decision suggested by the analysis so far performed. It is also used to help decide whether additional information, which would aid in screening the product (i.e., defining the location of the point), should be sought with a final decision being reserved for a later time.

At the conceptual level, the approach offers considerable improvement over its predecessors. However, there are practical difficulties in describing the density functions representing successful and unsuccessful products. Likelihood ratios of success to failure are, of necessity, exclusively based upon information about products which were passed through the screening process and were later dropped or put to the ultimate test in the marketplace. What is needed to improve the likelihood ratio is the knowledge of products screened out which would have ultimately been successful. This deficiency, however, exists in all screening models. The only way to overcome it is to bear the cost of passing favorably upon all ideas for a specified period, and then observing what actually does happen to each idea, as compared to what the screening decision would have been if the experiment were not taking place. Another approach would be to attempt simulation of the product idea's eventual performance in the marketplace, but the problem here is that of building a valid simulator. Most companies are not willing to bear the expenses associated with either of the preceding courses. We are thus left with not very satisfactory measures of the efficiency of the screening process.[12]

A further comment might be made concerning the character of the information which might be sought to reduce the risk in the decision being made. Considerable improvement would result from being able to learn more about the two probability distributions of successful and unsuccessful products when a particular product idea is the current focus of activity. All too often, however, any additional information sought is relevant only to reducing uncertainty via improved information estimates of data already introduced into the decision. But it might sometimes be appropriate to obtain different kinds of information than are usually considered in the screening process. An example of this kind of information might be market acceptance data. Attempts to measure market acceptance with substantial accuracy are typically not made until much later in the product development process. Measures of consumer tastes and preferences to guide formulation of specific product ideas, and the assessment of their profitabilities, are rarely available. Thus, the earlier availability of data not normally available until later would do much to improve the efficiency of the screening model. One possible way to obtain such data is through pilot studies (reduced versions of the data collection procedures which might be utilized later). In providing preliminary data and testing research instruments, such studies would help expedite the entire product development process. Again, this deficiency is not unique to this screening model.

THE POTENTIAL FOR IMPROVING SEARCH AND SCREENING

In the course of our brief review of significant approaches to improved search and screening, we already have had occasion to mention contributions from relatively recent developments in statistical methodology. The Stefflre approach makes use of techniques of non-metric multi-dimensional scaling; the Freimer-Simon approach employs multiple discriminant analysis and statistical decision theory. It is our contention that multivariate statistical techniques hold considerable promise for effecting improvements to the search and screening process.

It should be apparent from the earlier discussion of Market Structure Studies that one, and possibly the major, contribution multivariate statistical techniques can make to search and screening is to give effect to conceptualizations of consumers in terms of their product-market characteristics and to product-markets in terms of their consumer characteristics. Search and screening thus becomes directly associated with the whole body of research aimed at understanding consumer behavior (*e.g.*, research concerned with such topics as the diffusion and adoption of innovations, market segmentation, brand loyalty, the dimensions of product quality, and market response surfaces). The multivariate nature of these techniques allows a more complex structuring and representation of the variables that affect and are manifested by consumer behavior. The statistical nature of these techniques permits measurement of the separate effects of individual variables and of their *interactions* and provides the facility for controlling chance phenomena. Further, since many of the relevant measurement inputs to behavioral processes are ordinal in nature, the capability of these techniques in handling non-metric data does much to enhance their usefulness. The improved ability these techniques provide for managing complexity can only lead to our improved understanding of consumer decision processes.

In this section we will discuss, briefly, various of the currently available multivariate statistical techniques in order to differentiate them, but our major purpose will be in suggesting their applicability to search and screening. Clearly, our discussion will not be adequate to distinguish all their features or to discuss their limitations. We have referenced additional material to achieve these purposes.[13]

Non-metric multi-dimensional scaling can be accomplished in a variety of ways.[14] Such techniques primarily use rank ordered data as inputs (preference or similarity data tend to be of this type, where A is more preferred to B than to C or is judged more similar to B than C.) One technique (the Kruskal-Shepard method) starts with an arbitrary scattering of points (objects of interest) across a specified dimensional space. The computer program shifts the points until the pairs that were declared most alike are close together in the space and those less alike are farther apart. The program terminates iteration when further shifting of points cannot affect further improvement. One criterion for evaluating an array of points is to calculate the correlation between the rank order of inter-point distances and the rank order of pairs of objects in the original data. By changing the specified dimensionality of the space, it is often possible to further improve the fit. Deciding the dimensionality of the space and giving meaning to these dimensions is a *subjective* undertaking apart from the multi-dimensional scaling techniques themselves.

As we have already noted, the ability of multi-dimensional scaling to handle non-metric data inputs is very useful. Moreover, calculated inter-point distances can be used as a metric surrogate for the non-metric inputs, and thus, the output from multi-dimensional scaling can serve as the input to other multivariate statistical techniques which require metric data. Multi-dimensional scaling permits a more complex representation of consumer preferences than was previously possible. Preferences for products and brands can be seen in hierarchical form, which intuition argues is a more logical way of representation than focusing upon a single most preferred (or most frequently purchased) brand. The ability to discern this structure and the dimensions which comprise it will allow a more realistic model of consumer decision-making and consequently better understanding and prediction of differential responses to the offerings of the firm.

Factor analysis[15] is a set of procedures developed for the purpose of analyzing the intercorrelations within a set of variables. Most factor-analytic applications have used metric input data but such methods exist for non-metric inputs. Intercorrelations become the measures of proximity between variables. Using these intercorrelations it is possible to summarize the relevant information contained in a large set of variables into a smaller, more manageable set. Factor analysis is the technique most often used when the task is to find the minimum number of independent dimensions needed to account for most of the variance in the original set of variables.

For new product search and screening, a principal application of factor analysis would be in trying to identify the critical and meaningful dimensions of a multivariate domain. This might involve identification of a number of factors for a set of socio-demographic characteristics, measured personality traits, advertising exposure scores, and the like. The interpretation of such factors could give insight into the underlying reasons for peoples':

1. Willingness to try a new product
2. Perceived needs for a new product or service
3. Actual purchase behavior
4. Attitudes toward hypothetical new product concepts

In the development of improved screening devices, factor analysis might be used to identify more complex variables (*i.e,* the factors) from the many that comprise screening checklist. As a consequence of the manner in which they are obtained, these factors would have the advantage of being independent (see the rationale for the Freimer-Simon approach). Moreover, factor analysis should prove useful in identifying which of the variables comprising the checklist contribute importantly to the underlying factors associated with successful products.

The object of *multiple discriminant analysis*[16] is to produce a linear function that will help in distinguishing members of mutually exclusive sets. In the Freimer-Simon model, the technique is used to identify the weights to be attached to each screening variable in order to distinguish between successful and unsuccessful products. In this sense, multiple discriminant analysis is used to affect only a two-way classification (however, n-way

classifications are possible). It should be noted that when the sets determined by the criterion variable are not mutually exclusive, the potential
discriminating power of the criterion function is greatly reduced. Thus, in
estimating weights for a linear discriminant function to distinguish successful from unsuccessful products, the fact that product success is in reality a
continuum, rather than a dichotomy, will affect the predictive value of the
functions.

The linear discriminant function for a two-way classification can be
expressed as:

$$F = w_1 x_1 + w_2 w_2 \ldots + w_n w_n$$

where F = the value of the discriminant function. If individual i has a value
above F, he is classified as as member of group 1; if below F he is classified
as a member of group 2.

w_j = the discriminant coefficients or weights.

$(j = 1,2, \ldots ,n)$.

x_j = the independent variables used.

$(j = 1,2, \ldots ,n)$.

The weights are assigned to the variables such that the ratio of the
difference between the means of two groups to the standard deviation
within the groups is maximized. This is analagous to the one-way classification in analysis of variance. One can also determine the relative importance of the independent variables $(x_1, x_2, \ldots , x_n)$ by measuring the
contribution of each variable to the difference in F statistics between the
two groups. Thus, in the context of product screening it is possible to
determine which of the screening criteria are most useful and to measure
their relative importance in discriminating between successful and unsuccessful products. Clearly, the success-failure dimension is not the only one
relevant to search and screening. It may be possible to relate various
product-market characteristics (such as variety of product sizes, package
functions, intensity of distribution, relative price, number of competitive
brands, and produce appearance or taste), socio-economic and psychological dimensions of consumers, and the like to dependent variables such as
the intensity of use of the product (none, light, medium, heavy) or to
measures of brand loyalty.

In applying discriminant analysis it was known in advance into which
groupings the dependent variable was to be partitioned. *Cluster analysis*[17] is
the name for a set of numerical procedures for classifying objects. These
procedures may be termed preclassification techniques since their purpose
is to aid the description of *natural groupings* that occur in large masses of
data. From these natural groupings (or clusters) the research must later
develop the conceptual framework for classification. Factor analysis, and
multi-dimensional scaling, discussed earlier, can be used for these same
general purposes. The researcher must specify the characteristics on which
each of a set of objects (people, products, advertisements, etc.) are meas-

ured. The researcher has no external criterion for grouping the objects into similar subsets; instead he is looking for natural groupings in terms of the characteristics upon which the objects are measured.

Three general categories of proximity measures can be used to identify clusters. These are Euclidean distance measures (such as were earlier described in discussing multi-dimensional scaling), correlation measures (which are those normally used in factor analysis), and similarity measures based upon the matching of attributes. The nature of the input data— nominal, ordinal, interval, or ratio scaled—usually determines which pairwise proximity measure can be utilized in expressing the relationships among objects.

There are a number of clustering routines. The type of proximity measurement used and the purpose of the cluster analysis will often guide the selection of a routine. Illustrative of these are node building and hierarchical grouping routines. Node building might start by selecting an object closest to the centroid of all the data to serve as a prime node around which other points are clustered until some threshhold distance level is reached. An unclustered object farthest from the centroid of the first cluster may then be chosen as a new prime node. The process is continued, the third and subsequent prime nodes being selected on the basis of largest average distance from the centroids of clusters already formed. Hierarchical grouping routines may start either (a) by splitting the data into two groups (using procedures involving the least squares criterion) and then repeating the procedure sequentially to split each group in half again until individual objects are reached or (b) by starting with clusters of one object and building new clusters hierarchically until one overall cluster results (or until some criterion of proximity or within cluster variance is exceeded).

Cluster analysis, like the first two techniques already discussed, can be used to identify the dimensions of a space or the features associated with various product groupings. As the potential applications for these techniques are similar to those earlier discussed for multi-dimensional scaling and for factor analysis, no further discussion will be attempted here.

By no means have we exhausted either the types of multivariate techniques or their applications. Many of the authors previously referenced have reported either applications of these techniques or conjecture about them in many areas in marketing. Such techniques offer great promise if administered by competent hands. Statistical methods afford only mechanical means for analyzing data. The meanings of interpretations arising from such analyses are provided by the research-analyst. The techniques are useful for their ability to reduce complexity and they may be invaluable for providing insight, but confidence in one's interpretations can only come about after the hypotheses developed from previous work are objectively tested in independent settings.

CONCLUDING REMARKS

With this article we have reviewed and evaluated several models which have recently been proposed to aid the new product search and screening process. These models have in significant measure served more to improve the conceptual bases for carrying out search and screening activities than to offer immediately implementable solutions. The Stefflre Market Structure Studies approach, while implementable, appears to suffer from incompleteness and questioned validity. We have conjectured that further research contributions to search and screening will probably involve the use of multivariate statistical techniques, and we have suggested a few of the possible applications for these techniques. Search and screening can only benefit from closer ties with ongoing research in such areas as diffusion and adoption of innovations, market segmentation, brand loyalty and switching, and measurement of market response surfaces which also make use of these same statistical techniques.

We hope to see search and screening more adequately tied to the changing nature of the marketplace. The emerging field of endeavor known as technological forecasting promises to aid product development. Forecasts of new technology may indicate the emergence of different product-markets or indicate the possibility of effecting a closer matching of products with changing consumer preferences for product characteristics. Such forecasting procedures may aid in predicting changes in consumer preferences for existing products as a consequence of new technology affecting seemingly unrelated product-markets. The integration of search and screening with technological forecasting may even lead to facilitation of the latter process. The identification of new product opportunities which cannot be accommodated by existing technology may lead to research aimed at creating the necessary technological breakthroughs.

We desire this article to provide impetus to research aimed at improved decision-making in product development. But we would caution those prepared to travel this road. The improvements to search and screening which we have noted here have all involved greater use of analytic methods that the procedures they replaced. Many of the relevant measurement inputs will continue to be ordinal in nature. Moreover, subjectivity will not be eliminated in decisions affecting product development, only reduced in its effect by increased use of analysis. Uncertainty will always be present to make any approaches to search and screening fallible. But the importance of successful new products to the growth of a business enterprise will continue to encourage efforts to achieve a better management of such risks.

NOTES

1. For examples see A. Charnes, W. W. Cooper, J. K. DeVoe, and D. B. Learner, "DEMON: Decision Mapping Via Optimum GO-NO Networks - A Model for Marketing New Products," *Management Science* (July, 1966), pp. 865-887. W. F. Massy, "Stochastic

Models for Monitoring New Product Introductions," and P. Kotler, "Computer Simulation in the Analysis of New Product Decisions," both in F. Bass, C. King, and E. Pessemier, eds. *Applications of the Sciences in Marketing,* New York: John Wiley (1968), pp. 85-111, 283-331; G. L. Urban, "Sprinter: A Tool for New Product Decision Makers," *Industrial Management Review* (Spring 1967), pp. 43-55.

2. There are a few which exist. Such models tend to be highly descriptive and hence are not evaluative. Within marketing, see G. E. Larsen, "Locating Ideas for New Products" in T. L. Berg and A. Schuchman, *Product Strategy and Management,* New York: Holt, Rinehart and Winston (1963), pp. 420-430 and D. B. Montgomery and G. L. Urban, *Management Science in Marketing,* Englewood Cliffs, N. J.: Prentice-Hall (1969), pp. 296-298. Within organization theory a few models of organizational problem-solving have implication for search. See R. M. Cyert and J. G. March, *A Behavioral Theory of the Firm,* Englewood Cliffs, N. J.: Prentice-Hall (1963), pp. 120-122 and F. J. Aguilar, *Scanning the Business Environment,* New York: Free Press (1967). The closest to an evaluative model is J. B. MacQueen, "Optimal Policies for a Class of Search and Evaluation Problems," *Management Science* (July 1964), pp. 746-759.

3. J. T. O'Meara, Jr., "Selecting Profitable Products, *Harvard Business Review* (January-February 1961), pp. 83-99; W. Alderson and P. Green, *Planning and Problem Solving in Marketing,* Homewood, Ill.: Richard D. Irwin, Inc. (1964), pp. 204-207; or H. Terry, "Comparative Evaluation of Performance Using Multiple Criteria," *Management Science* (April 1963), pp. 431-442; E. A. Pessemier, *New Product Decisions: An Analytical Approach,* New York: McGraw-Hill Book Co., (1966); C. H. Kline, "The Strategy of Product Policy," *Harvard Business Review* (July-August 1955), pp. 91-100; B. M. Richman, "A Rating Scale for Product Innovation," *Business Horizons* (Summer 1962), 37-44.

4. See Alderson and Green, *loc. cit.* and M. Freimer and L. S. Simon, "The Evaluation of New Product Alternatives," *Management Science* (February 1967), pp. 279-292.

5. See M. Freimer and L. S. Simon, "Screening New Product Ideas," *Marketing and the New Sciences of Planning,* American Marketing Association Proceedings of the Fall Conference (1968), pp. 99-104.

6. E. A. Pessemier, *op. cit.,* pp. 39-71.

7. The comments in this paragraph are developed from those of D. B. Montgomery and G. L. Urban, *op. cit.,* p. 303.

8. V. Stefflre, "Market Structure Studies: New Products for Old Markets and New Markets (Foreign) for Old Products" in Bass, King, and Pessemier, *op. cit.,* pp. 251-268.

9. For an interesting case description applying Stefflre's techniques (in which this problem presents itself), see "Maxwell House Division" in M. P. Brown, R. N. Cardozo, S. M. Cunningham, W. J. Salmon, and R. G. M. Sultan, *Problems in Marketing,* New York: McGraw-Hill (1968), pp. 439-466.

10. Stefflre, *op. cit.,* pp. 252, 257-8, 265-6.

11. M. Freimer and L. S. Simon, "The Evaluation of New Product Alternatives," *op. cit.*

12. Efficiency of search and screening activities is extremely difficult to measure because of the difficulty of separating out the net contribution of these activities in the total product development process. Examining the profitability of successfully commercialized new products is not useful since the product's success may be due, for example, to the design engineers having found a way to halve the cost of producing the item. Totaling the number of products which reached commercialization and failed has the same faults. Even though objectives of search and screening activities are readily defined, *i.e.,* to identify those product ideas which will be successful if commercialized and screen out those which will not, this does not help in providing a criterion for evaluating the effectiveness of the activity. One could think in terms of minimizing the errors of making wrong decisions or alternatively maximizing the profits of those products passed to commercialization, but problems of measurement limit the value of such an approach. Thus, the essence of the problem of evaluating the efficiency of the search and screening activities lies in two, possibly insurmountable, issues: (1) determination of the "real" worth of ideas eliminated from further consideration even prior to the formal search activity, and (2) evaluation of the net contribution of search and screening activities when a product is successfully commercialized. Given this substantial difficulty of measuring overall effectiveness, it is readily apparent why much attention should be paid to evaluating on whatever other bases are feasible, the worth of the models and technology utilized within the search and screening phases themselves.

13. A number of general references to multi-variate statistical techniques should be useful. See P. E. Green and D. S. Tull, *Research for Marketing Decisions,* Englewood Cliffs, N. J.: Prentice-Hall (1966), pp. 336-364. W. W. Cooley and P. R. Lohnes, *Multi-variate Procedures*

for the Behavioral Sciences, New York: John Wiley (1962): and T. W. Anderson, *Introduction to Multi-variate Statistical Analysis,* New York: John Wiley (1958).

14. For a comprehensive review of available methods see P. E. Green, F. J. Carmone, and P. J. Robinson, *Analysis of Marketing Behavior Using Non-metric Scaling and Related Techniques,* Technical Monographs, Cambridge, Mass.: Marketing Science Institute (1968); and P. E. Green, F. J. Carmone, and P. J. Robinson, "Non-metric Scaling in Marketing Analysis: An Exposition and Overview," *Wharton Quarterly* (Winter-Spring 1968), pp. 27-41. Discussion of an application of one such approach is provided by D. H. Doehlert, "Similarity and Preference Mapping: A Color Example" in *Marketing and the New Sciences of Planning,* American Marketing Association Proceedings of the Fall Conference (1968), pp. 250-258.

15. In addition to mention in the general references cited in footnote 13, factor analysis is extensively discussed in H. H. Harman, *Modern Factor Analysis;* Chicago: University of Chicago Press (1967), second edition. See also W. F. Massy, "Applying Factor Analysis to a Specific Marketing Problem," in R. Frank, A. A. Kuehn, and W. F. Massy, *Quantitative Techniques in Marketing Analysis,* Homewood, Ill.: Richard D. Irwin (1962), pp. 100-104.

16. For an exposition, see W. F. Massy, "Discriminant Analysis of Audience Characteristics," *Journal of Advertising Research* (March 1965), pp. 39-48. W. R. King, "Early Prediction of New Product Success," *Journal of Advertising Research* (June 1966), pp. 8-13; and T. S. Robertson and J. N. Kennedy, "Prediction of Consumer Innovations: Application of Multiple Discriminant Analysis," *Journal of Marketing Research* (February 1968), pp. 64-69.

17. An excellent introduction to clustering techniques is provided by R. E. Frank and P. E. Green, "Numerical Taxonomy in Marketing Analysis," *Journal of Marketing Research* (February 1968), pp. 83-94. The authors include an extensive bibliography.

ADDITIONAL SELECTED BIBLIOGRAPHY

Exploration and Screening

Baty, E. B., "Generating a Flow of New Product Ideas," *Machine Design,* Vol. 35 (July 4, 1963), 76-79.

Benge, E. J., "That New Product Idea," *Sales Management,* Vol. 88, No. 7 (April 6, 1962), 95-96.

Eldridge, R. G., "How to Fish for New Product Ideas and When to Throw Them Back," *New Products: Concepts, Development, and Strategy,* R. R. Scrase, ed., Michigan Business Papers, No. 43, Bureau of Business Research, The University of Michigan (1966), 1-10.

Ellington, C. E., "Sources of New Product Ideas," *New Products/New Profits,* Elizabeth Marting, editor, American Management Association (1964), 61-75.

Freimer, M. and Simon, L. S., "The Evaluation of Potential New Product Alternatives," *Management Science B,* Vol. 13 (February, 1967), 279-292.

————"Screening New Product Ideas," *Marketing and the New Science of Planning,* Robert L. King, ed., AMA Fall Conference Proceedings, Series No. 28, American Marketing Association (August, 1968), 99-104.

Harris, J. S., "The New Product Profile Chart: Selecting and Appraising New Projects," *Chemical and Engineering News,* Vol. 39, No. 16 (April 17, 1961), 110-118.

"How to Generate Ideas for New Products," *Business Management,* Vol. 33, No. 1 (October, 1967), 83-91.

Lanitis, T., "How to Generate New Product Ideas," *Journal of Advertising Research,* Vol. 10, No. 3 (June, 1970), 31-35.

O'Meara, J. T. Jr., "Selecting Profitable Products," *Harvard Business Review,* Vol. 39, No. 1 (January-February, 1961, 83-89.

QUESTIONS FOR DISCUSSION AND REVIEW

1. Where can a firm look for new product ideas?

2. Can you suggest some techniques used by firms to generate new product ideas internally?

3. Why is it important to explore many new product ideas?

4. Who should be responsible for the search program? Why?

5. What are the responsibilities of a search committee?

6. Why is screening of new product ideas necessary?

7. What are several methods used to screen new product ideas?

8. What guidelines should be set up to screen these ideas?

9. Do you feel that company objectives are of prime importance in ascertaining a screening device? Why?

10. Is it possible to forgo this step and continue to develop new products? Why?

11. Under what ideal conditions can a firm accept all new product ideas?

BUSINESS ANALYSIS

The new product ideas that have been screened and have received tentative approval will be evaluated quantitatively. Further study will determine whether or not plans will be drawn up to produce an iconic or analogue model. The company can use cost-benefit analysis by determining and projecting demand for the possible new product and ascertaining all costs and pricing of the product. By this means the new product can be compared with a risk spectrum for further judgment. Should the judgment be positive, the product idea will be passed on to the development stage. Should the product be judged too risky an investment because of the possible lack of sufficient demand, or because of excessive start-up costs, the need to borrow capital funds externally, or because close substitute products are being sold in the market place at a lesser price than the new product ideas can be sold at profitably, the new product ideas may be shelved. In estimating costs, companies have used break-even analysis, Bayesian analysis, and simulation in their methodology. Where there is need to ascertain cash flows, capital requirements, and the interest paid for new capital for developing new product ideas, net present value formulas or methods such as return on capital investment and payback analysis can be used. Also theoretical models help one determine profit optimality. The following articles underlie the nature and methods of determining whether the firm should proceed to the development stage. Is the new product idea a worthwhile risk for investing development dollars? The methods used today eliminate uneducated guesses to a large extent.

A RATING SCALE FOR
PRODUCT INNOVATION
BY BARRY M. RICHMAN

In an increasingly dynamic environment resulting in more rapid innovation and product obsolescence, a more precise method must be found to improve the chances of success in the introduction of new products. Poor product planning has resulted in poor product decisions. This situation can be corrected by the application of more scientific tools and techniques in the screening and selection process. This article considers such tools and techniques.

What determines the success of a new product in terms of over-all profitability to the company? Most executives would probably agree that the success a new product enjoys is directly related to the nature and extent of the competitive advantage in a market that has a demand for this class of product. It is the result of price and product differentiation with respect to specific attributes, characteristics, and features—tangible or intangible—that gives one product a greater degree of acceptance within a certain segment of the market. The degree of profitability, therefore, could be said to result from two major factors: (1) the nature and extent of competitive advantage; and (2) the size of the market segment where the advantage is appreciated and transferred into consumer preference and hence profitable sales.

In selecting new products, many companies have a tendency to estimate success and profitability in some ad hoc manner without systematically

EDITOR'S NOTE: From *Business Horizons,* Summer 1962, pp. 37-44. Reprinted by permission of the publisher and the author.

analyzing competitive advantage as it relates to consumer acceptance. A profit target is established without carefully considering whether it is realistic in terms of the company's talents, resources, and capabilities, or whether this product possesses the characteristics necessary to achieve this profit goal.

Considering the extremely high failure rate[1]—as compared with the successful development, commercialization, and marketing of new products by most companies—it appears that there is much room for improvement in the selection and screening procedures now in use. The approach presented here entails the quantification of qualitative considerations in a systematic and structured manner. In this way decisions will be more meaningful since the crucial factors to be analyzed will be ranked and assigned weights and values. This will by no means supplant management judgment or completely eliminate the environment of uncertainty; however, it will offer a more scientific approach to the decision-making process. A case example will be used to illustrate the practical utilization of the tools and techniques.

The term "new product" will refer to an innovation or to a product addition already marketed by other companies. It should be noted that the screening process to be presented can also serve as a useful tool in evaluating company acquisitions and mergers.

SCREENING AND SELECTION

In order to arrive at a proper decision concerning new product additions, a company may best approach the problem by deducing specific integral elements from broad general factors until a meaningful profit estimate can be made. The initial factors that should be considered are:

1. Total potential market for this class of product and the related determinants of demand (It is assumed that the company has the proper tools and techniques for such forecasting.)
2. Company talents, skills, capabilities, and resources
3. Competitive environment and the company's position in the industry.

Before the company can arrive at any meaningful estimate of profitability, it should, by use of the second and third factors, define and deduce the optimum competitive advantage the new product may enjoy. This is so because the nature and extent of competitive advantage depend on all of the company resources in relation to the competitive environment and the company's position in the industry. The nature and extent of the competitive advantage, in turn, define the size of the market segment within the total potential market. Only when competitive advantage and size of the

---

1. For current figures see *Management of New Products* (New York: Booz, Allen, and Hamilton, 1960), p. 14.

related market segment are determined can a realistic profit estimate be made.

Tools and Techniques

An effective tool and certain techniques are required to determine (1) whether the company is in a position to endow the new product with the necessary features that would result in profits, and (2) what type of advantage the company can more readily provide. The selection of product ideas and new products should be limited to those that can be translated into the necessary competitive advantage, which in turn can be transferred into a minimum desired level of over-all company profits. It is felt that new product proposals may best be screened and evaluated by use of an evaluation matrix (to be discussed later), which reflects product fit and compatibility with the company.

Initial Screening

The screening process begins with the inception of the product idea, which may originate from both internal and external sources. The company may wish to consider the idea in terms of any special reasons it may have at that time for adding new products. At different times in the life of a company some product ideas may be of greater significance than others. For example, the company may be more interested in replacing obsolete products than in expanding its line, or it may be interested in adding a new product that will balance the seasonal nature of its operations. Whatever the case, it will be assumed that management wants to pursue the product idea for purposes of development and commercialization. If there are clearly some insurmountable obstacles and limitations, such as lack of funds or legal considerations, the product proposal will be eliminated at an early stage. The study will relate only to new products where no such obstacles are apparent.

In some cases the company will adopt a new product regardless of its fit with respect to the company as a whole, for reasons of opportunism and large profits in the short run. The products to be considered here, however, will be only those that have long-run implications for the company inasmuch as they would become a permanent part of the organization, at least for the foreseeable future.

EVALUATION MATRIX

The evaluation matrix has two major functions and involves a two-part analysis. First, it is concerned with ranking and weighting the various spheres of company performance in relation to the over-all future success of the company. This will serve as a guideline in determining the nature of the competitive advantage the new product may offer. Second, it indicates the degree of product compatibility in relation to these spheres of performance by the assignment of values, thus reflecting the over-all product fit with the company as a whole. The over-all result derived by the application of this tool is reflected in one quantitative figure. An estimate of profitability is not provided for in this matrix. Such an estimate, however, would evolve directly from the findings and conclusions resulting from the application of this tool.

The following hypothetical example will illustrate the practical application of the evaluation matrix.

Case Study: The Matrix in Action

A large manufacturer of a wide line of photographic equipment, cameras, projectors, and other related supplies is considering the addition of a transistor radio to its product line. The company has undertaken a preliminary study of the total market potential for this class of product, and at present the management believes that the idea should be pursued and translated into a product with specific characteristics. The company must decide whether an expenditure is warranted for the development and eventual commercialization of a line of transistor radios.

By concentrating its efforts on certain determinants of demand relating to consumer preference, the company may be able to obtain an adequate share of the market through demand manipulation, and perhaps even alter the conditions of the market. This would, of course, be within the limits set by various uncontrollable factors such as population and level of incomes. This focus on specific determinants of demand would result in a differentiated product that would offer certain advantages over competing products in a particular segment of the market. An analysis of the nature of major strength of the company is required for this purpose.

Spheres of Performance

The success and survival of this or any other company depend on the magnitude and extent of the over-all competitive advantage enjoyed. The competitive advantage is derived from the extent and nature of the company's resources and the utilization of these resources along with talents and skills present in the company. The totality of this competitive advantage depends on the performances and contributions in different spheres of operation. These spheres, although not completely independent and mutually exclusive, can be subdivided for the sake of analysis. Each one has varying degrees of significance in terms of over-all company success. In ranking and assigning weights to the individual spheres, the company must consider all its resources with respect to the particular sphere of activity and in relation to the competitive environment.

The greater the competitive advantage the company has in a specific sphere, the greater would be the assigned weight, since it would be more significant in relation to over-all company success. In most cases the weights assigned would reflect the historical development of the company in terms of talent, know-how, and resources. It is the future relationship that is important, however, and a planned major change of emphasis in terms of the significance of some spheres should be reflected in the assigned weights. The total of the assigned weights should always equal 1.0, which is a reflection of the over-all company performance and success. This ranking and assignment of weights should also reflect the company's relations with various interest groups such as distributors, suppliers, creditors, and unions. This in turn indicates the ability to achieve a maximization of contributions to the company at minimum cost.

Assignment of Weights

In this company there are six operational or functional spheres in which success and performance are determined by the extent and nature of company capabilities and resources, and the effectiveness of company policies with respect to the utilization of these resources. In addition, there are two nonoperational spheres that must be considered since they play a role in determining over-all company success. Most companies would probably lend themselves to a somewhat similar breakdown. The spheres and their weights in this particular company follow:

Marketing (.20) This industry is highly marketing oriented, and the company feels that its capabilities and talents in this sphere are above average in relation to competition. This appears to be a major area in relation to over-all company success, and the company plans to capitalize further on its flair for promotion, strong brand name, and broad quality product line. Worldwide distribution and servicing of the products are probably major strong points. The company provides guarantees for its products and, although few of the retail outlets are owned by the company, good relations and servicing are expected to prevail in the future.

Research and Development (including design, styling, engineering, and market testing) (.20) Along with marketing, this operational sphere is expected to be the most integral with respect to future success. The company is a leader in the industry in terms of design, styling, and ability to develop durable products with special features that permit precision and ease of handling. In several cases the company obtained patents for products and plans to do the same in the future.

Personnel (.15) The company expects to maintain a slight advantage with respect to managerial talent as a result of its recruiting selection, training, and compensation policy. It is expected that high morale will continue among employees, provided that the organizational structure is not disrupted too quickly or too extensively. The company expects good union relations to continue, but no competitive advantage is anticipated in this respect.

Finance (.10) The majority of the firms in this industry are financially strong, as is this company. No distinct competitive advantage is expected to be derived from this area.

Production (.05) While this company has modern methods and processes of production enabling the output of durable and high quality goods, no distinct competitive advantage is anticipated in terms of cost or know-how.

Purchasing and Supply (.05) The company does not anticipate any special advantage with respect to cost or the attainability of special materials.

Location and Facilities (.05) Although this is a nonoperational sphere, it should be considered since it contributes in varying degrees to the over-all success and performance of a company, but especially so if the company has a preferred location in terms of cost or special access to supplies and markets.

The location of this company offers no distinct advantage, and its facilities are not expected to result in any competitive advantage in the future.

Company Personality and Goodwill (.20) This nonoperational sphere can be treated independently even though it has evolved as a result of the performances in other spheres. It would be more significant in an industry dealing in highly differentiated products than in an industry dealing in products with a high degree of standardization. This sphere relates to the character, traditions, customs, and personality of the company, as well as its reputation and clarity of identification in the minds of its employees and consumers. This in essence reflects loyalty and consumer preference.

This particular company feels that its future success and performance depend greatly on its character, image, and personality. It has developed pride among its employees and a reputation for dependable, durable, and high quality products. The company has won consumer confidence by standing behind its products with guarantees and warranties.

A management team should be responsible for ranking and assigning weights, and the field of operations research presents some approaches that can be utilized. The most applicable one appears to be the Standard Gamble Technique for measuring utilities.[2] This technique could be extended and applied to determine the quantitative weights of each sphere based on subjective appraisals.

2. See, for example, David W. Miller and Martin K. Starr, *Executive Decisions and Operations Research* (Englewood Cliffs, N.J.: Prentice-Hall, Inc., 1960), pp. 69-72. The use of this technique may be facilitated by regrouping the above spheres into broader spheres and then subdividing this grouping and repeating the process.

Product Attributes

In translating the product idea into an actual product that offers optimum competitive advantage, the company must consider its areas of major strength. It is best to select products that do not divert company attention from the structure of its over-all success pattern. Since this company is highly marketing oriented and has a flair for sales promotion, the company need not offer an advantage in terms of price. In order to capitalize fully on its reputation and personality, the company feels that the transistor radio, if adopted, should derive its advantage through innovative style and design, high quality in terms of durability and tone, and a guarantee at least as good as those offered by competitors.

It is felt that a very compact, durable, high quality transistor that would also give a good, clear tone in an automobile would appeal to travelers, especially those who travel abroad and rent or buy foreign cars, which are seldom equipped with radios. Many of these travelers would be the consumers of existing company products. Such a radio could probably command a higher price than competing products but a price somewhat lower than car radios.

It is necessary to consider whether a transistor radio with the above attributes and features can be effectively developed and marketed by the company, in light of all its resources. In addition, it must be determined whether the new product ties in with future company operations. The better the fit, the greater the probability of achieving the desired competitive advantage without hindering the over-all success of the company. If it is ascertained that the product has a good fit and can derive the desired competitive advantage, a meaningful estimate with respect to the scope and extent of consumer preference, and hence profitability, can be made.

It should be noted that in many instances the new product being screened may already be a developed product rather than merely an idea. In this case, many of the attributes of the product must be taken as given. The company could then influence the extent of competitive advantage only through price or its promotional policy. The degree of product fit and compatibility with the company should still be determined in order to decide whether the new product ties in with the future over-all success and performance of the company and whether the company is capable of successfully undertaking its commercialization. If there is a poor fit, the likelihood of deriving an increase in over-all company long-range profits would be highly questionable.

Assignment of Values

The new product proposal reflecting the desired attributes and characteristics should be analyzed in terms of compatibility with each separate sphere, and with the company as a whole. This is best accomplished by assigning values that reflect the product fit in each sphere. In each case a value between 0.0 and 1.0 is assigned depending on the degree of product fit with respect to the policies, resources, and other features of the sphere under consideration. Near-perfect fits call for values approaching 1.0, and very poor fits have values approaching 0.0. The assigned values in each case are multiplied by the assigned weights, and all the new results are added, thus reflecting over-all product fit in one quantitative figure.

Marketing (.9) The company believes that the proposed product fits in well with anticipated marketing policies and activities. The same channels of distribution, outlets, and sales promotion policies can be utilized. The company expects it to appeal to many of the same customers as the old products do. The company has the ability to effectively promote the significant product attributes and features. In addition, the radio will not upset the pricing policies of the company or replace any part of its product line. The brand name of the company does not tie in perfectly with the new product, but it is felt that there is some degree of compatibility in this respect.

Research and Development (.7) The company feels capable of developing, designing, and testing a transistor radio that would possess the tangible attributes necessary to obtain the desired competitive advantage. Although the company is confident that it can obtain the required basic skills, the services of some outside experts will be necessary. This will also call for some new research and development activities, but they are not expected to disrupt or hinder the other necessary activities and policies of this sphere. It is unlikely that a patent can be acquired for this product.

Personnel (.6) The necessary labor and executive resources can be obtained, although some additional training will be required. There will be some organizational disruption, but this is not expected to be of a very significant or serious nature. There is no anticipated change in the area of industrial relations.

Finance (.9) The necessary funds for development, commercialization, and promotion of the new product are readily attainable at favorable terms. Furthermore, it does not appear that expenditures for other important purposes will be restricted. Only if the product is highly unsuccessful will dividend payments have to be curtailed.

Production (.8) A new production line will be required, but no difficulty is expected. The processes used for other products will not be disrupted. The company anticipates using the same extent of mechanization and specialization that it uses in the manufacturing of several other items.

Purchasing and Supply (.9) Several of the existing sources of supply can be utilized, and a few new ones will have to be obtained. Materials required for the development and production of the transistor radio are readily obtainable.

Location and Facilities (.3) The company will have to acquire new facilities in a new location, preferably near one of its existing plants, be-

Table 8-1   Evaluation Matrix—Product Fit

	(A) Relative Weight	(B) Product Compatibility Values											(C) A × B
Sphere of Performance		0	.1	.2	.3	.4	.5	.6	.7	.8	.9	1.0	
Company personality and goodwill	.20							x					.120
Marketing	.20										x		.180
Research and development	.20								x				.140
Personnel	.15							x					.090
Finance	.10										x		.090
Production	.05									x			.040
Location and facilities	.05				x								.015
Purchasing and supply	.05										x		.045
Total	1.00												.720*

*Rating Scale: 0–.40, poor; .41–.75, fair; .76–1.0, good. Present minimum acceptance rate: .70.

cause the present facilities have no excess capacity for this purpose. A special location is not required, however, and the company is confident that it can obtain a fairly desirable location.

Company Personality and Goodwill (.6) It is felt that the new product does not coincide exactly with the company image and personality. The transistor radio is not actually a related or complementary product, but the management has a reputation for being aggressive rather than conservative, and therefore the addition is not expected to endanger company reputation and loyalty in the future. Since the transistor radio is expected to derive its main advantage through promotion, quality, dependability, and design, the goodwill built up by the company will in some respects be compatible with the new product.

PRODUCT FIT

The results of the new product evaluation are presented in Table 8-1. It can be seen that the new figure obtained for the over-all product fit is .720, which places the product high up in the "fair" category in terms of compatibility with the company as a whole. (The maximum rating of 1.0 indicates a perfect fit.) The company may have differing minimum cutoff rates at different periods of time in light of economic and other conditions. In cases where consideration is being given to several new products, the company would be inclined to give priority and preference to those with the highest ratings.

The minimum cutoff rate could best be determined through experience by evaluating actual new product success in relation to product fit indicated during the screening stage. It is also possible to reflect back and consider what the product fit of currently successful products would have been in the idea and screening stage. Some type of post-completion audit could expand the usefulness and accuracy of this tool.

By selecting new products with a good over-all fit, the company can increase the probability of effective development and successful commercialization. Those products with the best fit are the ones most likely to succeed in terms of over-all profitability, since the company is capable of providing the necessary promotion, product attributes, and features in terms of competitive advantage. While the purpose of this paper is not to estimate profitability, a meaningful estimate could evolve once the company knows the nature and extent of competitive advantage desired in terms of the total potential market, and is confident of achieving this advantage. The estimation of profitability would be the last step in the screening process before a decision for adoption or rejection is reached. This would be preferable to a situation in which the company establishes a somewhat arbitrary profit target without analyzing and evaluating whether the new product will possess the attributes necessary for a great enough competitive advantage, and hence attainment of the profit goal. Nor should the company fail to consider the new product in relation to the skills, capabilities, and resources of the company, and its impact on anticipated over-all company success and performance.

With the utilization and application of the tools and techniques presented, management may be in a position to make more meaningful decisions with respect to new product additions. The approach outlined could also be useful for teaching purposes as a guide to the implications and problems that relate to the area of product planning.

In practice, it is evident that the above tools and techniques would not necessarily be utilized in a manner identical to the one presented. However, the approach could be adapted to fit many company situations relating to the screening and selection of new product ideas and new products.

MARKETING MIX DECISIONS FOR
NEW PRODUCTS
BY PHILIP KOTLER

Companies are increasingly recognizing that new products are basic to their survival and growth. According to one study "it is now commonplace for major companies to have 50% or more of current sales in products new in the past ten years." [1]

At the same time, the development of new products is a costly and risky business undertaking. Some new product ideas turn out to be technically unfeasible after good money has been spent and others turn out to be commercially unsuccessful after still more good money is gone. As many as three out of four new products introduced on the market may fail to attain commercial success.

Thus management finds itself in a dilemma: it must develop new products and yet the odds weigh heavily against their success. The answer lies in making the innovation function a more rational process through administrative reforms and improved decision-making procedures. Management is coming to recognize the desirability of centralizing responsibility for overseeing the process in new product committees and departments. Furthermore, it is recognizing the need for better theory and decision procedures at each stage of the new product development process *(search, screening, profit analysis, product development, test marketing,* and *commercialization).* At each stage, a basic decision is called for on whether to abandon the project or continue it. The purpose of this paper is to describe

EDITOR'S NOTE: From the *Journal of Marketing Research,* February 1964, pp. 43-49. Reprinted by permission of the American Marketing Association and the author.

a methodology for improved decision-making at the third stage, that of profit analysis.

THE PROFIT ANALYSIS STAGE

Suppose a new product idea has been screened and found to be compatible with the company's objectives and resources. The next task is to evaluate the profit potential of the product. In practice, this evaluation tends to be conducted in the following manner. On the basis of inspiration or previous research, management develops a particular conception of product attributes and a marketing program for the new product. Based on this specific conception of the marketing mix, management develops two different estimates. One is an estimate of the required sales volume to break even. The other is an estimate of the sales volume which is likely to be stimulated by the marketing mix. If the sales potential estimate comfortably exceeds the break-even volume estimate, the product idea is judged to be profitable, If profits promise to be large in relation to the required investment, the product idea is likely to pass to the fourth stage, that of product development.

Yet a more refined model for the analysis of new product profit potential is both desirable and practical. Instead of considering only one marketing mix and whether break-even volume is likely to be achieved under it, the more refined model provides for a simultaneous evaluation of the profit potential of several marketing mixes. The refined model can be illustrated by the following example:

The ABC Electronics Company is a small manufacturer of transitors and clock radios and is presently engaged in reviewing other electronic products for possible addition to the product line. One of these is a small portable tape recorder. Small novelty tape recorders have appeared recently on the market, and they retail at prices between $20-$50. The company's marketing research department has surveyed the market and found that interest in this type of unit is substantial and growing.

An executive committee is appointed to examine the potential profitability of this product. The production department estimates that $60,000 would have to be invested in specific new equipment and facilities and that this investment would have an estimated life of five years. The accounting department submits that the product would have to absorb $26,000 a year of general overhead to cover the value of supporting facilities, rent, taxes, executive salaries, cost of capital, etc. The marketing department advises that the product be supported initially with an advertising budget of approximately $20,000 and a personal selling budget of approximately $30,000 and furthermore that it should be priced at approximately $18 F.O.B. factory with no quantity discounts. Finally, the various operating departments estimate that the new product would involve a direct material and labor cost of $10 a unit.

In the light of these estimates, should the ABC Electronics Company develop this new product? Is the marketing mix proposed by the marketing department sound?

What Is the Break-Even Volume?

The first step in the business analysis of a new product idea is to estimate how many units would have to be sold in order to cover costs. This break-even volume is found by analyzing how total revenue and total cost vary at different sales volumes.

Total revenue at any particular sales volume is that volume times the unit price adjusted by allowances for early payment, quantity purchases, and freight. The adjustments are fairly straightforward and total revenue as a function of sales volume is generally simple to estimate.

The total cost function is more difficult to estimate. Total costs often bear a non-linear relationship to output. It is difficult enough to establish the shape of the total cost function for existing products because the statistical data are impure; the total cost function for a new product is even more difficult to estimate because the statistical data are non-existent. But as a practical matter, the break-even analyst usually assumes a linear total cost function. This assumption may be faulty for very low and very high levels of output but may be sufficiently accurate for intermediate levels, according to some recent statistical cost studies [3].

The total cost function is composed of variable and fixed cost elements. In the example, variable costs are assumed to be constant at $10 a unit. The following fixed costs are found in the example. The tape recorder requires additional fixed investment of $60,000 with an estimated life of five years. On a straight line basis, this amounts to an annual depreciation cost of $12,000. The new product is also charged $26,000 a year for its share of general overhead. This figure presumably represents a long-run estimate of the opportunity value of the corporate resources required to support this new product. In addition, the company is considering an annual expenditure of $20,000 on advertising and $30,000 on personal selling. Fixed costs therefore add up to $88,000 ($12,000 + $26,000 + $20,000 + $30,000).

The break-even volume can now be estimated. At the break-even volume (Q_B), total revenue (TR) equals total cost (TC). But total revenue is price (P) times the break-even volume and total cost is fixed cost (F) plus the product of unit variable cost (V) and break-even volume. In symbols:

$$TR = TC$$

$$P \cdot Q_B = F + V \cdot Q_B$$

Combining similar terms, and solving for Q_B, we find that

$$Q_B = \frac{F}{P - V}$$

P — V is the difference between price and unit variable cost and is called the unit contribution to fixed cost. It is $8 in the example. The company would have to sell 11,000 units ($88,000 ÷ $8) to cover fixed costs.

At this point it would be useful to express the break-even volume (Q_B) not as a constant but rather as a function of elements in the marketing mix. The break-even volume will vary with the product price and the amount of marketing effort devoted to the new product:

$$Q_B = \frac{\$12,000 + \$26,000 + A + S}{P - \$10} = \frac{\$38,000 + A + S}{P - \$10}$$

where A = advertising budget
       S = sales budget
       P = unit selling price to wholesaler

In Table 8-2, eight alternative marketing programs are listed for this product along with the implied break-even volumes. In the case of mix #5, the company could sell as few as 4,143 tape recorders to break even; while in the case of mix #4, the company would have to sell as many as 23,000. This high sensitivity of the break-even volume to the marketing mix decision is often overlooked in profit analysis.

Table 8-2   Minimum Volume Requirements as a Function of Marketing Mix

	Price	Advertising	Sales Budget	Break-even Volume Q_B
		Some Possible Marketing Mixes		
1.	$16	$10,000	$10,000	9,667
2.	16	10,000	50,000	16,333
3.	16	50,000	10,000	16,333
4.	16	50,000	50,000	23,000
5.	24	10,000	10,000	4,143
6.	24	10,000	50,000	7,000
7.	24	50,000	10,000	7,000
8.	24	50,000	50,000	9,857

The eight marketing mixes in Table 8-2 are a small sample from the very large number of mixes which could be used to market the new tape recorder. They were formed by assuming a high and low level for each of the marketing variables and elaborating all the combinations. Suppose executive opinion held that $16 is a price on the low side while $24 is a price on the high side; and that $10,000 is a low budget for advertising and personal selling respectively, and $50,000 is a high budget. This yields eight strategy combinations ($2 \cdot 2 \cdot 2 = 2^3$) and makes the marketing mix problem manageable.

Each mix is a polar case. For example, mix #1 represents the common strategy of setting a low price and spending very little for promotion. This works well when the market is highly price conscious, possesses good information about available brands, and is not easily swayed by psychological appeals. Mix #4 represents a strategy of low price and heavy promotion. The interesting thing about this mix is that it produces a high sales volume but also requires a high sales volume to break even. Mix #5 consists of a high price and low promotion and is used typically in a seller's market where the firm wants to maximize short-run profits. Mix #8 consists of a high price supported by high promotion; this stragegy is often used in a market where buyers are sensitive to psychological appeals and to quality. The other mixes (#2, 3, 6, 7) are variations on the same themes, with the additional feature that different assessments are made of the comparative effectiveness of advertising and personal selling. But it should be noted that while the division of a given budget between advertising and personal selling affects the actual sales volume, it does not affect the break-even volume.

Different marketing mixes not only imply different break-even volumes, but also differences in the sensitivity of profits to *deviations* from the break-even volume. For example, the break-even volume is approximately the same for mixes #1 and #8. Yet the high price, high promotion character of #8 promises greater losses or greater profits for deviations from the break-even volume. This is because there are higher fixed costs under mix #8 but once they are covered, additional volume is very profitable because of the high price.

Break-even analysis is necessary, but not sufficient by itself to identify the optimal marketing mix. It indicates what volumes have to be achieved but does not indicate what volumes are likely to be achieved. Missing is an account of how various elements in the marketing mix will affect the actual volume of sales.

Ideally the company requires a demand equation showing sales volume as a function of price, advertising, personal selling, and other important marketing mix elements. Such equations are difficult enough to derive for established products where there are historical data, let alone for new product ideas where there are none. Yet though the product is only an idea at this stage, there are some research procedures which can yield useful information for estimating sales. A survey could be made of the attitudes and interests of various consumers toward alternative product features and prices. It might help to develop some prototypes of the tape recorder in order to get firsthand reactions. The survey may indicate what socio-economic groups constitute major prospects for this product. The approximate number of persons in each prospect group can be estimated from census data. In addition, an analysis can be made of the relative strength of competitors in different segments of the market. Since information is expensive to collect, a Bayesian analysis of the value of specified types of additional information should be performed at each juncture [2].

Through this type of research and analysis, the executives will have a better idea of what sales volumes are likely to be achieved with different marketing mixes. For each particular mix, the executives can develop a subjective probability distribution of possible sales volumes. The mean of this probability distribution shows the expected sales volume for this marketing mix. Let the expected sales volume be denoted by Q. The fourth column in Table 8-3 shows an (hypothetical) expected sales volume for each of the eight marketing mixes. It should be noted that sales are expected to move inversely with price and directly with the amounts spent on advertising and personal selling. However, increased promotion is expected to increase sales at a diminishing rate.

What Is the Best Marketing Mix and the Implied Profit Level?

At this point, the expected volume (Q) and the break-even volume (Q_B) can be compared for each mix. The results are shown in column 6 of Table 8-3. The greatest extra volume $(Q - Q_B)$ is achieved with mix #1. But extra volume is not a sufficient indicator of the best mix. The extra volume must be multiplied by the unit value (P — V). A high price mix delivering a small extra volume may be superior to a low price mix delivering a large extra volume. Therefore $Z = (P - V) \cdot (Q - Q_B)$ has to be calculated for each marketing mix. These results are shown in column 7 of Table 8-3.

Z is a measure of the absolute profits expected from different marketing mixes. Of the mixes shown in Table 8-3, mix #5 appears to promise the largest amount of profit. This mix calls for the product to be sold at a high price with little promotional support. This strategy is often used when a company believes its product has been smartly designed and essentially sells itself. But before ABC Electronics can be sure that it has found the best marketing mix, or that the product should be produced at all, it must examine some additional issues.

1. *The profit estimates for the eight marketing mixes may not be equally reliable.* The profit estimates were derived from prior cost and sales estimates. Management may have a varying amount of confidence in these different estimates. Suppose management has much more confidence in its sales estimate for marketing mix #6 than #5. This greater confidence may arise because the executives have more experience in using strategy #6. The choice they face is between a highly uncertain profit expectation of $18,998 and a more certain profit expectation of $16,800. Most managements have a risk aversion and are willing to accept a strategy with a lower expected profit if the accompanying risk is *sufficiently* less. However the specific amount of trade-off of expected profits for risk reduction will vary among managements.

How can management's taste for risk be measured and introduced into the formal analysis? There are at least two different ways to accomplish this. One is through the preparation of an indifference map in which

Table 8-3   A Comparison of Expected Volume (Q) and Break-even Volume (Q_B) for Various Marketing Mixes

	(1)	(2)	(3)	(4)	(5)	(6) Volume above Break-even	(7) Absolute Profits
		Marketing Mix					
	P	A	S	Q	Q_B	$Q - Q_B$	$Z = (P - V)(Q - Q_B)$
1.	$16	$10,000	$10,000	12,400	9,667	2,733	$16,398
2.	16	10,000	50,000	18,500	16,333	2,167	13,002
3.	16	50,000	10,000	15,100	16,333	−1,233	−7,398
4.	16	50,000	50,000	22,600	23,000	−400	−2,400
5.	24	10,000	10,000	5,500	4,143	1,357	18,998
6.	24	10,000	50,000	8,200	7,000	1,200	16,800
7.	24	50,000	10,000	6,700	7,000	−300	−4,200
8.	24	50,000	50,000	10,000	9,857	143	2,002

management expresses its preferences between different combinations of expected profit and risk. Let us recall that in considering each marketing mix, management developed a subjective probability distribution of possible sales outcomes. Only the mean, Q, of the distribution was used. Now assume that the standard deviation of this distribution is used as a measure of risk. A low standard deviation means that management is fairly sure of the sales outcome and a high standard deviation means that management is very unsure. The standard deviation of the profit estimate can be calculated form the standard deviation of the sales estimate.[3] Let us use σ_z to denote the standard deviation of estimated profit. Let $(Z, \sigma_z)^*$ represent the expected profit and standard deviation of profit, respectively, of the marketing mix with the highest Z; in our example, this is mix #5 and assume it is ($18,998, $12,000). Then management can be asked to list other (Z, σ_z) such that it is indifferent between them and $(Z, \sigma_z)^*$. For example, management may be indifferent to ($18,998, $12,000), ($16,000, $6,800), ($13,000, $4,200), ($10,000, $2,000), and ($7,000, $0). An indifference curve has been fitted through these sample points in Figure 8-1. The region to the left of this curve consists of inferior profit situations while the region to the right of this curve consists of superior profit situations. Then the (Z, σ_z) for the other marketing mixes can be plotted. If these points all plot in the inferior region, then mix #5 remains the best mix, subject to further qualifications. If any points plot in the superior region, the foregoing

3. Expected profit is given by $Z = (P - V)(Q - Q_B)$. Suppose both Q and Q_B are estimated with some uncertainty. The uncertainty of Q reflects the difficulty of estimating sales; and the uncertainty of Q_B, the break-even volume, reflects the difficulty of estimating costs. Suppose further that the degree of uncertainty in estimating sales is independent of the degree of uncertainty in estimating costs. Let σ_Q and σ_B, the standard deviations, represent the respective degrees of uncertainty. Then σ_z, the standard deviation of profit, can be derived by applying elementary theorems on variances. Specifically, $\sigma^2_{ax} = \alpha^2 \sigma^2_x$ and $\sigma^2_{x+y} = \sigma^2_x + \sigma^2_y$. Applying these theorems to $Z = (P - V)(Q - Q_B)$, $\sigma_z = (P - V)\sqrt{\sigma^2 Q + \sigma^2 Q_B}$.

procedure can be repeated to establish a new indifference curve to the right of the old one and the remaining contending points can be tested again.

If management has difficulty in thinking of risk in terms of standard deviations, an alternative procedure can be used instead. Management can be asked to express its preferences between various gambles where the risks are stated. The preferences become the basis for preparing a corporate utility scale for various money sums. For a management with risk aversion, the chance to earn twice the profit tends to carry *less* than twice the utility. For each marketing mix, the possible profit outcomes are re-stated as utility outcomes. Then the probabilities are used to find the expected utility for that marketing mix. The best marketing mix can be defined as the one with the maximum expected utility [5].

2. *The absolute profit estimates for the eight marketing mixes must be converted into rates of return on investment in order to choose the best marketing mix and to decide whether to develop the new product at all.* For example, management estimates that 5,500 units will be sold in the first year with marketing mix #5 and 8,200 units will be sold with marketing mix #6. But mix #6 will tie up more dollars than mix #5 because production, inventory, and marketing are carried out on a larger scale. For each mix, Z should be expressed as a ratio to the required investment. Mix #5 is still likely to stand out as the best choice in the example. But now a second question also can be answered: is the expected rate of return greater than

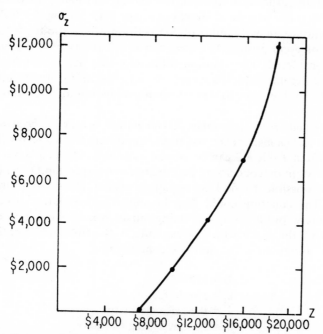

Figure 8-1. Company indifference curve for expected profit (Z) and risk (σ_z).

the company's target rate of return? The company is not likely to develop a new product whose expected rate of return falls short of the target rate.

3. *The use of expected profits ignores the variability and duration of profits implied by different initial marketing mixes.* At the outset, it should be emphasized that management is *not* trying to determine a permanent marketing mix to be used over the lifetime of this product. Both costs and sales will change over time because of competition, market saturation, business fluctuations, and the like. The company may start with mix #5 and if strong competition enters the market with a reduced price, the ABC Electronics Company may find it expedient to change its mix. It may reduce its price and/or change its promotion. Either reaction is tantamount to adopting a new marketing mix.

By examining different marketing mixes in the profit analysis stage of new product development, the company is trying to ascertain an initial strategy and its implied initial profit level. Thus $18,998 represents the amount of profits expected in the first year with mix #5. The company is interested in discovering the strategy which will enable it to recover as much cost as possible as soon as possible because of the difficulty of foretelling the fate of the product beyond a few years. Yet it is also a fact that the initial marketing mix can have an important effect on the company's long-run success with this product. A low price, medium promotion mix like #2, in creating a high initial sales volume, tends to bring about an earlier saturation of the market and hence a shorter period of profits. Mix #5, because it employs a high price and brings high profits, is likely to induce an early influx of competition which also tends to shorten the period of good profits. The long-run implications of the initial mixes must be considered. The solution ultimately may lie in simulating on a computer different time sequences of mix decisions under alternative assumptions and events to derive some indication of alternative profit possibilities.

4. *The previous analysis assumes that no marketing mix has been overlooked which might yield a higher expected profit than the eight listed mixes.* The sales estimates (Q) in Table 8-3 can be viewed as a sample from a larger universe of executive opinion concerning the functional relationship Q = f (P, A, S). It may be possible to find an equation which closely describes these estimates. The equation could then be solved to estimate expected sales, and ulitmately profits, for marketing mixes which were not explicitly considered by the executives. For example, a plausible mathematical form for demand functions is the multiple exponential:

$$Q = kP^aA^bS^c$$

where k = a scale factor
      a = the price elasticity
      b = the advertising elasticity
      c = the personal selling elasticity

The multiple exponential equation has provided a useful fit in several demand situations [4]. This form fits quite well the sample values of (Q) in Table 8-3. This is more by design than by accident. The least squares equations is

$$Q = 100,000 \ P^{-2}A^{1/8}S^{1/4}$$

Price has an elasticity of —2, that is, a one percent reduction in price, other things equal, tends to increase unit sales by 2 percent. Advertising has an elasticity of 1/8 and the sales budget has an elasticity of 1/4. The coefficient 100,000 is a scale factor which translates the dollar magnitudes into the appropriate physical volume effects.

Several of the preceding equations can now be drawn together:

$$Z = (P - 10)(Q - Q_B) \qquad \text{(1) profit equation}$$

$$Q = 100,000 \ P^{-2}A^{1/8}S^{1/4} \qquad \text{(2) demand equation}$$

$$Q_B = \frac{38,000 + A + S}{P - 10} \qquad \text{(3) break-even volume equation}$$

The best marketing mix was defined initially as the one which maximized Z, that is, profits. Solving equation (1) in terms of (2) and (3), Z can be re-written as:

$$Z = (P - 10)\left(100,000 \ P^{-2}A^{1/8}S^{1/4} - \frac{38,000 + A + S}{P - 10}\right)$$

$$Z = (P - 10)(100,000 \ P^{-2}A^{1/8}S^{1/4}) - 38,000 - A - S$$

$$Z = 100,000 \ P^{-1}A^{1/8}S^{1/4} - 1,000,000 \ P^{-2}A^{1/8}S^{1/4} - 38,000 - A - S \qquad (4)$$

Thus Z is a function of three marketing variables.

The next step is to find that unique set of values of P, A, and S which maximizes Z in (4). This is a problem in differential calculus. The work is carried out in the appendix where the following values emerge:

$$P = \$20$$
$$A = \$12,947$$
$$S = \$25,894$$
$$Z = \$26,735$$

It is interesting to compare this mix with mix #5 which yielded the highest Z of the eight mixes considered in Table 8-3. Mix #5 called for a price of $24 and an advertising and sales budget of $10,000 each. The new calculation calls attention to the possibility that a somewhat lower price, a slight increase in advertising expenditure, and a substantial increase in personal selling expenditure might boost profits by several thousand dollars. Thus it may be possible to employ mathematical analysis to overcome the limitations of considering only a small set of marketing mixes. Though we have illustrated this in terms of Z, a more complicated mathematical analysis can be prepared for finding the best marketing mix under conditions of uncertainty, different investment requirements, and more than three marketing variables.[4]

SUMMARY AND CONCLUSIONS

The overall challenge of new product development is to weed out the impracticable ideas as early as possible and to process the remaining ideas as efficiently as possible. The profit analysis stage is where a product idea which has been found to be compatible with the company's objectives and resourses must be analyzed for its profit potential. It is not sufficient to confine the analysis to one specific conception of how the product will look and be marketed, thought this is the typical practice. For the marketing mix will influence both the costs and the sales of the new product, and it is not obvious in advance which mix will maximize expected profits.

The method outlined in this article requires management to develop estimates of likely costs and sales under different marketing mixes on the basis of the best available information. These estimates become the raw data in an analysis which seeks to determine the best marketing mix and whether this mix promises a sufficient level of profits, in the face of uncertainty and the required investment, to justify developing the product. Admittedly there is no way to prove that the suggested analysis does in fact lead to better decisions at the profit analysis stage. Its claim is that it calls attention to the relevant factors and outlines a systematic way to consider them.

APPENDIX

The objective is to find the unique set of values of price (P), advertising (A), and personal selling (S), which maximize profits (Z) in the equation:

$$Z = 100{,}00P^{-1}A^{1/8}S^{1/4} - 1{,}000{,}000P^{-2}A^{1/8}S^{1/4} - 38{,}000 - A - S \qquad (1)$$

First find the first three partial derivatives of Z and set them equal to zero:

4. It possesses a number of plausible properties. First, it provides that the effect of a specific marketing variable depends not only upon its own level but also on the levels of the other marketing variables. Thus a price of $16 will have one demand effect if advertising and selling are each set at $10,000 and another if advertising and selling are each set at $50,000. This interdependency does not exist with linear equations. Second, the exponential equation shows diminishing marginal returns to increases in the advertising and sales budgets and this accords with intuitive expectations. Finally, the exponents represent the respective elasticities of the marketing variables, provided there is no intercorrelation between the independent variables.

$$\frac{\delta Z}{\delta P} = -100{,}000P^{-2}A^{1/8}S^{1/4} + 2{,}000{,}000P^{-3}A^{1/8}S^{1/4} = 0 \tag{2}$$

$$\frac{\delta Z}{\delta A} = 12{,}500P^{-1}A^{-7/8}S^{1/4} - 125{,}000P^{-2}A^{-7/8}S^{1/4} - 1 = 0 \tag{3}$$

$$\frac{\delta Z}{\delta S} = 25{,}000P^{-1}A^{1/8}S^{-3/4} - 250{,}000P^{-2}A^{1/8}S^{-3/4} - 1 = 0 \tag{4}$$

Rearrange the terms in (2):

$$\frac{\delta Z}{\delta P} = 100{,}000P^{-2}A^{1/8}S^{1/4}(20P^{-1} - 1) = 0 \tag{2a}$$

Assuming that $P \neq \infty$, $A \neq 0$, and $S \neq 0$, it follows that $(20P^{-1} - 1) = 0$ or

$$P = \$20 \tag{5}$$

Next, rewrite (3) and (4):

$$12{,}500P^{-1}A^{-7/8}S^{1/4}(1 - 10P^{-1}) = 1 \tag{3a}$$
$$25{,}000P^{-1}A^{1/8}S^{-3/4}(1 - 10P^{-1}) = 1 \tag{4a}$$

Divide (3a) by (4a), term for term:

$$\tfrac{1}{2}A^{-1}S = 1$$
$$S = 2A \tag{6}$$

Next substitute (5) and (6) in (3a):

$$12{,}500(20^{-1})(A^{-7/8})(2A)^{1/4}[(1 - 10(20^{-1})] = 1$$
$$A = \$12{,}947 \tag{7}$$

Substitute (7) in (6):

$$S = 2(12{,}947) = \$25{,}894 \tag{8}$$

The optimal marketing mix (P, A, S) is (\$20, \$12,947, \$25,894). The executives would forecast that this mix would produce a sales volume of:

$$Q = 100{,}000^{-2}A^{1/8}S^{1/4}$$
$$= 100{,}000(20^{-2})(12{,}947^{1/8})(25{,}894^{1/4})$$
$$= 10{,}358$$

The break-even volume implied by this mix would be:

$$Q_B = \frac{38,000 + A + S}{P - 10} = \frac{38,000 + 12,947 + 25,897}{20 - 10} = 7,684$$

Finally, profits (Z) under the optimal mix would be:

$$Z = (P - V)(Q - Q_B)$$
$$= (20 - 10)(10,358 - 7,684)$$
$$= \$26,735$$

REFERENCES

1. Booz, Allen, and Hamilton, *Management of New Products,* third ed., 1960.

2. P. E. Green, "Bayesian Statistics and Product Decisions," *Business Horizons,* 5 (1962), 101-109.

3. J. Johnston, *Statistical Cost Analysis,* New York: McGraw-Hill, 1960.

4. E. Nemmers, *Managerial Economics,* New York: John Wiley and Sons, 1962, 96ff.

5. R. Schlaifer, *Probability and Statistics for Business Decisions,* New York:McGraw-Hill, 1959, Chapter 2.

ADDITIONAL SELECTED BIBLIOGRAPHY

Business Analysis

Cord, J., "A Method of Allocating Funds to Investment Projects When Returns Are Subject to Uncertainty," *Management Science,* Vol. 10, No. 5 (January, 1964), 335-341.

Murdock, J. R., "Financial Evaluation of New Product Opportunities," *The Professionals Look at New Products,* Brand, Gruber and Co., eds., Michigan Business Papers, No. 50, Bureau of Business Research, The University of Michigan (1968), 182-197.

Pessemier, E. A., "Analyzing the Economic Potential of a Consumer Product," Reflections on Progress in Marketing, L. George Smith, ed., AMA Educators Conference Proceedings, American Marketing Association (December, 1964), 23-39.

Scheuble, P. A., Jr., "ROI for New-product Policy," *Harvard Business Review,* Vol. 42, No. 6 (November-December, 1964), 110-120.

Spitz, A. E. and DeKorvin, A., "A New Theoretical Model for Determining Profit Optimality," *Journal of Financial and Quantitative Analysis,* Vol. 6, No. 4 (September, 1971). 1117-1121.

Wilkinson, J. D., "Profit Performance Concepts and the Product Manager," *Management Services,* Vol. 5, No. 4 (July-August, 1968), 17-25.

Winer, L., "A Profit-Oriented Decision System," *Journal of Marketing,* Vol. 30, No. 2 (April, 1966), 38-44.

QUESTIONS FOR DISCUSSION AND REVIEW

1. What are the advantages and disadvantages of the methods used to determine a go-no-go decision to develop a new product idea?

2. Discuss break-even analysis as a quantitative tool for management decision making.

3. How would you define profit optimality?

4. Explain how the holistic approach "fits" into business analysis of a new product idea.

5. Assuming that the new product idea "passes inspection," what means are available to generate funds for developing, testing, and commercializing the product?

9

DEVELOPMENT

After the business analysis step, many of the new product ideas will have been eliminated or shelved. Since the committee or new product decision-maker has been favorably impressed, however, by some of the new product ideas which have been analyzed and given an affirmative judgment, the next step is to develop a model and/or build a pilot plant to ascertain the usefulness and profit possibilities of the new product idea. The new product idea then can be transformed into a physical entity. The idea has borne a product sample. The thinking behind the development of a working physical model is to determine whether or not the product can be produced on a mass basis technically, and it is just as important at this stage to determine whether or not the time is right.

Is production being planned so that sales will be made immediately? Does the firm have to inventory the product until product information is made available to the buyers? Is it a seasonal product which will be purchased only during the season? Development of a new product can move in various directions, for the product can be improved, changed, modified, or produced as approved earlier. If changes are made, and the new product is later tested, it may or may not become a successful new product. Though a modification in design may reduce costs by switching raw materials, or by reducing packaging costs, it may also bring on a change in the minds of the purchasers. There is always the possibility that the product objectives will not be reached, particularly should a change in the development of the product take place that was not anticipated in the earlier steps of product planning. Some firms develop and test raw materials that make up the finished product so as to avoid error and reduce the risk element in bringing the product to market. The following series of articles discuss the development stage of product planning.

TIME LAG IN NEW
PRODUCT DEVELOPMENT
BY LEE ADLER

New product development is crucial to the success of many companies
... and likewise the time dimension is crucial to successful new product
development.

But this temporal aspect has several facets. Some of these factors are well
understood. Marketing executives are aware of the advantages that accrue
to the new product that hits the market first. They are also aware of being
too late—hitting the downside of a product cycle; becoming the victim of
changing consumer habits, tastes and styles; or of having an idea fail
because it is ahead of its time.

However, there is one temporal aspect that is often underrated. This is
the length of time it takes to develop new products. To put it another way,
one of the prime causes of product failure lies in "underestimating the time
... needed for orderly market development and growth."[1] *The fear of wrong
marketing timing leads to faulty development timing.*

That is, anxiety about timing in the market makes time an enemy in the
laboratory. Ironically, the outcome is that time kills the very thing it is
designed to save.

The insufficient time allowed for proper development is then expressed
in other ways in accounting for the high rate of new product failures. Such
explanations as inadequate market analysis, failure to discover product
defects until after launching, skipping or glossing over steps in development

EDITOR'S NOTE: From the *Journal of Marketing*, January 1966, pp. 17-21. Reprinted by
permission of the American Marketing Association and the author.

Table 9-1. New Product Development Time.
I. Consumer Packaged Goods.

Product	Company	Date Development Started or Idea Born	Test or Initial Markets	Large-scale or National	Elapsed Time	Reference	Remarks
Birdseye frozen foods	Birdseye Division, General Foods	1908	1923		15 years	*Printers' Ink,* 5/29/64	
Ban (roll-on deodorant)	Bristol-Myers	About 1948	1954	March, 1955	6 years	*Printers' Ink,* 6/5/59 *Sponsor,* 4/16/56	Roll-on idea came from an outside inventor, hence presumably predates 1948. Bristol-Myers developed product that failed in test markets in 1951. Company researchers worked on plastics, finally assigned outside company job of making plastic marbles. Consumer-panel studies favorable in fall, 1953. Final test markets, summer, 1954. National advertising, March, 1955.
Calm powder deodorant in aerosol can	Alberto-Culver	1959		February, 1964	5 years	*Printers' Ink,* 1/24/64	Non-spray powder deodorants were tried about 1948–50, did not "get off the ground" then.
Chlorodent (tooth paste)	Lever Brothers	1930s	March, 1951	Early 1952	Between 11 and 21 years	*Tide,* 3/28/52	Idea developed in 1930s; two J. Walter Thompson vice presidents formed a company, Rystan, with a patent for chlorophyll products. Idea subsequently presented to Lever, and Lever licensed to produce tooth paste.
Citroid (cold compound)	Grove Laboratories	1954–55		1956	1 to 2 years	*Advertising Agency,* 10/26/56	

Product	Company					Reference	Notes
Coldene (cold-remedy liquid)	Pharma-Craft	1954	1955	1956	1 year	Printers' Ink, 2/7/58	
Crest (fluoride tooth paste)	Procter & Gamble	1945	January, 1955	January, 1956	10 years	Advertising Age, 8/1/60	Discovery that stannous fluoride is a preventive against tooth decay first made by Dr. Joseph C. Muhler in 1945, when he was a sophomore at School of Dentistry, University of Indiana. Since P&G had a parallel interest, Dr. Muhler continued to work on the project.
Decaf (decaffinated instant coffee)	Nestlé	1947	1953		10 years	Tide, 1/25/57 Nestlé Company	
Flav-R-Straws	Frontier Foods Corp. and others	1953	April, 1956	Early 1957	3 years	Food Business, 4/57	Inventor sold idea to Frontier in 1955. By January, 1956, Frontier was in trouble, and product taken over by others.
Gerber (strained baby foods)	Gerber	1927	1928		1 year	Business Decisions That Changed Our Lives, Sidney Furst, Milton Sherman (Random House, 1964), p. 167.	
Hills Brothers (instant coffee)	Hills Brothers Coffee	1934	1956		22 years	New York Times, 11/16/56	
Johnson liquid shoe polish containers that are also applicators	S. C. Johnson	1957	February, 1960	Early 1961	3 years	Printers' Ink, 7/14/61	

Table 9-1 *(Continued)*

Product	Company	Date Development Started or Idea Born	Test or Initial Markets	Large-scale or National	Elapsed Time	Reference	Remarks
Lustre Creme (liquid shampoo)	Colgate-Palmolive	1950		June, 1958	8 years	*Drug Trade News,* 5/19/58	Five years of product tests, three years of consumer research.
Marlboro (filter cigarettes)	Philip Morris	May, 1953	March, 1955		2 years	*Advertising Age,* 2/28/55	Marlboro had previously existed as a premium non-filter cigarette; development of filter, hard package, flip-top were new; red ("beauty") tip derived from earlier non-filter product.
Maxim (concentrated instant coffee)	General Foods	1954	May, 1964		10 years	*Printers' Ink,* 5/1/64	Preserves flavor and aroma of freshly brewed coffee. Process involves freezing of freshly percolated coffee. To use, crystals are dropped into cup of boiling (or iced) water.
Minute Maid (frozen orange juice)	Minute Maid	1944	1946		2 years	*Sales Management,* 4/1/49 *Advertising Age,* 3/14/49	Introduced in 1946 under private label; and in 1947 under Minute Maid name.
Minute Rice	General Foods	1931		First quarter, 1949	18 years	*Food Field Reporter,* 12/13/54 *Advertising Agency,* 11/49	Idea originally came from member of Afghanistan royal family. GF had plant ready in 1941. World War II interrupted; army used plant. Consumer-tested in spring, 1946. Began national distribution in late 1948.

Product	Company					Source	
Purina Dog Chow	Ralston-Purina	1951	February, 1955	April, 1957	4 years	*Wall Street Journal*, 1/2/58	Began search for a dry dog-food in 1951; developed light aerated feed using new formula in 1953; began testing February, 1955; in four additional test markets in 1955–56; achieved national distribution by April, 1957.
Red Kettle (dry-soup mixes)	Campbell Soup	Before 1943		August, 1962	19 years	*Advertising Age*, 9/24/62 *Food Field Reporter*, 8/28/61	Campbell first tested dry noodle soup in 1943–44, withdrew product because "we were dissatisifed with the processes and packages available." Resumed testing in 1959.
Stripe (tooth paste)	Lever Brothers	1952	1957	Early 1958	5½ to 6 years	*New York Times*, 1/15/58	Inventor spent four years developing the striping device. Took Lever engineers six months to design a production machine. Product then in test markets for 14 months.
Wisk (liquid detergent)	Lever Brothers	1955	January, 1956		1 year	*Fortune*, 6/59	
Wrinkle-removing creams	(Many)		1963–64				Protein used in these creams, developed during World War II.

Table 9-2. New Product Development Time.
II. Other Consumer Goods.

Product	Company	Date Development Started or Idea Born	Test or Initial Markets	Large-scale or National	Elapsed Time	Reference	Remarks
Bendix (washer/dryer)	Bendix	Prior to World War II		March, 1953	12 years plus	*Fortune, 3/53*	
Eversharp ("Fountain Ball" ball pen)	Eversharp	January, 1958	September, 1958	January, 1959	8 months	*Sales Management, 1/2/59*	Eight months in product development; one year in product and market testing.
Fairchild (Mark IV 8mm. sound projector)	Fairchild Camera & Instrument	Late 1961	August, 1963		2 years	*New Products, New Profits,* American Management Association, 1964	Fairchild describes as "better than average effort," due to technical advances in dealing with the complexities involved.
Floron (plastic floor tile)	Pabco Products	1947–48		October, 1953	5 to 6 years	*Sales Management, 1/1/55*	
GE (electric tooth brush)	General Electric	1958–59	October, 1961	April, 1962	3 to 4 years	*Printers' Ink, 7/20/62*	Electric tooth brushes available for 30 years; wall-socket recharging, new.
Polaroid Land Camera	Polaroid Corp.	1945–46	1947–48		2 years	*Business Week, 9/3/49 and 1/19/63 Printers' Ink, 5/29/64 Standard & Poor's Corporate Records,* 1965, p. 9745.	

Polaroid Color-pack Camera	Polaroid Corp.	1948	January, 1963	May, 1963	15 years plus	Business Week, 1/19/63	
Scripto Tilt Tip (ball pen)	Scripto	1959	April, 1961	Mid-1961	2 years	Advertising Age, 1/30/61	
Sinclair (Power X gasoline; Extra Duty Motor Oil)	Sinclair Oil	Late 1952		April, 1953	6 months	Printers' Ink, 6/18/54	
Smith Corona (portable electric typewriter)	Smith Corona	1952	Early 1957		5 years	New York Times, 11/17/57	
Sunbeam (electric tooth brush)	Sunbeam Corp.				5 years	Sales Management, 9/4/64	
Talon (zippers)	Corporate predecessor of Talon, Inc.	1883	1913	1918	30 years	Business Decisions That Changed Our Lives, Sidney Furst, Milton Sherman (Random House, 1964), p. 115.	Zippers first thought of as shoe-fastening device in 1883. In 1894, product first developed for use in shoes. First modern zipper concept, emerged in 1908. First successful mass production, 1913; and first applications to clothing in 1913–18. In 1918, an ex-GI suggested use of zippers for money belts, and this was really the first commercial success.

Table 9-2 *(Continued)*

Product	Company	Date Development Started or Idea Born	Test or Initial Markets	Large-scale or National	Elapsed Time	Reference	Remarks
Television	(Many)	1884	1939	1946-47	55 years	Federal Communications Commission, "Broadcast Primer," Bulletin 2-B, 1961.	In 1884, Nipkow, a German, patented a scanning disk for transmitting pictures by wireless—this is credited with being the first development that led ultimately to what is now known as television. In 1890 Jenkins began his

studies in the U.S. In the 1900s, Rignoux and Fournier conducted "television" experiments in France. In 1915, Marconi predicted a "visible telephone." In 1923, Zworykin applied for patent on the iconoscope, a TV camera-tube. In 1925, Jenkins demonstrated a mechanical television apparatus. In 1927 the first experimental television program from New York to Washington made by Bell Laboratories. In 1928 the first station, WGY, established in Schenectady. In 1930 RCA demonstrated large-screen TV in New York. In 1936 RCA tested outdoor TV pickup in Camden. By 1937, 17 experimental stations in existence. The first commercial program authorized on July 1, 1941 by WNBT–New York, but the first TV sets shown to consumers at New York World's Fair in 1939, and available to consumers in 1939–40.

New Product Development Time.
III. Industrial Goods

Product	Company	Date Development Started or Idea Born	Test or Initial Markets	Large-scale or National	Elapsed Time	Reference	Remarks
Dictet (portable recording machine)	Dictaphone Corp.	1954	Early		20 months		A Critical Look At The Purchasing Function, Robert F. Logler, American Management Association Bulletin No. 13

Product	Company					Source	Notes
Isothalic (chemical component to improve house paints)	Oronite Corp. (subsidiary of Standard Oil of California)	1951	Late 1957–early 1958		6 to 7 years plus	*Sales Management*, 9/19/58	Specific development of superior house paint begun in 1951. Oronite began work on Isothalic during World War II. Isothalic reported to be ten years in development.
Krilium (soil conditioner)	Monsanto	1939	May, 1952		12½ years	American Management Association Bulletin No. 13, 1961, pp. 122–41.	
Page Master (selective pocket-paging system)	Stromberg Carlson	1955		March, 1957	2 years	American Management Association Bulletin No. 13, 1961, pp. 122–41.	
Penicillin	(Many)	1928	1943		15 years	*Business Week*, 3/3/45	Discovered by Sir Alex Fleming.
Transistors	Bell Laboratories	1940	1955–56		15 to 16 years	*Business Week*, 3/26/60	First discovery accidental, in 1940. First laboratory transistor, debut in 1948. Prototype qualities available, 1954. First consumer applications in hearing aids and radios, 1955–56.
Xerox (electrostatic copying machines)	Xerox Corp.	1935	1950		15 years	*Forbes*, 9/15/62 *Fortune*, 7/62 *New York Times*, 12/10/61 *Standard & Poor's Corporate Records*, 1965, p. 4472.	

such as pilot production or market testing—all of these are ways of saying that the felt pressures of market timing resulted in an unfortunate telescoping of development timing.

The fact is that it takes much longer to develop new products than usually is thought to be the case. The conventional rule of thumb about allowing two to three years will be wrong more often than not.

This point is documented by a review of published accounts of new products. This search of literature uncovered 42 case histories. See the accompanying table; it provides information on *consumer packaged goods, other consumer goods, and industrial goods.*

It would be misleading to average the length of time it took to develop these new products from the time they were a "gleam in the eye" until actual market introduction, simply because of the various possible definitions of a new product. A new product can be new to an individual company but not to the industry. Or it can be a new ingredient, feature, package, strength, flavor, etc. added to an existing product. Or it can be new in every sense, for example, the Polaroid camera and Xerox electrostatic reproduction.

In the accompanying table, elapsed time is calculated from the date that development began or that the idea was conceived until test marketing or initial marketing. These elapsed times are approximations for several reasons. As a careful examination of the literature made clear, dates are often vague because company records are poor, recollections foggy, and cases reported unsystematically. Moreover, chronologies are further confused by gaps between birth of idea and beginning of development.

Nonetheless, these cases clearly demonstrate that on the whole product development is more time-consuming than commonly recognized. The range was from 6 months for Sinclair Power-X gasoline to 55 years for television. Many new products took 5 years, 10 years, and even longer to bring to fruition.

Marketers need to allot considerably more time to the development process than most of them do.

B

BUILDING THE
PROTOTYPE MODEL
BY SEYMOUR W. HERWALD

One of the most crucial stages of product development is that awkward period between the establishment of the feasibility of a device in the laboratory and the existence of prototype models of that device which can be economically produced in quantity. Considerable planning must be done if the product is to pass through this difficult period with the maximum possible efficiency.

INCREASED COST OF PROTOTYPE MODELS

First of all, in the area of engineering alone, real production prototypes will cost anywhere from 5 to 10 times as much as the laboratory breadboard model. Since there is no absolute definition of a laboratory model, the cost figures may vary somewhat with each company's definitions. At Westinghouse, a laboratory breadboard is defined as "a model constructed to demonstrate the feasibility of a new principle." In using this definition, it is soon apparent that most considerations of packaging, the interchangeability of parts, reliability, environmental suitability, production rates, and cost of manufacture have been minimized. The development of the prototype then includes the cost of engineering the literally thousands of detailed items so important and necessary to successful production.

EDITOR'S NOTE: Reprinted by permission of the publisher from *Developing a Product Strategy,* AMA Management Report #39. Copyright © 1959 by the American Management Association, Inc.

It is extremely important the the initial enthusiasm occasioned by seeing a new invention working in laboratory breadboard form be properly tempered by the sobering thought that the spending has just begun. It is quite possible that, even after a production prototype model is available (at 10 times the laboratory breadboard cost), as much as 10 times the cost of the prototype itself may have to be spent for production tooling and marketing of the new device. In other words, a company may have to spend as much as 100 times the original breadboard costs to get a new product on the market, selling in forecast quantities.

It is quite important, therefore—despite the initial laboratory success of an invention—to judge carefully whether manpower, facilities, organization, and capital are available to develop it into a successful product. The inventor who has not had sufficient experience will usually tend to underestimate the time and cost of this effort. He should be shown, by someone he respects, that the accomplishment of what may appear to him to be mere details is really necessary, and is costly because of the sheer number of these details.

CHECKLIST OF PROTOTYPE-PLANNING FACTORS

In preparing to go ahead, a number of factors must be checked, including many which have been reviewed previously and to which the answers may appear obvious:

1. Is there a real and profitable market for the device?

2. Who did the original laboratory work? Has the group assigned to develop the production prototype had previous experience with the activity that conceived the laboratory breadboard, or must some allowance be made for development of communications and individual personality adjustments? It is usually possible to alleviate difficulties of this type by transferring some of the laboratory personnel to the development group, even if only temporarily.

3. Has the group assigned to make the prototype *actually* made a careful analysis of the performance and theory of operation of the laboratory model? In the members' opinion, does it *in theory* meet the needs of the customer?

4. Has a definitive specification of prototype performance been arrived at? Does it meet the needs and approval of the customer?

5. Has the group selected to do the production-prototype development had experience along the lines of the product being considered? If not, a factor varying with the degree of inexperience should be applied to the time, money, and manpower estimates.

6. Do new components have to be developed? Are suitable suppliers available, or must they be developed?

7. Does a planned schedule exist which contains key check points that are readily demonstrable? Do the checks really show that the device will perform in its ultimately intended environment?

8. Has there been adequate planning of the facilities, manpower, organization, and capital which must be available in order to complete the prototype developments?

9. Are there one or more critical items in planning—such as time, money, or facilities—that cannot be exceeded without the complete failure of the project?

CHECKLIST OF PROTOTYPE DESIGN FACTORS

Similarly, there are many facets of the actual design that must be checked fully during the prototype-development period. Some of the most important ones are:

1. Can the laboratory model be made to operate in the actual environment in which it is to be used? In the field of airborne equipment, for example, is there something critical in the laboratory device that will make it function improperly at the extremes of altitude, speed, and temperature that the aircraft of today and tomorrow must withstand?

2. Can the device be controlled and operated by the type of personnel who will use it, or was the laboratory model pampered into operation by a group of skilled scientists?

3. Is the laboratory model capable of being packaged in a form that is acceptable to the user insofar as space, weight, and appearance are concerned? A new cigarette lighter that does not fit conveniently into the palm of the hand or in the pocket probably will not sell, regardless of what other performance advantages it may have in the laboratory.

4. What degree of cost reduction must be effected to make the selling price of the device agree with the price that market research has estimated as desirable for customer acceptance?

5. Will the design be reliable enough that the people charged with maintenance responsibility can keep it in operation?

6. Is the design such that the model can be tooled economically?

7. How much do the most expensive items contribute to the performance? Can they be eliminated? If not, can they be redesigned with an acceptable degradation in performance?

8. Are the design and proposed tooling compatible with the facilities contemplated for manufacture?

MANPOWER AND FACILITY REQUIREMENTS

Companies, such as Westinghouse, which manufacture a wide diversity of products find it desirable to do prototype development and design in the plant at which the particular product under development is to be manufactured. In other manufacturing organizations, it may be desirable to carry on development in a central location, particularly where the same or a similar product is manufactured in multiple locations. Typical examples might include industries that process such basis commodities as steel, copper, petroleum products, fabrics, or automotive equipment.

At the Air Arm Division of Westinghouse, a large portion of the effort is devoted to developing production prototypes from both our own laboratory breadboards and those of others. Since our business is military airborne electronic equipment, we have found it necessary to plan for the following manpower and facility requirements to handle our particular development problems:

1. Large groups of competent engineers and scientists.

2. Long-range planning and market research to determine the usefulness of the contemplated product and consequent marketability.

3. Suitable laboratory facilities, including adequate instruments and tools.

4. A flight-test facility, so that we can prove the suitability of our prototypes in an environment as similar to the ultimate one as we can achieve.

5. Adequate environmental facilities which simulate the airborne military environment.

6. Quality control compatible with the reliability required in military service.

7. Manufacturing techniques and know-how compatible with the light weight, size, and performance requirements of airborne equipment.

8. Project reviews at appropriate times in the development schedule.

Usually, those factors which cause the most trouble in planning for the future are most obvious when viewed in retrospect. Monday-morning quarterbacks are invariably better than the fellow on the field who has to call the right plays in advance and then run interference. Adequate planning greatly increases the probability of calling the right plays at the right time.

NOTE

1. Clarence F. Manning, "Principles of Product Strategy," speech before 12th Annual Marketing Conference, National Industrial Conference Board, October 28, 1964.

ADDITIONAL SELECTED BIBLIOGRAPHY

Development

Hennessey, R. G., "The Accelerated Program: From Idea to Product Faster," *New Products/New Profits,* Elizabeth Marting, ed., American Management Association (1964), 237-244.

Kemm, T. R., "Scientific Experimentation in Product Innovation," *New Ideas for Successful Marketing*, John S. Wright and Jack L. Goldstucker, eds., AMA Proceedings of the 1966 World Congress, American Marketing Association (June, 1966), 241-246.

Kuehn, A. A., and Day, R. L., "Strategy of Product Quality," *Harvard Business Review*, Vol. 40, No. 6 (November-December, 1962), 100-109.

Saporito, D. A., "New Product Success through Industrial Design," *The Professionals Look at New Products*, Brand, Gruber and Co., eds., Michigan Business Papers, No. 50, Bureau of Business Research, The University of Michigan (1968), 83-94.

Starkey, E. A., "Business Development: A New Concept," *Marketing in a Changing World*, Bernard A. Morin, ed., AMA Conference Proceedings, Series No. 29, American Marketing Association (June, 1969), 91-95.

Urban, G. L., "A New Product Analysis and Decision Model," *Management Science*, Vol. 14, No. 8 (April, 1968), B490-B517.

Utech, K. H., "Testing New Products during the Development Process," *The Professionals Look at New Products*, Brand, Gruber and Co., eds. Michigan Business Papers, No. 50, Bureau of Business Research, The University of Michigan (1968), 83-94.

Wong, Yung, "Critical Path Analysis for New Product Planning," *Journal of Marketing*, Vol. 28, No. 4 (October, 1964), 53-59.

QUESTIONS FOR DISCUSSION AND REVIEW

1. Discuss the meaning of an analogue and iconic model. Give examples of each.

2. Of what use is a single physical model?

3. What methods would you suggest using to determine the purchase intentions of prospective buyers utilizing a physical model?

4. What are some key points to keep in mind for demand creation when developing a model of a product?

5. Would you combine development and testing techniques in product design? Why?

10

TESTING

In some industries the testing of a new product goes hand in hand with development. Although the technical force within a company could develop a product which it deems satisfactory, it is far more important to have the approval of the final users. So the engineer-production men have to "pretest" the product before an inventory can be built up. Aside from engineering the physical entity of a product, the firm must look to the consuming public for approval before the dollars and energies of the firm are committed to producing and selling it. Test marketing is an absolute necessity with some products, even though a few firms make little effort in the direction of testing.

Labeling and packaging play important roles in consumer purchasing. Products that vie for shelf space at retail outlets must, in a matter of seconds, be recognized by the purchasers. A label that attracts the attention of the buyer may induce a purchase response. Attractiveness of the physical package in products such as perfumes and colognes elicits purchase responses because the packaging is unique and different. The perfume package, however, becomes an expensive item greater than the cost of the perfume contained in the package. The product per ounce (or less) costs less than the container which holds the perfume. Decanters that contain various alcoholic beverages also show how packaging plays a role in product sales during holiday periods. The size and shape of packages, their composition (glass, plastics, etc.), color, and weight must be tested for purchaser approval. The size and color of the label as well as its message aid in the successful sale of the product.

Another factor important to the success of a new product is the type of promotion appeals that will disseminate product information calculated to induce purchase action. Promotion programs should also be tested. Not all unsuccessful products are due to poor quality or high price; often a poor promotion program can cause the demise of a new product. The following articles deal with testing a new product.

A NEW APPROACH TO
TEST MARKETING
BY DAVID K. HARDIN

One of the sacred institutions in grocery and drug marketing today is the test market. The high cost of marketing failures has made this a cornerstone of marketing plans.

Yet test marketing has not been an accurate prediction device. Too often managements have found that test marketing results are ambiguous. As a result, the test market fails in its real job—to reduce uncertainty about basic product marketing decisions.

LIMITATIONS OF TRADITIONAL TEST MARKETING

Moreover, the failure of the test market to deliver accurate sales predictions has led managements down many costly roads. Test market plans may include many separate test areas at great cost; but there is no evidence that this proliferation is providing the answers.

In fact, the limitations of traditional test marketing are such that further increases in the number of separate test markets would not overcome them. Certainly taking into account the high cost of test markets, in terms of management effort and corporate resources, the level of prediction accuracy has *not* been encouraging. And yet test marketing technology and related research efforts have been a focal point of management attention for several decades.

EDITOR'S NOTE: From the *Journal of Marketing,* October 1966, pp. 28-31. Reprinted by permission of the American Marketing Association and the author.

Interestingly enough, test marketing technology also has failed to produce axioms or theories from which to interpret test market results. Instead, there is mythology.

In examining the test marketing of a new line by a major food products company, one researcher observed that the various management hypotheses were subjective, numerous, and diverse: "The executives invariably had a pet hypothesis as to the intrinsic characteristics of market areas which accounted for differences in performance in future areas. These hypotheses had been generated both from observation in the test areas and with past sales of similar product lines."[1]

Nevertheless, test markets and similar new product planning devices absorb the bulk of the total new product marketing research expenditures of major American companies. Each of several major grocery product manufacturers individually spend more on marketing research than other entire industries—such as furniture, home building, and clothing.

REASONS FOR UNSATISFACTORY RESULTS

Since many extremely competent marketing researchers and marketing executives have devoted considerable attention, time, and funds to test marketing, why are the results so far from satisfactory? The reasons are several.

1. *The salesmen in the selected areas are stimulated beyond normal activity levels* by mere awareness of the fact that a test is going to be conducted in their market. No matter how many times the salesmen are urged to make only "normal" sales efforts, the fact that his area is being scrutinized by the top management of his company causes a more intensive effort. For example, if sales are not up to the salesmen's subjective expectations, sales pressure is almost unconsciously increased through unplanned selling efforts—they want it to be "successful." The performance becomes a test of the salesmen, not of the product.

2. *The trade is alerted to the fact that a test is being conducted in the area.* In fact, this is often the reason the trade are asked to accept the product. For a variety of reasons, important elements of the trade are usually interested in the performance of a new product; and thus, the manufacturer may receive considerable artificial distribution and retailer support.

3. *Special introductory offers and promotions are often made* which would not otherwise be made, because it is so important to *get* distribution (to measure consumer acceptance) and to *maintain* distribution for specified time periods within specified retail outlets. Some of the introductory offers are so low that the real retail price of the test item is depressed below the

1. William R. King, "Toward a Methodology of Market Analysis," *The Journal of Marketing Research,* Vol. 11 (August, 1965), pp. 236-243.

price at which the manufacturer could profitably produce the item for marketing.

4. *Competitive efforts, both deliberate and coincidental, have profound effects on the test market results.* These efforts take place through the entire spectrum of marketing action: advertising, display, special promotion, sampling, couponing, special pricing, special retailer margins or allowances, and actual buying actions.

5. *Measurement accuracy is a major source of ambiguous data.* Store auditing is often quite inaccurate, due to inadequate store records and incomplete knowledge of store billing and handling systems. Also, the ability to obtain representative sampling of all major outlets—chain and independent—causes data adjustments to be made to account for incomplete market coverage. This level of data inaccuracy can be particularly high when the measurement is of an *ad hoc* nature and involves temporary arrangements and relationships.

THE CHANGING FUNCTIONS OF TEST MARKETING

The limitations of test marketing are causing managements to seek other prediction devices to explore traditional test marketing. The need for more accurate measurement is further compounded by the *changing needs* of today's marketers.

Management's uses of test marketing results are rapidly changing. *Greater* accuracy than ever is required.

No longer are test markets used largely to separate the very successful from the very unsuccessful product—a relatively easy task that is now taking place in advance of the test market. This goal is being achieved by improved product and concept testing techniques prior to test marketing introduction. Management is no longer willing to risk the cost (up to $500,000) and competitive warning (up to two years) that a traditional test market represents merely to uncover a winning product.

As a rule, management is test marketing only those products for which there is an expectation of going national. Evidence of this is that leading grocery product companies—such as General Foods, General Mills, Pet Milk, and Pillsbury—are now going into national distribution with 75 to 85% of the products that are test marketed. Obviously the "winners" are selected in advance of test marketing.

What, then, is the new role of the test market? It is becoming the first phase of national distribution. It is increasingly viewed as an aid to capital budgeting and facility planning. How large a plant is needed for national sales? What is the optimum promotion spending level? How many dollars will produce how many sales? What is the return on investment? A company averaging 20% return may well reject a new product that produces only 8%. Another company might embrace the same product because its average return is 7%.

Most companies have budgeted fixed payout periods for new product investments; and the role of the test market is to indicate the levels of marketing spending and support which will meet these payout goals. Which combination of spending level and sales support produces the profit maximization?

Truly bad products are no longer test marketed—good products are mismarketed. In the last ten years a significant proportion of the "unsuccessful" new convenience food product entries failed because of *over*spending or *under*spending on product introduction—a failure of budgeting as much as of consumer rejection.

To answer the changing demands made of the test market, new research techniques and approaches are evolving. Test marketing is no longer asked to say "yes" or "no" to a new product. Instead, it must answer in fairly precise terms a much more demanding question: How much will product X sell?

ELEMENTS OF SUCCESSFUL MEASUREMENT

For purposes of analysis, test market prediction can be divided into two elements:

1. *Consumer acceptance,* as measured in terms of initial and repeat purchase levels.

2. *Trade acceptance,* or the ability of the manufacturer's sales force to secure, maintain, and expand distribution of the new product.

Consumer acceptance is increasingly subjected to accurate measurement under controlled conditions; trade acceptance is not. Each is vital to the success of a new product and should be measured separately. Yet many manufacturers persist in continuing to try to measure the two in the same test. Unless they are measured separately, the basic problem of accurately allocating marketing resources cannot be solved.

By measuring *consumer acceptance* through tightly controlled market *experimentation,* the marketing executive is able to determine *trade acceptance* through more normal test marketing efforts. In the past, the marketing executive was often unable to tell whether a new product failure was a consumer or trade problem. Now, by separating the measurements, the nature of any problem is determinable.

Techniques have now been developed which focus on the determination of *consumer acceptance* of new products in an actual marketing environment. In a sense, management has come to recognize the need for letting research personnel control the test market, in order to ensure the kinds of controls and designs necessary to accurate measurement and prediction.

Thus, management is beginning to recognize the need for increased *control* over the test marketing environment and situation—recognition that this is a *research device and not a sales device.* Closely related is an improved understanding of what is really taking place under test marketing conditions.

CONTROLLED MARKET EXPERIMENTATION

In a sense, manufacturers are learning that the establishment of *ad hoc* research measurements in test marketing environments simply are not adequate or rigorous enough for accurate measurement and prediction. Increasingly, manufacturers are showing a willingness to bring the test marketing problem to an established research environment or marketing laboratory.

Some major grocery product companies are running as many as a dozen controlled experiments of this type concurrently over a wide range of products and problems. Five years ago, these same companies were running none.

Test marketing is, of course, an experiment. Like all experiments, the test should be designed to test one hypothesis or several. In most new product tests the hypothesis to be tested is that the new product can obtain a given brand share within a given time under given conditions.

The establishment and maintenance of all experimental controls and designs are simply not within the competence framework of the wholesaler or the manufacturer's sales force. Moreover, they cannot be overly temporary. Temporary facilities lack the measurement precision possible with a permanent arrangement—in terms of both measuring personnel and the establishments to be measured.

Permanent operating facilities need to be established in selected markets. As a result, controlled marketing facilities are now offered by several independent marketing research companies. In some markets, permanent arrangements have been made which permit the researcher to place new products on the shelves of grocery and drug retailers. In order to ensure experimental validity, the researchers are often allowed to:

1. Handle the placing of products on shelves in retail stores.
2. Service these products regularly, to ensure that the required in-stock condition is maintained.
3. Audit product class sales.
4. Observe competitive actions that would affect the experiment.

For the experiment to be effective, the products need to be placed on retailer shelves in accordance with rigid conditions established by the manufacturer. These conditions generally include:

1. Retail price.
2. Number of facings or exposures the test product is to receive on the shelf.
3. Product location within the store.
4. Conditions of product display.

The conditions to be established are always with reason. Certainly the product should not be given an advantage that could not readily be duplicated.

However, the issue is increasingly one of *controlled* rather than *natural* conditions. Management is learning far more from consecutive experiments which contrast products given *identical* market treatments than formerly was learned from test markets which provided no real comparability. It is far more useful to contrast the sales results from products A, B, and C which were all based on two facings in the baked-goods department, than it is to know sales results where product A was out of stock one-fourth to one-third of the time and product B was granted far more shelf space than C because of favorable sales results when product A was launched.

Distribution must be immediate and as total as possible. The distribution period needs to be specified, so there is no discontinuance of distribution within the measurement period. By having continuous servicing of product, out-of-stock conditions are minimal or absent. Conditions of price, facings, and location should not be allowed to fluctuate during the study, unless such fluctuations are a condition of the research design.

Under these controlled conditions, the product sales data can then be related to management expectations and plans. In a sense, the researcher has virtually built a "marketing laboratory" within the test cities for the specific purpose of measuring consumer acceptance of new products. For measuring marketing alternatives, each market may be further divided into marketing zones. Each of the zones may contain matched store panels with matched customer demographic characteristics.

Because the experiment is tightly controlled, observation of competitive actions can be systematically monitored and evaluated. Constant checking in the stores and of local media produces measures of competitive activity that can aid in explaining apparent anomalies in the data. Stores with special activity can be eliminated from the measures, if necessary.

The sample of stores should be large enough to permit narrowing of the sample by this type of elimination. The permanent nature of the test relationships acts to dampen special activities that would constitute experimental interference.

Data based on controlled experimentation do *not* produce estimated national figures. But it has already been seen that traditional test market data also fail to permit national estimates, and at much greater cost. The experimental approach ties the data to history and earlier controlled experiments, thus permitting management to contrast the present product with known winners and losers. Moreover, the consistent development of these types of data on various product lines produces more and more precise prediction criteria.

Discussions with major food marketers make it clear that the use of experimental marketing data is rapidly increasing. Also, experimental measurements of the interactions of various marketing devices—such as advertising expenditures, retail allowances, shelf space, and displays—are essential to predictions of sales through the use of computer models.

"The interaction of a brand's advertising expenditure, retail allowance, allocation of sales force effort, and market share determine the relative measure of a brand's retail availability. This measure attempts to simulate the effect of retail distribution, the allocation of shelf space, and in-store special display promotions on the brand's sales. Once these interaction mechanisms are tested and developed to the point where they are reasonably correct determinants of sales effectivenesss, guidance can be provided to marketing executives in proper allocation of resources to these variables."[2]

The tightly controlled experimental test market understandably produces data precision vastly superior to classical test markets. Statistical sales variance in these tests *was found to be only 25 to 30% of the variance produced by traditional measures,* based on comparisons of controlled and uncontrolled brands in three product classes—moist dog food, cake mixes, and canned meats. And measurement error also was reduced.

Experimentation of this type provides a determination of the effectiveness of overall new product marketing strategy; and it also permits the evaluation of alternative tactics through matched store-panel experiments.

In a sense, experiments take place within experiments. By varying the promotional devices and emphasis given to each device, measurements of the value of these devices can be obtained. In this regard, the matching panels should include corporate chains, if possible. The uniform marketing and promotional policies within a corporate chain drastically reduce the effects of unbalanced outside stimuli. Competitive price reductions or special promotions are matched in each panel if the panels are balanced by corporate chains.

Such experiments might be used to uncover at what price and market spending level sales and profits will be optimized. Obviously, the lower the price, the smaller are the monies available for promotion, and the larger the volume required for comparable profits. Yet through judicious testing of price-level and market-support spending alternatives, optimization of profits can be approached.

By optimizing accurate and meaningful data on *consumer acceptance* of his new product, the marketer has already solved much of his problem in terms of *trade acceptance.* First, the data are helful in developing trade acceptance. Second, knowledge of the best tactics (such as price or display space) can be related to the effort required to achieve these tactics. Finally, and most important, the entire introduction can be devoted to trade problems because the product is *known* to have customer acceptance.

The use of traditional test markets largely to measure *trade* problems is not a serious research challenge. The focusing of the effort on this one objective makes the measurement relatively easy.

The trade-acceptance objective can be clearly and realistically defined,

2. Doyle L. Weiss, "Simulation for Decision Making in Marketing," *Journal of Marketing,* Vol. 28 (July, 1964), pp. 45-50, at p. 49.

and the funds committed with confidence that would not have been the case without a measurement of consumer acceptance. In a sense, the variable of trade acceptance has been isolated and can thus be measured and resolved. Unlike *consumer acceptance,* trade acceptance is subject to change through commitments of time and funds.

PRODUCT TESTING IN
SEGMENTED MARKETS

BY ROBERT N. REITTER

STATEMENT OF PROBLEM

Marketers adopt a segmentation outlook when they recognize that consumers have different tastes. In reality perhaps all markets are segmented, but only some activities seem to call for recognition of taste differences among consumers. Entry into an already crowded, competitive category requires such an outlook. Here, an unsatisfied consumer segment represents a major opportunity. As more markets become competitive, the search for opportunities intensifies, and managements more frequently adopt the segmentation outlook.

Increased attention to such consumer differences should change thinking about two proven product research methods, paired comparison and monadic testing. Both methods are used to select the product or concept preferred by the greatest number of people. Such a testing process is appropriate in new markets when an optimal product has yet to be established. However, the process is quite inconsistent with the segmentation outlook. The traditional testing methods were designed to locate optimal products and concepts for markets as a whole. But these are by definition inappropriate for segmented tastes. In scanning the field for just this product and concept, the traditional testing methods necessarily ignore segmentation opportunities.

EDITOR'S NOTE: From the *Journal of Marketing Research,* May 1969, pp. 179-183. Reprinted by permission of the American Marketing Association and the author.

It might seem as though the segmentation outlook could be accommodated by simply altering the rules for interpretation of standard research techniques. Instead of approving only a product that won in a paired comparison test, a loss could be tolerated for a product directed at only one market segment. However, more modest targets would not solve the problem. There is no assurance that a minority vote signifies the presence of a cohesive market segment that would really prefer the test product if it were available. In a paired comparison test, some respondents only choose the lesser of two evils when stating their preference. In reality, products not represented in the test but available in the market would better satisfy them. Still other respondents cannot discriminate between the two test products; their votes are arbitrary. Accordingly, one cannot determine to what extent a minority vote results from unenthusiastic preference or nondiscrimination and to what extent from special appeal to a particular market segment.

The problem is inherent in the traditional techniques themselves. Used consistently, paired comparison and monadic testing can help to achieve the probably unique mix of ingredients appealing to the greatest possible number of users. But these methods were not designed to help locate and satisfy groups whose tastes differ from those of the majority.

CHARACTERISTICS OF DESIRED SOLUTION

A testing method for segmented products should first be able to isolate the market segments in question. This should be accomplished directly, without using intermediate factors, such as demographic or psychological traits. Correlations between these factors and what people want in a product tend to be quite low [3], making their use as screening devices correspondingly inefficient.

A better and more direct approach is to *classify users by the features they desire in a product*. This way of looking at differences among consumers has been termed "benefit segmentation." The following hypothetical example will illustrate the advantages of the approach.

Example

A coffee manufacturer wishes to enter the market with a new blend of ground coffee. All of the blends he has tested have lost to the dominant established brand in blind preference tests. Realizing that the dominant brand must already maximize overall preference, he begins to think of finding a blend that is optimal for only one market segment—those who like a particularly strong, rich coffee.

Let us assume research has shown that upper-income people living in the East are more likely to prefer such a coffee. The next round of product testing is accordingly confined to this group. A blend produced to be especially strong and rich achieves 50 percent to 50 percent parity with the dominant brand.

It is not clear, however, whether this is the best blend for the marketer's purpose. Not everyone in the demographically screened sample desires a strong, rich coffee; perhaps some of the preference votes for the new blend come from people not in this market segment. These people would not be attracted by the concept of such a coffee and would be unlikely to try it in the marketplace; hence, their preference for it is of little practical value.

On the next round of testing, the manufacturer decides to use a subsample of respondents who describe themselves as preferring a strong, rich coffee. In effect, he decides to divide the sample by desired product attributes. This time, the new blend beats the dominant brand 60 percent to 40 percent among the strong, rich segment, and loses 35 percent to 65 percent among the rest of the sample. This result establishes that the test blend is at least suitable for the marketing purpose.

Classification by desired product attributes entails some additional advantages. The manufacturer can now obtain diagnostic information from his target market segment, which is isolated within the sample of respondents. He can determine whether the test blend is approximately optimal by comparing it with what the target segment ideally desires in a coffee. Perhaps an adjustment of its degree of strength and richness will further heighten preference for it. Moreover, he can compare reactions to the blend on a blind basis with reactions to a description of such a coffee, and thus determine whether the formulation and concept are compatible.

Testing Method and Objectives

Product and concept testing among market segments so defined allows the manufacturer to adjust formulation and concept to each other and to desires of the market segment in question. These adjustments can have great practical value. The formulation can be geared for compatibility with the communications about it and for superior performance as perceived by the target group. The effect is that those most likely to try the product are also most inclined to prefer it to other products once having tried it.

Ideally, the testing method would not require prior assumptions about market segmentation, but could scan the field for segmentation opportunities previously unknown.

The testing method should, therefore, accomplish these objectives:

   focus on the segmentation inherent in the market
   isolate segments in terms of desired product attributes
   test the appeal of given formulations among such market segments
   test the appeal of concepts or ads among the same segments
   test the compatibility of the product and communication about it.

PRACTICAL SOLUTION

Antecedents

The technique to be described here has several published antecedents. A few years ago, Kuehn and Day [4] proposed a highly rigorous method for eliciting distributions of consumer preference along major dimensions of brand choice. The method is not intended, however, for repeated use in testing individual products, since the sample sizes required are very large and the developmental work prior to implementation is time-consuming and costly.

Benson [1] suggested the addition of this question to preference tests: "If you had to choose between a product with more of characteristic Q and a product with less of characteristic Q, which would you rather accept?" Provided that consumer preferences are known to be distributed normally, i.e. with one mode and little skewing, responses can be used to estimate the distribution of preferences. But this two-choice procedure does not yield enough information to discover market segments—secondary modes in the distribution not located at the central mean. Accordingly the procedure is not applicable when these market segments become the main focus of interest.

Eastlack [2], in looking at this problem with respect to the coffee market reports the successful use of a modified semantic differential scale, permitting a graduation of response. The scale is defined by labeling its extreme points; for example, "less bitterness" at the left end and "more bitterness" at the right end. The nine choices separating these extremes are unlabeled except for the central one, which is marked "the brand I prefer to use." Respondents are thus asked to describe the given product with reference to their favorite brand on the criterion of bitterness and are given a series of graduated choices to express degrees of satisfaction in this respect. A modified version of these scales is used in the technique described next.

Description of Technique

This method has been used to test coffee, beer, carbonated beverages, and canned food products. Sometimes respondents tasted products in a central location; other times they were given products to use over time at home. Most of the tests elicited response to four unidentified formulations and several concepts or names. In all instances concepts and names were disassociated from formulations actually tasted.

Before responding to any test products, respondents described their ideal in the category under consideration by marking a series of semantic differential scales at the point that best represented what an ideal coffee,

beer, etc., would be like. The scales were developed to include the
dimensions considered important by every market segment of appreciable
size. A representative sample was asked to rate the importance of several
attributes. When necessary, items rated as very important were selected for
scaling after factor analysis had removed those among which high correlation existed.

Some of the scales used in testing coffee were:

Strong	_____	Mild
Not rich	_____	Rich
Bitter	_____	Not bitter

Respondents first marked these lines to describe an ideal coffee; the
marks of course represented purely verbal, approximate response. They
continued to describe the taste of actual formulations using the scales on
which the ideal had already been marked. The mark then functioned as a
reference point, against which to evaluate given taste sensations. In effect
the scales allowed nonverbal response to the implied questions, *Is this taste
just as I like it, or is it too strong or mild? To what extent is it too strong or
mild?* etc., for each of the scales used in the test.

Besides these qualitative taste ratings, respondents indicated preferences
by ranking all blind products on an overall liking scale.

Product concepts were presented in the form of print ads or simply as
brand names written on plain cards. Responses were again elicited on the
semantic differential scales, which by this time contained marks for the
ideal product and each of (usually) four unidentified formulations. Although each test was limited to four formulations to avoid taste fatigue in
central location testing and excessive fieldwork in home use tests, there is
no need to limit severely the number of concepts or brand names to be
presented.

This interviewing method elicited great quantities of data. Each scale,
marked by each respondent, often provided about 20 useful comparisons

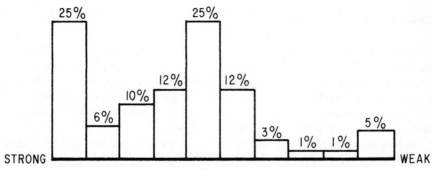

Figure 10-1. Distribution of ratings for ideal product.

from ideal to formulation and concept judgments, and among and between formulation and concept judgments. Since 10 or 12 scales were used in each test and these were usually completed by at least two hundred respondents, the resulting data tended to defy thorough analysis. Indeed, the value of the scaling devices used proved to depend heavily on the techniques used to tabulate and analyze the data. Even the sketchiest analysis would not have been possible without use of a computer. Presently, a computer program has been developed which, though far from exhaustive, presents the data in all of the forms that have yielded valuable insights thus far.

The program presents the distribution of ratings, mean, standard deviation, and standard error for the ideal product, for each formulation and concept on each scale used, among the following subgroups:

preferrers of each test formulation
preferrers to each test concept
brand usage
heaviness of category usage.

A separate series of tables shows overall preference cross-tabulated by location of the ideal mark on each scale. Here, the bases tend to be small, resulting from the wide dispersion of ideal marks typically found. Accordingly, these tables are used as interim data solely for analytical purposes. The distribution of ideal marks provides clues concerning the combinations that will produce the most meaningfull shifts in the preference data. The information is then presented in this form. Typically, on any one scale, two or three divisions are made to break up overall preference. These divisions are labeled for the scale in question; for example strong preferrers, medium preferrers, mild preferrers.

Inspection of the distributions guides the use of standard deviations to form the appropriate bands for statistical confidence. These simplify and shorten the analysis by screening out subsample comparisons that can reasonably be attributed to sampling errors. When the distributions deviate sufficiently from the normal so that nonparametric statistical methods must be used, few, if any, comparisons escape this screening. Accordingly, it is important that the scalar extremes be constructed to represent the real extremes of choice. The resulting distributions can still exhibit more than one mode but tend not to have the extremely non-normal forms requiring the use of less efficient statistical methods.

Examples of Results

Some examples, taken from actual test results, will illustrate these tabulations and their analytical uses.

An important but ambiguous tabulation is the distribution of ideal ratings (see Figure 10-1). Such findings reveal segmentation inherent in the market; the ambiguity lies in the unresolved distinction between consumer

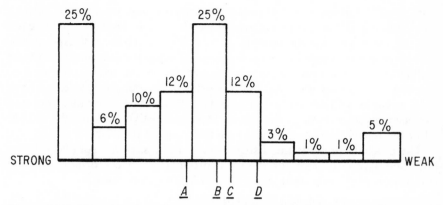

Figure 10-2. Mean blind product ratings in relation to distribution of ratings for ideal product.

differences based on words and images, and those based on actual tastes. The fourth of the sample choosing an extreme rating near the word "strong" may or may not enjoy what the producing technologist would consider a really strong product; perhaps they would only like to believe that their tastes operate this way. Despite this ambiguity, the distribution of stated preferences provides useful marketing information. This example indicates an opportunity for a product marketed as "strong." Just how

Preference among the test products would then be examined using the distribution of ideal ratings for cross-tabulation. Here, it might be most useful to contrast product preference among the 25 percent expressing an extreme desire for a strong product with the 75 percent distributed about the scale's midpoint (Figure 10-1).

With the distribution of ideal ratings as background, mean ratings can be plotted, showing reactions to the taste of the actual formulations tested (Figure 10-2). In this example, the four brands blind tested were considered fairly similar in strength; none appeared to have been formulated with the segment preferring a strong product as the target user group, although Brand A was the closest contender for this segment's choice.

The blind product descriptions sometimes provide surprising contrast with the disassociated response to what are in fact the corresponding concepts or brand names (Figure 10-3). Brand D, perceived as the weakest of the four on the basis of formulation alone, is considered the strongest of the four in terms of brand image. (Here, there was reason to believe that the manufacturer of Brand D, a leading brand, acted on the premise that people enjoy a product weaker then they would like to believe.)

Comparison of blind product preference with the stated ideal product has proved particularly valuable. That those preferring a given blind taste should differ from others in what they consider an ideal product is

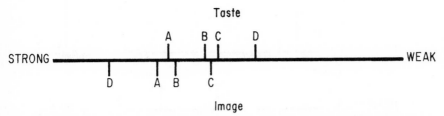

Figure 10-3. Mean blind product ratings in relation to mean concept ratings.

especially meaningful because the two sets of responses are collected quite separately in the interview. Thus the subjects form associations that they need not be aware of to reveal. In one case, for example, preferrers of the unidentified taste of a new brand were more likely than others to term their ideal product "nonfilling." The difference in mean ideal ratings between these subsamples represented 12 percent of the total scale length. Nonetheless, the difference proved to be significant at the 99 percent level. Accordingly, the idea of a nonfilling product was recommended as particularly appropriate in advertising the new brand.

One further analysis is useful to those responsible for the development of product formulations. This analysis is confined to preferrers of the formulation in question and compares ratings of the product against this group's stated ideal. On most criteria, it would be expected that the preferred product would deviate little from what is considered ideal. A study of the scales correlating most closely with overall preference can reveal the relative importance of the dimensions studied to this overall choice. Sometimes, however, the preferred product deviated from ideal on certain less critical dimensions (Figure 10-4). Here, Product Y, quite close to the ideal on other attributes, was judged too "tongue-tickling," a term interpreted by laboratory technicians as meaning excessive carbonation.

Flow of Information

Although the last analysis referred to is the only one specifically intended to provide information for the producing technologist, some of the other findings can also serve this function. Traditional product and concept tests have tended to produce summary scores. The preference rating is often followed by open-ended diagnostic questioning, but consumers' difficulty in articulating reasons for preference has often prevented the data from being useful. Hence, formulations and concepts are returned to those who developed them, often with a single number representing their degree of success. The analyses described here tend to improve this flow of information.

The scalar terms represent a partial bridge between the terminology used

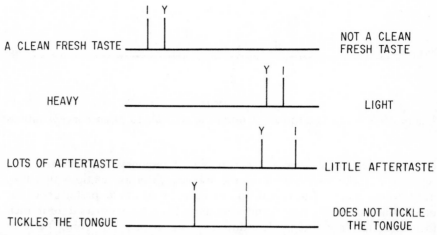

Figure 10-4. Rating of product Y and ideal product by preferrers of product Y.

by consumers and that used by developers of formulation and concept. To know that a product was liked by too few consumers because it was judged too "light" at least provides a clue for its developers. Although the clue tells neither the chemist nor the copywriter what elements to add or subtract, the finding may nevertheless suggest new directions. Subsequent tests will show how well the clues were interpreted. In the long run, the continued feedback process of diagnostic product research should improve the ability to match preferences as stated by consumer segments with products that will succeed in these segments.

CONCLUSION

Traditional tests of product concept and formulation ask,
How many prefer the test product?
In developing products for market segments, it is also useful to ask the following:
How close is the test product to the

best possible product?
product concept?
formulations of other brands?
image of other brands?

For how many people?

REFERENCES

1. Purnell H. Benson, "Fitting and Analyzing Distribution Curves of Consumer Choices," *Journal of Advertising Research,* 5 (March 1965), 28-34.

2. J. O. Eastlack, Jr., "Consumer Flavor Preference Factors in Food Product Design," *Journal of Marketing Research,* 1 (February 1964), 38-42.
3. Russell I. Haley, "Benefit Segmentation: A Decision-Oriented Research Tool," *Journal of Marketing,* 32 (July 1968), 30-5.
4. Alfred A. Kuehn and Ralph L. Day, "Strategy of Product Quality," *Harvard Business Review,* 40 (November-December 1962), 100-10.

ADDITIONAL SELECTED BILIOGRAPHY

Testing

Abrams, J., "Reducing the Risk of New Product Marketing Strategies Testing," *Journal of Marketing Research,* Vol. 6, No. 2 (May, 1969), 216-220.
Ash, W., "Test Marketing Simulation for Evaluating New Products," *The Professionals Look at New Products,* Brand, Gruber and Co., eds., Michigan Business Papers, No. 50, Bureau of Business Research, The University of Michigan (1968), 225-229.
Block, A. T., "How to Use Test Marketing," *The Professionals Look at New Products,* Brand, Gruber and Co., eds., Michigan Business Papers, No. 50, Bureau of Business Research, The University of Michigan (1968), 203-209.
Roscow, Y. S., "Can Success Spoil a Test-marketing Plan?" *Printers' Ink,* Vol. 295, No. 4 (August 25, 1967), 17-22.
Sherak, B., "Control and Reduction of Error in Marketing Tests," *New Ideas for Successful Marketing,* J. S. Wright and J. L. Goldstucker, eds., AMA Proceedings of the 1966 World Congress, American Marketing Association (June, 1966), 433-439.

QUESTIONS FOR DISCUSSION AND REVIEW

1. What is product testing? Product-line testing?

2. What types of testing are there?

3. Differentiate between product testing and consumer tests of a new product.

4. How can market testing prove beneficial to the firm?

5. What dangers can you describe in market testing?

6. Describe actual product tests that have been "interfered with" by competitive marketing strategy.

7. What alternatives to market testing are available?

11

COMMERCIALIZATION

Of the many new product ideas that have been analyzed by the firm, usually no more than a few are considered to be basically free from defects, considered satisfactory by a test market, and appear to have some cognition of future success. The guarantee isn't stamped on the product, but enough time, effort, and money have gone into the product to reduce the risk of failure. As an example of the number of new product ideas that have decayed and have been eliminated during the step-by-step new product process, a decay curve of new product ideas is shown below.

The stage in the new product process has been reached whereby the firm commits financial and human resources for building facilities or making present facilities available for producing the new product, and for pricing

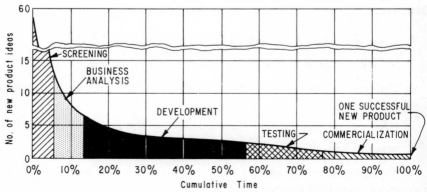

Decay curve of new product ideas (58 ideas). Reproduced courtesy Booz, Allen & Hamilton Inc.

the new product. These procedures involve more money and manpower, in most cases, than the cumulative costs of taking the new product idea through the stages of the new product process. As an example of cumulative costs, the following chart depicts the expenses incurred by a new product idea as it moves along the new product process.

The following articles discuss the commercialization stage of a new product and the adoption behavior of its buyers.

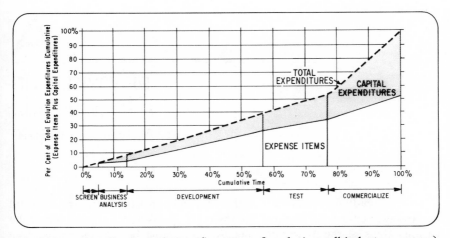

Cumulative expenditures and time (by stage of evolution—all-industry average). Reproduced courtesy Booz, Allen & Hamilton Inc.

A

READYING FOR
PRODUCTION
BY LAWRENCE D GIBSON

Getting ready for production and marketing consists of building the total marketing program and making the many decisions necessary in each of the various areas of the marketing mix. A name must be selected, a package designed, a price set, an advertising and promotion schedule developed. Literally hundreds of decisions must be made. Obviously we cannot consider each one separately. Faced with this kind of situation, the corporate controller of General Mills has often made the point that he cannot be concerned with all the decisions that have to be made in a corporation as large as his. And he has further suggested that there would probably be little profit to the corporation if he did examine each decision. In only a few cases would it be possible to evaluate the rightness or wrongness of specific decisions. The world is so complex that the effects of one decision become confounded with others, and thus each of us must wait for later events to prove a decision right or wrong.

However, it is possible to examine the *process* by which decisions are made. If the process includes the right inputs we can determine whether the decisions are based on sound premises. If they are, we then have some hope and confidence in the quality of the individual decisions. Two of the most essential premises of the process of getting ready for production for marketing are what is called "programming" at General Mills, and that

Editor's note: From *New Products: Concepts, Development, and Strategy,* Robert R. Scrase, ed., Michigan Business Papers No. 43, 1966, pp. 51-56. Reprinted by permission of the Graduate School of Business Administration, The University of Michigan, and the author.

well-worn phrase, "product concept," which we marketing researchers use
so effortlessly.

At General Mills we believe that programming is synonymous with
management. It is our word for the process of setting objectives and
checking our progress against those objectives. I won't labor the benefits of
programming, since they are self-evident. Programming forces us to a
careful examination of what our objectives should be, it ensures that each
involved person is aware of the objectives, and it disciplines our efforts to
make certain that everything we do is calculated to accomplish our
objectives. Finally, it makes us evaluate our progress in terms of the
objectives, so that we may see deviations quickly and take appropriate
action. We believe that programming is inherently a good thing. At the very
least, it attempts to guarantee that our decisions and efforts will be
internally consistent, and this is no small virtue. Unfortunately, though, it
guarantees only that they will be consistent, not that they will be right.

What then can we do to increase the odds that our programming will be
right—not merely consistent? Let me suggest that the answer lies in a far
more precise understanding of what we mean by product concept. We
really are awfully sloppy in the way we use this phrase. Our product
concept should be the focal point of our program. All of our programming
should be calculated to achieve, realize, and, if possible, enhance it. But just
exactly what is a product concept?

Webster says a concept is something conceived in the mind or an
abstract idea generalized from particular instances. That's no help. David
Hardin suggested earlier that a product concept may be defined as "a
synthesis or a description of the product idea embodied in the proposed
new product." That may be closer, but it is still too fuzzy for our purposes.
In the case of our new snack line at GMI—Bugles, Whistles, and Daisies—
our laboratory people could say, according to these definitions, that our
product concept was a shelf-stable line of salty snacks. Our packaging
people could point out that the essential idea was the use of a very high-
quality foil in the packaging to keep the product stable. At another level of
abstraction, our management people might say that the essence of our
product concept was the massive application of the resources and talents of
a major corporation to the solution of a technical problem which local
potato chippers simply couldn't face. Yet our real product concept, which
I am not free at this point to state precisely, is none of these.

Each of these statements about our product concept would be valid for
Webster, and many might be valid under the various definitions that we
researchers have traditionally used. But these definitions are inadequate.
If our programming is to be built around the product concept, then we must
understand exactly what we mean by product concept, and we must
communicate it precisely to each other and to the consumer.

Well, what are we aiming at when we use the words "product concept?"
What are some of the alternate words that we use to mean pretty much the

same thing? We say "product promise." We talk about "how the product will be positioned." Some people like the phrase, "consumer proposition." Folksy types like such phrases as "the real reason why they should buy," and even "what's in it for the people." This whole line of comment sounds very much like the old familiar question, "Why do people buy?" Let's look at this question to serve as the focal point for our program. We should at least be able to describe what an acceptable answer should look like.

Let me wander with a few stories. Why do we men buy fertilizer? Do we really want that 50-point paper bag of dry, granular material? I don't. That physical entity is a nuisance and an inconvenience. It's heavy. Sometimes it smells. Sometimes the bag leaks and spills all over the car. When I put it on the grass I don't do it evenly, and I burn the grass and skip spaces. It's really pretty silly. I don't want that bag of fertilizer. What I want is a green lawn—notice green, not necessarily healthy or growing. I want approbation from my friends and neighbors. I want a sense of pride in my home. I want to feel secure in my investment. And if someone can show me a better way to get a green lawn, approbation, pride, and security without that bag of fertilizer, you will see a very fast shift in my buying habits.

A can of oil is another useful example. Think for a moment about driving into a gas station and hearing those words, "You're down one quart." Do you want the oil itself, or do you buy it grudgingly? As a matter of fact, have you ever got out of the car to watch them put the oil in? How do you really know that they put in the oil you paid for? And yet you frequently drive away from the gas station feeling that your car is operating somewhat better because you paid the 65 cents. You didn't buy a can of oil. You paid for protection of a $3,500 investment, and you happen to be convinced that oil is necessary for that protection.

Well, here are two cases where we know something about the "real reason why." What are the common elements? First, we are not dealing with the real world. We are dealing with the world of perception or imagery. People act on the basis of their imagery, of the way they see things, of what's in their heads. How else can they act? Next we are concerned with people's needs for fiscal soundness, for personal pleasure, for sociological reinforcement. Please notice that we are using the word "needs" very broadly—not in a narrow or functional sense, but in a complete psychological and sociological sense. Incidentally, needs, so defined, are pervasive, expansive, and probably in the end insatiable. Then we are concerned with the attributes of the product—but as people see them, not necessarily as they "really are." Most importantly though, we are dealing with the consumer's perception of the *relationships* of those attributes to his needs. The critical issue is the relationship. When the attributes are seen as relating to the needs we have a "reason why."

What are these relationships? I like to call them perceived satisfactions. Other people prefer the term "values." Occasionally they may be dissatisfactions or negative values, but again the issue is a relationship. Obviously, then, I want to define a product concept in such a way that the customer will see the relationship between the attributes of the product and his needs. Often a simple statement of attributes is enough: "Butter Brickle Cake—the flavor of an old-fashioned candy parlor in a new cake mix by Betty Crocker." Sometimes we will work with statements of needs: "No more soggy sandwiches." But what we must always imply is the relationship between attributes and needs—the satisfactions.

This simple and fairly obvious notion is one that I find very satisfying. First it suggests the elusiveness of our task of defining product concepts, and of marketing. The reason we have difficulty grasping the problem is that we are not dealing with real attributes or real needs but with the *perceived relationship* between them. This definition implies that a product concept really doesn't exist independently of people. In turn, it suggests that all concepts face segmentation in the market place. We rarely sell all the people. Sometimes it is useful to define our marketing strategy in terms of the market segmentation. Either copy or media considerations may make this possible. However, segmentation is always with us in principle.

Product concepts, as we have defined them, are consistent with our whole pattern of marketing thinking, and, in fact, this is the essential issue of marketing. We as a corporation try to build attributes into our products which will be perceived by consumers to be peculiarly capable of satisfying their needs.

There are, of course, problems in attempting to apply this definition of product concept. If anything, the problems are more difficult under this definition. We can no longer feel safe in sticking to the attributes as a product concept. Some attributes may suggest satisfactions to people (One-Step Angel Food Cake); other may not (Bacon-flavored Isolate Soy Protein). So we believe that the old "we'll treat 'em equal with the bare-bones description" simply doesn't work. We have tried a number of approaches ranging from full-scale advertisements to the "bare-bones" approach. We have come back to the idea that we want the simplest possible statement that enables a consumer to see the satisfactions we believe she will derive.

One final thought. It is true that precise concept statements can be difficult to come up with. However, we think they are not only desirable but essential, and not just for marketing research but for marketing. If we can't come up with these statements, what are the implications about the difficulty that the advertising agency, the package-design firm, etc., will face?

With this definition of product concept as the focal point of our program our other tasks are simplified enormously. What is a good name for a new product? One that communicates its concept. What is a good package design? One that is consistent with and communicates the concept. What is good advertising? Advertising that communicates the concept. No more research about whether people like the name.

I thought you might be interested in a few examples of some consistencies and inconsistencies between concepts and products. The data I'm going to discuss are from a proprietary in-house technique, so you'll have to excuse me if I'm not able to tell you all the details of the research technique. The numbers I will use are indices of trial (a behavioral measure of reaction to the product concept) and repeat purchase (a behavioral measure of the product's ability to back up the concept).

A cereal was introduced recently which had an extremely high trial rate. In our technique fully 11 per cent of the people who were exposed to the concept bought the product. You will have to remember that in the cereal business a 1 or 2 per cent share of market makes a successful brand. And in our trial techniques most products are in the range of 4 to 6 per cent trial. The product's repeat index was only a little over .1, one of the lowest numbers we have ever seen in our technique. Why? The product doesn't back up the concept. It doesn't deliver the satisfactions implied by the concept. In contrast, one of our new products that looks very successful, Bugles, had only about 6 per cent trial but a repeat index of 1.0. Here's one that really delivers on its concept.

Finally, let me mention a test that we made using the same technique with one of our prepared food products. Using sample of 2,000 people per analytical cell, we tested this product with three different names and concept statements. We expected sharply different trial rates, but it turned out that the trial rates were very similar. On the other hand, one name and concept statement had twice the repeat index of the other two. When we talked to our home economists about this they insisted that the answer was obvious. The winning name and concept described more accurately what satisfactions the housewife could expect from the product. The women who selected the product on the basis of this concept were not disappointed. Apparently the others were.

So back to the original subject: getting ready for production, getting ready for marketing. We can't hope to examine each of the decisions individually. We have to understand what we are doing well enough to build a process that will work. We suggest that the key elements of the process are, first, programming—the simple act of managing—and, second, programming around a precise understanding of the product's concept. Finally, product concepts must be based not just on attributes of the product, not just on needs of the people, but on the relationships between the two—the satisfaction we want people to perceive between their needs and our product. Then it's easy.

B

NEW PRODUCT FORECASTING WITHOUT HISTORICAL, SURVEY, OR EXPERIMENTAL DATA

BY WALTER B. WENTZ AND GERALD I. EYRICH

"There is nothing more difficult to take in hand, more perilous to conduct, or more uncertain in its success than to take the lead in the introduction of a new order of things."[1]

Thus an Italian civil servant articulated the nature of innovation, over four hundred years ago. One doubts that a new-product manager, confronted with a new and novel good on one hand and the capricious and allusive tastes of the consumer on the other, would state matters much differently in the twentieth century.

The emergence of research as the fifth instrument of marketing (the others being price, product, promotion, and distribution) offers the firm the opportunity to reduce the uncertainty of new venture by forecasting demand. The basic tools of marketing research—historical data analysis, survey, and experimentation—are frequently missing when forecasting the demand for a revolutionary new product. Where could the electronics industry find sales data before introducing the television set? What kind of survey data could the container industry have gotten prior to the introduction of the tin can? How could one construct an experimental market problem for the diesel locomotive? Yet these were once new products with promising but uncertain markets. Each required substantial resources for their development, tooling, and market introduction. The rational alloca-

EDITOR'S NOTE: From *Marketing and the New Science of Planning*, Robert L. Kind, ed., 1968, pp. 215-221. Reprinted by permission of the American Marketing Association and the authors.

tion of such resources is dependent on several types of information, not the least being an estimation of total potential demand and the rate of market penetration—an allusive chore when restricted by the lack of historical, survey, and experimental data.

Given these restrictions, the normal market research techniques of multiple linear regression, factorial analysis, and statistical hypothesis testing are incapable of predicting sales. Marketing theory and analysis, when applied within the context of the theory of innovation diffusion, can be used to estimate demand.

First, a general model that identifies the determinants of demand must be constructed. This construction is then up-graded to an explicit form by estimating the parameters. The result is a function equating total potential demand to a series of terms representing the significant applications of the new product. Next, the theories and empirical findings of innovation diffusion are invoked to estimate market penetration rate. Applying this to the potential demand value, the market analyst can estimate the annual sales of the new product. Total potential sales is then adjusted for the firm's anticipated market-share, to arrive at a series of point estimates of yearly sales. If desired, the complete model can be converted into a stochastic model by explicit inclusion of probalistic factors through techniques such as Bayesian analysis. As experience is accumulated, variables can be added or deleted and parameters adjusted to reflect the realities of the market-place.

CONSTRUCTION OF A GENERAL MODEL

Selection of Variables

Presumably the dependent variable would be potential sales, hence the first task is to hypothesis the endogenous determinants of demand. In other words, list each of the various applications of the product and then select a variable to represent each application. Ideally a variable will have three properties: (1) It will be a reasonably precise index of the application. (2) Its past and present values can be readily found or can be estimated accurately and easily. (3) Its future values are forecastable. An example that conforms to these criteria would be adult female population as one the independent variables in a demand function for a new household product or service.

As the initial objective is to estimate total potential demand, the endogenous variables—price, promotion, and distribution—associated normally with the firm's demand function will presently be excluded. They will be introduced later, however, in the computation of market penetration rate. For now it is convenient to deal with the total demand for the new product.

As the product is defined as a new innovation, one can assume that the firm's demand curve should initially be synonymous with the industry's demand curve. If a strong patent is obtained, this situation will prevail. Even without patent protection the firm will likely enjoy a monopolistic position during the early part of the product's life cycle. It the firm lacks protection and the market accepts the new product, the firm will likely be displaced from its monopolistic position. This is almost certain in the long run. The Polaroid Land Camera is an example of near total protection. The Hula-Hoop illustrates the other extreme.

The search for applications and their companion variables should likely start with the innovator. Hopefully, he had some practical use in mind when he came forth with the idea. In fact, the idea itself may have resulted from the perception of a need or application in the marketplace. If not, the firm is well advised to discover such a need, unless it wants a warehouse full of homeless products. Orphans are expensive. This is precisely why such firms as the Carnation Company team a marketer with the innovator as soon as funds are allocated to a new product's development.

Having compiled a list of applications and their associated variables—a list that will doubtless grow after the item has been introduced to the market—one can state demand in the general form:

$D = f(X_1, X_2, \ldots X_n)$, where
D = Aggregate potential demand.
X = Independent determinants of demand $1, 2, \ldots n$

$1, 2, \ldots n$ = Applications $1, 2, \ldots n$.

To illustrate, assume the firm is about to introduce a closed circuit, computer-controlled television system which provides for the presentation of any published material for home reading through the use of telephone dialing. The particular applications might take the form:
1. Number of households in available coverage areas
2. Number of libraries
3. Number of major business firms
4. Number of hospitals, rest homes, and similar institutions
5. Number of educational institutions, above the eighth grade

Segmentation

A collateral benefit may emerge, namely segmentation of the market. If the applications and their variables indicate two or more separate and homogeneous markets, segmentation is possible. If segmentation is not a viable policy—due perhaps to manufacturing or distribution economies of scale—the identification of the market subsets will aid in the selection of product characteristics. This will help to design a good that can be more easily generalized to each of the market segments, when it is impractical to produce a separate product for each one.

At this juncture the firm has taken a step toward definition of the marketing problem, and has begun to frame the problem in manageable terms. Hopefully, significant determinants of demand have been isolated, so research can now be focused on them, and the firm can begin to allocate its resources with respect to the emerging product.

CONSTRUCTION OF AN EXPLICIT MODEL

The task of upgrading the general demand model to an explicit one is accomplished through estimating the potential demand of each variable. As the object is to predict aggregate potential sales, a summation of the individual elements of demand yields an explicit form of the demand equation as shown below.

$$\hat{D} = \hat{\gamma}_1 X_1 + \hat{\gamma}_2 X_2 + \dots \hat{\gamma}_n X_n, \text{ where} \tag{2}$$

$\hat{D}$ = Estimate of potential sales

$\hat{\gamma}_i$ = Estimate of the parameter of demand determinant X_i

X_i = Variable representing an application of the product

$1, 2, \dots n$ = Applications $1, 2, \dots n$.

Thus each $\hat{\Upsilon} X$ term represents the total demand for a particular application. If one or more terms are identified with applications unique to a particular market segment and there are no applications common to that and other segments, then their sum represents the potential sales for that market. A relatively high or low value indicates the relative importance of each market segment.

This technique is illustrated by using the previous postulated innovation. If variable X_1 is total households (50 million in 1960) and variable X_2 is public libraries (8,000 in 1960) and if total market saturation is estimated to be one "TV reader" installation per 1,000 households and one "TV reader" installation per public library, then total potential demand is 50,000 units for home usage and 8,000 units for library usage. The parameters Υ_1 and Υ_2 would be .001 and 1 respectively. This illustrates the method by which total potential demand, as a function of different applications, can be computed.

The estimation of the parameters involves an analysis of the applications. This may be done within the firm or with the assistance of the potential customers. The latter can also serve as a source of data for the manipulation of the product and promotional instruments. For example, in the construction of an aggregate demand function for helicopters in the petroleum industry, pipeline patrol emerged as an application. Discussions with pipeline operators and helicopter pilots provided insights that allowed for the computation of the number of miles of pipeline that could support one helicopter. Hence, the reciprocal of that distance became the parameter, and interterminal pipeline mileage (published data) became the variable of a significant application.

The final result of this phase of the problem would be an explicit demand equation, equating the estimates of total potential demand, $\hat{D}$, to a group of variables, X_1, X_2, ... X_n, which represent the significant applications— and possibly the market segments—of the product. An illustration of the form might be:

$$\hat{D} = .001X_1 + X_2 + .03X_3 + 2.7X_4 + .83X_5, \text{ where} \tag{3}^2$$

$\hat{D}$ = Total potential demand for the postulated product, television readers.

X_1 = Number of households in available coverage areas.

X_2 = Number of libraries.

X_3 = Number of major business firms.

X_4 = Number of hospitals, rest homes, and similar institutions.

X_5 = Number of educational institutions, above the eighth grade.

ESTIMATION OF PENETRATION RATE

Innovation Diffusion

The wealth of theoretical and empirical work on innovation diffusion provides a basis for estimating the rate at which the market will assimilate a new product.[3] If plotted against time, total adoptions will typically take the form of the S-curve shown in Figure 11-1.

The length of time from introduction to maturity varies considerably. Some products have been successfully marketed for many years, but are still on the early adopter portion of the growth curve. An example is electricity. Others, notably vogue items, experience a life cycle measured in months. The Hula-Hoop is illustrative. Although it is difficult to generalize to all new products, one can generalize with some precision by industry or product class. For example, women's fashions, toys, and movies have typically short cycles; automobile styles, men's clothes, and furniture have moderate longevity; and machine tools, aircraft, and computers have relatively long life cycles. Figure 11-2 shows the rate of market penetration for a cross-section of industrial products.

The buyer categories—both consumer and industrial—can be stereotyped with respect to psychological, sociological and economic properties. This is useful in the selection of promotional media and the preparation of

advertising copy, especially during the initial penetration when the innovators and early adopters must be identified and reached. Hence the
construction of a market penetration (adoption) model is very useful in the
manipulation of the promotional instrument.

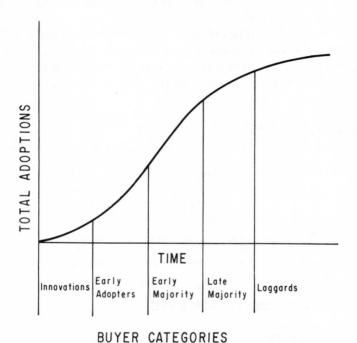

Figure 11-1. Adoptions vs. time and buyer categories.

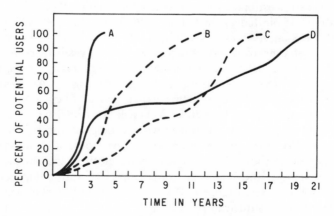

Figure 11-2. Market penetration vs. time.

Gompertz Function

The S-shaped form of the cumulative sales curve associated with the life cycle of a product suggests the use of a growth function in order to determine market penetration rate. The Gompertz curve is a commonly used growth function because of its unique properties. The mathematical form of a Gompertz curve is

$$Y = Ka^{b^x} \tag{4}$$

If $0 \leqslant a \leqslant 1$ and $0 < b < 1$, then $Y = Ka$ when $X = 0$ and Y approaches K as X approaches infinity. Such a function would trace out a curve similar to that shown in Figure 11-1. If we let:

$\hat{Y}_x$ = Estimated total sales X years after product introduction

K = Total potential sales

then the Gompertz curve can be used to solve for the rate of market penetration of the new product.

The computation of $\hat{Y}_X$ is simplified by transforming the function into logarithmic form:

$$\log \hat{Y}_x = \log K + (\log a)\, b^x \tag{5}$$

The graphical expression of $\hat{Y}_X$ is shown in Figure 11-3.

The K value, which is a constant, is the aggregate potential demand, $\hat{D}$, computed by formula (2). Like all exponential functions, the Gompertz curve is asymptotic to a limit, in this case $\hat{D}$, as X increases. This conforms to most real-world experience where there are almost always some potential customers who refuse to adopt a product. Even if these nonadopters could

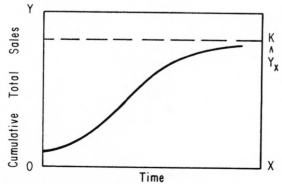

Figure 11-3. Gompertz function.

$$(\hat{Y} = Ka^{b^x}, 0 < a \leqslant \& \ 0 < b < 1)$$

be converted into late laggards, it is doubtful that the time and the marginal cost of the additional promotion, production, and price discounting would be justified by the marginal revenue from this final increment of sales. For example, as the firm approaches market saturation, large additional advertising expenditures produce very few additional sales.

Having estimated K by equating it to $\hat{D}$, the total potential sales, a and b must then be estimated in order to compute $\hat{Y}_X$ for each period 0 through $X = n$. A convenient solution is to first estimate $\hat{Y}_x$ at the start of the product's life cycle, $\hat{Y}_0$.

$\hat{Y}_0$ would equal the sales forecast for the first year of the new product introduction, X_0. As the Gompertz function is asymptotic to both K and the X axis, $\hat{Y}_0$ can never be zero. Hence the starting period (X_0) should be the period of the first expected sales. These starting-year sales would be based on management's evaluation of the size of the innovator population, the initial production release, the introductory promotional budget, and marketing estimates. Since X equals zero, the exponent b becomes 1 (by definition) and the formula for $\hat{Y}_0$ is reduced to simply $\hat{Y}_0 = Ka$. As both K and $\hat{Y}_0$ have been previously determined, a is the remaining unknown and is quickly revealed by simple algebra.

The next step is to estimate $\hat{Y}_m$ where m denotes the year of product maturity. Again one defer to similar products for insight into the percentage of market saturation that can be expected at maturity. The number of time periods, m, from introduction to maturity is suggested by experience with comparable goods.

By assuming $\hat{Y}_m$ is a particular percentage of K at $X = m$ (maturity), $\hat{Y}_m$ is readily computed. At this point all values have been estimated except b. The solution of b is most easily obtained by solving the equation in its logarithmic form after division by K as shown below.

$$\frac{\hat{Y}_m}{K} = a^{b^m}$$

$$\log\left(\frac{\hat{Y}_m}{K}\right) = \log(a)\, b^m$$

$$b^m = \frac{\log \frac{\hat{Y}_m}{K}}{\log a}$$

$$b = \sqrt[m]{\frac{\log \frac{\hat{Y}_m}{K}}{\log a}}$$

The Effect of Mortality and Obsolescence

If the product experiences either mortality or obsolescence, then the projected sales for each year, ΔS, should allow for their effect on sales. For example, if the life span of the product is 10 years, then replacement sales in the period X-1 to X would equal ΔS for the period $X - 1$ to X plus the sales at period $X - 11$ to $X - 10$. Total sales would then equal:

$$\Delta S_x = (\hat{Y} X - \hat{Y} X - 1) + (\hat{Y}_{x-10} - \hat{Y}_{x-11}) \tag{7}$$

$$\underbrace{\text{new}}_{\text{sales}} \qquad \underbrace{\text{replacement}}_{\text{sales}}$$

Similarly, if the product has an annual rate of attrition, as is the case with some categories of aircraft, then annual sales would be:

$$\Delta S_x = (\hat{Y}_x - \hat{Y}_{x-1}) + \lambda \hat{Y}_{x-1}, \text{ where} \tag{8}$$

$$\underbrace{\text{new}}_{\text{sales}} \qquad \underbrace{\text{replace-}}_{\text{ment sales}}$$

λ = Coefficient, representing replacement rate as a percentage of beginning year inventory.

$\hat{Y}_{x-1}$ = Inventory at start of period X.

The Effect of Exogenous Variables

The previous model holds K constant throughout the range of X. This may be an untenable assumption if product sales would be effected by the almost continuous increases in population, GNP, disposable personal income, and the industrial community growth. A convenient accomodation to this reality is the use of a variable K value—designated K', which reflects the increase of K with time. One reasonable relationship is

$$K' = \alpha K, \text{ where} \tag{9}$$

$$\alpha = (1 + i)^x, \text{ and} \tag{10}$$

i = the annual rate of increase in the market saturation level due to the effects of exogenous variables.

Thus our estimate of cumulative total sales, $\hat{Y}_x$, becomes

$$\log \hat{Y}_x = \log K' + (\log a)b^x \qquad \text{or} \tag{11}$$

$$\log \hat{Y}_x = \log \alpha K + \log K + (\log a)b^x \tag{12}$$

A graphical presentation of the effects of growth in endogenous variables is presented in Figures 11-4 and 11-5. Figure 11-4 presents the total sales and Figure 11-5 presents annual sales. In both figures $K = 1000$, $a = .01$, and $b = .8$. Three conditions are portrayed: (1) no annual growth, (2) an annual growth rate of 3%, and (3) an annual growth rate of 6%.

It is obvious that under a growth situation, a market saturation level in the maturity stage of the product's life cycle does not assure the decline and fall of the product. On the contrary, the replacement market and the

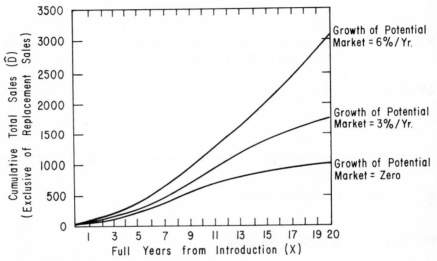

Figure 11-4. Cumulative total sales vs. time.

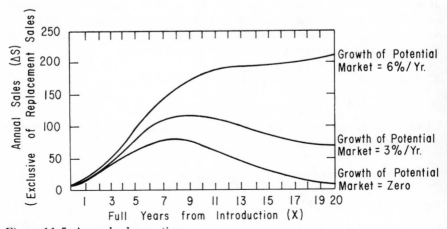

Figure 11-5. Annual sales vs. time.

upward movement of the market saturation level itself can provide continuous significant demand sales. Two examples are the automobile and private housing.

There are important implications of the maturity stage, however, It suggests a timing for the introduction of new products, especially in vogue product lines such as women's fashions, and the need for product variation. The latter is especially important if the firm has a large market share, but is threatened with the emergence of competition, particularly if the competitors were to engage in price competition and a strategy of product generalization. In addition, innovation diffusion theory suggests that the buyers who dominate the market at the maturity stage have different personalities and socio-economic status than those who accept the product early in its life cycle. For example, contact with previous acceptors of the product becomes very important as a source of information as impersonal contact, particularly printed material, declines in its effectiveness as the product enters the maturity stage. This implies a need to shift, or even reduce, promotional resources as sales pass the second inflection point on the Gompertz curve.

TEST AND REFINEMENT

A model built on assumptions is uncertain at best. Yet this does not deny its usefulness, expecially when the alternatives are abstention and pure speculation. In fact, the uncertain nature of the problem of new product forecasting suggests certain merit for the construction of a model if only to define the problem and reveal areas where further study is needed. It also reduces the problem to manageable dimensions. Perhaps more important, it provides a basis for construction of a more realistic model once experience and data have begun to accumulate.

The goodness of fit between the sales forecast and the reality of the marketplace can be inferred initially by plotting actual sales against the forecase curve. After time series observations are recorded, the parameters can be easily recomputed.

After initial market penetration, additional market insight can be gained through a cross-sectional or time series regression analysis. If the total market is segmented into homogeneous subsets and an accelerated effort is made to reach saturation in several of those cells, then a regression of sales against the supposed determinants of sales may reveal coefficients (Υ_1, Υ_2, etc.) which are appropriate to the demand model. If the market segments are not homegeneous—say they vary in respect to per capita income, family-cycle distribution, etc.—one might adjust the parametric values to correct for these differences through the use of time series analysis.

The use of a stochastic model is suggested by the uncertainty of the problem. Risk is inherent in virtually all new ventures. The explicit introduction of chance can be made by assuming the original estimate to be the most probable, or mean outcome, and then estimating a range of possible error. If the firm keeps tally on its estimates of parametric values, especially k and m, it might compute the distribution of the actual values about the estimates. An alternative is to examine the experience of the industry as a whole, or to query the firm's management. Managerial estimates might be tallied with a mean and standard deviation computed to render an error distribution about the estimated sales or by use of Bayesian analysis techniques.

SUMMARY

The uncertainty inherent in introduction of a truly new product suggests the need for a predictive model of both cumulative and annual sales. Yet the very nature of an innovation often denies the use of the more familiar techniques of market research. The lack of historical data, the impracticality of a survey, and the impossibility of market experimentation force us to look elsewhere for a measuring and forecasting method.

One technique is to first construct a general demand equation, identifying the determinants of sales by qualitative analysis of the product's applications. This model can then be developed into an explicit form, by quantitative analysis of potential applications. The result is an estimate of the total potential market.

As the firm cannot expect to capture the entire market in the first year—in fact the diseconomies of a 1-year production run would make it undesireable—the analyst must turn to innovation diffusion theory to estimate the rate of market penetration.

Experience with product life cycles indicates that cumulative total sales will likely take the shape of a growth function which can be expressed mathematically as a Gompertz curve. By assuming the estimate of the total potential market is the K-value, or asymptote, of the Gompertz function and estimating the probable time from product introduction to maturity, one can make estimates for each year's cumulative sales as well as annual sales. After initial market penetration, conventional market analysis techniques can be invoked for refining the demand model.

NOTES

1. Machiavelli, *The Prince,* 1513.
2. Note that this is not a regression equation although its form is similar.
3. See Gerald Zaltman, *Marketing: Contributions from the Behavioral Sciences* (New York: Harcourt, Brace and World, Inc., 1965), or Everett M. Rogers, *Diffusion of Innovations* (New York: Free Press, 1961), for a comprehensive introduction to innovation diffusion theory.

ADDITIONAL SELECTED BIBLIOGRAPHY

Commercialization

Charnes, A., Cooper, W. W., Devoe., J. K. and Learner, D. B., "DEMON: A Management Model for Marketing New Products," *California Management Review,* Vol. 11, No. 1 (Fall, 1968), 31-46.

Davidson, T. L., "In-use Product Evaluation," *New Products: Concepts, Development, and Strategy,* Robert R. Scrase, ed., Michigan Business Papers, No. 43, Bureau of Business Research, Graduate School of Business Administration, The University of Michigan, (1966), 77-84.

Day, C., "How to Set the Stage for a New-product Success," *Sales Management,* Vol. 94, No. 1 (January 1, 1965), 35-41.

Dusenbury, W., "CPM for New Product Introduction," *Harvard Business Review,* Vol. 45, No. 1 (January-February, 1967), 124-139.

Holliday, J. R., "Promotion during the National Introduction," *The Professionals Look at New Products,* Brand, Gruber and Co., eds, Michigan Business Papers, No. 50, Bureau of Business Research, The University of Michigan (1968), 230-238.

Wallack, L., "Why Certain New Products Survive," *Printers' Ink,* Vol. 282 (February 8, 1963), 21-28.

QUESTIONS FOR DISCUSSION AND REVIEW

1. What does commercialization of a product mean to a firm? In effect, what decisions are made?

2. Describe reasons for further testing at this stage in the product process.

3. What market strategy must be developed simultaneously with commercialization of the new product?

4. Should periodic testing be done? If so, what kinds of tests?

PART IV
PRODUCT AUDITING

A majority of the major firms in the United States are considered to be multiproduct firms. They would have to be if the firms are planning to remain in business for decades. Substitute products introduced by competitive firms, or similar products introduced after the expiration of patents, can and do curtail sales of the major producer. This chapter deals with a product's life cycle, the ways and means of pumping continual life into the product so as to reap profit benefits, and the demise of unprofitable products. Product auditing deals with cost/benefit analysis of each product so as to determine whether or not to find new markets for a product, change its design or packaging, institute a new promotional campaign, or curtail production and drop the product from the line.

PART IV

PRODUCT AUDITING

12

THE LIFE CYCLE OF PRODUCTS

What most product managers consider to be the normative form of a product life cycle is depicted below.

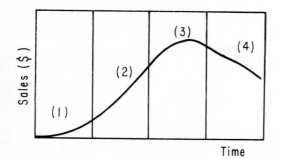

(1) introduction

(2) growth

(3) maturity

(4) decline

It takes time for the users to become aware of a new product, to use the product and if satisfied with it, to purchase it again. This is the introductory period. The reusers and new users combined form the growth period. After national coverage of the markets is attained, the product is said to have reached the mature stage in sales. When substitutes are introduced and loyal users are tempted to try competitors' products, sales begin to slip. If sales move down during successive quarters and are maintained at lower levels or decline further, the product has reached the declining state. It must be understood, however, that not all products go through the above stages during the same time span. For instance, a new product's life cycle could appear like A, B, or C.

The following articles deal with the life cycle of products and explain its variance. They also discuss methods and means to extend the life cycle, thereby creating additional profits for the firm, and the validity of the life cycle as a measuring tool.

PRODUCT LIFE CYCLES AS
MARKETING MODELS
BY WILLIAM E. COX, JR.

Product life cycles have been widely discussed in marketing literature. The discussions universally conclude that it would be desirable to determine the life cycles of the products of the firm and its competitors. But can product life cycles actually be calculated and used in marketing management? Product life cycles not only *can* be determined; they are particularly useful as marketing models.

The concept of the product life cycle basically describes the evolution of a product, as measured by its sales over time. Every product passes through a series of stages in the course of its life, with the total of the stages considered as the product life cycle. At any given time, therefore, every product is located within one of four life-cycle states—Introduction, Growth, Maturity, and Decline.

Various writers have emphasized the value of a product-life-cycle model as a basis for product planning and control.[1] In these sources, however, the product life cycle is presented as a qualitative concept. These writers indorse the use of the product life cycle as a framework for management analysis but fail to consider problems encountered in the measurement of product life cycles. Since measurement problems must be resolved prior to the quantification of product life cycles, this article emphasizes this neglected area. In addition, there is an examination of promotional strategy

EDITOR's NOTE: From *The Journal of Business,* October 1967, pp. 375-384. Reprinted by permission of the publisher and the author. Copyright © 1967 by the University of Chicago Press.

in each stage of the life cycle, and statistical evidence regarding the nature of product life cycles is provided for a select group of products.

THE LIFE CYCLES OF ETHICAL DRUGS

In the development of the concept of the product life cycle as a management tool, it is desirable to collect empirical data in order to formulate the life-cycle model proposed by Forrester and others. The collection of empirical data in turn requires that the scope of such an investigation be limited, preferably to a single industry or market. The ethical-drug industry was selected for the initial development of a product-life-cycle model. The products of ethical-drug firms are called "ethical" because they may be purchased only upon the prescription of a physician. In addition, ethical drugs are promoted to physicians and druggists, rather than the ultimate consumer.

A sample of 754 ethical-drug products introduced in the United States in the years 1955-60 forms the basis for the construction of the model of the product life cycle.[2] The sample was drawn from records of new product introductions in the drug industry. These records are prepared and maintained by an industry consultant, Paul de Haen, and are widely used in the drug industry. Access to the records was provided by Mr. de Haen; the development of product life cycles for ethical drugs was greatly facilitated by the availability of such records. The absence of records of product introductions for most industries means that the construction of life-cycle models in these industries must begin with a compilation of new product introductions. The difficulty of preparing such a compilation is perhaps the most serious obstacle to the widespread development of product life cycles for a variety of industries and products.

If a record of new product introductions is available, the next step in the construction of quantitative models of the product life cycles in an industry requires that "product life" be carefully defined and measured. Product life may be initially defined as the time span between birth and death. But how should product birth and death be defined and measured? A search of the literature failed to reveal any previous attempts to define product life, birth, or death in precise, measurable terms. In the absence of precedent in any industry, the task of defining these term becomes critical in the development of quantitative models of the life cycles for ethical drug products.

CATALOGUE VERSUS COMMERCIAL LIFE

The determination of the product life of ethical drugs was initiated through the development of two measures of product life:

1. *Catalogue life* is defined as the length of time that a product is carried

in the catalogue of a drug firm or in the *Drug Topics Red Book*. Catalogue life begins with catalogue birth, which occurs when the product first appears in the firm's catalogue or in the *Red Book*. Catalogue life ends with catalogue death, defined as the removal of the product from the firm's catalogue or the *Red Book*.

2. *Commercial life* is defined as the length of time between the following:

a) Commercial birth requires that a product achieve a national sales volume of five thousand new prescriptions in a single month. This requirement was established by a drug-industry committee of subscribers to the reports of Medical Data Services, Inc., Darien, Connecticut. While five thousand new prescriptions are considered to be the best single measure of commercial birth, it is an inappropriate measure for many products and firms. (Medical Data Services provided the data on prescription volume and manufacturers' revenue which was required to develop the product life cycles of ethical drugs.)

b) Commercial death occurs when the total dollar revenue for a drug product falls to 20 per cent of the maximum monthly total dollar revenue during the commercial life of the product. An alternative death rule of 10 per cent of maximum revenue is also calculated for comparison with the findings resulting from the 20 per cent rule.

The employment of two measures of product life permits an evaluation of the temporal relationships among the introduction of a new product (represented by catalogue birth), the attainment of commercial birth, commercial death, and the removal of the product from the market and the catalogue (catalogue death). A graphic representation of the relationship of catalogue and commercial life is shown in Figure 12-1. Two measures of product life are as appropriate for other industries as for ethical drugs, since the distinction between catalogue and commercial life is of a universal nature. Examples of products which attain catalogue birth, yet fail to reach commercial birth (success), are common to most firms. Equally common are products which have reached commercial death but are retained in a firm's product line, so that catalogue life continues after commercial life has ended.

In applying the concept of the product life cycle to certain industries, it might be preferable to substitute the term "market life" for "catalogue life." Market life would then be defined as the length of time between market introduction and removal of the product from the market. The development of definitions of commercial birth and death which have broad application is one of the most important tasks ahead for the improvement of product-life-cycle models. In the ethical-drug industry, the definition of commercial birth was framed in terms of the number of new prescriptions filled in a given month. An alternative approach would be to use the total number of prescriptions filled in a given period. Different standards would be employed in other industries—units sold, sales revenue (in dollars), and similar measures of commercial success.

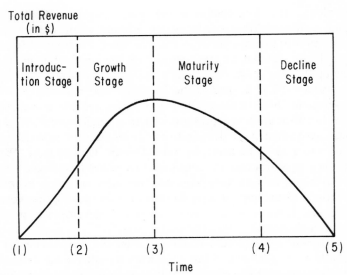

Figure 12-1. The graphic relationship of catalogue and commercial life and the stages of the product life cycle. Relationship of catalogue and commercial life: (*1*) catalogue birth—product is introduced in the catalogue of the firm; (*2*) commercial birth—product attains five thousand new prescriptions in one month; (*3*) maximum monthly revenue; (*4*) commercial death—either 20 per cent or 10 per cent of (*3*); (*5*) catalogue death—product is dropped from the catalogue. Stages of the product life cycle: Introduction stage—the time period between catalogue birth (*1*) and commercial birth (*2*); Growth stage—the time period between commercial birth (*2*) and maximum monthly revenue (*3*); Maturity stage—the time period between maximum monthly revenue (*3*) and commercial death (*4*); Decline stage—the time period between commercial death (*4*) and catalogue death (*5*).

Interviews with marketing managers of ethical-drug firms were valuable in formulating a definition of commerical death for ethical-drug products. These managers tended to define the commercial death of a product in terms of its commercial history. Thus a product which achieved a high level of prescriptions (e.g., fifty thousand new prescriptions in a month) at one time would be considered "commercially dead" at a higher level of new prescriptions than a product which never achieved such a high level of commercial success. (A product with a peak of fifty thousand new prescriptions per month would be commercially dead when volume dropped to ten thousand new prescriptions per month, under the 20 per cent death rule mentioned earlier. A product with a maximum level of five thousand new prescriptions per month would be commercially dead at one thousand new prescriptions per month under the same rule.) In summary, commercial death is relative to the level of commerical success attained during product life. This formulation thereby recognizes the influence of scales of production and distribution upon commercial death, a recognition which would be absent in the use of an absolute measure of commercial death.

If the four components of product life (catalogue birth, commerical birth, commerical death, and catalogue death) are combined with a measurement of the maximum revenue attained during product life, the resulting five components may be used to define precisely the four stages of the product life cycle, as shown in Figure 12-1. In addition, the development of measures of product life is valuable in planning the firm's product line and its promotional strategy. Estimates of expected product life may be employed in planning the introduction of new products and the retirement of old products. Measures of expected life, together with the estimated sales revenue and profits during the expected life, provide an important part of the information necessary for planning promotional timing and expenditure.

The division of the product life cycle into four distinct stages makes it possible to study the characteristics of each stage. The ethical-drug industry again provides the setting for this analysis. Promotional strategy for ethical-drug products in each stage is examined, drawing upon the findings of the author's doctoral dissertation.[3]

THE STAGES OF THE PRODUCT LIFE CYCLE

Introduction Stage

The Introduction stage of the product life cycle is the time period between the catalogue birth of a product and its commercial birth. In the ethical-drug industry, this time period is short, with a median length of one month for the products studied. Only 313, or 41.5 per cent, of the 754 products studied reached commercial birth; it is therefore apparent that an ethical-drug product must quickly establish a market position if it is ever to achieve commercial success.

A short time period, together with the need to establish market position early, would seem to call for aggressive promotional effort in the Introduction stage. Among ethical drugs, however, promotional expenditures are usually at a very low level in this stage. Is it possible to increase the probability of attaining commercial birth by promoting products heavily in the first month following catalogue birth? This question is typical of those produced by the application of a product-life-cycle model to the problem of planning promotional strategy. In addition, the model provides a framework for establishing management controls as a means of checking on the fulfillment of plans.

Growth Stage

The second stage of the product life cycle, the Growth stage, may be defined as the time period between commercial birth and the maximum monthly revenue for the product. A study of the products reaching commercial birth established that the average length of time in the Growth stage is six months. Virtually all products (95 per cent) reach maximum revenue within thirty months following commercial birth. If the first two stages are combined, the average time between catalogue birth and maximum monthly revenue is only seven months.

Promotional expenditures for most ethical-drug products are at a peak in the Growth stage. What percentage of the total promotional expenditures over a product's expected life should be expended in the first two stages of the product life cycle? Use of the life-cycle model results in such questions and directs the organization of data necessary to answer the questions.

Maturity Stage

In the third stage of the product life cycle, the Maturity stage, an objective definition requires that rules of commercial death be established. In the study of product life, two rules were employed—20 per cent of maximum monthly revenue and 10 per cent of maximum monthly revenue. The Maturity stage may therefore be defined as consisting of the time period between maximum monthly revenue and commercial death (which occurs when monthly revenue declines to 20 or 10 per cent of maximum monthly revenue).

It was established that the median time span between maximum monthly revenue and commercial death is fifteen months under the 20 per cent death rule and twenty months under the 10 per cent rule. If the median time spans for the first three stages are combined, the average time between catalogue birth and commercial death is twenty-two months under the 20 per cent rule and twenty-six months under the 10 per cent rule. A typical ethical-drug product will therefore be commercially dead just two years after its market introduction.

Ethical-drug firms frequently spend more for promotion on products in the Maturity stage than is warranted by expected sales and profits. Product-life-cycle models are particularly useful for this type of analysis.

Decline Stage

The final stage of the product life cycle, the Decline stage, may be defined as the time period between commercial death and catalogue death. Only a small proportion (approximately 2 per cent) of the products reaching commercial death also reached catalogue death during the period of the study, resulting in insufficient data to determine the length of the Decline stage for the ethical-drug industry. On the evidence, it seems likely that average length of this stage is longer than the other three stages combined. The low incidence of catalogue deaths indicates that, if an ethical-drug product attains commercial birth, it is virtually certain to be retained in the product line regardless of its subsequent level of commercial success.

Non-price promotional expenditures should be and are generally negligible in the Decline stage, but there is an opportunity to compete on a price basis during this stage. Ethical-drug firms rarely use price as a promotional tool, however, preferring a general policy of establishing a competitive list price in the Introduction stage and maintaining that price over the life cycle.

NON-PRICE PROMOTIONAL STRATEGY OVER THE PRODUCT LIFE CYCLE

A group of forty-five products introduced in 1959 which reached commercial birth was analyzed to develop additional, more precise information about the relationship between non-price promotional effort and the stages of the product life cycle. Data on promotional effort were obtained from the same consulting firm which provided the data for the calculation of the life-cycle curves of the products in this study.

Analysis of the promotional efforts on behalf of each of the forty-five products within the stages of the product life cycle reveals that promotional strategy may take one of three forms:

Form A.—Promotional effort in the Introductory stage is zero or at a relatively low level, rises to a peak in the Growth stage, and declines to a moderate level (above the Introductory stage level but below the peak) in the Maturity stage. The Decline stage is not considered, because few products in the study reached this stage of the product life cycle.

Form B.—Promotional effort is at a peak in the Introductory stage and declines through the Growth and Maturity stages, with promotional effort at a higher level in the Growth stage than in the Maturity stage.

Form C.—Promotional effort rises through the Introductory and Growth stages to a peak in the Maturity stage. Promotional effort in the Growth stage is at a higher level than in the Introductory stage.

The majority of the products studied, 70 per cent of the total, followed Form A with respect to detailing (personal-selling) strategy. Thus detailing effort was at a maximum in the Growth stage of the product life cycle. Form B was employed by 25 per cent of the products and Form C by 5 per cent of the products. Medical-journal advertising strategy among the forty-five products also showed an emphasis on Form A, with 72 per cent of the products in this category. Approximately 18 per cent of the products followed Form B, and 10 per cent may be classed as a Form C strategy.

Direct-mail advertising strategy for the forty-five products again favors Form A, with 72 per cent of the products in this category. Form C was adopted by 18 per cent of the products and Form B by 10 per cent of the products. Direct-mail advertising strategy varies slightly, therefore, from the other two forms of promotional effort, as a result of the greater tendency to adopt a Form C strategy.

Table 12-1 summarizes the findings of the analysis of promotional strategy within the stages of the product life cycle and shows that a Form A strategy is the basic promotional strategy adopted by the ethical-drug industry.

Another approach to the analysis of the relationsip of promotional effort and the product life cycle is that of examining the timing of the initial promotional effort with relation to the product life cycle. Using catalogue birth as the time base, Table 12-2 shows that, for those products reaching commercial birth, the most common practice is to begin promotion in the same month as catalogue birth. There appears, however, a tendency for direct-mail advertising to be instituted after catalogue birth almost as frequently as it is started coincident with catalogue birth.

A group of thirty-seven products introduced in 1959 which did not reach commercial birth was then analyzed to determine whether or not there is any difference in promotional timing between products reaching commercial birth and those that do not. When products not reaching commercial birth are studied, it is apparent that there is a pronounced tendency to begin promotion after catalogue birth. Unfortunately, there is no information available as to the reason for this situation.

TYPES OF PRODUCT-LIFE-CYCLE CURVES

Pioneering studies on the product-life-cycle concept have generally employed a basic curve form which may be described as a simple parabola, represented by the equation: $Y = a + bX + cX^2$. Figure 12-1 in this article

Table 12-1   Non-Price Promotional Strategy over the Product Life Cycle of Products Introduced in 1959

	Introductory Stage	Growth Stage	Maturity Stage	Decline Stage
Detailing effort (in minutes)	49	97	35	. . . . . .
Medical-journal advertising (in dollars)	$5,472	$19,489	$9,432	. . . . . .
Direct-mail advertising (in dollars)	$3,399	$16,255	$8,816	. . . . . .

Note: Data shown are the arithmetic means of the monthly averages in the promotional forms.

Table 12-2   The Relationship between the Timing of Promotional Effort and Catalogue Birth in the Product Life Cycle

	Timing of Initial Promotion (Per Cent)		
	Prior to Catalogue Birth	Coincident with Catalogue Birth	After Catalogue Birth
Products reaching commercial birth:			
Detailing effort (in minutes)	27	55	18
Medical-journal advertising (in dollars)	13	62	25
Direct-mail advertising (in dollars)	7	49	44
Product not reaching commercial birth:			
Detailing effort (in minutes)	15	38	47
Medical-journal advertising (in dollars)	7	33	60
Direct-mail advertising (in dollars)	5	27	68

displays this basic curve. May has noted that there are many exceptions to this basic form and presents five examples of variations in life-cycle curves, with four of the five examples devoted to changes in skewness and kurtosis from the basic curve type.[4] May's fifth example may be described as a linear function, with sales (plotted on the Y or vertical axis) remaining relatively constant at a low level over time.

May notes that this example "shows the sales curve for a type of product of which there are probably more than any other—the product which was never during its entire life able to find a niche, grow and perform the mission for which it was designed." This conclusion is applicable to the ethical-drug industry, since 58.5 per cent of the ethical-drug products studied did not reach commercial birth. Thus the establishment of a commercial-birth rule (five thousand new prescriptions must be written for a product in a given month) results in the assignment of most ethical-drug products to a subthreshold category in which there is little interest in studying the variations in sales over time. An analysis of product-life-cycle curves is meaningful, therefore, only for those products which attain commercial birth.

A sample of 258 ethical-drug products introduced during 1955-59 which attained commercial birth was studied to determine the types of product-life-cycle curves present in the ethical-drug industry. It was found that six types of life-cycle curves were needed to describe the 258 products in the sample. The six types of curves and their mathematical equations are presented in Figure 12-2.

It has been noted that earlier studies of the life cycle have employed a simple parabola as the basic curve form, and this curve has been designated as a Type I curve in this study. This curve form may also be described as a polynomial of the second degree. The Types II, III, and IV curves are

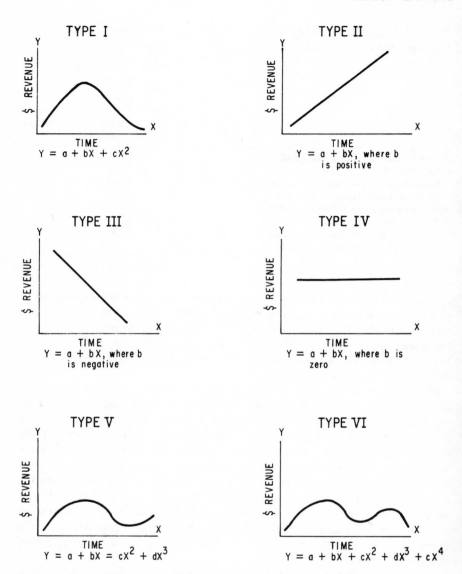

Figure 12-2. Types of product-life-cycle curves for ethical-drug products.

linear functions, with positive, negative, and zero slopes, respectively. The remaining curves, Types V and VI, are polynomials of the third degree and higher. These curves are cyclical in nature, in contrast to the Types I-IV curves, in which a clear secular trend is in evidence.

The frequency of the six types of product-life-cycles curves in the ethical-drug industry is:

Curve Type	Per Cent
Type I	28.3
Type II	5.4
Type III	12.8
Type IV	5.1
Type V	9.3
Type VI	39.1
Total	100.0

Type VI curves (polynomials of the fourth degree) may be considered the basic curve form the ethical-drug industry. Not only does this curve form occur most frequently in the study (39.1 per cent), but further studies have shown that Type V curves eventually become Type VI curves. The original study covered drugs introduced from 1950 to 1960, so that many products were in the early stages of their life cycles in 1960. By extending the analysis to 1963, it was possible to show that drugs with Type V curves in 1960 displayed Type VI curves by 1963.

Extension of the analysis beyond 1960 also provided evidence of a tendency toward a Type VI life-cycle curve for drugs showing Types I, II, and III curves in 1960. Only the Type IV curves (5.1 per cent of all drugs studied), therefore, failed to show a tendency toward the Type VI curve over time. Some drugs with Types I and III curves in 1960, in failing to transform into Type V or VI curves by 1963, apparently (1) were allowed to decline as a result of the introduction of substitute drug products or (2) had little price or promotional elasticity in the Decline stage of the product life cycle. Most Type II curves had evolved into Type I, V, or VI curves by 1963.

The principal reason for the predominance of the Type VI curves in the ethical-drug industry is the use of a promotional "hypo." A study of the promotional expenditures on behalf of the 258 products in the sample revealed that it is common practice to increase promotional expenditures sharply when an ethical-drug product reaches the end of the third, or Maturity, stage of the product life cycle. The promotional effort or hypo almost invariably results in increased sales of the product. There is a consequent transformation of the typical parabolic or second-degree life-cycle curve (Type I) into a third-degree (Type V) and, finally, the fourth-degree polynomial (Type VI), which is characteristic of the life-cycle curves of the ethical-drug industry.

Product life cycles in the ethical-drug industry, in taking the form of fourth-degree polynomials, may be said to represent a combination of "natural" and promotional market responses. Over the first three stages of the product life cycle, the typical parabolic form may be considered a "natural" response by the market to a product innovation. In the fourth (Decline) stage of the product life cycle, the promotional hypo will bring

1234567890

forth an additional market response, with the accompanying transformation of the life-cycle curve from a parabolic form to that of a fourth-degree polynomial. If there is no promotional effort in the final stage of the product life cycle, the parabolic (second-degree polynomial) curve stands as the basic form. In this case, the product life cycle represents the "natural" response of a market to product innovation.

There is an alternive mathematical treatment of the Type VI life-cycle curve that appears promising, although research is still in progress. The Type VI curve may be considered as a sinusoidal function with damped oscillations, with the amplitude of the temporal oscillations measured from their average level. If life-cycle curves can properly be considered as sinusoidal functions, three features of the curves could be described (period, amplitude, and phase), thereby improving the specification of the form of life-cycle curves. In addition, the potential applicability of Fourier Series analysis to the sinusoidal functions might further increase the descriptive and normative capacity of these functions when applied to life-cycle curves.

Interest in the regularity of product-life-cycle curves is based primarily on the potential use of these curves for forecasting purposes. Sales may be projected over the expected life of a product on the basis of a point estimate of the maximum sales level for the product. The estimate of maximum sales, when combined with the curve form associated with the given product, makes it possible to forecast the sales growth or decline with each stage of the product life cycle. The length of each stage may also be forecast, providing an estimate of the expected life of the product.

Analysis of competitive products may be incorporated with that of a given firm's product for the purpose of forecasting market share over the life cycle of the product. Product-life-cycle analysis may thereby provide the basis for the development of market-development models and facilitate the adoption of a comprehensive system for product planning and control in the firm.

CONCLUSIONS

In a multiproduct firm, operating within a variety of market structures, there is an important need to develop methods for allocating the limited resources of the firm in an optimum manner. The product-life-cycle concept appears to be particularly appropriate in this respect. In either structural or quantitative form, a product-life-cycle model emphasized the examination of product evolution, in which the current position of a product is scrutinized in relation to its past and future. Each product may also be investigated in relation to other products in the firm and the products of competing firms. A comparative analysis of the firm's product line within the framework of a product-life-cycle model may thereby provide a superior basis for optimizing the allocation of the firm's resources. Much additional work remains to make product-life-cycle models fully operational for planning and controlling marketing activities, but the paths and prospects for further development are clear.

LEVERAGE IN THE PRODUCT
LIFE CYCLE
BY DONALD K. CLIFFORD, JR.

Not long ago, a leading packaged goods maker was promoting a brand of toilet soap. Growth had been fair but not spectacular. Finally, product and market tests suggested that an increase in spot television advertising, backed by a change in copy, could help the product to reach the "escape velocity" it needed to become a sales leader. But management, feeling that the funds would be better spent in launching a new product, vetoed the proposal.

The new product was, to be sure, a moderate success. But the promising soap brand went into a gradual sales decline from which it never recovered. Management had pulled the props out from under the product at a critical point in its growth period.

Again, a product manager at a firm making light industrial equipment felt that his principal product was not getting the sales support it deserved. Unconvinced by the salesmen's claims that the product was "hard to sell," he developed new presentations and sales kits and persuaded sales management to run special campaigns. At year-end, however, volume had shown no improvement. With the power of hindsight, management recognized that this product had long since passed its zenith and that no amount of additional sales support could have profitably extended its growth. Yet the expensive promotion drive had cut into the marketing budgets of several promising new products. In short, management had failed to consider each product's position in its life cycle.

EDITOR'S NOTE: From *Dun's Review,* May 1965, pp. 62-70. Reprinted by permission of the publisher and the author.

As these two cases suggest, the concept of the product life cycle—familiar as it is to most business executives—is frequently forgotten in marketing planning. Yet there is conclusive evidence that if properly used it can transform a company's profit-and-loss statement. The concept is based on the fact that a product's sales volume follows a typical pattern that can be charted as a four-phase cycle *(see chart)*. After its birth, the product passes through a low-volume introduction phase. During the following growth phase, volume and profit both rise. Volume stabilizes during the period of maturity, although unit profits start to fall off. Eventually, in the obsolescence stage of the product, sales volume declines.

The length of the life cycle, the duration of each phase and the shape of the curve vary widely for different products. But in every case, obsolescence eventually occurs either because the need disappears (as when frozen orange juice hit sales of orange juice squeezers), because a better or cheaper

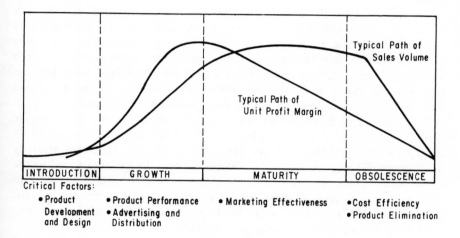

Profile of a Product. The wise marketer is aware of the critical factors underlying the course of his product's sales volume and profits. More importantly, he knows how to manipulate those factors to swell earnings. The chart above shows the typical shape of a product's sales volume and profit. The table shows a life-cycle "audit" of a product in early maturity.

Product XYZ, March 1965		Change in Past Year	Average Annual Change Over Past Five Years
Annual sales volume	$28.6 million	+2.5%	+11.8%
Gross margin	31.0%	−5.0%	−17.0%
Profit contribution	9.0%	−5.0%	−12.0%
Return on invested capital	14.0%	−4.0%	−12.0%
Price	$.85/lb.	−$.04	−$.11/lb.
Market share	16.0%	−	+8.0%

product may be developed to fill the same need (oil-based paint is losing its position in the home to water-based paint, and plastics are replacing wood, metal and paper products ranging from dry-cleaning bags to aircraft parts) or because a competitive product suddenly gains a decisive advantage through superior marketing strategy (as happened to competing products when Arthur Godfrey promoted Lipton Tea and again when the American Dental Association publicly endorsed Procter & Gamble's decay-prevention claims for Crest toothpaste).

The profit cycle of a product is quite different from its sales cycle. During introduction, a product may not earn any profit because of high initial advertising and promotion costs. In the growth period, before competition catches up, unit profits typically attain their peak. Then they start declining, although total profits may continue to climb for a time on rising sales volume. (In the chemical industry, for example, rapid increases in volume often more than offset the effect of price reductions early in the growth phase.)

During late growth and early maturity, increasing competition cuts deeply into profit margins and ultimately into total profits. For instance, as a result of drastic price-cutting, general-purpose semiconductors, once highly profitable, now return so little unit profit that major companies such as the Columbia Broadcasting System and Clevite Corp. have left the business entirely. Finally, in the obsolescence phase, declining volume eventually pushes costs up to a level that eliminates profits entirely.

What does this mean for the marketing manager? At the very least, he should always bear in mind that the factors behind a product's profitability change with each phase of its life cycle, and plot his sales strategy accordingly. Typically, product development and design are crucial in the introduction phase. For industrial products, where customers are slow to change from a proven product, technical superiority or demonstrable cost savings are often needed to open the door. For consumer products, heavy marketing spending may be critical in building volume.

During the growth period, reliability is vital to the success of most industrial products and technically complex consumer products. A well-grounded reputation for quality can win a manufacturer the leading position in the market, as it did for Zenith Radio Corp. in black-and-white television sets. For consumer packaged goods and other nontechnical products, on the other hand, effective distribution and advertising are crucial.

The key requirement during maturity, though harder to define, can be described as "overall marketing effectiveness." Marketing skill may pay off in a variety of ways; for example, by cutting price so as to reach new consumers, by promoting new uses for the product, or by upgrading distribution. During obsolescence, cost control is the key factor in generating profits. The product of the low-cost producer and distributor often enjoys a profitable "old age" long after its rivals have disappeared from the scene.

But although they are valid within their limits, these generalizations about the product life cycle do not really go far enough. For they fail to take into account a key fact: life cycles can be managed.

Life-cycle management, which adds a vital new dimension to the traditional life-cycle concept, has two basic aspects: (1) Controlling individual product life cycles to generate new profits. (2) Controlling the mix of product life cycles in the product line by carefully planned new-product introduction, product-line pruning and allocation of money and manpower among existing products according to their profit potential.

A product's introduction phase can often be shortened by increasing marketing expenditures or securing national distribution more quickly. In the next phase, growth can be speeded and sales and profits ultimately pushed to higher levels by exploiting additional markets, by pricing the product to encourage wider usage, and by more productive advertising or sales efforts; in short, by more effectively planned and implemented marketing strategy.

CHEATING OLD AGE

But it is in maturity that the shape and duration of a product's life cycle can be changed most radically. Is the product really approaching obsolescence? Or does it merely seem to be because consumers' needs are not being truly filled or because a competitor has done a superior marketing job? The question is crucial, since often the real challenge of "maturity" is not to adapt to it but to change it by revitalizing the product—through repackaging, for example, or by product modifications, repricing, appealing to new users or adding new distribution channels. And often a successfully revitalized product offers a higher return on management time and funds invested than does a new product.

Take, for example, the case of E. I. du Pont, which as a major force in packaging materials has been strongest in cellophane, a product so well-known it has become almost a synonym for transparent packaging. After World War II, flexible packaging, and cellophane in particular, entered a period of rapid growth. By the 1950's, however, new products began to meet certain packaging needs better. Polyethylene film, for example, was not so easily ruptured in cold weather, and in time it also became lower in price. As a result, cellophane began losing its share of the flexible-packaging market, and it was clear that sales would soon begin falling unless strong corrective action was taken.

Faced with this threat, du Pont launched a series of product modifications. These included special coating to reduce winter breakage and increase protection, new types of cellophane for different products and lighter grades of cellophane more competitive in price with the newer packaging materials. All in all, the customers' choice of cellophane types mushroomed from a handful to well over 100.

The results have been impressive. In the face of widespread prediction of rapid decline, cellophane as a whole has maintained its sales volume—of which the traditional grades now represent a relatively small fraction.

Further testimony to du Pont's effectiveness in life-cycle management is its control of the life-cycle mix of its flexible packaging products. Recognizing the maturity of cellophane, de Pont has developed a strong position in polyethylene and in other new packaging materials. So while maintaining its position by reshaping the life cycle of cellophane, the company has also provided for growth by adding new products to strengthen its product mix.

Another success in life-cycle manipulation was scored in the cake-mix market, where P&G introduced a large number of new cake types. This built sales in three ways. First, by broadening its line, P&G appealed to a wider market. Second, by increasing the variety of cakes, it persuaded women to make them more often. Third, by vastly increasing the number of cake mixes to be stocked in supermarkets, P&G achieved a billboard of cake mixes on shelves that inevitably drew the shopper's eye. In brief, Procter & Gamble increased the demand for cake mix and then filled that demand through the strength of its distribution.

Not all products, of course, can be revitalized in maturity. Maturity is forced upon some products by a basic change in consumer habits or a radically superior new competitor. In such cases it is important to recognize the fact promptly, and to cut back on the time and money invested in the product. In obsolescence, finally, marketing effectiveness is a matter of knowing when to cut short the life of a product that is demanding more that the small share of management attention it deserves.

Not long ago, a small candy company drastically changes its life-cycle mix by eliminating no fewer than 796 of the 800 items in its product line. By putting its muscle behind a single strong growth brand, and maintaining just three other products to offset swings in production, the company shifted its life-cycle balance from early obsolescence to growth. From a marginal producer, it has become one of the most profitable small companies in the confectionery business.

This type of successful product and product-line strategy is clearly the result of imagination, courage and sound judgment. It took imagination and initiative for P&G to expand its cake-mix line rather than modify its prices or advertising approach. It took marketing courage as well as judgment for the small candy company to cut its line by 99.5% rather than seek new brokers or start a fresh promotion program.

These companies, and others like them, were able to manipulate the life cycle of their products by making disciplined, periodic reviews of their progress. Such reviews should include not only a formal audit of each product's progress and outlook that pinpoints its position in its life cycle, but a profile of the life-cycle mix of the product line as a whole.

TRACING A LIFE STORY

Although the steps involved in the first part of a life-cycle analysis often vary, the following are typical:

¶Developing historical "trend" information for a period of three to five years, using such data as unit and dollar sales, profit margins, total profit contribution, return on invested capital, market share and price.

¶Tracing trends in the number and nature of competitors, the number and market-share rankings of competing products and their quality and performance, shifts in distribution channels and the relative advantages of competitive products in each channel.

¶Analyzing developments in short-term competitive strategy, such as competitors' announcements of new products or plans for expanding capacity.

¶Developing (or updating) historical information on the life cycles of similar or related products, to help suggest the shape and duration of the life cycle for the product under study.

¶Projecting sales for the product over the next three to five years and estimating an incremental profit ratio for the product during each of these years. The incremental profit ratio is the ratio of total direct costs to pretax profits. Expressed as a ratio—for example, 4.8 to 1 or 6.3 to 1—it measures the number of dollars required to generate each additional dollar of profit. The ratio typically improves (that is, falls) as the product enters its growth period, then begins to rise as the product approaches maturity, and climbs even more sharply as it reaches obsolescence.

¶Estimating the number of profitable years remaining in the product's life cycle and—based on all the information at hand—assigning the product to one of seven positions on its life-cycle curve; introduction, early or late growth, early or late maturity, early or late obsolescence.

Once the life-cycle positions of all the company's major products have been determined, a life-cycle profile of the company's entire product line can be drawn up. It works this way: Management first determines what percentages of sales and profits fall within each of the seven stages of this product life cycle, thus creating a "life-cycle profile" in terms of both sales and profits; it then calculates the change in the life-cycle and profit profiles over the past five years, and projects these profiles over the next five years; and finally it develops a *target* life-cycle profile for the company as a whole.

The target profile shows the desirable share of company sales that should fall within each phase of the product life cycle. It is determined on the basis of obsolescence trends in the industry, the pace of new-product introduction in the industry, the average length of product life cycles in the company's line, and management's objectives for growth and profitability. As a rule, the target profile for companies whose life cycles tend to be short, and for companies aiming for ambitious growth, will call for a high proportion of sales in the introductory and growth phases.

By comparing the company's target profile and its present life-cycle profile, management is now in a position to assign priorities to such functions as new-product development, acquisitions and product-line pruning. And once corporate effort has been broadly allocated in this way among products at various stages of their life cycles, marketing plans should be developed for individual product lines. Since each product's life-cycle position and outlook has been calculated, marketing executives, from the product managers up to the marketing vice president, have a far sounder basis for setting up individual product plans.

TIME FOR AN AUDIT

To illustrate the use of life-cycle analysis, consider a well-diversified company in the packaging business—a field where new materials and new forms of packaging are being introduced every year and where mature and obsolescent products still account for the bulk of sales volume. As a basis for planning individual product and product-line strategies, this company carried out a life-cycle audit, developing sales and profit information for each of its products.

For product XYZ, a packaging film *(see table, page 269)*, sales growth slackened last year. Gross margins, profit contribution and return on investment, which had all been declining since 1959, fell more sharply last year. Prices were largely to blame, but increased costs were also significant. Market share, meanwhile, had doubled in the previous five years, but showed no gain in 1964.

Two new competitors and four new competitive products had appeared, eliminating a former quality advantage of product XYZ. Sales analysis indicated that the top fifty accounts did 82% of product XYZ's volume in 1964, as against 68% five years earlier. In the same period, the total number of customers somewhat decreased. Finally, the incremental profit ratio appeared about to deteriorate from 11-1 to 12-1 in the coming year, rising to 15-1 by 1969.

On the basis of this analysis, marketing executives determined that product XYZ was in early maturity, with at least ten more years of profitable life in prospect. They decided, however, that a further increase in maturity could be offset, and additional growth achieved, if the film's tensile and tear strength could be improved by 25% at no increase in cost—an objective that appeared technically feasible. This then became a major element of their marketing strategy.

In similar fashion, the company developed life-cycle and profit profiles of its entire line. Only 6% of its current sales were represented by products in the introduction and growth stages, a far cry from the target profile of 25% called for (based on the expected length of life cycles in the business and growth and profit objectives). Management therefore decided to step up its acquisition program and new-product development sharply and to eliminate two obsolescent products. These steps cut the share of total volume represented by obsolescent products from 15% to 11%—close to the target profile of 10%.

The depth of life-cycle analysis, and the factors it must consider, vary almost as widely as do company needs, objectives and product lines. There is, then, no reliable formula for weighting the various factors that determine the life-cycle position of a product. But a management that makes good use of life-cycle analysis knows that it is this very flexibility that makes life-cycle analysis such an effective and widely applicable route to profits.

NOTES

1. Jay W. Forrester, "Industrial Dynamics," *Harvard Business Review,* Vol. XXXVI, No. 4 (July-August, 1958); and Arch Patton, "Stretch Your Products' Earning Years—Top Management's Stake in the Product Life Cycle," *Management Review, XXXVIII (June, 1959), 9-14, 67-79.*

2. Each ethical-drug product included in this study has the following characteristics: (1) a brand name, (2) a single manufacturer or distributor as the marketer, (3) a specific dosage form, and (4) a specific strength or potency. E.g., one of the products in the sample is Frenquel, manufactured by the Wm. S. Merrell Co. The product is more specifically defubed as Frenquel 20-mm tablets.

3. William E. Cox, Jr., "Product Life Cycles and Promotional Strategy in the Ethical Drug Industry" (unpublished Ph.D. dissertation, University of Michigan, Ann Arbor, 1963).

4. Charles K. May, "Planning the Marketing Program throughout the Product Life Cycle" (unpublished Ph.D. dissertation, Columbia University, New York, 1961), pp. 57-58.

ADDITIONAL SELECTED BIBLIOGRAPHY

The Life Cycle of Products

Brockoff, K., "A Test for the Product Life Cycle," *Econometrica,* Vol. 35, Nos. 3-4 (July-October, 1967), 472-484.

Buzzell, R. D., "Competitive Behavior and Product Life Cycles," *New Ideas For Successful Marketing.* J. S. Wright and J. L. Goldstucker, eds., AMA Proceedings of the 1966 World Congress, American Marketing Association (June, 1966), 46-67.

Kotler, P., "Competitive Strategies for New Product Marketing over the Life Cycle," *Management Science,* Vol. 12, No. 4 (December, 1965), B104-B119.

Levitt, T., "Exploit the Product Life Cycle," *Harvard Business Review,* Vol. 43, No. 6 (November-December, 1965), 81-94.

Patton, A., "Stretch Your Product's Earning Years: Top Management's Stake in the Product Life Cycle," *The Management Review,* Vol. 18, No. 6 (June, 1959), 9-14, 67-71, 76-79.

Polli, R. and Cook, V., "Validity of the Product Life Cycle," *The Journal of Business,* Vol. 42, No. 4 (October, 1969), 385-400.

Van Dyck, K., "How to Lengthen the Life of a Profitable Product," *Business Management,* Vol. 25, No. 4 (January 9, 1964), 30-33, 58-60.

QUESTIONS FOR DISCUSSION AND REVIEW

1. What does a graphic presentation of a life cycle predict?

2. How valid is the use of the life cycle of a product as a measuring tool?

3. Discuss several methods of extending a product life cycle.

4. Give reasons for differentiation of spans of product life cycles.

5. How can you determine the success of two products by comparing their life cycles? Can you assume their contribution of margin to be the same?

6. What methods or procedures can be used to exploit the product life cycle?

13

THE MORIBUNDITY OF
PRODUCTS

As mentioned previously, not all products go through a normal life cycle. Some products have fleeting success, then die rather rapidly. Other products go through an extended life cycle. Whether the demise of a product comes quickly or after a protracted period of time, steps must be taken to assure an orderly withdrawal from the market. Both internal and external factors must be taken into consideration. Internally, the firm must curtail production, make a decision on whether to sell off the inventory piecemeal or "dump" the inventory, decide whether to keep the fixed assets that made the product (machinery and equipment), and arrive at a solution about what to do with the productive labor resources as well as the sales manpower. Externally, the firm must make a decision on what to do with distributor or dealer inventories, whether to inform them immediately about the decision to drop the product from the line or wait until the inventory level is reduced, whether or not to accept immediate reorders at existing price levels, how to approach the dealer organization, and how to determine the future relationship with the dealers concerning other products of the firm's product mix. These decisions are especially important where the product has been accepted regionally or nationally, where a firm's selling organization is tied directly to a dealer representation.

Firms can also consider the possibility of selling the patent and all rights allowed under the law to the dying product. Ipana toothpaste is a perfect example of another firm buying the name and rights attached to the product and making a successful reappearance in the marketplace. It is important for the financial well-being of the company to set up a procedural mechanism and assign the responsibility to handle the activities which will bring the demise of a product to the most profitable end for the firm. The following articles depict the dilemmas faced by the firms who have dying products on hand.

WHY DO MOST
NEW PRODUCTS FAIL?
BY THEODORE L. ANGELUS

In 1968, 9,450 supermarket items were introduced into the market. Less than 20% met sales goals. The cost of these failures is extremely high. A single product failure can cost from $75,000 in test market to $20,000,000 for a national introduction. The waste in new product development alone represents 70% of the investment, not to mention the time and talent costs which are unrecoverable.

To determine why new products fail, our company has just completed an extensive survey in the consumer packaged goods field. We talked to over 150 advertising and manufacturing executives to get the facts on 75 major new product failures in the food and drug trade over the past several years. Where necessary, we cross-checked individual brand information to make sure the findings were reliable. We then spent two months analyzing and interpreting the data.

One overriding conclusion: The major reason for new product failure (and the most damaging) unquestionably is a lack of a real consumer point of difference. It is not a question of "me-tooism." Of these new products 80 percent have a point of difference in packaging or formulation. Unfortunately, the difference in most cases is important only to the manufacturer and not to the consumer, where it counts.

These unreal product differences generally result in the more costly new product failures. Manufacturers invest heavier behind a new product if they believe it has unique qualities.

EDITOR'S NOTE: From *Advertising Age,* March 24, 1969, pp. 85-86. Reprinted by permission of the publisher and the author. Copyright © 1969 by Crain Communications Inc.

To give you an idea of the range of products included in our study, a listing of some 25 out of the 75 new products we classify as unsuccessful are listed below.

NEW PRODUCTS THAT FAILED TO MEET DESIRED SALES GOALS

FOOD: Campbell's Red Kettle Soups
Corn Crackos Cereal
Dynamo Liquid Detergent
Easy-Off Household Cleaner
Gablinger's Beer
Heinz Happy Soups
Hunt's Flavored Ketchups
Knorr's Dry Soup Mix
Post Cereals with Freeze-Dried Fruit
DRUG: Code 10 Hair Dressing
Cope Sedative
Cue Toothpaste
Duractin Analgesic

Fact Toothpaste
Hidden Magic Hairspray
Measurin Analgesic
Manicurist Nail Polish
Mighty White Toothpaste
Noxzema Medicated Cold Cream
007 Men's Toiletries
Revlon's Super Natural Hairspray
Reef Mouthwash
Resolve
Subdue Shampoo
Vote Toothpaste

INSIGNIFICANT PRODUCT DIFFERENCES

When Menley & James introduced Duractin regionally in late 1962, they had a sustained release analgesic which gave pain relief for eight hours. This difference proved unimportant to the broad segment of consumers who wanted speedy relief. Cost of failure for the western region only is estimated at $1,500.000.

In 1964, Hunt introduced a line of flavored ketchups (Pizza, Hickory and Steak House). Consumers didn't respond to the difference and Heinz was virtually unaffected. Pizza and Hickory were ultimately withdrawn from the market. Cost of failure—at least $1,200,000. Del Monte tried again with the same idea with a slight variation: it was called Barbecue and contained onions. It failed in test market as well. It is interesting to note that the primary users of ketchup are kids who detest onions.

One of the most frequent failures in this area results from new product forms (tablets for powders, liquids for tablets, aerosols for liquids or pastes, frozen for canned). As an example, last year American Home lost approximately $850,000 introducing Easy-Off Household Cleaner. Easy-Off's point of difference was an aerosol foam formulation in a market dominated by liquids, Formula 409 and Fantastic. Consumers couldn't see any advantage to the aerosol foam because there wasn't any. Proliferation of brands and inadequate support were given as other reasons for the failure. Under the most favorable circumstances, Easy-Off never could have made it; it had no consumer point of difference.

POOR PRODUCT POSITIONING

Positioning problems fall into one of three areas—insignificant, confused or mismatched. Insignificant means the consumer could care less, confused means she doesn't understand and mismatched means product performance doesn't match the appeal.

Insignificant positioning is highly overrated and in most cases is a direct reflection of insignificant product differences. It follows that if a manufacturer develops an insignificant product, the advertising will reflect this. For example, Easy-Off's advertising was forced into using aerosol foam as a point of difference as the basis for a campaign. Introductory commercials showed Easy-Off in a side-by-side demonstration in which Easy-Off did not run as liquids do, but soaked up dirt. Advertising could not be faulted. The recall score was 38%, one of the highest Boyle-Midway had received on any of its brands.

Duractin's "Eight-hour relief" story attempted to give meaning to the sustained release difference, but without success. Even repositioning against arthritic sufferers where chronic and prolonged suffering is a real problem would have been rough, because arthritics have great loyalty to Bufferin, and the potential is severly limited.

Generally, when the product difference is real to the consumer, advertising will fall into place naturally. Usually, the most straightforward execution of the difference is the most effective. Examples of real consumer differences with non-gimmicky straightforward advertising are Head & Shoulders dandruff shampoo, Maxim freeze-dried coffee, Nyquil nighttime cold remedy and Piels draft beer.

A classic example of confused positioning occurred when Revlon introduced Super Natural hairspray in the early 1960s, and subsequently lost millions. Super means "more holding power"; natural means "less holding power." The consumer really didn't know what the product represented. Executives said the market was shifting to lower-priced brands, the Aqua Nets and Just Wonderfuls. Of course they were, because the higher-priced brands were not offering any real advantages, like Hidden Magic from Procter & Gamble, or new brands were confusing, like "Super Natural."

Mismatched positioning is the greatest single problem in the advertising communications business because it is prevalent on both new and established products. Mismatched positioning results in tremendous media inefficiencies. The challenge in positioning a new product is to determine the most effective combination of consumer appeal and product performance.

A mismatch occurs when the most effective combination has not been found. For example, Right Guard deodorant was positioned as a man's deodorant until 1963. When a switch in advertising was made with the claim, "The perfect family deodorant because nothing touches you but the spray itself," sales increased by $20,000,000 annually. Today Right Guard has a $50,000,000 franchise because of a more effective combination of appeal and product performance.

Mismatched positionings result when a product is developed with marginal product differences. The advertising generally takes the direction of the highest potential appeal area which may not relate to the performance characteristics of the particular product. Here's an interesting thought. In most product categories, there are at least 100 combinations of appeal and performance.

For example, in the shampoo market, possible appeal areas may be cleanliness, shine, body, manageability, softness, dandruff control, color hold, economy, unbreakable tube and non-drying formula. Against these ten appeal areas (and there probably are ten more), there are some 10 to 15 product performance characteristics to choose from. All told, there are 100 to 150 possible positioning combinations to choose from to achieve the most effective and efficient shampoo advertising story.

NO POINT OF DIFFERENCE

When you consider that 80% of all new products have a point of difference, "me-tooism" may be the overworked term in the marketing man's vocabulary.

"Me-too" products can be highly successful in certain situations, such as line extensions where a "me-too" can trade off a brand name. In 1966, Heinz successfully introduced its Heinz Barbecue Sauce, a "me-too," to "Open Pit." Heinz product line and quality image readily lent itself to an additional condiment line extension.

"Me-too" products can be highly successful in a market which is not completely saturated, so that advertising and promotional pressure become the determining wedge in building a franchise. But generally, "me-too" products under a new brand can never be marketing successes.

Several years back, Kaiser withdrew its aluminum sheet foil product from the market because it had no advantage over Alcoa or Reynolds Wrap. The market wasn't large enough to sustain a third entry, especially with rising price competition from private label brands. Pepsi-Cola's "Tropic Surf," a "me-too" of Fresca, may ultimately have to be withdrawn from the market.

In certain types of markets (cigarets, toilet soaps, hairsprays, men's after shave lotions and colognes, floor waxes, shaving creams, etc.), it is difficult, if not downright impossible, to develop a product that has a real point of difference. In markets that are flooded with "me-toos," product positioning takes on greater significance and flexibility.

BAD TIMING

Many new products fail because they get caught in a market explosion when several new entries are introduced simultaneously. Many manufacturers rush into these situations, in many cases with inferior product entries, hoping to gain a foothold before consumers get married to competitive brands. Inevitably, a spending spiral occurs, a shake-out results and the smaller or medium-size manufacturer gets squeezed out first.

A few years ago we saw the toothpaste and mouthwash market explosion, resulting in a combined loss of over $40 million from brands like Fact, Vote, Cue, Reef and several others. Last year, we saw the household cleaner market explode (17 new brands in nine months), and an estimated $5 million to $7 million loss from failures like Easy-Off, Clean & Kill, Whistle, Power-On, Crew, etc.

PRODUCT PERFORMANCE

True product problems seem to be occurring with less frequency each year. More sophisticated interpretation of product tests and greater emphasis on prolonged market testing give the manufacturer a greater chance of uncovering and solving product problems.

Manufacturers will, in certain situations, delude themselves into believing that a point of difference will outweigh a product problem. Many times a product test will not reveal a product problem because the unique aspects of the product are artificially highlighted in a product test. For example, in 1966 General Foods nationally introduced Post Cereals with freeze-dried fruit. Product tests did not reveal the extent of the consumer problem. Three separate market tests showed high trial and low conversion because the fruit did not reconstitute fast enough, and the cereal became soggy. Nevertheless, GF went national and lost close to $5 million.

Currently, Procter & Gamble is testing Echo in Indianapolis, a "one-step" clean and floor wax product. Unless the directions are adhered to word-for-word, consumers become dissatisfied with Echo's cleaning and shine performance. P&G is taking its time evaluating this problem, which, if serious enough, could cause the product to go back to the drawing board.

Performance problems seem to occur most often in food products because of the difficulty in assessing consumers' taste preference in other than prolonged testing situations. Campbell's Red Kettle and Knorr's dry soups were failures because of the difficulty in assessing the taste appeal relative to Lipton. Knorr's taste problem was a quality control difficulty which never was resolved satisfactorily. In any case, if manufacturers do learn anything worthwhile from product testing, it seems that a successful product test should not be sufficient reason for a national introduction. After all, 90 percent of the brand failure in this study had successful product test results.

WRONG MARKET FOR COMPANY

Procter & Gamble failed on two occasions to successfully introduce a hair-spray product (Hidden Magic and Winterset/Summerset). Colgate flopped miserably in the men's after shave lotion and cologne market with 007 in 1965. Colgate never made it in the food business, and American Home is failing in the dry laundry bleach market with Daybrite. Countless numbers of small or medium-size manufacturers are experiencing repeated failures in entering new markets alien to their existing product line.

These failures come about because the manufacturers do not have experience to generate a feel for the business, or else they overestimate their production, marketing or financial capability.

"Shimmer," a low-calorie gelatin dessert from Louis Sherry Co., has been achieving fantastic consumer acceptance since it was introduced in the New York market last May. Current projections show that the brand will be in the black within 12 months. A look behind the scenes reveals that the key man with Louis Sherry is an ex-General Foods executive who knows and understands the gelatin dessert business, having been intimately involved with Jell-O. Technical development on Shimmer was conducted by an ex-Jell-O research and development specialist, who joined the Louis Sherry team specifically to develop Shimmer. In short, these men were able to transfer their know-how and experience to the introduction of a new quality product with a real consumer point of difference.

As you would expect, few marketing men will admit their company entered a market that did not fall within its capability, because, in a very real sense, it reflects poor business judgment which could have been avoided.

A few conclusions have come about as a result of our study in the new product area:

NEW PRODUCT OPPORTUNITIES

1. A new product opportunity can exist in just about any type of market situation—large or small, growth or decline, multi-brand or single brand, commodity or brand items.

2. New product opportunities exist when a manufacturer has developed a product that has a significant point of difference.

3. Certain prevailing market conditions can make a particular market ripe for new product expansion. A few of these include:

Insignificant product differences between brands.

Unusually high profit returns and low advertising and promotion to sales ratios.

Lack of innovations over past several years.

High gross profit category.

Innovations in related fields that have application in other product categories.

New uses for appliances; toaster pops for example.

Low consumer loyalty and high brand switching.

Limited appeal of major brands in a market.

RESEARCH

1. Standard research methods are inadequate for new products.

2. There are no reliable predicative measurements in new products.

3. Product testing should not be the basis for introducing a new product, because 90% of the failures have had successful product test results. In many companies today, the final decision to introduce is predicated on an over-all win on a blind or identified product test. It is as dangerous to introduce a new product because of an over-all preference as it is not to introduce because of an over-all loss.

The key is to determine if a new product is preferred significantly on an isolated product attribute that can be related to a primary appeal area. (Ultra Brite, Colgate's tremendous dentifrice success over the last year lost all product tests, but enough consumers preferred Ultra Brite's sharp taste to indicate a viable franchise potential.)

NEW PRODUCT POSITIONING AND RESEARCH & DEVELOPMENT

1. Research and development projects should be started after brand name, package copy and advertising has been settled.

2. Successfully positioning a product after R&D is generally a hit or miss proposition, because the appeal area may not relate directly to the outstanding performance characteristics of the product. If this is the case, the entire brand presentation to the consumer would be seriously dissipated.

3. New product success does not have to be a technological breakthrough which should, in most instances, be left to the giants of the industry. As evidence of the high R&D waste on new products, greater success and less risk would be incurred if a portion of R&D funds were allocated to conceptual development and conceptual research techniques.

ADVERTISING AGENCIES

1. Most agencies are unwilling to make the same new product investment as their clients.

2. Agencies tend to employ inexperienced, low-priced talent on new products, putting their top people on going billing brands.

3. Most agencies tend to present a new product opportunity to clients in terms of marketing statistics rather than gettting to the guts of the problem, which is showing how to enter a market with a product that has a real point of difference to the consumer.

B

THE PRODUCT
ELIMINATION DECISION

BY JAMES T. ROTHE

The management of products throughout their life cycles is of great and growing importance in our economy. In less developed economies, functions are performed by the same physical means over such extended periods of time that the life cycle of products can hardly be observed and certainly is not of major concern to the businessman. In our economy, particularly since 1945, rapid technological advancement and high levels of income have induced such frequent shifts in customer preferences for products that the management of products over their life cycles is becoming one of the high priority managerial concerns.

While an enormous amount of attention has been paid to new product development efforts, little thought has been devoted to product elimination efforts.[1] This neglect is unfortunate because a planned and systematic product elimination program may contribute substantially to the firm's profitability and future growth. Profits can be enhanced by eliminating certain costs associated with products in the later stages of their life as well as by increasing the productivity of the resources released from the older products.

Most contributions to the product elimination issue have been theoretical in nature. Articles published by Kotler, Alexander, Berenson, and Kline develop a theolry of product elimination, but little research has been done on this

EDITOR'S NOTE: From *MSU Business Topics,* Autumn 1970, pp. 45-52. Reprinted by permission of the Division of Research, Graduate School of Business of the Michigan State University, and the author.

aspect of business.[2] Consequently, factual knowledge is extremely limited in an area where it could be quite useful to management.

This article reports on a study which surveyed the product elimination decision as it is currently being made by management. The study focused on: the importance of elimination decisions to firms, organization for and participation in product elimination decisions, the structure of elimination decisions, the degree of formality in elimination programs, and typical management problems with elimination programs. The study was limited to manufacturers of consumer products since consumer products tend to have shorter life cycles than industrial products. On the basis of buying habits, consumption patterns, distribution similarities, product similarities, and price similarities, a five category industry classification was developed: drugs, major appliances, food, clothing, and minor appliances. A sample of 100 firms was selected systematically for each of the five categories and two mailings of the questionnaire were used. Responses to the questionnaire were classified by industry type and by the degree of formality of their product elimination programs. These responses, where practicable, were then converted to means per industry and fomality categories on a 100-point basis. The equality of these means was then tested statistically.

Product elimination proved to be of interest to respondents. More than 40 percent of firms contacted responded to the study and approximately 30 percent of these responses were usable. The minor appliance category reported the largest product lines as well as the shortest life cycles for their products. For each industry category, the mean number of new products introduced annually exceeded the mean number of products eliminated yearly. This apparent proliferation of product line accentuates the need for improved total product management including product elimination efforts.

Firms rated product elimination activities approximately one-third as important as new product activities of the firm. Table 13-1 shows how different industry respondents rated each of the product planning and development activities. The respondents were asked to note the relative importance on a scale 0-100, 100 being most important; their average scores are shown in the table.

An interesting pattern of response is indicated in Table 13-1. Each industry rates new product activities as most important, changing or revitalizing existing products second most important, with the development of new uses and product elimination activities about equally valued and ranking third in importance. However, the drug industry rates new product activities higher than other industries while product elimination activities were rated most important by the appliance categories.

Marketing and corporate management executives dominate the elimination activity. Table 13-2 shows responses related to organization participation. The lack of financial executive participation in the decision was not expected and suggests an imbalance which should be corrected.

Professor P. Kotler recommended the three stage approach to product

Table 13-1. Importance of Product Planning and Development Activities

Activity	Drugs	Major Appliances	Food	Clothing	Minor Appliances
Planning for new products[a]	51	40	40	37	40
Developing new uses for old products	15	12	17	16	14
Changing and/or revitalizing existing products	24	32	31	35	31
Eliminating products from the product line[a]	10	16	12	12	15
Other			Few observations		
Total points	100	100	100	100	100

(a) Significant statistical differences were found among the means at the δ level of .05, using the one way analysis of variance, fixed effects model. Specific hypotheses were tested for all possible combinations of two means by the student t ratio at the same level of significance. This was done without added risk of Type I error because the within group variance provided an unbiased estimate of the variance of the treatment population. The results of this statistical analysis are interpreted as: (1) the drug industry respondents placed more value on new product activities than other industries, and (2) the drug industry respondents valued product elimination activities less than the major appliance and minor appliance industries while both appliance categories rated elimination activities higher than other categories.

Table 13-2. Organizational Participation in Elimination Programs

Functional Group	Most Important Participant		Second Most Important Participant	
	Number	Percentage	Number	Percentage
Accounting	1	*	14	8
Engineering	1	*	12	7
Finance	3	2	17	10
Marketing	130	75	27	15
Production	4	2	41	24
Purchasing			4	2
Corporate management	27	16	48	28
Committee	8	5	11	6
Total	174	100	174	100

*Insignificant Fraction

elimination decisions, as represented below in Figure 13-1. The approach was purely normative and represents an excellent starting point from which data can be generated to substantiate the framework offered. Modeling this part of the study after Kotler's approach, respondents were asked to indicate how they handled each stage of the process.

Recognition. Responses to the recognition state of the decision (see Table 13-3) show that minimum sales volume proved to be the most popular variable in recognizing products for possible elimination. Respondents

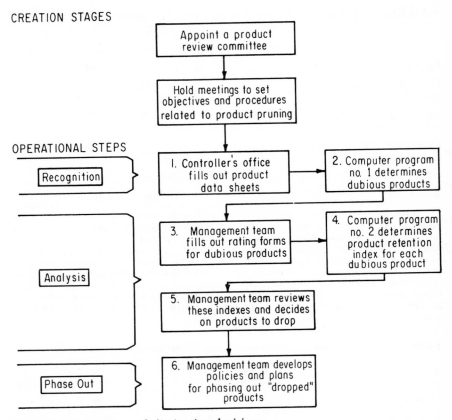

Figure 13-1. Structure of elimination decisions.

again were asked to note the relative importance on a scale 0-100, with 100 being most important. The average scores are shown in the table. Surprisingly, little attention was given to product profitability at this stage of the analysis. Life cycle theory would suggest that profitability analysis would be vital at this stage of the process because profitability figures tend to lead sales figures. This may represent a serious flaw in the recognition phase of elimination programs.

Analysis. Five factors were used by the respondents to analyze products previously recognized as potential candidates for elimination. Table 13-4 shows these factors and their relative importance; respondents again were asked to note the relative importance on a 0-100 scale, and the table shows the average scores.

The pattern of responses shown in Table 13-4 can be interpreted several ways. A general pattern emerges with respondents rating profitability first in each industry and market position second in four of the five industries.

Table 13-3. Recognition of Weak Products

Variable Used	Drugs	Major Appliances	Food	Clothing	Minor Appliances
A minimum sales volume	36	33	29	32	29
A minimum product volume	15	22	19	12	19
A minimum market share percentage	13	13	13	12	13
Some percentage figure of actual dividend by forecast sales volume	14	7	7	11	10
Some comparison of today's market share with previous years	10	10	13	12	10
A percentage figure of actual divided by projected production	3	6	7	5	7
Percentage of total company sales this product contributes	9	9	12	16	12
Other			Few observations		
Total points	100	100	100	100	100

Table 13-4. Factors Used to Analyze Weak Products

Major Factors	Drugs	Major Appliances	Food	Clothing	Minor Appliances
Product profitability[a]	45	31	45	31	36
Product costs[a]	11	17	13	16	14
Product investment	16	14	16	13	15
Company alternatives[a]	10	15	12	19	13
Market position[a]	18	23	14	21	22
Others			Few observations		
Total points	100	100	100	100	100

(a) Denotes significant statistical differences among the means, as explained in footnote to Table 13-1.

A wide degree of significant statistical variation exists among the industries with respect to how they rate a given factor. Four of the five factors employed by respondents were rated significantly different in importance for this phase of the elimination process.

Phase Out. Respondents were asked which phase out strategy they most often used. Surprisingly, the quick drop strategy was preferred to the slower phase out often suggested as a better strategy; the answers are categorized in Table 13-5.

Table 13-5. Phase Out Strategies

Elimination Strategy	Drugs	Major Appliances	Food	Clothing	Minor Appliances
Drop immediately	44.4%	53.0%	53.1%	78.3%	61.8%
"Milk" or slow phase out	33.3	41.7	34.0	15.0	28.7
Both drop and "milk"	21.2	5.3	12.9	6.7	9.5
Total percentage	100.0%	100.0%	100.0%	100.0%	100.0%

FORMALITY IN ELIMINATION PROGRAMS

Much of the literature dealing with product elimination dwells on the formality issue. An almost universal appeal for formal systems is readily apparent. Part of the purpose of this study was to look more closely at the formality issue. To do this, respondents' programs were placed in one of the three categories: highest formal development, intermediate formal development, or lower formal development. Results of this classification are shown in Table 13-6.

The data in Table 13-6 suggest that the drug and food industry respondents were less formal in their elimination decisions while both appliance categories were more formal. This is consistent with each industry's rating of the importance of elimination activities as shown in Table 13-1. The drug industry rated elimination activities significantly lower than the four other industries, while the appliance categories rated elimination activities higher than the other categories.

The most important issue is whether or not the degree of formality influences the factors used in the decision. An analysis of the responses to this study suggest that formality does not influence choice and rating of importance of factors used in elimination decisions. This is shown in Table 13-7.

The pattern of responses shown in Table 13-7 is similar to that of Table 13-4 in that the general pattern of results is the same. In each category, product profitability is rated most important while market position is rated second. However, at this point, one very real difference is apparent. When the responses to the analysis stage of elimination decisions were categorized by type of industry, widespread statistical differences were noted in how firms rated factors (4 of 5 cases in Table 13-4). Note that in Table 13-7, *no* significant differences were found. This type of finding was evident throughout this part of the study.

It seems evident that elimination decisions vary with industry category. That is, the relative importance of factors used shows significant statistical variation across industry type not found when responses were classified by degree of formality.

Does formality matter? This question can be answered by scrutinizing the industry category with the greatest percentage of "highest formal

Table 13-6. Formality in Elimination Programs

HIGHEST FORMAL DEVELOPMENT

Type	Number	Percentage of Highest	Percentage of Total Industry Category
Drugs	6	15	18
Major appliances	10	26	26
Food	6	15	19
Clothing	5	13	17
Minor appliances	12	31	28
Total	39	100	—

INTERMEDIATE FORMAL DEVELOPMENT

Type	Number	Percentage of Intermediate	Percentage of Total Industry Category
Drugs	12	17	36
Major appliances	16	23	42
Food	9	13	29
Clothing	16	22	53
Minor appliances	18	25	43
Total	71	100	—

LOWEST FORMAL DEVELOPMENT

Type	Number	Percentage of Lowest	Percentage of Total Industry Category
Drugs	15	23	46
Major appliances	12	19	32
Food	16	25	52
Clothing	9	14	30
Minor appliances	12	19	29
Total	64	100	—

Table 13-7. The Influence of Formality on Decision Factors in the Analysis State

Major Factors	Highest	Intermediate	Lowest
Product profitability[b]	38	37	36
Product costs[b]	13	16	14
Product investment[b]	15	15	15
Company alternatives[b]	14	14	13
Market position[b]	20	18	22
Total	100 pts.	100 pts.	100 pts.

(b) No significant statistical differences. (See note to Table 13-1 for explanation of methodology.)

development" responses—minor appliances. Minor appliance firms also had the largest product lines, the shortest life cycles, and rated elimination activities as very important. In short, formality of elimination programs is related to need rather than structure or content of programs. As such, it is not correct to assert that more formal programs are necessarily better programs, but that formality as an ingredient of the firm's elimination program should be tempered by need.

The responses suggested that several typical problems affected the management of elimination programs. The most common of these problems were: lack of top management interest and participation, resistance to elimination of products by sales personnel, lack of interdepartmental coordination in elimination programs, and lack of a regular routine for the program. These problems do not seem insurmountable, but the lack of recognition by top management of the importance of life cycle management at this end of the cycle would seem to be dangerous.

CONCLUSIONS AND IMPLICATIONS

If management becomes more aware of opportunities afforded by product elimination programs, the purpose of this study will have been achieved in part. While it is to be expected that the contributions of product elimination programs to the operations of a firm will vary, the proper performance of the program should result in increased profitability for the firm, through an improved growth rate since resources will be reassigned to more productive uses, and through the enhancement of the planning function in the firm through better exploitation of the life cycle concept. This study has attempted to show how a number of firms are currently making the product elimination decision. Unfortunately, it is not possible to prescribe an elimination program or system with numerically specified variables for all firms. Variation does and should exist in elimination programs since individual firm needs vary. In addition, it is not as easy to develop an index of effectiveness for product elimination programs as it is for new product programs (for example, the percentage of new product programs expenses devoted to successful new products). Rather the findings of this study with respect to the organization, structure and management of elimination activities can be used by firms to design elimination programs which will fit their individual needs. In doing so, management will increasingly recognize that product elimination efforts are a normal and necessary part of product planning and development activities. Certainly as increased competition and improved technology place more and more emphasis on managerial competence for success in the marketplace, the product elimination decision will demand more attention.

NOTES

1. D. U. Clifford, "Managing the Product Life Cycle," *Management Review,* June 1965, p. 137; and Peter F. Drucker, "Care and Feeding of the Profitable Product," *Fortune,* March 1964, p. 133.

2. Philip Kotler, "Phasing Out Weak Products," *Harvard Business Review,* March-April 1965, pp. 107-18. Ralph S. Alexander, "The Death and Burial of Sick Products," *Journal of Marketing,* April 1964, pp. 1-7. Conrad Berenson, "Pruning the Product Line," *Business Horizons,* Summer 1963, p. 63. Charles H. Kline, "The Strategy of Product Policy," *Harvard Business Review,* July-August 1955, p. 100.

3. Kotler, "Phasing Out Weak Products," p. 257.

ADDITIONAL SELECTED BIBLIOGRAPHY

The Moribundity of Products

Alexander, R. S., "The Death and Burial of Sick Products," *Journal of Marketing,* Vol. 28, No. 2 (April, 1964), 1-7.

Berenson, C., "When to Kill Sick Products," *Industrial Marketing,* Vol. 49, No. 9 (September, 1964), 98-102.

Constandse, W., "Why Companies Fail," *Business Management,* Vol. 39, No. 1 (October, 1970), 13, 42.

Kotler, P., "Phasing Out Weak Products," *Harvard Business Review,* Vol. 43, No. 2 (March-April, 1965), 107-118.

Sommers, M. and Kernan, J., "Why Products Flourish Here, Fizzle There," *Columbia Journal of World Business,* Vol. 2, No. 2 (March-April, 1967), 89-97.

QUESTIONS FOR DISCUSSION AND REVIEW

1. What are the primary causes of failure of products?

2. What steps should be taken when the decision is made to curtail production of a company product?

3. Who should be held responsible for the phase out?

4. Why does a product prove successful in one market while failing in another market?

5. Why do some firms feel that organization problems should be given primary attention?

6. Why do you think there are differences of opinion among marketing men, accountants, and production men as to when a product should be phased out?

14

THE REJUVENATION OF PRODUCTS

Many products that have reached a declining stage in their life cycle, whether or not they have been successful products, have been changed in such a manner that sales and profits have shown an upward trend. A rejuvenation can look like the following:

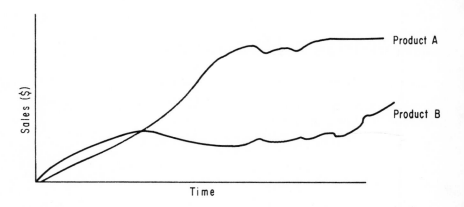

The reasons for the increased growth can be a change in the physical structure of the product, an addition to the product such as a new or different ingredient, a change in the label or the package, a new promotional campaign, or the discovery of new markets or new buyers. How many of us have seen product changes in automobiles, tractors, lamps, homes, etc., to denote physical changes of a product? Soap and toothpaste manufacturers have added bleaches, or whiteners, and protective compounds to their products. These additives have increased sales. Beer producers and food processors have made label changes to rejuvenate their products. Manufacturers have found new markets for their products that were thought to be nonexistent before the sales decline. The "jeep," helicopter, and candles are just a few of the hundreds of products that attained a "new lease on life."

If a firm introduces market planning techniques earlier in the life cycle of a product with the integration and use of market research, the life cycle of a new product can be extended. To rejuvenate a dying product, a firm can investigate the characteristics of the market, its present market penetration, its channel and its management, product characteristics and demand from potential users. The following articles discuss the problem of product rejuvenation.

NEW PRODUCTS FROM OLD: SHORT CUT TO PROFITS

BY KENNETH VAN DYCK

Most companies are afflicted with myopia when it comes to the opportunities for profit through creative redesign of existing products.

They know, of course, that a healthy budget for new product research is necessary. But they don't recognize that, in most cases, a far smaller amount applied to "product renaissance" can pay off more quickly.

The chances for success with any totally new product admittedly are slim. Dealing with your present line means starting on a more solid foundation with greater opportunity to increase your market and profits.

REQUIREMENTS

How do you know when a product is "ripe" for redesign? Here are four sure symptoms:

1. Profit slipping—Redesign to reduce cost or justify a price increase.
2. Share of market declining—Keep present customers while attracting new one.
3. Sales steady—give them a spurt with a redesigned product.
4. Absence of change—The very fact that a product has not been changed for a few years probably is reason enough to consider redesign now.

Recognizing redesign opportunities is only part of the job. You also must create a climate that welcomes changes.

If you must, resort to such gimmicks as "Product Evaluation Week" or "Product Audit Month." Announce an "anything goes" policy—any suggestions based on improvement of present products will be welcome. Create an atmosphere that will allow the people in your company to release whatever ideas they have.

You also should seriously consider the stimulation that external creative product development people can bring. Many companies that ordinarily follow a strict do-it-yourself philosophy use outside design consultants for evaluation of existing products, processes and packaging—just because of their objectivity.

START NOW

A redesign program does not have to wait for creation of a special climate or evaluation by outsiders. Here are some things you can do right now, with examples of how they have led other companies to profit-making decisions.

1. Tell your production department to dis-assemble your key product and re-examine the three components with the highest labor cost content. There may be a chance to reduce costs and maybe even price.

Stanley Power Tools had an objectively oriented team of specialists (insiders and outsiders) look at their low-cost power-tool line recently and cut the cost of one item by 8.5%, according to Jim Godfrey, director of product engineering.

At Baldwin-Lima-Hamilton's Instrumentation Division, in a similar "second look" program, sheet metal cases for their strain-gauge line of instruments were replaced with Formica-covered wooden cases—lower cost, more durable, and lighter. Harry Lockery, manager of engineering at B-L-H, says that the resultant quality increases and the improved human engineering features have significantly increased sales.

2. Suggest that your chief marketing executive give a one-hour report to your key department heads. Subject: "What Today's Typical Customer Is Looking For."

International Equipment Co. is the world's largest manufacturer of laboratory centrifuges. When its engineers heard that customers in biological and hospital laboratories wanted the centrifuge to harmonize architecturally with new cabinet installations, Richard W. Schmader, executive vice-president, asked his design team to completely redesign the product.

This resulted in a new machine with several important new features (electrical braking and electrical speed indication) as well as new modern appearance. Savings of 15% in manufacture permitted adding the new features without raising prices, and sales more than doubled over the next two years.

3. Ask your salesmen to find out what feature of your product the competition is "knocking" most.

Sperry Products Division, Automation Industries, found its Reflectoscope (an ultrasonic flaw-detection instrument for field use) was being criticized as "too heavy" and "old-fashioned looking." Sperry modified the electronic circuits to include modular capability, redesigned the case and front panel. Weight was cut by 40 pounds, and the redesigned instrument looked as new and professional on the outside as it was inside. Richard Nealey, sales manager, reports that sales increased significantly.

4. Have your market research people heard your chief competitor's sales pitch?

It's easy to find an outlet that sells both your products and a competitor's. Even at trade shows it's not unheard of for friendly competitors to visit each other's booths.

5. Tell your chief engineer to have another look at the basic product concept.

Encourage your engineers to use the knowledge built up over the years— bring out their creativity. Ask the head of your engineering department to re-evaluate your product in terms of its basic concept. Remember, the customer only cares about *what* your product does—not how its done.

Perhaps, if you stop thinking in terms of the present design or today's manufacturing methods, you'll come up with a new approach—a redesigned product that achieves the same result for the customer, but in an entirely different way. Engineering is a good place to go for this kind of thinking.

6. Ask your designer if the product really "looks" like the price it carries.

How much better it is to have the customer pleasantly surprised at how low your price is, rather than shocked at how high it is. The difference, to some extent, can be good design.

This is an area that has long been neglected for most industrial products—the accent has been on function rather than appearance. Today, however, especially with the accent on improved factory environment, the product that looks more modern, has "cleaner" design, will usually get the nod over the product that does the job but exhibits pedestrian design—if prices are comparable.

7. Talk to some of your customers—through a third party if necessary—to get their true reactions to your product and suggestions for its improvement.

It was partially as the result of customer suggestions that Fasco redesigned its line of kitchen hoods a few years ago. Reports president

Harry Sylvester: "Not only did the design improve, but we also cut manufacturing costs. As a result, sales doubled in a short time."

IMPLEMENTATION

It is very important that you prevent departmental rivalries from interfering with possible improvements developed by these steps.

Don't let the marketing or production departments, for example, feel so strongly about present methods that they won't entertain new ideas. Let someone in a neutral position, possibly an outside consultant, assemble, referee and evaluate all the suggestions you receive.

Even if you score some successes on the first product, don't relax. Try another one next month.

Press for reevaluation of every product you make at least every three to five years—if you want to take full advantage of this concept.

B

MARKET PROBING EXPANDS TO AVERT PRODUCT FLOPS

Judging by inquiries it receives, says the National Industrial Conference Board, one of the more pressing concerns of the industrial marketer is the high rate of new product mortality. With the rate of product obsolescence accelerating, he wants to know: How can I reduce the risk of failure in developing and launching new products?

In a just-released study, "Appraising the Market for New Industrial Products," NICB supplies some answers drawn from the experience of more than 100 U.S. and Canadian industrial firms. The 112-page book, which includes detailed descriptions of the methods employed by 15 companies, is No. 123 in NICB's "Studies in Business Policy" series.

The study suggests there is increasing emphasis in the industrial field on improving and broadening the scope of marketing planning and research for new products.

"Many managements acknowledge that the factors contributing to their companies' new product failures in the past have often been largely within their own control," it says. "Typically, they voice less concern with their companies technical research and development programs than with the need for better market planning and more effective use of marketing research."

EDITOR'S NOTE: From *Industrial Marketing*, November, 1965, copyright 1965 by Advertising Publications Inc., Chicago, Illinois.

EARLIER START

The steps commonly being taken to remedy this defect include introduction of marketing planning techniques earlier in the new product development cycle, integration of marketing research with all segments of the cycle — from research and development out to sales and promotion — and establishment of market monitoring systems to check the product's potential at different points in the development cycle.

The degree to which marketing research techniques are utilized depends heavily on the amount of risk involved in launching a particular product, says the report. For some companies, the stakes are so small that practically no advance spending on marketing research can be justified, as in the case of a manufacturer having a very broad line or relatively inexpensive products, no one of which contributes a dominant portion of gross income.

At the other extreme stands the company introducing a complicated big-ticket item into an unfamiliar market. It willingly foots the bill for painstaking research at all stages.

All industrial manufacturers, however, are coming under greater pressure to make products pay off. An NICB survey conducted late last year revealed that half of 173 industrial producers questioned derive 10-30% of current sales from products first marketed within the preceding five years, and 19% draw 50% of sales from such products. About seven out of 10 anticipated greater dependency on new products over the next five years.

INFORMATION GAP

According to the latest survey, a major cause of new product trouble is insufficient knowledge of:

Product characteristics or features required by prospective users;

Demand for the product, present and future size, trends and characteristics of the market;

Degree and rate of market penetration that the company can realistically expect for the product;

Appropriate methods of distribution for the product, and what is required to operate successfully through them, especially when these differ from those used in marketing established product lines;

The strengths and weaknesses of competitive products.

Other bugaboos include misdirected or inadequate marketing efforts, failure to consider the probable reactions of competitors, changes in external factors that alter the product's life expectancy and poor timing.

Systematic marketing planning and research is of "great value" in judging the merits of new products and in guiding their development from concept to market stages, said the study participants. In particular, they cited the advantages of applying research to the following four areas:

1. Pretesting of product ideas.

2. Estimating the potential market for new products.

3. Product and market testing prior to full-scale marketing.

4. Determining the most effective ways of selling, distributing, pricing, packaging and/or promoting the product.

They stress that the research needs to be comprehensive and properly timed if it is to contribute effectively to the development program.

CONCEPT TESTING

The logic of pretesting new-product ideas, as stated by one chemical company executive, is that it "provides a clear checkpoint for decision to continue or kill programs, with obviously concomitant advantages such as the acceleration of promising programs, and the diversion of people and funds to more promising projects." At the same time, it entails some risk of disclosing project plans to competitors.

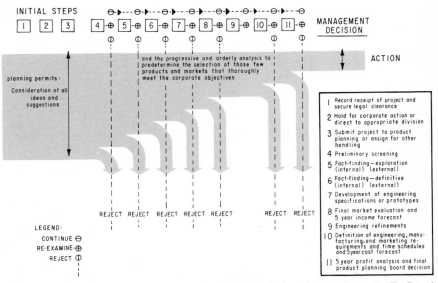

Monitoring. In the development cycle of a new industrial product, B. F. Goodrich Co., one of the NICB study participants, builds in stop-or-go decisions at seven different points.

During the concept testing phase, market research tries to ascertain appropriate uses for the new product, who the users will be and their needs, relative importance of product functions to different classes of users, design parameters for the product, pricing possibilities and economic utility to users, indications of potential sales volume, and the best ways to market the product.

A common practice is first to present new product proposals to the company's own marketing and sales personnel for their opinion. The next step is to seek the opinions of prospective users.

Many researchers like to get views from several different areas within those firms pinpointed as users of the new product. The market research staff of National Lead Co., for example, regularly interviews "technical research, to determine the trends of usage of the proposed product in the prospect's end product; marketing, to determine the market outlook for the prospect's end product; and purchasing, to determine historical and anticipated purchase patterns of the proposed product."

One of the obstacles of concept testing is for product sponsors to communicate and respondents to comprehend new product ideas during early abstract stages. Respondents find it difficult to visualize the unknown, and tend to think in terms of products and technology they are familiar with. Thus, according to the study, demonstration aids are normally required. The more closely they resemble the actual product, the better, because the more clearly a respondent understands the new product concept, the more meaningful his reactions.

ESTIMATING MARKET POTENTIAL

It is difficult enough to measure current demand for existing products, but to measure future demand for unlaunched products is really a slippery proposition, the study indicates. The likelihood of inaccuracy varies according to how much market data is available for the product in question, how precise an estimate is required, what kind of market the product will sell in, and how new the product is.

Market estimates are usually based on information from several different sources, the most common being public and commercial publications, the company's own sales and market data, its sales personnel and distributors and prospective product users.

Relevant statistical measures to gauge demand for a new product differ with each situation. Sometimes the new product can be related to the production, shipment, sale, or usage of some other product. If the product were a new kind of roadbuilding equipment, for instance, the market researcher might relate demand to highway construction volume on a dollar or mileage basis.

Occasionally researchers resort to analogy, examining market growth from some earlier product whose pattern of acceptance approximates that of the new product. Sprague Electric Co., for example, studied the displacement of receiving tubes by transistors in order to estimate the extent to and rate at which integrated circuits would replace these earlier products. The problem with this method is finding a true parallel.

USER SURVEYS

In making his sales forecast, the researcher seldom feels confident applying an estimated market-share ratio to the total market projection. So he employs other methods, namely sales force estimates, surveys of prospective users (both of which are used for measuring total market potential as well) or limited marketing of the product. In any case, review and revision of estimates is even more necessary than for total market forecasts, since estimate sources are less stable.

Advantages of basing sales forecasts on users' expectations are proximity to the source of sales, exposure to the reasons behind user buying, and availability of information in the form and detail required. Problems occur in markets where users are numerous or not easily located, and when product users are ill-informed or uncooperative. Furthermore, user expectations are often subject to change.

One advantage of the sales force composite method is that it taps specialized knowledge of men closest to the market. On the other hand, salesmen can be poor estimators, either too optimistic or too pessimistic, and unaware of the broad economic patterns shaping future sales.

PRODUCT PRETESTING

Information accrued from testing at this point is twofold. First there are the technical considerations of how the product functions in actual use. Secondly, there are such marketing planning considerations as user reaction, price possibilities, key purchasing influences and effective sales approach.

The three possibilities for pretesting are product-use tests, tests involving product displays at trade shows or dealer showrooms, and limited marketing operations.

The most common method is the product-use test. An instrument company reports that "trial usage is beneficial: (1) from a standpoint of determining if the product meets the user's needs, and (2) from an engineering standpoint of design, location of controls, and convenience of operation to the user, etc." Thus any weaknesses can be corrected before full-scale production.

Some manufacturers give a product to the user at no charge, while others charge a minimal amount in the belief that the user is more apt to feel a vested interest in the test results and to report objectively on the product's performance if he has paid.

It is best if, when tests are run, someone from the company is present to see that the product is used correctly, said several respondents. Otherwise the customer might misuse the product and broadcast his dissatisfaction to others.

HOW TO PROBE

Since most industrial products have limited markets and since pertinent information about an industrial product is often technical, most industrial market researchers rely heavily on personal interviews to gather their information, according to the latest National Industrial Conference Board study. When probing complex product concepts, this allows the interviewer to sense the extent of the respondent's comprehension. Also personal contact stimulates responses, perhaps even eliciting useful, unsolicited information about market situation, competitive products, etc. Drawbacks, however, are the time and money involved.

Telephone interviews are used when information is needed regarding well-defined basic product concepts or specific product features, or when supplemental data is needed. The telephone normally is not used to conduct first stage interviews, at which product concepts generally should be illustrated with demonstration aids.

Almost half of the companies in NICB study have used mail surveys in their new product research, usually to broaden the base of an investigation and/or to supplement first hand findings obtained in personal interviews.

DRAWBACKS

Limitations of the product-use method are that users are sometimes biased in their reports, inclined to be more critical or more favorable under test conditions than under ordinary conditions, and that the expense of producing prototypes hinders placement of a sufficient number in representative test situations.

The merits of product display tests are that they are cheaper, quicker, and more easily controlled than other premarket tests. At the same time, information obtainable through trade show and dealer display tests may be scant or superficial, prospects may not be representative, and expressions of interest may be invalid reflections of willingness to buy. Also tests publicly reveal plans to competitors.

Test marketing is the small-scale trial distribution of a new or modified product. To achieve realistic results, the limited market should contain the same combination of product, price, selling effort, advertising, and other marketing elements as will be employed in the full-scale distribution. Common objectives are to determine acceptability of the product, the effectiveness of its marketing program, shortcomings in either the product or marketing program, evidence of sales volume, and unforeseen uses for the product.

Some companies find it advantageous to make limited production runs of the new product. Others enter the market on a tentative basis after arranging for the product to be manufactured by non-company sources.

One Canadian company imported products from abroad which were then sold under conditions similar to those likely for its new product. Another company relies upon subcontractors to produce the quantities needed to fill orders, so that it does not have to invest in capital equipment initially.

HOW TO PLAN NEW PRODUCTS, IMPROVE OLD ONES, AND CREATE BETTER ADVERTISING

BY DIK WARREN TWEDT

The term "brand loyalty" has semantic implications of consumer fidelity and allegiance that are a brand's due, *and no brand has ever had that right.* In our competitive economy, a branded product or service will succeed only to the degree that it offers consumers more total satisfactions than other available brands.

These satisfactions, of course, can be of different kinds—economic, physical, or psychological—but unless a given branded product can legitimately claim that it does a better job (at a given price) than its competitors in providing one or more of these consumer satisfactions, it has not really established its right to be represented in the marketplace. Although this principle has always been true for products in abundant supply, natural selection (and the resulting "survival of the fittest") operates more swiftly today than ever before. There are four major reasons why this is so:

1. Increasing consumer sophistication resulting from higher educational levels, and changes in income distribution which permit more people to exercise greater brand choice.

2. Exponential proliferation of consumer choice, both within and between product categories.

3. Higher absolute levels of media promotion, and more effective mass advertising.

4. Increased sophistication of retailers (often aided by computerization),

EDITOR'S NOTE: From the *Journal of Marketing,* January 1969, pp. 53-57. Reprinted by permission of the American Marketing Association and the author.

which is reflected in quicker decisions about a given brand's viability.

Alert marketing management has recognized these trends and has responded by even greater attempts at product differentiation, thus quickening still further the tempo of competition for the consumer dollar. It would appear that now and in the foreseeable future marketers are caught in a competitive spiral, in which competitive pressures will always be "more than yesterday, but less than tomorrow."

If this is to be the nature of the competitive environment, what is the most appropriate strategy for the individual marketer? The answer is twofold: (1) to continue to improve present products so that they will maintain or extend their differentiation and (2) to plan new product entries so that maximum differentiation is built in from the very beginning.

A deceptively simple but powerful, three-step method exists to accomplish both objectives. During the past two decades, this method has been applied successfully in new product planning and product improvement for more than a score of major marketers in this country and abroad. Here is how it works. (In the first step, *carpet sweepers*—a mature product category—will be used as an example.)

STEP 1—IDENTIFICATION OF POSSIBLE PRODUCT ATTRIBUTES

Step 1 is a *systematic creative exploration* of all the ways in which (carpet sweepers) can vary. Note that the analysis is not restricted to ways in which carpet sweepers *do* vary, or have varied in the past; we inquire rather into all conceivable ways in which carpet sweepers could be made to vary! This approach owes much to the "brainstorming" technique pioneered by the late Alex Osborn.[1]

As in brainstorming sessions, the small group working on the initial listing of ways in which product attributes can vary should carefully avoid any mutual criticism, or even attempts to prematurely evaluate suggestions. "Hitchhiking" is encouraged, that is, the constructive elaboration of another group member's idea. At this stage, primary emphasis is on sheer quantity of ideas; the objective evaluation comes later. By striving for as long a list of attributes as possible, the chances are greater that more areas of the product domain will be explored.

Obviously there is no magic number at which the listing of possible attributes should stop; listings will vary in length with products of different complexity. But don't stop too soon! In one analysis, more than 80 cigarette attributes were recorded before someone thought to add a key attribute, "flavor."

In an actual application of this method almost 20 years ago, one of the product attributes that an advertising agency group conceived for carpet sweepers was "color." Until that time, carpet sweepers had been available in only two colors, black or dull gray. By introducing a line of pastel "decorator" colors, the Bissell Company was able to reverse a declining sales trend. What might have been considered a minor, non-functional change in an unimportant product attribute, actually resulted in a major change in marketing position.

For new product conepts, the same logic is followed as for mature products. The first step is to list systematically all of the ways in which the product or service can vary. Suppose, for example, that prior to the introduction of aerosol packaging, a marketer of dairy products had wanted to expand his share of the market for high butterfat cream. One of the product attributes that could have been assigned to cream was "greater convenience." From this identification of the opportunity for product differentiation could have come the concept of whipped cream in ready-to-use form.

One of the more obvious product attributes, but one that is seldom fully explored for its differentiation potential, is sheer *size*. The market for a branded product may often be expanded considerably merely by offering a larger range of sizes. Of course the size variations must make sense to consumers; needless proliferation is likely to be confusing to the public and discouraged by Congress.

STEP 2—ASSIGNMENT OF DIFFERENTIATION RATINGS

When the product attribute list is long enough to suggest that most of the possibilities for product differentiation have been considered, it is time to proceed to the second step: an assignment of one of three *differentiation ratings* to each product attribute. For each attribute, a judgment is made as to whether our brand is *superior, equal,* or *inferior* to most competitive brands. As a beginning, this judgment can be based upon informed marketing opinion. Eventually, depending upon the size of the risk involved, it may be appropriate to test the validity of such judgments with consumer research.

In designing a new product, step 2 calls for a series of decisions about what attributes should be built into the product, rather than merely assigning competitive comparison values to attributes of existing products.

Let us suppose that we are members of a group that has been asked to devise a marketing strategy for typewriters to be sold to the home market. We begin with the almost purely theoretical, exhaustive listing of the ways in which typewriters can vary. In step 2, we judge how our present typewriter actually compares with most competitive brands on each attribute listed. An example of a partial listing follows:

Step 1. Listing of Typewriter Attributes	Step 2. Assignment of Differentiation Ratings. Compared with most competitive brands, our brand is . . .		
	"Superior"	"Equal"	"Inferior"
	+	=	−
1. Price		=	
2. Portability	+		
3. Esthetic design (geometric)	+		
4. Esthetic design (color)	+		
5. Versatility of use		=	
6. Availability		=	
7. Service guaranty	+		
8. Convenience of cleaning		=	
9. Convenience of replacing ink element		=	
10. Adjustability to different touches			−
11. Convertability to different fonts		=	
12. Ruggedness and so forth			−

If we made competitive judgments objectively, and if we can be reasonably confident of their validity, a preliminary evaluation of the product's marketing future can be made at the end of step 2. If honest self-appraisal turns up no plus marks, but only a few equalities and the balance minuses, it is probably time either to drastically improve the product or retire it.

It is self-evident that not all product attributes are of equal importance to consumers, and also that one golden virtue may compensate for many minor shortcomings. In planning for product differentiation, an attempt should be made to move as many ratings as possible to the left in this three-column analysis—from equalities to pluses, and from minuses to equalities, or even pluses.

It is rarely possible to move all ratings to the first column of plus marks. Some of the attributes in a given product profile require tradeoffs. For example, if a typewriter were clearly superior in attributes 2 through 12 in the listing shown, it is likely that such superiority would be reflected in higher price. Whether non-competitive prices are "inferior" or "superior" product attributes is debatable. The traditional viewpoint that high prices tend to deter sales (which would lead to classification of high price as "inferior" product attribute) may not be true in our present affluent economy.

STEP 3—TRIVARIANT ANALYSIS

The third step is to determine the relative marketing potency of the attributes identified in step 1 and evaluated in step 2. Originally, this determination was made by simply asking consumers, "How desirable to you is (the attribute in question)?"

In 1951, Dr. Perham Nahl, now with the Leo Burnett Company, and I were working on the advertising campaign of a large manufacturer of canned pet food. It was found that the product attribute "Government inspected" was considered to be highly desirable by purchasers. However, after further investigation, it became clear that advertising based upon this selling idea was not likely to have much impact; people thought this attribute was already true for all brands. (It happens that most brands of canned pet food are *not* Government inspected, but remember that the model deals with attitudes and opinions rather than with matters of fact.)

In addition to *desirability,* then, a product attribute, to provide effective consumer motivation, must have some degree of *exclusivity.* Development of this simple two-dimensional model, with its assumptions that advertising will be more effective if it stresses product attributes that are desirable, and also relatively exclusive to the brand advertised, led us to a search for other dimensions—such as believability, meaningfulness, ego-involvement, and so forth.

The results of our empirical research was "trivariant analysis," in which the position of each product attribute is located on three scales: *desirability, exclusiveness,* and *believability.* A simple mathematical expression of this relationship is:

$$MP = \int (D)\,(E)\,(B)$$

in which MP (marketing potency, or the extent to which a given product attribute will effectively promote sales) is assumed to be a function of a multiplicative relationship among the three factors—multiplicative because the reduction of any of the three right-hand terms to zero or near zero sharply reduces the attribute's marketing potency.

This general formula is obviously naïvely stated because equal weight is assigned to each of the three factors. It is hardly likely that this is true for all product attributes and all product categories. The model has been useful, however, in determining relative potency of a wide variety of attributes for many categories of products and services.

The basic assumptions are not new. Creative people have known since the beginning of advertising that to interest consumers, advertising must say something desirable about the product. At the same time, it must say something that doesn't automatically apply to any and all brands in the product category. Finally, the statement must be either believable or provable. Trivariant analysis is simply a convenient way to express these three factors in quantitative terms.

An intercorrelation matrix of the three factors, based upon 105 attributes taken from studies of seven different product categories, suggest that although the factors are not wholly independent, they are worth measuring separately.

	−.24	1 Desirability
−.29	.52

2   1

1 Desirability
2 Exclusiveness
3 Believability

These correlation coefficients indicate that if a product attribute was thought to be desirable, there was a slight tendency for it to be thought of as "not exclusive," but there was a moderately strong tendency for consumers to believe the claim. If a product attribute was thought of as "exclusive," consumers had a slight tendency not to believe the claim.

HOW PRODUCT ATTRIBUTES (OR COPY CLAIMS) ARE EVALUATED BY TRIVARIANT ANALYSIS

The mechanics of measuring the three factors are straightforward. Each product attribute is briefly described in a "copy capsule." The copy need not be an unemotional recital of dull fact; it can and often should be an enthusiastic presentation of a single argument as to why the consumer should buy. The test themes or copy paragraphs are typed on 3 x 5 cards. A few examples of such copy capsules are:

"A hair spray that lasts through three shampooings"
"A wrist watch that varies less than two seconds a day"
"The bourbon that makes even the rocks taste better"
"A refrigerator with a 10-year guaranty on all moving parts"
"The first completely nourishing breakfast you don't have to cook"
"This dog collar flea-proofs your dog for three months in 28 seconds"

Unless the basic selling idea depends heavily upon the brand name, it should be tested without the support of the brand name. If the product attribute has high potency, linkage with a well-accepted brand should make it even more acceptable to consumers.

All cards are rated by each respondent on a rating scale for *desirability* of each attribute, then the same cards are shuffled and rated again for *exclusiveness*, and finally for *believability*. A description of each operation follows:

1. Here are a few brief descriptions about some (product category) you might buy. For each description, which number on this scale (refer to scale 1) comes closest to your opinion? If your opinion comes somewhere in between these numbers, give a number in between that best represents how *desirable* each description is to you personally.

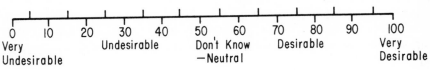

2. Here are the same brief descriptions again. Now this time, please give the number on this scale (or some number in between) that comes closest to the way you feel about how *exclusive* each description is to you.

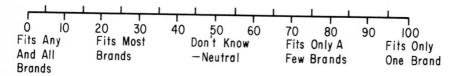

3. Now here is the last scale. Here are the same descriptions again, and this time please give the number on the scale (or some number in between) that comes closest to your own *belief* in the description as it might apply to a particular product.

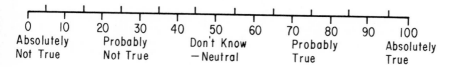

This technique allows a large number of product attributes to be tested, including an advertiser's present copy claims, experimental claims, competitive claims, and even new product concepts not yet fully developed. A computer program is available that yields mean scores and measures of variance for 22 attributes, and that also provides separate scores for such dichotomous variables as light versus heavy users, men versus women, exposure to advertising versus non-exposure, and so on. The program also prints out differences in scores that are significant at the 1% and 5% confidence levels for any dichotomy selected.

Trivariant analysis has an important limitation. Although it is an efficient way to test the probable effectiveness of *factual* claims, it seems less applicable to advertising approaches that depend heavily upon *emotion*, or upon *graphics*. (Copy research has not yet found a way to obtain from consumers their belief in such a theme as "Modess—Because," and it is also rather difficult to establish the desirability of such illustrative devices as the Marlboro tattoo.)

A report is made in the form of a two-dimensional chart (the third factor, believability, is shown in parentheses) that locates the desirability and exclusiveness of each attribute. Figure 14-1 shows how consumers evaluated different potential attributes of refrigerators, information which was subsequently used in planning specifications for a new line of refrigerators.

After mean scores for each claim are plotted on the desirability and exclusiveness scales (with believability scores shown in parentheses), quadrants I through IV are established by drawing dotted lines so that half the claims fall above the line and half below, and half fall to the left of the

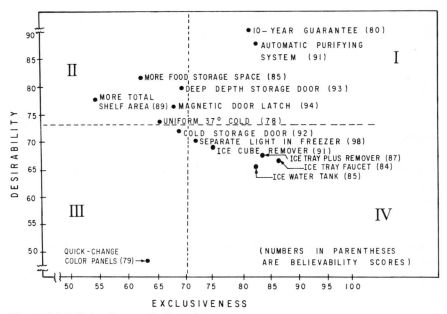

Figure 14-1. Trivariant analysis: refrigerators.

vertical line and half to the right. Product attributes in quadrant I (upper right-hand of chart) are considered to be relatively desirable, and yet they are not commonplace characteristics of brands already available. They are thus better candidates for developing what Rosser Reeves has called the USP, or Unique Selling Proposition.

Believability scores provide an indication of the amount of assurance the consumer requires before he is willing to accept the selling proposition. Low believability scores suggest cognitive dissonance, but they are not always bad, provided there is a way to prove the claim's validity (through such means as demonstration, testimonial, case history, expert witness, and so forth).

These charts have also been useful to creative groups planning advertising copy strategy because they provide diagnostic profiles that suggest ways in which particular copy claims may be strengthened. If, for example, a claim is strong on desirability and exclusiveness but low on believability, the creative objective becomes one of furnishing adequate proof for the claim. Or if a claim happens to be low on desirability, it may be because the claim as stated has not yet made clear how the attribute really benefits the consumer, or it may be because the consumer simply doesn't care.

The three-step approach described here obviously depends greatly upon the quality of operations performed by the smallest but most powerful of all computers—the one located midway between the ears. Much of what has been described requires good, hard thinking. If the thinking has been productive, the methods outlined are likely to be helpful in developing orders of priority for new product planning, for improvement of present products, and for selecting those attributes of advertised products that are most likely to motivate customers to buy. With such working priorities established, the probability is substantially increased that consumers will be better served and that corporate net earnings will be increased.

NOTES

1. Alex Osborn, *Applied Imagination: Principles and Producers of Creative Problem Solving* (New York: Charles Scribner & Sons, 1963). For an interesting and somewhat different approach to the same problem, see William J. J. Gordon, *Synectics: The Development of Creative Capacity* (New York: Harper & Row Publishers, 1961).

ADDITIONAL SELECTED BIBLIOGRAPHY

Rejuvenation of Products

Lazo, H., "Finding a Key to Success in New Product Failures," *Industrial Marketing,* Vol. 50, No. 11 (November, 1965), 74-77.

Stanton, F. W., "Rejuvenation of Old Products," *Innovation: Key to Marketing Progress,* Henry Gomez, ed., AMA Proceedings of the 46th National Conference of the American Marketing Association (June, 1963), 607-618.

QUESTIONS FOR DISCUSSION AND REVIEW

1. How do you determine when a product needs rejuvenation?

2. What role does research play in finding success from product failures?

3. What is the appropriate strategy for a firm in today's market?

4. How does "brainstorming" help in rejuvenation?

5. Describe how product attributes can be rated.

PART V
NEW PRODUCTS
AND THE LAW

There have been many news items appearing in journals and newspapers depicting secrecy and security precautions, because of burglary and theft, of new product plans, blueprints, and the like. There have also been news articles dealing with unethical practices of firms that introduced poorly developed products, products that can be considered dangerous to human use, and products whose prices are manipulated through collusionary practices. The chapters in Part V deal with the above aspects as new products are introduced into the market place.

15

CORPORATE
RESPONSIBILITIES

Top management must take decisive measures to guard new product ideas from theft. Theft can take more than one form. It can mean loss of company knowledge concerning new product development to competitors as well as loss of disclosure of blueprints, technical data, other research and development, and promotional data. New product secrecy and new product invention are two distinct concepts when discussed in a court of law. Careful data concerning new product invention can be utilized to contest any prepatent application by competitors. New product secrecy has an altogether different connotation. Patents, copyrights, or any new legal maneuver should be utilized to protect the research of a firm.

Corporate responsibility also means that close substitute products should be investigated at the patent office to determine whether the firm's present products are patentable. The following articles spell out the need for top management to take the proper steps to protect the firm's interest in research and development from both endogenous and exogenous factors. The importance of understanding patent laws and product patent protection is also underscored.

SECRECY AND
INVENTION AGREEMENTS
BY WILLIAM F. WEIGEL

The growth and complexity of industrial activity here in the United States have had a very profound effect upon many of the law's earlier concepts with respect to employer-employee relationships. American business today is of necessity more impersonal, and research and know-how have become more integral facets of today's corporate existence-no longer confined to the progressive organization but virtual necessities of the survival of all business. This changing system has produced new problems for the employer in the protection of his intangible assets.

If the corporate employer is to succeed in the modern, research-oriented competitive struggle, he must constantly protect himself from his own employees. I do not mean to imply that the interests of the employer and the employee are not compatible, but I do believe the employer should make sure that he will benefit from the research and inventions of his technical employees and that he will be protected against the loss or disclosure of his trade secrets and know-how. Although these two subjects—secrecy and invention—are often treated as one, particularly in employment agreements, they do involve two distinct legal concepts and should be considered separately. I would like to examine each of these subjects, pointing out some of the problems which exist and exploring the possibilities of avoiding some of them by establishing a contractual relationship. I must caution, however, that this is an area of the law that is

EDITOR'S NOTE: From *Research Management,* Vol. 7, No. 4 (1964), 241-251. Reprinted by permission of the publisher and the author.

constantly changing and which is not as yet uniform throughout the 50 states. The general concepts which will be discussed might not be applicable in your particular jurisdiction or in your particular situation and should always be discussed first with your own attorney.

THE PROBLEM OF INVENTION

Closely related to our subject of trade secrets is the problem of title to employee inventions for these are often embryo trade secrets. Although this knowledge has its genesis with the employee, it is equally important that it be protected by the employer. I reverse the title of this paper and deal with it first.

Presumably, most people who are involved in research activity have signed a contract with their employer, agreeing to assign to him any inventions originated or developed by them during the course of their employment. Few large corporations today would hire or keep in their employ anyone in research or related activity without such a contractual arrangement. In the absence of such an agreement to assign, it is fairly well settled in law that an employee who develops or conceives an invention during the course of his general employment has title to the invention and the right to ownership of any patent which may issue on it. This is true even where the invention is developed during business hours, on the employer's premises, at his expense, and with his facilities and equipment. The reason for this rule is apparently the underlying public policy of the law to encourage and reward inventive genius.

The rule that title to inventions rests in the inventor is not without exception. There is an important limitation on this rule. In the absence of an express agreement to assign, the courts will on occasion spell out an implied agreement to assign, if the circumstances surrounding the employment are of such a nature as to indicate that this was, in effect, the intention of the parties. For example, an agreement would be implied where one was specifically employed to invent for the benefit of the employer or where one was paid to accomplish a particular objective. Such an employer-employee relationship may arise during the course of employment and need not necessarily have existed at the time of the original employment.

It is often a question of fact whether the nature of employment is general, so that the title to inventions rests in the employee, or specific, so that the assignment of title to the employer will be required. If the invention is closely related to the specific scope of the employment such as the solution of a particular problem or the development of a process for a specific need, title will be in the employer. Also, some courts have required assignment, where the employment was in an area where invention was common or expected. In order to avoid the necessity of establishing what the relation actually was, however, it is far preferable to spell this out by a written agreement with each employee engaged in research activity.

The contract should provide that the employee will assign to the employer all inventions pertaining to the business (whether patentable or not) devised during the course of employment. It should also provide that the employee, both during and after his employment, will assist the employer in the obtainment, maintenance, and enforcement of patents pertaining to the invention. Mere employment will usually be adequate consideration to support the obligation to assign. To make it more palatable to the employee, however, many companies include a provision providing for the additional payment of a predetermined sum (e.g., $100, $500) for each invention assigned on which a patent issues, or they agree to reassign to the employee any inventions which are found to be inapplicable to the company's business. This additional consideration is not necessary, however, to establish a valid contract.

In the absence of an agreement or other legal obligation to assign, the employer is not entirely without rights in the inventions of his employees, but acquires what the law calls a "shop right." This is a right first formulated by the courts of equity about 100 years ago in an effort to minimize the harsh effect upon the employer of granting title to inventions to the employee. It grants to the employer, who in most instances has provided the tools, equipment, and facilities to make the invention possible, a qualified right to use the invention in his own business. In effect, under a "shop right" the employer is entitled to a non-exclusive, royalty-free license under the patent which rightfully issues to the employee. This right to use may be defeated only if the inventing employee clearly and affirmatively indicates from the very outset that he intends to reserve all rights to the invention for himself and does not acquiesce in use of it by his employer.

As far as the employer is concerned, the "shop right" is better than nothing, but is certainly far less satisfactory than having outright title to the invention. A "shop right" may not be assigned, but it does inure to the benefit of a successor in business. Once the right arises there is no obligation to compensate the employee for use of it, and it will endure for the entire life of the patent, whether or not the inventing employee continues to be employed. It is an unsatisfactory arrangement which may be easily avoided by a preexisting contract to assign of the nature we have discussed. Indeed, its shortcomings are largely responsible for the almost universal practice of large companies' requiring their research personnel to execute invention agreements.

PROTECTION OF TRADE SECRETS

The protection of trade secrets and confidential information has become a more serious problem to most employers than that of title to inventions. Even though the law is well defined in this area, and it is universally recognized that no employee has the right to disclose his employer's trade secrets, there are practical difficulties which transcend the law. Unfortunately the loss of trade secrets is often occasioned by a dishonest or unscrupulous employees who has little respect for the law. On other occasions, competitors purposely hire technical personnel with the hope, or the predetermined understanding, that the employee will divulge the trade secrets of his previous employer. And there is of course, the honest employee, trying to please his new employer, who is uncognizant of the fact that his previous employment involved a confidential relationship. A money judgment against any such employee is often not collectable, and an injunction will not necessarily protect or compensate the owner of the trade secret. Therefore, an employer of technical personnel is hardly in a position to rely upon the basic legal tenet which prohibits disclosure.

In the recent *Carter* case there was an employee disclosure to the Colgate Company of Carter's trade secret with respect to the manufacturing know-how essential to its "Rise" shaving cream. This unauthorized disclosure permitted Colgate to develop its own "Rapid Shave" as a competitive product. Even thought Carter was granted an injunction and was awarded more than $5,400,000 in damages, Colgate did achieve a competitive market position, which it presumably will maintain, but which might not have occurred without the unlawful disclosure. Likewise the *Goodrich* case, even though the Ohio Supreme Court has now enjoined the erstwhile Goodrich space suit engineer from disclosing any Goodrich trade secrets to his new employer, International Latex, such an injunction is certainly difficult of enforcement by Goodrich and may not permit the employee to perform to the best of his abilities in his new job. Thus, we can see that, although the law against disclosure may be clear, the relief is not always satisfactory. There may be a practical solution to these problems, but let us first see what the problems are.

The courts have not always been in agreement on whether one has a property right in the usual sense in a trade secret. Unlike a patent right, however, one may not prevent another from making use of trade secrets if they have been discovered by honest means. All that the owner of a trade secret does have is a personal right against one who discloses or receives a trade secret under unlawful circumstances. For example, the owner of a secret formula for a patent medicine has no redress against one who, by analysis, discovers the formula and duplicates the product. He does, however, have a right to proceed against a faithless employee who discloses the formula to a competitor or against the competitor if he knowingly induced such disclosure.

In order to protect a trade secret, the subject matter of the secret need not be patentable, so long as the owner has invested money, time, or effort in acquiring it and has treated it as secret. It cannot, however, be a matter of common knowledge or something generally known in the trade. Nor, can it be a part of the "personal skills, knowledge, and experience" of an employee or another. This distinction, however, has been the source of much litigation in the trade secret field.

There is implicit in every contract of employment, whether written or oral, a prohibition against the disclosure of any trade secret acquired in the course of employment. There would, thus, not seem to be any necessity to require an employee to execute a specific agreement not to disclose his employer's trade secrets. Such agreements, however, do serve a very practical purpose. They put the employee on notice that his employment does involve certain confidential relationships and that at least some of the information acquired by him during his employment is considered to be in the nature of trade secrets. These contracts should prohibit disclosure both during and subsequent to the period of employment. Their duration should be measured by the expected life of the value of the confidential information to be protected.

There is a constant problem—whether or not there exists a secrecy agreement—in defining what is or is not a trade secret. It is particularly difficult with respect to scientific and technical information. This type of information is often of substantial commercial value. The scientific employee, however, may wish to claim that it is actually part of his professional know-how and not confidential information exclusive with his employer. These subtle differences are usually impossible to foresee or to delineate by legal jargon in a written contract. In theory what is confidential information depends simply upon the intent and understanding of the parties. In practice, however, many problems will, of necessity, arise if an attempt is made to agree upon this in advance. In resolving these controversies the courts have tended to favor the employee in close situations in order to assure his mobility and freedom. This tendency has caused more and more employers to look for new methods to protect their trade secrets which will not necessarily be dependent upon judicial whim but which will justify their high outlay in research activity and permit a freedom of communication within the company and with other outside organizations.

The most practical solution to the trade secret problem, and the one to which more and more employers are resorting, is the use of restrictive covenants not to compete in employment contracts. Such restrictions cannot restrain the employee who sells his employer's trade secrets for personal gain, nor can they minimize the growing problem of industrial espionage. They should, however, permit the free interchange of technical and scientific information and help curtail the flow of confidential information from the employee who is employed by a competitor and either does not recognize that much of what he has learned in his previous employment was of a confidential nature or obligingly shifts his loyalties to his new employer. They also have the advantage of preventing a disclosure from ever occuring, rather than giving the employer an ineffectual cause of action for money damages after the real injury has happened.

The restrictive covenant is simply an undertaking by an employee that when he severs his employment he will not compete with his former employer, either for his own account or in the hire of another. Basically, the only limitation on such restrictions is that they be reasonable and be designed to accomplish some legitimate purpose. The law abhors most restrictions on freedom of movement and the right to earn a living and, unless otherwise justified, they will be classified as unlawful restraints of trade. Since what is or is not reasonable has been construed differently in the various juridictions, these agreements, perhaps more than the others we have discussed, should be carefully considered by each company's own counsel. For example, I understand that all such restrictive covenants against subsequent employment have been prescribed by statute in Michigan, North Dakota, California, and Oklahoma.

As a general rule, a covenant not to compete as part of an employment contract will be held to be valid if the restriction placed upon the employee is no greater than is reasonable under the circumstances. In determining what is reasonable, the courts uniformly apply three tests.

(1) The scope of the restriction should not be greater than necessary to protect the employer's legitimate interests.

(2) The restriction should not be unduly harsh or oppressive on the employee.

(3) The restriction should not be contrary to public policy.

Protection against loss of clientele or loss of trade secrets or confidential information are the usual "legitimate interests" of the employer to be protected. We are principally interested in the latter and, if one is to take advantage of restrictive covenants for such purposes, he should be able to demonstrate that there existed a confidential relationship with the contracting employees, that this relationship was known to the parties, and that the employer took reasonable steps to keep the information in question secret.

There are three principal factors to be considered with respect to the scope of the restraint—space, time, and activity. The restriction on each must be reasonable and each will be weighed against the other two.

Originally, the most attention was given to the geographical area in which the restraint operated. When businesses were local in nature, it was said that one could not be restricted from plying his trade throughout the realm. Although some state statutes retain such geographical limitations, the general yardstick will now be the area in which the employer does or is likely to do business. Thus, whereas a worldwide limitation would not be unreasonable in many businesses, even a city-wide restriction would probably not be upheld for a baker, cobbler, or retailer.

The courts were less concerned with the duration of the restriction when businesses were generally local and the geographic restriction was naturally limited. Now, with nationwide and worldwide businesses, a compromise will usually have to be made in the duration of the restriction if an adequately broad geographic restriction is desired. Where technology and scientific achievement is advancing so rapidly, the value of confidential information is often short-lived. Accordingly, restrictions against employment in competitive activity are often limited to a period of three or five years. One must also take into account, in devising a restriction, the period of time during which the employee has been employed and the skills and experience he brought to the job. With respect to a retired employee, a restriction unlimited in time is usually justifiable.

The restriction with respect to activities should not exceed the extent of the employee's previous activities with the contracting employer. A restriction not to work for a competitor of a company such as Du Pont or General Electric would be so broad that it would probably be invalid as applied to an engineer. On the other hand, it might be reasonable for the president of the company. In each instance one must make a realistic appraisal of the likelihood of any particular employee becoming a potential competitor or using his previous employer's confidential information to that employer's detriment in his new position.

Let us assume each of the three restraints—space, time, and activity— are reasonable and necessary for the protection of the employer. This, however, does not assure us that the restriction will be enforced and particularly does not assure injunctive relief, even if it is held to be valid. If it is too harsh upon the employee, if it will cause him to be unemployed or force him to take work more menial than that for which he is qualified, or if it would require a substantial change in his personal life, a court will be very reluctant to enforce the restriction. With this in mind, some corporations provide in their contracts for at least partial payment of salary to the employee during the period that he is unemployed as a direct result of the restrictive covenant.

Few restrictions have been invalidated as contrary to public policy. They will be, however, if the employer's business is unlawful, if the restriction would tend to create a monopoly, or if the restriction would deny a community a needed service. For example, no court would be likely to sanction a restrictive covenant which deprived a town of its only doctor.

It may seem that it is virtually impossible to draft a restrictive covenant which will satisfy the reasonable test in all respects. Granted, it is difficult, and for that reason I believe each one should be tailored to the particular employee and circumstances involved, or there should at least be several different forms for different classes of employees. It would seem well not to attempt to bind employees who do not have access to trade secrets, since courts will look at the overall policy of an employer to determine the reasonableness of one of his particular contracts. Although many restrictive covenants have been declared invalid, the courts have shown a recent tendency to adopt what some writers refer to as a "blue pencil" approach to these covenants. Rather than declare one of these restrictive covenants unreasonable and thus completely void, the courts often rewrite them in a manner so that will be reasonable and uphold them to that extent. This is a very hopeful trend for the employer, since he no longer is faced with an "all or nothing" proposition. Nevertheless, every effort should be made in the first instance to draft the contract within a framework of legality.

We have spoken of three types of employer-employee contractual arrangements—contracts to assign inventions, agreements not to disclose confidential information, and restrictive covenants not to compete. Ordinarily, all three may be embodied in one document, bearing in mind the special circumstances attendant upon the restrictive covenant. There is no question but that such contracts can afford the employer a certain measure of protection and are virtually a necessity if his business involves any substantial amount of research activity. In my opinion, however, none of these measures provides an adequate substitute for employee loyalty fostered by mutual trust and understanding.

COMBINING "OLD" ELEMENTS ISN'T INNOVATIVE, SUPREME COURT RULES IN VOIDING A PATENT

By a WALL STREET JOURNAL *Staff Reporter*

WASHINGTON—The Supreme Court reemphasized that new products, to be patentable, must represent true "innovation" and "add to the sum of useful knowledge."

It isn't enough that a product "filled a long felt want and has enjoyed commercial success," the Court declared.

The High Court thus reversed a lower court that had upheld the validity of a patent held by Pavement Salvage Co., Pittsburgh, on a process for road laying with asphalt.

THE PATENT CASE

In the patent case, the Pittsburgh concern's patent covered a machine that combined a radiant-heat burner for heating asphalt adjacent to the new strip being laid, a spreader for putting down the new strip and a tamper for shaping the newly placed blacktop.

The case began when Pavement Salvage Co. brought a patent infringement suit against Anderson's-Black Rock Inc., a Charleston, W.Va., road builder. The road builder simply placed a radiant heat burner on the front of a standard paving machine and the Pittsburgh company claimed the combination infringed on its patent.

EDITOR'S NOTE: From *The Wall Street Journal,* December 9, 1969, p. 4. Reprinted by permission of the publisher, Dow Jones & Co.

The Supreme Court ruled unanimously that Pavement Salvage's patent is invalid. Justice Douglas, writing the Court's opinion, said all three elements of the concern's machine are "old" and held that the combination of the three didn't represent a patentable innovation. The combination may have been "of great convenience," but it "did not produce a new or different function" as required by patent law, Justice Douglas said.

ADDITIONAL SELECTED BIBLIOGRAPHY

Corporate Responsibilities

Auber, R.P., "New Products: Beware of Outside Ideas," *Management Review*, Vol. 54, No. 8 (August, 1965), 22-26.

Bate, F.L., "The Protection of Company Knowledge from Theft—Legal Remedies," *Research Management*, Vol. 7, No. 4 (1964), 253-259.

Bryant, W.S., "The Patent Mess," *Fortune*, Vol. 66, No. 3 (September, 1962), 111-113, 226, 231-232.

Coghlan, D.B., "Protecting Trade Secrets in Contract Research," *Trade Secrets: A Management Overview*, J.W. Blood, ed., AMA Bulletin No. 64, American Management Association (1965), 14-16.

"One Approach to Protecting Company in the Matter of Unsolicited Business," *Trade Secrets: A Management Overview*, J.W. Blood, ed. AMA Bulletin No. 64, American Management Association, (1965), 17-21. (From the General Electric Company's booklet "Policies Concerning Submitted Ideas," supplied by Harry R. Moyers, General Patent Counsel, Patent Legal Service, General Electric Company, New York, N.Y.)

Preston, L.E., "Patent Rights under Federal R & D Contracts," *Harvard Business Review*, Vol. 41 No. 5 (September-October, 1963), 6-7, 10, 12, 198-206.

Questions For Discussion And Review

1. Explain the need for secrecy concerning new products.

2. Suggest various means to protect new product development.

3. How did the Supreme Court rule on combining old elements of a product into a new product?

4. What remedies are available to a firm when secrets are stolen?

16

CORPORATE ETHICS

This section deals with product liability and the ethical considerations of the firm. No longer does the principle "caveat emptor" prevail in American industry as it flourished decades ago. There are many statutes on the books today that "enforce" firms to protect the users of the products they produce. Most of the laws on the books today are, in effect, disclosure laws. That is, the firms, by inserting on the package or by label have to disclose the composition, ingredients, side effects, dangers, etc., if there are any. These laws run the gamut from the Food, Drug & Cosmetics Act of 1938 down through The Substance Labeling Act of 1965, and the Fair Packaging and Labeling Act of 1967. In addition, there is the law of negligence. Every firm that manufactures products to be sold for public consumption is under an ethical and moral obligation to exercise reasonable care in the production and sale of its products. If the product is harmful or defective and causes injury to the user, the user may become the plaintiff in a law suit. The plaintiff has cause for legal action under any one of the following:

1. Failure of the firm to test the product to attempt to discover defects
2. Failure to give adequate warnings of possible danger (side effects) to the user
3. Inadequate or misleading direction in the use of the product
4. Failure to explore the consequence of normal wear, tear, and abuse

Planned obsolescence may very well come under on-trial review by the judge or jury in the not too distant future. In addition to the law of negligence, corporate ethics have also brought into being the law of warranty. The firms assume, voluntarily or otherwise, that the products they manufacture and sell will meet certain standards. Should an injury be caused by a product, in essence a breach of such warranty has occurred; thus, because the manufacturer did not exercise proper care or was at fault in causing said injury, the user of the product may have cause for legal action.

Aside from the legal action than can be brought against firms who knowingly or otherwise produce and sell "defective" products, ethics play a marketing role, in addition to the economic role. Many industrial firms employ quality control features or "flying auditors" (trained quality control men sent to suppliers' premises to check quality of product, the books, etc.) to cut down on rejects, transportation costs, and loss of time. It is less costly and less time-consuming to be more ethical in the production, sale, and advertising of new products.

PRODUCT LIABILITY:
GET IT ON THE RECORD
BY THOMAS H. F. SMITH

The rising tide of consumerism and the high cost of product liability suits have combined to make manufacturers more conscious than ever of the reliability of their products. Many companies are taking additional precautions in the design and testing of their products. Another method of preventing liability losses, however, is frequently overlooked by many of them—detailed record keeping to prove that the company exercised proper care in the manufacture of its products.

What makes this consideration so important is the attitude of the court toward the doctrine of "strict liability." This legal doctrine holds that a plaintiff need not prove negligence in manufacture, but simply that a defect in the product existed, whether or not the manufacturer knew that the defect existed or could have prevented it.

In many cases, the courts have held the manufacturer responsible even for unintended but forseeable misuse. In other words, the manufacturer has a duty to anticipate any possible misuse that may be made of its product. In the hands of a plaintiff's counsel, this becomes a potent weapon, because the jury and the court are convinced that a lack of foreseeability can be equated to a lack of "due care," and this by definition, is a "tort." Consequently, the manufacturer may lose its case.

Can this situation be prevented? In many cases it can be if the manufacturer has kept proper records from the research and development phase through the production of the product.

RELIABILITY COORDINATOR

The first step in setting up a record-keeping system is the establishment of a firm and thoroughly developed management philosophy or policy regarding manufacturing control procedures and record keeping. This charter should include specific provisions for the appointment of a single qualified individual who will act as chairman or coordinator for product reliability or assurance.

This employee will become one of the company's most important key operating personnel. He must have the insight and imagination as well as experience and education. Above all, he must be capable of operating under pressure and able to make a proper technical presentation when the occasion should arise that he appear in court as an expert witness on behalf of the company in a liability case.

Once such a person has been selected, the company must then establish his authority through a directive to all its operating personnel. Top management must make it completely clear that the product reliability coordinator is in a position of responsibility and reports directly to highest company level. His efforts will be futile if his decisions are overridden by top management in order to meet production or marketing schedules and quotas. Some companies may feel that they are in business to produce and sell, and that any interference in this cycle is a direct impediment to profit. This may well be true. But in today's liability atmosphere, a company stands a slim chance in defending a claim if an attorney can convince the jury that its prime concern was with cost and not quality or safety.

A company that feels a reliability control program is too constricting should contemplate how many units of its product it would have to sell to make up for a $100,000 loss from a single liability claim. It should also consider the possibility that the adverse publicity that may accompany this settlement might even more severely affect its profits and the popularity of its product.

TWO KINDS OF RECORDS

Assuming that a company accepts the importance of the product reliability coordinator, what kinds of records should it expect him to collect and maintain, and how are these related to liability prevention and protection?

Basically, the necessary records fall into two categories—those that are generated from within the organization and those from external sources, such as customer letters, testing laboratory reports, and information and data obtained from vendors of components, ingredients, subassemblies, containers, or other elements of the product. Both the internal and external categories are equally important parts of a liability prevention record.

For companies that may not be aware of it, there have been some recent changes in the law regarding "discovery procedures" in liability cases. The manufacturer no longer enjoys the protection of the confidential nature of his company files and records that it formerly did. Disclosure and interrogatory investigative procedures are now designed for the benefit of the plaintiff and permit an almost total examination of the company's files. This allows an examination of all the intricate details of a manufacturing operation: obviously, any deficiencies, however slight, will be brought to light and used against the company. Because this is a situation that should be prevented, it is imperative for the manufacturer to keep all record files ready for inspection at any time.

In the establishment of the records systems, two participants are vital members of the team: the claims representative of the company's insurance carrier and its corporate legal counsel. The great value of the advice these two representatives can offer cannot be estimated. Their suggestions will guarantee that the time and money a company spends on record keeping will be well invested.

WHERE TO BEGIN

The record keeping must begin where product begins; in most cases, this is research and development or engineering and design. Every investigator, developer, designer, engineer, or technician must be trained in the proper methodology of individual record keeping. Bound notebooks with daily dated and witnessed entries are critical not only for patentability, but also for liability protection. When blueprints, design drawings, models, or other information that cannot readily be entered into such a record are required, appropriate entries, notations, and references to them should be made

It is essential that continuity of the project is verifiable. Changes and alterations made to improve the product or its performance should be shown.

There is also an advantage to indicating the reasons why the final design was accepted and other prototypes were rejected. These constitute the first stage of the product history record and must be carefully preserved.

Naturally, before proceeding with full-scale production, performance testing for efficacy, durability, and, of course, safety should be conducted. Most of these tests are done within the organization, but on occasion an outside laboratory will be engaged for this purpose. All reports on this phase of the product's development must also be retained for the entire market life of the item.

From these preliminary activities, the manufacturing standards for the product evolve. These should be thoroughly thought out so that each progressive step in the process can be understood and followed clearly and concisely. Particularly critical are inspection instructions for each individual part, component, or ingredient. Specifications must be provided that give tolerances for acceptance or rejection. Reference should be made to the criteria from which these limits were established. This is important because it authenticates the reliability or authoritativeness of the tolerances.

Equally important is an indication of the frequency and consistency with which these tests are conducted and the rate of acceptances and incidence of rejections that take place. Obviously, a procedure that accepts all is not a true quality control measure and would have negligible value in court. Conversely, one that demonstrates a degree of severity and judgment can be used advantageously to demonstrate a company's efforts to manufacture and market a safe product.

STANDARDS

At this point, top management may ask if some of the standards for products established by law are sufficient. According to one expert in the product liability field, "The government can establish the floor, but doesn't determine the ceiling." Thus, established standards can serve as a minimal guide, but only the company itself can decide the extent to which it wishes to protect its own interests.

The next record to be considered is the unit item production record. This may be simple or complex, depending on a company's product. Whichever it may be, the records should reflect certain basic facts. It should indicate in some readily identifiable fashion the date on which the product was manufactured. If a serial numbering system is possible, this would be an ideal approach. The record also should contain an indication of the source or lot number of any of the functional component parts. Who tested, checked, or approved this item should be noted. When an individual employee is aware that a failure is directly traceable to him, he is less likely to be slipshod.

Two other important documents that belong in a company's liability protection file are a Hold Harmless Agreement and a Certificate of Insurance (issued by a responsible carrier) provided by each vendor from which the company purchases parts, materials, or subassemblies. These certificates should be examined carefully for both validity and scope by both the company's insurance representative and its legal counsel.

Contracts should not be entered into haphazardly with suppliers; the financial stability of the supplying company should be thoroughly investigated. Although a company must ultimately defend itself in a liability suit, the proper records of its contractual agreements with its suppliers may enable the company to distribute the blame and cost if it is determined that an item obtained from them was the faulty part causing the damage or injury.

USER DOCUMENTS

The records that have been described so far are never seen by the ultimate user of a product. Important as they are, even greater significance is attached to the group of documents that the user of the product will actually come in contact with. These documents include labels, brochures, instruction manuals, directions for use, guarantees and warrantees, service contract agreements and policies, and even advertising.

Properly prepared, these documents can protect the company against liability judgments and may even preclude the filing of a suit. Improperly handled, they can spell financial ruin for the company.

Guidelines are available for the preparation of most of this literature. Federal and state statutes, national and local codes, industry standards, and the company's own design and development departments will all play a part in this process. In every case, the company's legal and insurance advisers should examine the *ifs, ands,* and *buts* and the clarity of the language in which these documents are written.

The unsuspecting user might be unaware that there is a distinct difference between "Directions for Use" and a "Warning.' Directions required to assure effective usage may say nothing about the danger of misuse and, hence, would not fulfill the "duty to warn."

A company must also keep in mind that directions are removed from most products prior to use and are then promptly misplaced or irretrievably lost. Precautionary warnings, unless firmly affixed to the product, will follow the same route. The lawn mower manufacturer that has the word "Caution" actually molded into the cast aluminum discharge chute of his machine is in a better defensive position than the competitor who dismisses his responsibility with a paper label or decal that will quickly scratch off.

SERVICE CALL REPORTS

Records relating to service agreements or actual product service not only should be carefully preserved, but also should be complete and thorough down to the minutest detail.

For example, a simple service call report can be prepared so there will be no reason for omitting any critical items of information. The following questions will elicit the necessary information:

1. What was the purpose of the service call or visit? The service representative should identify the item by serial number.

2. What specific repairs were made to the product? Were any parts replaced? If so, for what reason? Were any adjustments made? If so, for what reason?

3. Does it appear that the product was used for some unintended purpose?

4. Does this misuse to appear to create an unsafe condition? If so, what steps were taken to correct this?

5. Has the product been altered by the customer?

6. Have any safety devices been removed or tampered with?

7. Did the customer make any peculiar or unusual inquiries regarding the operation or use of the product and particularly about the function of safety features?

8. Has the customer read and signed the report?

It may seem easier to maintain good customer relations by soothing an irate customer with a quick replacement or a token gift rather than asking him a lot of bothersome questions, but in many cases the entry of the answers to the questions in the company's permanent record file is an additional safeguard in liability proceedings.

Suppose, for example, that the company replaces without examination an item that reportedly caused a fire in a house. The customer relations/ service department neglects to determine the extent of the fire damage or the contribution the company's product made to causing it. The fire marshall, on the other hand, has entered into his report that a defective product, made by the company, was at fault.

Where does the company stand when it is named as defendant by the insurer of the house in its attempt to affix blame and collect damages? Obviously, not in an enviable position.

If, on the other hand, the company had followed a standard policy of examining the damaged product to ascertain any defect and notifying its insurance carrier, it would be in a substantially better position.

COMPLAINT LETTERS

Service records and even consumer complaint letters also provide evidence that for a given number of product units sold, the incidence of failure, defect, or other problems was either low or high. If high, this is a signal to the company that it should redesign the product or modify quality control procedures. Perhaps standards for rejection or acceptance required revising. A complete file showing a minimum of complaints is a perfect Exhibit B for the defense. Exhibit A, of course, would be the internal records discussed earlier.

All correspondence, written or verbal, that relates to a complaint or claim should be retained not only until the entire matter is settled, but afterwards as well, because it can help with subsequent cases and save much time and effort.

The final document needed for a liability protection file is a well-developed plan for tracing the distribution and sale of the company's products. In the event a faulty or potentially dangerous condition exists, the company should be prepared to trace down all units involved and either recall or repair them.

B

IS YOUR BUSINESS ON A COLLISION
COURSE WITH THE PUBLIC?

What can business look forward to in 1971? The picture is not entirely in focus . . .

In the past, business could safely assume that almost every year, the cost of labor and materials would continue to go up, prices would increase and that higher costs, as usual, could be passed along to the consumer.

That assumption is still reasonably safe but it no longer is a major premise. Something new has been added to our economic mix and its ingredients are giving businessmen an unaccustomed and unsettling set of jitters. The new element is consumerism. This was the nut of a recent Conference Board seminar in New York at which industrial, governmental and academic pundits made their predictions for the future.

The jitters are such that some businessmen are now talking about compensating sales and marketing heads not only on the sales they generate—but on the performance of the wares they sell and the amount of reduced complaints from customers; a startling concept, this.

Just how serious is consumerism? How widespread is it? And how can its subtleties be expected to affect the fortunes of American corporations, big and small?

The crystal-ballers differed in their estimates. But on one point all agreed: Consumerism is here, it is big, and growing and serious. If business is to survive as we know it American businessmen cannot shrug it off as a passing fad.

The keynote of the conference was sounded by Betty Furness, former movie actress, television personality, refrigerator peddler and consumer affairs advisor to Lyndon B. Johnson. She is now chairman and executive director, State Consumer Protection Board of New York State.

"Consumers are just beginning to find their collective voice; just beginning to sense their collective strength. It has suddenly dawned on us that laissez-faire isn't fair. That if our money is good there is no reason why we can't demand that what we spend it on be as good."

As her business audience stirred uncomfortably, Miss. Furness laid it on the line: "The consumer game is a game everybody plays whether they want to or not. The world is roughly divided into two teams. On one side is the consumer, on the other, the people producing things for them to consume. . . . But one team has the advantage of putting up other people's money while consumers put up not only their own money but their health, safety and convenience as well."

Miss Furness contends that business, more often than not, conceals the flaws in its products; it does not tell the truth about them, what they can and cannot do. Moreover, business hides behind warranties "that sell the product in big type and take away the consumer's protection in the fine print."

Cataloguing the failings of everyday products, Miss Furness cited shirts that consumers "discovered weren't washable right after they had washed them, fabrics that couldn't take heat right after they had ironed them and colors that weren't color-fast after they had ruined a wash."

Such discoveries, she maintains, are "expensive and irritating" and when consumers complain about them to manufacturers they get little satisfaction. These however, were only "nuisance disaster;" consumers were "in for a lot worse."

OUR POISONOUS TECHNOLOGY

American scientific genius has given us detergents whose phosphates choke our rivers and lakes, high-test fuels that poison our air, nylon stockings that melt, color television sets that emit radiation, insecticides that can kill people as well as bugs, diet foods that do little or nothing for a consumer's health, indeed "may even harm it."

Add soft drinks that "unfortunately included an ingredient many doctors believe is dangerous and that the government eventually had to ban." For another, the pill was heralded as the answer to pregnancy but "privately it was acknowledged as an experimental drug. It was not until the first women developed blood clots and died that the early pill-takers realized they were being used as human guinea pigs without being told, without being asked and without their consent."

Thalidomide was unleashed on an unsuspecting public before its fetus-deforming qualitites were exposed. Cigarette advertising seduced consumers so successfully "with promises of romance if we would only learn to smoke" that eventually the government had to step in with a king-size advertising campaign to convince Americans that cigarette ad claims weren't necessarily Holy Writ.

These experiences, Miss Furness contends, changed the atmosphere of the marketplace and led consumers to wonder about corporate reliability. "Consumers are growing more and more suspicious and more and more questioning. The myth that just because a product is on the market it has been tested and proved safe and okey has been exploded. Trapped by inflation and a growing awareness of pollution both personal and environmental, people are beginning to demand that the rules in the consumer game change."

Change, yes. But how much? In what form? And to what extent?

Miss Furness's antidote for consumerism, as prescribed for businessmen, is more information. Advertising and packaging should tell the whole truth, and nothing but, about a product. If marketers stop glamorizing their wares and simply give the facts, consumers will be able to make more intelligent buying decisions.

Not necessarily so, counters Edward L. Bond Jr., chairman of the board, Young & Rubicam Inc., a giant advertising agency which drumbeats the virtues of many consumer products. Bond admits that marketers are not always on the side of the angels. On the other hand, he contends, the attacks on advertising "are out of all proportion to the wrongs."

Bond says he is "fed up to the eyeballs with the tolerance our society shows to its critics; with the nonachievers who scorn the achievers; with the anti-materialists who sing their songs of protest accompanied by electric guitars played in airconditioned auditoriums built by the entrepreneurial system."

He "refuses to apologize" for industry's pursuit of profit. The profit motive "has led to innovation, greater efficiency and to a gross national product that increased by $411 billion between 1961 and 1969."

This gain, Bond emphasizes, is larger than the *total* output of any other nation except the Soviet Union. It has made possible the growth of a vast middle class of Americans who "enjoy more comforts, more education, more vacations, more security than any other people anywhere."

Thirty-seven million American families own their own homes. Seven out of 10 homes have washing machines; 99.8 percent own refrigerators. Half of our people have finished secondary school—more than in any other country. This year 7.4 million students are enrolled in colleges and universities.

"Show me a country without a free enterprise system." Bond challenges, "and I will show you a country without free art, free elections, free speech.

The wealth of our society—much of which we give away in foreign aid and in assisting developing nations—is due to the ingenuity found in such profusion in our marketplace."

WHAT PRICE GENIUS?

All of this may be so, consumerists concede. But the ingenuity and innovative genius of marketers do not always work to the advantage of the consumer for a number of reasons.

One reason is the basic structure of our economic system. To keep afloat and competitive in an increasingly dog-eat-dog marketplace, manufacturers are forced to worship at the shrine of cost-cutting. This inevitably results in goods that, too often, are not as good as they might be. Or as efficient as marketers know how to make them.

To compensate for this incursion on quality—perhaps even to cover up for it—marketers have taken to exaggerating and overglamorizing the virtues of their wares.

The glamor age of marketing, however, could be passing. And faster and more assuredly than most businessmen anticipate or want. Notes Commissioner Mary Gardiner Jones of the Federal Trade Commission (FTC) the governmental agency that monitors the manners of major advertisers: "The complexities of management, distribution and personnel which beset all business today have developed an institutional blindness (in business) to the immediate problems which their customers actually face. "It is almost as if business is so preoccupied with solving the many internal problems which hamper its ability to provide the kind of service it really wants to provide its customers that it has forgotten to take care of the real problems which bug them"

The commissioner took dead aid at one of the sacred icons of modern corporate religion. "Marketing cannot simply serve the manufacturer's desire to grow and increase sales." Marketing which sees its goals exclusively in such terms "must ultimately be self-defeating if it is done at the *expense* of the customer's goodwill and in the end, of his patronage."

To eliminate deception the FTC typically requires "disclosure of material information" on a product or service. Failure to disclose such information, says Jones, could mislead consumers "as to the actual properties of the product in question . . . and unfairly detract their attention away from what might be superior product either in terms of price or quality."

NAIVE OR NECESSARY?

Marketers, understandably, consider this approach naive. Quips the president of one national package goods company who prefers anonymity: "These fired-up consumerists and bureaucrats who are all for nothing but the truth in advertising and who bleed so copiously for the public overlook one vital point: What advertiser would be willing to spend millions telling the world his product may not be quite as good as the other guy's?"

Bond of Young & Rubicam agrees and makes the further point that complete truth in advertising must result in companies producing ads that are "no more than mere rating sheets or performance charts."

Moreover, Bond maintains he isn't sure consumers really want or need complete truth in advertising. Does a woman really yearn to know that the basis of her most seductive perfume is ambergris, the excrement of a sperm whale? Or that an important hormone, Premarin, in wide medical use, is extracted from the urine of pregnant horses?

Bond concedes business should provide information that the consumer truly needs, but "imagination, fantasy, hope and aspiration,"—prime ingredients of modern promotion —"all have their place in advertising." Without them, life would be dull indeed.

So claims, counterclaims, indictments and defenses shuttle back and forth from consumer to producer—and vice versa. Cleared of the smog of verbiage, however, the consumerism issue seems to boil down to this: Just how big a dose of truth can most products survive? As big as the increasingly strident voice of consumerism demands? Or as little as public opinion and regulatory taboos may allow a company to get away with?

The future alone can tell. One thing, however, is sure: Marketers can expect mounting resistance and resentment from consumers who, for one reason or another, believe they are not getting a fair shake in the marketplace.

Marketers are not unaware that they are on the hot seat; and the seat is getting constantly hotter. They know that sooner or later they must do something about consumerism besides fret over it. The question that makes management toss in its bed is: Who will do the doing?

Business, already awash in a sea of regulations, wants no part of further government regulation. The alternative, of course, is self-regulation. Thus far the history of self-regulation in industry has been less than exemplary. Nevertheless, Steven L. Osterweis, president, Associated Merchandising Corporation, believes business can handle the job on its own.

Equating consumerism with "motherhood, ecology, peace and sex" in today's public consciousness, Osterweis says that "in the 1970s everyone must be for, and can't be against, improving quality standards."

Osterweis assumes business will take a responsible posture toward this end, forestalling any need for government intervention. To achieve this immunity, business must concern itself with three major elements—the safety, public effect and performance of its products.

Safety is an obvious requirement. no company can afford to put out an unsafe product although the recent history of certain pesticides indicates some still do.

The areas of public effect and product performance are less definable. As of now, many manufacturers claim, the public's concern over how a product may affect the environment isn't as pressing as ardent consumerists protest it is.

Women, for example, have been warned repeatedly about the lake and river poisoning effects of phosphate-laden detergents. But their wash is "whiter;" let someone else worry about rivers (although recently, New York's Suffolk county became the first in the nation to ban the sale of all detergents). Farmers know of the toxic qualities of many pesticides but such pesticides are cheap and plentiful. Motorists still demand high-powered, leaded gasolines. The list of self-serving, even if dangerous, products is a long one.

It is this selfish interest—the "men's room mentality" one conservationist calls it—that discourages business from producing products that could be easier to live with it less efficient. Here, Osterweis concedes, governmental regulation is both necessary and desirable. One overall rule for all would remove the temptation that becomes practically a marketing "must" in today's competitive economy.

Business, Osterweis points out, can do a lot—and probably should do more—to improve the quality and life span of its products. Consumers, however, must do their part by being willing to pay more for a better product and learn how to take better care of it.

The "built-in obsolescence" so many consumers complain about, Oster-weis says, may not be the horrendous bugaboo they make it out to be. Most drivers wouldn't buy a car that would last forever even if Detroit could make one. Women's buying urges go up or down with the rise and fall of hemlines dictated by fashion. Washing machines, television sets, dishwashers and innumerable other products constantly add the improvements and refinements that stimulate demand and are the heart and soul of marketing.

Still another factor encourages business to produce products that lead short if not always merry lives. Many corporations assign the responsibility for marketing a product to product managecs and division heads, and set a time limit that prescribes how soon a product is expected to earn its keep.

"What have you done for me lately?" says Osterweis, "is not too far from the mark in describing the manner in which these product managers are judged." Understandably, most product managers are more concerned with peddling their products—and fast—than in improving them.

While such a compulsion exists, Osterweis concedes, self-regulation must remain more of a myth than a reality. There are other dangers. Companies might be tempted to establish minimal industry-wide standards that would discourage others from getting into the business. Any such ploy must attract the unwelcome interest of antitrust. Or an industry might dictate standards low enough not to affect its pocketbook but far from what a militant consumer movement would expect. Which would leave us just about where we are now.

Instead of badgering product managers to get their products out of the house and earning a living as fast as possible, Osterweis would have product managers compensated on the net profit they generate. They would also be rated in relation to the performance of their products and the reduced numbers of complaints registered against them.

Such a system, Osterweis hopes, would result in personnel becoming "more consumer-oriented and responsible." Perhaps. One not-so-altruistic vice president of a manufacturing company comments dourly: "It's a noble thought. And maybe some day the chairman of the board will invite the night porter for lunch."

As of now there are some 200 "consumer bills" before Congress. This, in addition to the vast body of consumer law that already exists. *The Wall Street Journal* notes that "there are already nearly 1,000 consumer-related activities being conducted by existing Federal departments and agencies not to mention those at the local and state levels."

So imposing an array of law and enforcement agencies could encourage some to believe that Congress is genuinely interested in the consumer movement. But one skeptical consumerist remarks: "There's also a law that will give you a year in jail and a $1,000 fine for spitting in the subway. But how many of our jails are bulging with subway spitters?"

The fact that Congress until now has not split its pants rushing to enforce consumer legislation isn't an indication that it never will. Public opinion and pressure are potent inducers of political action. And business is worried about the form such action, political or public, might take.

How imminent is the threat of a government "czar of consumerism" ala Will Hays whom the movie moguls called in to police them when their product was under fire?

What about boycotts? Could hundreds of thousands, possibly millons of aroused and resentful consumers band themselves in a league that would publicly proclaim the deficiencies of certain products and snub them in the marketplace?

Could regional, local or state legislation be enacted that would compel industry to retool to meet their standards? California today, for example, requires pollution-controlling devices on cars. Spiked snow tires are banned in some states. DDT is taboo in certain localities, permitted in others. A crazy quilt of laws and regulations could seriously hamper business and increase the cost of marketing its products.

Such fears are real. The voices of the consumer are loud in the land and not all are those of the lunatic fringe—the professional militant, hippie student, dreaming altruist. Many belong to the most respected and influential members of government, academia and business itself.

Warns Secretary of Commerce Maurice H. Stans: "Businessmen must replace the outmoded and unequal principle of caveat emptor—let the buyer beware—with a new and fairer rule of conduct—doceatur emptor—let the buyer be informed."

Arjay Miller, former Ford Motor chief, now dean, graduate school of business, Stanford University, believes that "the key to a successful response by corporate management to the present consumerism is recognition that we are playing in a new ball game and that new ground rules are necessary."

David Swankin, Washington representative of Consumers Union, rocked businessmen by citing "countless numbers of unresolved consumer grievances" and cautioned that "like all other institutions the marketplace must become responsive to legitimate complaints or change will be *forced* upon it."

Zeroing in on "corporate neglect of its customer," Corwin D. Edwards, professor of economics, University of Oregon and former member of the Consumers Advisory Council charges that "When sold, new products often need further adjustment, repair or service. . . . Service and repair are often hard to get, slow, incompetent, expensive and dishonest." Moreover, warranties are "often obscure, tricky, meaningless or ineffective." The professor laments that "thus far responses by business to these new pressures have been very uneven."

Another professor, Richard W. Gumz, graduate school of business administration, Rutgers University, believes that "the major failure of marketing today has been to understand the significance of the fact that the consumer is and always will be supreme. In the future marketers will have to make a concerted effort and come to grips with this problem or face the consequences of serious and effective government reprisal."

Where is business heading in 1971—and the years after? Business alone can answer. Among businessmen the consensus is that those companies that recognize and react intelligently to the new, powerful and potentially dangerous wave of consumerism will survive, even prosper.

For the others it could be later than they think.

ADDITIONAL SELECTED BIBLIOGRAPHY

Corporate Ethics

"The Lengthening Reach of Liability," *Business Week* (September 16, 1967), 100-101.

"Backgrounder and NCFA Position Statement on Class Action Legislation," *Consumer Finance News,* Vol. 55, No. 4 (October, 1970), 4-5, 13, 18, 24, 26.

Arnold, R. T., "Professional Ethics and Protection of Trade Secrets," *Trade Secrets: A Management Overview,* J. W. Blood, ed., AMA Management Bulletin No. 64, American Management Association (1965), 9-13.

Austin, Robert W., "Code of Conduct for Executives," *Harvard Business Review,* Vol. 30, No. 5 (September-October, 1961), 53-61.

Baumhart, Rev. R. C., "How Ethical Are Businessmen," *Harvard Business Review,* Vol. 39, No. 4 (July-August, 1961), 6-19, 156-176.

Cox, A.A., "Product Liability," *The Southern Journal of Business*, Vol. 4, No. 2 (April, 1969), 80-86.

Hursh, R.D., "The Products Liability Problem," *Journal of Marketing*, Vol. 27, No. 4 (October, 1963), 9-14.

"Searle Loses New Case on Birth Control Pills," *The Wall Street Journal* (April 27, 1970), 12.

Southwick, A. F., Jr., "The Disenchanted Consumer—Liability for Harmful Products," *Michigan Business Review,* Vol. 18, No. 1 (January, 1966), 5-11.

Zaretsky, E. W., and Kraig, J. B., "Current Trends in Product Liability," *Management Review,* Vol. 58, No. 11, (November 1969), 49-53. (This article condensed from original article found in *Automation* (August, 1969), published by the Penton Publishing Co.

Questions for Discussion and Review

1. Should a code of ethics be spelled out for all businessmen? How would you begin to form a code?

2. Do you believe that some business organizations abide by a code of ethics? Can you name any?

3. Why is product liability so massive a problem today?

4. Can you explain why firms today are losing hazard suits at an ever increasing rate?

5. Does liability hold true for professionals? Explain.

6. What ideas can you express concerning standardization of consumer products?

17

BUYER DILEMMAS

Many organizations have come into being to protect the consumer or to enlighten the consumer. Federal and state laws have been enacted through the years to reduce the danger to the consumer of products sold in the open market. Magazines such as *Consumer Reports* also direct the consumer to the quality and price aspects of goods and services sold throughout the country. Consumer education at the senior high school level and in college curriculums is providing the background, knowledge, understanding, and utilization of this information for the purchase of products and services. Adult education classes held in public schools in the evenings also provide information and guidance in helping buyers to be more responsible. In the end, however, it becomes the responsibility of the buyers to become familiar with the various product offerings. Many firms pride themselves in their product line and zealously guard the reputation of their products. This is one major reason for developing brand consciousness. Products, by law, must be described by content of material, ingredients, instruction for use and care, side effects, any dangers surrounding their utilization, their weight, or a combination thereof. Distributing this information to users of the products permits the buyers to make more rational buying decisions. However, it still remains the responsibility of the buyer to be more astute or to ask questions about products before purchase, rather than entertain cognitive dissonance after purchase or make product purchases without reason or need.

It is also the buyer's responsibility to perform some comparison shopping before purchasing, so as to locate and decide on the best purchases. A mass educational program is one method to inform the buyer of his responsibility as a consumer. Indirectly, the product manufacturer will benefit from this, too, should he value his reputation and future success. The following articles espouse buyer dilemmas and costs facing buyers other than the price of the product alone.

THE COSTS OF INADEQUATE
STANDARDS TO THE CONSUMER
BY WALTER SANDBACH

INTRODUCTION

Since the end of World War II, and coming into full public view for the first time with President Kennedy's issuance of his consumer's "Bill of Rights" message in 1962, the U.S. has witnessed a swelling of interest in the consumer's welfare. In the field of safety, it has engulfed the automobile industry. The textile manufacturers have announced the intiation of a voluntary program of care-labeling for finished garments. Drugs, food and packaging and have been affected by this rising tide of interest in the welfare of the consumer.

More than mere prosperity lies behind the new wave of concern for the consumer. Consumers Union, when it embarked on its work thirty years ago, quickly found the interest for its publication not, as anticipated, among working men, but rather among the educated middle class. America is now rapidly approaching a homogeneous middle-class society. More and more people are willing to read to get information. No less a watchtower of our economic scene than *Business Week* asks itself, "What has caused all the excitement about consumer legislation and protection at this particular time?" In answer to its own question, "The best answer seems to be that the American consumer is, indeed, the best educated in the world, and he's

EDITOR'S NOTE: From *New Ideas for Successful Marketing,* J.S. Wright and J.L. Gold-stucker, eds., 1966, pp. 169-177. Reprinted by permission of the American Marketing Association and the author.

beginning to demand more information on which to make purchasing decisions."

Some auto executives probably wish that they had taken to heart the wisdom in a scene from the play, "Born Yesterday," as remembered by Clayton Fritchey in a recent newspaper column. In this scene the wheeler-dealer's not-so-dumb blonde companion is somewhat unimpressed with his bragging about how he can buy and sell people in government. "To hell with the public," says the wheeler-dealer. "You better watch your step, Harry," retorts the blonde, "they're getting more prominent all the time."

Of course, being "professional consumers" as our critics like to call us, we at Consumers Union hope that the wheeler-dealer's blonde was right and that the consumer will continue to rise in prominence. The need for this to happen was never greater. The famous designer, Raymond Loewy, stated the problem and the need for end-use standards for consumer products, as he spoke at the American Standards Association's 15th Annual Conference on Standards. Mr. Loewy said:

"Taking a hard look at the total output of American industry, I am amazed at its output and the brilliance of those who have created it. At the same time, I am dismayed by the diminished quality of some of our most popular products. Good old goods-hungry United States, nation of gadget-lovers, of implements and sophisticated machinery, consumers-extraordinaires of the most glittering and diverse heap of products any country has ever produced, is developing a case of mild indigestion. For a great, creeping nausea is rising over products that don't work, that fall apart in the hand, that buzz and rattle and fail and fail and fail again, and generally make themselves unpalatable.

"The ingredients, if I can believe the claims of producers of basic materials, are superior. Or, if they are not superior, at least they are honestly labeled. But while I hear tongue-clacking over how many transistors there are in the set, what percentage of genuine down feathers and what of unpedigreed barnyard chicken feathers, how pure the gold, how thick the salami, where is the standard for how good the end product?

"There has been an incredible scientific and technological explosion in recent times. Except for some major benefits to people in medicine, the chance to move around and communicate faster, the ability to over-kill, just plain consumers haven't very·much to show for this admirable and unprecedented human activity."

Raymond Loewy's statement echoes the thousands of letters we receive from consumers every year, complaining about products that have been built to too low a standard and have been marketed with advertising that gives the impression that the millennium has arrived. Is it any wonder that consumers are unhappy?

STANDARDS

At Consumers Union, inundated by these letters of complaint about products that do not live up to their promises, we are in danger of developing a warped viewpoint about products that are available in the market place. Fortunately our testing convinces us that there have been marked improvements in recent years in the design and performance of many products. Unfortunately, our testing also shows that there has been no improvement in many products, and even regression in some.

Our testing at Consumers Union is an effort to set standards for the end use of products. We find this goal entirely feasible. Wherever standards do exist, CU examines them for application to our tests: ASA, ASTM, GSA, Military Specifications, USDA standards for grades, and SAE performance standards for autos and automotive equipment. Our question is always this: Do the standard and the test for it reflect the kind of use to which the product will be put and the situation of that use?

Standards in the CU reports have either been originated by us or have been modified, adapted, or accepted from existing standards for use in testing and rating several hundred different kinds of products. The limitations have been mainly those of our own financial rescources and, with some products, the lack of identifiable brands with a reasonable expectation of shelf life before yielding to model changes.

End-use standards, consumer standards, marketing standards, call them what you will, are calculated to liberate, not enslave, the shopper. They should liberate him from the task of trying to skim off the product puffery, liberate him from having to sort out the conflicting and often meaningless performance claims, and finally liberate him from the emotional appeals that promise him status, or popularity, or sexual irresistibility.

THE GOALS OF STANDARDS

Present marketing standards, as dictated by the marketing departments of our corporations, need not be judged from the viewpoint of morality. They should, rather, be judged by how the consumer economy functions under them. Do they promote consumption and thus production? Undoubtedly they do. Do they serve the ultimate, or even the immediate ends of the production-consumption system?

What are the ends? To us at Consumers Union, the ends are these:

1. An adequate, varied supply of goods and services.
2. A steady improvement of quality and open-ended innovation.
3. A respect for the limitations of our natural resources.

4. A positive contribution to the quality of life.

Very few would disagree with these as the objectives of our producer-consumer economy. Success in reaching these goals depends in large measure, not only on the conscience of the manufacturer, but also on the critical judgment of the consumer. How can the consumer make critical judgments, and make them well, unless he is supplied with information? The label on the goods he selects must speak to him in clear and universally understood language. This language must include standards of quality, quantity, durability, safety, and performance. How well does the consumer fare with regard to these various standards as he makes his purchases in today's market place? Here are some examples from our testing and observations at Consumers Union.

THE COST OF INADEQUATE STANDARDS

Except for a home, the largest single expenditure most people make is for an automobile. The recent announcement that 8.7 million new cars had been called in since 1959 to correct manufacturing defect was treated by Congressmen as shocking news. It was no shock to many consumers and certainly not to our auto test division at CU. For a long time we have known that the consumer frequently got the short end of quality when he purchased one of these magnificent chariots, marvels of our manufacturing genius.

During 1963, Consumers Union purchased 32 cars for test. Here is what we had to say near the end of that year: "In anything as complicated as a car, pure chance will pay a part in the presence or absence of troubles. But something more than chance is at work when 32 out of 32 cars chosen at random for testing show troubles on one kind or another in the first few thousand miles. That's what CU found with the 1963 cars tested this past year. And CU's automotive consultants know what the 'something other than chance' is, it's bad quality control in the automobile industry. All the . . . '63's CU tested had something wrong with them either to begin with or very shortly thereafter."

In 1964, as the eight-million-new car goal was reached for the first time, faulty cars continued to plague dealers and consumers. In the judgment of our auto test division, the condition of the 1965 cars CU bought for testing was about the worst so far as sloppiness in production goes in the whole ten year stretch of deterioration that began in 1955.

Is it any different in 1966? Here's what we say in our April issue of *Consumer Reports:* "The gremlins in the automobile industry control are still at work and appear to be just as impartial as ever, judging by the 1966 cars CU bought for testing. It would be some small comfort to find that the defects in cars, as delivered, are all of the trivial, if annoying type, such as screws missing from trim or inoperative lighters. Unfortunately, they aren't.

Your car is just as likely to be delivered to you with a transmission fluid leak, or with the power steering hose almost chafed through by the fan belt."

1966 cars were delivered with rain leaks, a shock absorber control broken off, a power window inoperative, a defective engine block which requred replacement, from wheels improperly aligned, something the ordinary consumer is not apt to notice until his tires are badly worn; and cars arrived with headlights aimed at the ground, or at the eyes of approaching motorists, or at birds in the trees.

Remember that these were new cars, cars that retail from $1800 to $5500. Isn't the automobile consumer entitled to a standard of quality and of quality control better than this record would indicate?

Standards for auto safety are a story and several speeches, in themselves. Ralph Nader, who wrote an article on auto safety for *Consumer Reports* last February, has already focused nationwide attention on this issue. There is not time to review here all the charges and contercharges in the controversy which has arisen; but there does now seem to be general agreement that safer cars can be built and that the consumer has the right to ask for, and expect to get, the highest of standards in this critical area.

A part of the auto safety picture is the need for adequate production and marketing standards for tires, standards that are available to the consumer at the point-of-purchase. Recently *The New York Times* carried a news story about a Congressional hearing on tires, including this item: "The Federal Government's chief auto safety expert, Heinz A. Abersfeller, today testified that two-ply tires were 'not adequate for safe operation.'" The news story goes on: "Representative John E. Moss, Democrat of California, held up a piece of flimsy looking material, identified it as part of the sidewall from a two-ply tire and asked: 'Did you find that these two-ply marvels were safe?'

" 'In our judgment it meets the current General Services Administration requirement,' Mr. Abersfeller replied.

" 'Is it adequate for safe operation?' Mr. Moss asked. 'It is not,' the witness said."

Or listen to Senator Gaylord Nelson as he appeared recently on National Educational Television: "The auto industry, in equipping their cars with original equipment tires, and the tire industry, have not really been concerned or interested at all, in my judgment, about being careful about the safety factors on the automobiles. They have calculatedly and intentionally avoided giving the consumer any indication of what the quality of the safety factor in the tire was so that he can make an honest judgment."

The interviewer queries the Senator: "Intentionallly is a very serious word. ... " And again Senator Nelson: "I don't think there's any doubt about that. They have intentionally avoided ... as a matter of fact, when they started out putting on 2 ply tires called 2 ply tire/4 ply rating, they put the tire marking on the inside of the wheel on the automobile, so that the only way the consumer buying a new automobile could discover that he had a 2 ply/4 ply rated tire was to get underneath the car and look at the inside. Well, this is obvious that they had to put it on the tire, but they didn't want the consumer to know it. When they label tires with all these adjectives, you can have tires with the fanciest name, such as super supreme, and maybe they're third grade tires. So they have intentionally avoided putting information on the tire that would be of any value whatsoever."

These are very serious charges to make against two of our greatest industries, but there is little doubt left in the public mind that they are basically true. What has been the cost in money, and in lives, from inadequate and unknown standards for tires? Who is to say? Let us hope that the situation will soon be changed through pending legislation.

The move to automatic washing machines involves much more complex circuitry than in the old wringer washer. While a great boon to the housewife, the automatic machine has not been an unmixed blessing. Recently, Consumers Union asked its members about their experiences with their washing machines. We tabulated replies from 78,000 homes; they dealt with 13 brands purchased during the preceding nine years. These are generally well known brands, and one can assume that both performance and durability was considered in their design and production. What levels of performance and durability have been achieved? What kind of troubles did people encounter? Here are a few of the tabulations. Out of 78,000 washing machines reported on 13,400 did not complete washing cycle correctly; 10,800 leaked or flooded; 9,000 failed to spin; 8,900 had the pump blocked by an item escaping from the tub; 8,400 were excessively noisy or vibrated too much; 5,400 had transmission trouble.

As expected, the older machines required more repairs at higher costs, but 7 per cent of even the two-year-old machines had already needed repairs costing over $50, and 2 percent of the two-year-old machines cost more than $100 to fix. The standards involved with regard to washing machines were primarily adequate performance and durability. Is it really beyond the state of the manufacturing art to do better than this record indicates? The cost in money to consumers as a result of these low standards is enormous. To this cost must be added the housewife's inconvenience, and unhappiness, as she waits from a day to several weeks to get her machine back in operation.

In the field of textiles and clothing a revolution has occurred. This revolution has created vast new problems for the consumer. Consider what has happened. First came rayon, and after a time, nylon. Then followed Dacron, Orlon, Acrilan, Creslan, Lycra, and dozens of other fibers and yarns. Soon these synthetics appeared in combination with natural fibres. Chemical manipulation also modified familiar natural fibers into substantially new products: cotton that has some properties of the synthetics, and wool that doesn't shrink and retains a crease.

There has been no lack of troubadours to sing the praises of this revolution. Perhaps it is enough to state that objective tests done by Consumers Union and other disinterested institutions do provide a record of new and often desirable properties found in the so-called miracle fibers and fabrics. At the same time, few would deny that consumers have fallen hopelessly behind in their understanding of modern textiles. The most knowledgeable people have trouble identifying the fabric of which a garment is made, and even when given this information they cannot adequately predict the garment's performance.

The textile revolution can raise or not raise the standard of living depending on whether the consumer can take full advantage of its benefits. The consumer will not be able to take full advantage of those benefits until industry or government, or both in collaboration, have developed adequate standards for end use. Labels on textile goods must, indeed, state plainly the proper instructions for cleaning and maintenance, as now proposed by a textile industry committee. But labels must state much more. What is needed by the consumer is information on performance: durability, crease retention, shrinkage, stain resistance, and other properties that are appropriate for the intended use of the item. But before reliable statements can be made, there must be standards.

What would be wrong, for example, with letting the consumer know how well a carpet can be expected to wear under normal conditions? Is that really too much to ask? In *Home Furnishings Daily* appeared this news item: "Retailers should try to fight the fallacy in the public mind that carpets should last a lifetime, the Wisconsin Floor Covering Association was told here. Mrs. Lee Kolker, director of styling for C.H. Masland and Sons, pointed out that automobile builders have gotten themselves into the ideal situation, where they sell a product which will be next to worthless in five years and which will give trouble in the meantime."

There are certainly affluent people who, for style or decorating reasons, would change carpets every few years no matter what the cost. But there are many more who would like to know which carpet will give them the most service for their money so that they could use the money saved on carpets for some other purpose, perhaps even for buying other consumer goods. At the present time there is no way for them to find out this information. Research on the durability of most textile products is at a primitive stage with very little effective work being done to bring it up to date. What is required, therefore, is to undertake the necessary research for a number of important products.

Recognizing this need, Consumers Union, in 1964, offered to underwrite a Research Associate at the National Bureau of Standards to work in the area of carpets and rugs. The offer went a-begging, mainly because the National Bureau of Standards could not get the carpet industry to cooperate in setting up a programm of research. The NBS was unwilling to set up a research program without industry cooperation, even when CU was willing to underwrite the cost.

The case for end-use standards could be made for many other product categories, furniture, for example. Recently, Walter N. Rothschild, Jr., president of Abraham & Straus, a Brooklyn department store, said, in speaking of quality standards: "Probably the saddest tale of all is furniture. The industry's standards of construction leave much to be desired. Look at drawer bottoms or dresser backs. We have to maintain what is in effect a furniture rebuilding department to repair new furniture before some of it can go out to our customer." We at CU would add to Mr. Rothschild's remarks also that marketing standards for furniture also leave much to be desired.

CONCLUSION

Anyone who wants further documentation of the need for standards can find it by reference to *Consumer Reports.* Our reports of such staple products as refrigerators, toasters, television sets, kitchen ranges, to name a few, are replete with reference to the too low level of total quality. We have found over and over again that name brands, or price, are very seldom an accurate guide on which the consumer can depend in choosing the best product for his intended use. In a recent test project on blenders, and this is not an untypical example, the blender that did the best overall job retailed for $24.97. A blender retailing at $64.95 received a lower rating in our tests, and one selling for $62.95 was rated NOT ACCEPTABLE for safety reasons. What would be the savings to American consumers if they had sufficient information for them to be able to always buy the best value for their money? The amount saved would be astronomical!

For the sake of preserving the bountifulness of our continent we, sooner or later, are going to have to wean ourselves away from the wasteful production-consumption practices of today. There are warning signs wherever one cares to look. We simply can no longer afford waste of the prodigious scale practiced in the U.S.A.

In a way we are asking our industrial system, under Government sponsorship if necessary, to become its own Consumers Union. If this goal is realized and the present CU is put out of business as a result, so be it. What we think we have proved is that standards for end use are feasible-imperfect, yes-but not to be condemned for that, certainly.

Let the public decide what it wants. Give the consumer meaningful information, which requires standards of quality, quantity, safety, durability, and performance. The trend in one hundred years of mass-produced consumer goods unfortunately argues against our having too much hope for industry self-improvement in this regard. However, what is happening with the auto industry should give ample warning that if industry will not act voluntarily to give the consumer the standards and the information he needs, the consumer does have a final recourse-the Government. The hour is late, but in most product areas there is still time for industry to take the initiative in establishing standards which will enable the consumer to "vote" for or against a product on the basis of full information.

THE CONSUMER'S NEEDS PERSIST

BY SIDNEY MARGOLIUS

LIMITED PROGRESS

The past two years have seen much discussion and many hearings on behalf of the consumer, but little real progress has been made since the enactment of the landmark truth-in-lending bill in 1968.

The truth of the matter is that after all the sensational but fleeting publicity, consumers are still exploited on almost every front—from chinchilla promotions and other schemes operated by small deceivers to misleading packaging and advertising and overpriced products by huge food and drug manufacturers. And the money lost by the average family to these schemes has been especially costly in the last two years—a period of destructive inflation in which the moderate-income consumer daily runs a hazardous financial obstacle course.

Part of the problem of lack of progress is the welter of legislative proposals on behalf of the consumer. Many of these deal with peripheral problems which—while sometimes fairly important—obscure the real needs or are easier for congressmen and state legislators to attack.

For example, only a few states have had much effort to try to reduce the high finance charges paid by consumers, with local labor councils taking the lead in what effort has been made. On the other hand, many hearings and other legislative actions have been related to regulating credit bureaus

EDITOR'S NOTE: From the *AFL-CIO American Federationist,* January 1971, pp. 1-6. Reprinted by permission of the American Federation of Labor—Congress of Industrial Organizations and the author.

and credit-card mailings. Some people are adversely affected by unfair activities of credit bureaus and credit-card operators. But everybody, and the nation itself, is seriously affected by high interest rates. Similarly, much attention has been paid to "open dating" of food; relatively little to the high cost of food.

Much is made of small concessions to consumers such as Virginia Knauer's success in getting the Agriculture Department to reduce its proposed limit on fat content of frankfurters from 33 percent to 30. But the proposal for an independent federal consumer agency that could press various federal departments for more adequate standards and labeling on all foods, among other consumer needs, was blocked by the House Rules Committee. It refused, in a 7-7 tie vote, to let the full House consider the proposal. It had already passed the Senate by an overwhelming vote.

EFFORTS WASTED

Often the consumer organizations and other community groups themselves are led by the congressional staffs and federal agencies and commissions into campaigning for the less-important objectives instead of stimulating these staffs to more important goals that might truly reduce some of the great waste of family and national resources.

Some of the confused and unsuccessful activity on behalf of consumers results from haste, or perhaps even opportunism, rather than from an expert understanding of basic needs. For example, five different senators and several congressmen introduced proposals for various kinds of federal consumer departments or agencies. The bill that finally did move through the Senate only to be blocked by the House Rules Committee was a catchall of a number of proposals. But it did include the sorely-needed independent federal agency.

Another example of heavily-publicized activity on isolated problems was the hearings on breakfast cereals held by a Senate consumer subcommittee late in 1970. The main result of the inexpert and confusing testimony was to persuade much of the public that ordinary cereals have little or no nutrition and to encourage the sale of several over-priced, vitamin-fortified products.

But the much broader and economically significant report of a House subcommittee on the need for more adequate meat supplies was lobbied into oblivion by the American Cattlemen's Association and other farm groups. "Oblivion" came when the House Government Operations Committee didn't even release its subcommittee's report, much less act on it.

THE ADMINISTRATION'S ROLE

The Nixon Administration itself quite apparently has given just enough of the semblance of help to keep consumers from outright rebellion without actually remedying their problems. For every truly determined effort on behalf of consumers, the Administration and the business community have made a counter-proposal which would weaken the original proposal.

When a "class action" bill was proposed to facilitate suits by consumer groups for recoveries of overcharge, the Administration countered with a proposal to require first a successful suit by the Department of Justice before consumers could sue. When an independent consumer agency was proposed, the Administration countered with a proposal, endorsed by the Chamber of Commerce, to make statutory the present voluntary position of Consumer Assistant to the President and to institute a consumer division in the Department of Justice. The Justice Department is not noted for any persistent pursuit of consumer remedies.

Similarly, the Commerce Department has done a little but not much to relieve the problem of package-proliferation as was promised in the truth-in-packaging act, while the Food & Drug Administration seems determined to ignore the urgings of some congressmen to require more informative food labeling and standards—such as labeling the drained weights of canned fruits and vegetables and the percentages of ingredients in processed foods. Cleverly-deceptive illustrations and labeling continue to appear on packages under the Agriculture Department's juridiction even though the department has both the existing power and mechanism to require more honest packaging.

BUYING POWER DOWN

All of these missed opportunities have meant a serious plight for the consumer, who has had his buying power heavily eroded by the accelerated inflation of 1968-70. And more of the same is threatened in 1971, especially from still-rising medical, housing and car-owner costs.

In fact, by November 1970, the sharp rise in living costs had wiped out all the wage gains made by the average industrial worker in the past six years. In 1964 the average production worker with three dependents had spendable earnings after taxes of $76.38 in terms 1957-59 dollars. Currently he has just $77 a week of buying power calculated on the same basis. The average worker in manufacturing industries actually is even worse off than in 1964, with $84.43 in spendable dollars now, compared to $85.27 then.

CONSUMER PROBLEMS

There are six overriding problems today on which consumers are seriously in need of help. Presently little or no help is available, and "consumer education" or piecemeal legislation or hearings are no way to solve these problems. They are:

The high cost of food.

The pervasive effects of high interest rates, coupled with collection laws stacked on the side of the sellers, which affect consumers directly in financing homes, cars and other needs and lead to higher property and other taxes.

Booming medical costs and inadequacies of present private medical insurance, causing real anxieties in many families and a resurgence of high-pressure promotion of low-value insurance plans seeking to capitalize on those anxieties.

High housing costs.

Serious quality problems which have led to high repair costs especially for cars and household appliances and even create safety hazards as shown by the recent investigations of the National Commission on Product Safety.

High, and still rising, cost of auto insurance, which has made it the largest cost of car ownership for many moderate-income families and a particular burden on workers who must drive to a job.

Several of the federal and state proposals now pending will help alleviate some of these problems.

Food Costs

High food costs are still the basic problem. Food costs affect all other costs. But the general public has less voice in the decisions affecting its food costs than in almost any other consumer issue.

You would never be able to tell it from the prices you have to pay in the stores, but some farm prices, especially of livestock and poultry, dropped sharply in the fall of 1970. Processors and stores have been reluctant to pass on these decreases. By November, prices of farm products in general were 4 percent below a year ago, but retail prices were about 3 percent higher.

The result is that the "spread" between what a costs on the farm and at the market has widened to the point where farmers recently have been getting only 38 cents of the dollar you spend for food while the distributing industry's take has increased to 62 cents.

The current 38-62 division contrasts with the 40 cents going to farmers and 60 to the distribution industry in recent years and the 50-50 breakdown which was customary before and immediately after World War II.

Food prices have become an obvious sacred cow, so to speak. Both the Agriculture Department and farm organizations, to the benefit of distributors and processors but the detriment of farmers, have offered as their only contribution to solving the problem, the slogan that "food is a bargain." Congress itself, while willing to consider lesser proposals related to food, has been afraid to tackle the gut issue of prices. Congress completely ignored the recommendations of the National Commission on Food Marketing in 1966 for quality grades and other reasonable proposals, even though Congress itself had established the commission to seek ways to restrain food prices.

The futility of the government's mock war on inflation is that it has failed to attack such basic living cost problems. In fact, several times during the past few years, while the Administration was trying to quench the fire of inflation by pouring on the gasoline of higher interest rates, the Agriculture Department was encouraging farmers to keep up food prices by reducing supplies, as in the specific cases of tomatoes in 1969 and eggs in 1970.

At least three current proposals would help restrain food prices or help consumers select better value, thus indirectly restraining costs.

One is the proposal, still kept underground by the House Committee on Government Operations, to establish a national commission to gather information on present and future meat requirements. With meat alone taking 25 percent of a working family's food budget, the supply of meat is an influential factor in living costs—too influential to leave up to cattle raisers' associations alone.

The second proposal is to require unit pricing of foods. In addition to price per package, the retailer would have to show the price per pound or quart. Unit pricing would give consumers what the final version of the truth-in-packaging law failed to provide: a uniform way to compare prices on the basis of standard weights and measures.

Recognizing the fairness and economic usefulness of unit pricing, several states and a number of supermarket chains already have installed or plan to install partial systems of unit pricing. For example, when Esther Peterson, the first presidential consumer adviser, recently became consumer consultant to a chain of food stores in Washington, D.C., one of her first roles was to shepherd the chain's entry into unit pricing. Massachusets became the first state to actually require unit pricing, effective in 1971. In New York, Betty Furness, chairman of the New York State Consumer Protection Board, has held meetings with retailers with a view to recommending a unit-pricing law to that state's legislature.

Demand also is developing for more-informative labeling of processed foods in order to help consumers determine food values in an era of many processed and even imitation foods. Often these new ready-to-eat and invented foods, while priced high, tend to cut down on actual food values through addition of cheap fillers such as fats, water, sugar and starch. While manufacturers now must list ingredients of processed foods in order of importance, consumers have no way to know how much water has been added to frankfurters and lunch meats (legally, up to 10 percent) or to frozen poultry (up to 8 percent) or pre-sweetened breakfast cereals (any amount of sugar, but usually 45 percent). And those are just a few of the many examples which could be cited.

Federal agencies have the authority to require such percentage listing now, without further legislation. But food manufacturers are resisting this proposal intensely and suggesting instead a list of nutrients, such as the amount of protein and various vitamins. By itself, such a listing would be less than helpful to consumers and even misleading. Protein varies in nutritional quality and manufacturers also can draw attention away from basically low or only moderately nutritious products by adding cheap, synthetic vitamins. This presently is being done with the vitamin-fortified breakfast cereals.

Judging from various comments of officials, there is a danger that government agencies, and also congressmen unversed in nutritional economics, will acede to the nutrient-labeling counter-proposal without also requiring a showing of the percentages of actual ingredients.

Interest Rates

The prime interest rate has recently been reduced slightly, but these reductions have been of small direct help to consumers so far, although an indirect benefit has been the reduction of federal and municipal borrowing costs.

The direct help so far has consisted of a reduction of 25 cents per $100 in finance charges for loans by some banks—and even this small reduction was occasioned not so much by eagerness to reduce rates as by a decline in consumer borrowing in late 1970.

Similarly, the government has reduced the maximum interest rate of FHA and VA mortages to 8 percent from the previous 8 1/2. The reduction is much too small to enable most moderate-income families to finance individual houses, or even to reduce significantly the total cost of such high-rate mortgages. A borrower will repay a total of $53,000 on a $20,000 mortgage at 8 percent for 30 year.

In at least four states, efforts have been made or are underway to limit retail credit rates to 12 percent per annum. The Washington State AFL-CIO succeeded in 1968 in getting a state referendum which reduced the maximum rate from 18 to 12 percent. In 1969, the AFL-CIO called for a national campaign by state labor bodies to secure similar rate reductions. The Minnesota AFL-CIO has initiated a lawsuit against one retail chain, charging that its revolving credit rate of 18 percent a year violates that state's 8 percent usury law. In Oregon and Wisconsin, similar reductions have been made or are pending.

Harsh collection laws in most states are one of the reasons lenders and credit dealers often can get away with high interest and deceptive selling practices based on easy credit. Already five states have eliminated or restricted the holder in due course doctrine. This legal provision permits finance companies to escape responsibility for deception or non-performance by dealers who turn over sales contracts to them.

The National Commission on Consumer Finance currently is investigating such presently-permitted collection devices as holder in due course; fast repossessions coupled with court judgments and wage assigments; "sewer service;" inconvenient venues; harassment tactics; post-bankruptcy suits and misuse of small claims courts by creditors.

The commission's recommendations are due in mid-1972. If the commission recognizes the harmful nature of this bag of collection tricks, its findings may accelerate the present painfully piecemeal trend among the states to ameliorate these practices.

Medical Costs

The relentless increase in medical costs has caused a good deal of fear among moderate-income families. Medical costs in general have risen 68 percent in little over a decade. Eliminating drug costs from the combined figure, medical-care services have gone up 85 percent, led by the frightening rise of 200 percent in hospital service charges.

As a result, requests for information and complaints about various privately-sold health insurance plans have become the leading type of letter I receive from the column I write for labor papers.

Some of the letters are pathetic. A California couple pays $167 a year for a health insurance policy but the insuror would pay only $15 toward a minor operation for the wife. An Illinois couple is unable to find medical insurance for an invalid son. A Florida man took out a policy with one of the companies currently advertising heavily in newspapers and now is worried whether the policy is any good.

What is most pathetic is that these people have no place at all to turn for expert guidance on what supplementary health insurance to buy, or for evaluation of the multiplicity of varying policies offered by the high-pressured insurance sellers. Meanwhile these sellers, judging from the volume of letters from working families, are successfully persuading a great many moderate-income people to buy policies. Such policies usually promise to pay up to $100 a week for hospitalized illnesses at a time when hospital costs are approaching $100 a day. While the price of such insurance seems low, the benefits are so minimal as to be almost nominal.

Because of the crisis nature of the runaway health-care costs, several plans for National Health Insurance have been formulated. The experience of Medicare, as well as that of unions in other insured plans, has shown that insurance alone is not enough. Medical fees rise to meet the available insurance.

The Nixon Administration is reportedly preparing a proposal to attempt to cope with excessive costs of establishing yet unspecified controls and standards for fees. The program endorsed by the AFL-CIO would seek to provide not only National Health Insurance but to encourage more economical delivery of health care through prepaid group care and an increased supply of health care personnel.

Housing Costs

The average wage-earner has been effectively priced out of the new housing market. The median sales prices of new homes sold in mid-1970 was approximately $24,000, according to the Department of Housing and Urban Development. You need an income of about $10,000 a year—and possibly more—to afford this kind of price tag on a house.

In fact, with rising property taxes and mortgages in the 8 percent bracket, HUD Secretary George Romney has estimated that it takes close to $300 a month to finance the median new home today, including mortgage payments, maintenance and utilities.

While labor costs often are blamed for high prices of homes, the fact is that construction costs, which include both labor and materials, actually have risen less sharply than the price of land, interest and other contractor costs and overhead. Construction costs rose 22 percent from 1964 to early 1970, compared to the increase of 29 percent in the median sale price of the houses. Construction costs of publicly-owned housing increased even less—about 14 percent in that period.

Even middle-income families now often need help in the way of subsidized housing, especially younger families seeking their first homes. It has been estimated that the building or financing of perhaps half of the dwelling units built in 1971 will be subsidized in part by various federal programs such as the Emergency Home Finance Act of 1970.

Repair Costs

One of the most potentially useful proposals that can help alleviate the pervasive quality problems involved in cars, appliances and other equipment is the warranty and guaranty bill.

It was sponsored by Senator Warren Magnuson (D-Wash.) and Frank E. Moss (D-Utah) and was passed by the Senate in 1970 but got lost in the House, possibly because its full potential value may not have been understood. The bill specifies that only warranties which provide for unrestricted service could be called a "full warranty." Others would have to be labeled "partial warranty." The real value is that requiring such truth in warranties would influence manufacturers to build more durable, better-quality products or admit that they are providing only a partial guarantee. This bill will be re-introduced in Congress in the forthcoming session.

The proposed Product Safety Act recommended by the National Commission on Product Safety also would help eliminate quality defects that create unnecessary user hazards. The bill expected to be considered by the Senate Commerce Committee in 1971 would establish an independent Product Safety Commission with powers to ban unsafe products and set safety standards.

Auto Insurance Costs

The steadily rising cost of auto insurance—and the difficulty sometimes in getting insurance at all—are making a critical problem for workers who often need cars to get to work in this era of outlying plants. No single gimmick will alleviate this problem. Many consumer organizations have oversimplified the needed cures by seizing on the rather-oversold "no fault" plan. This plan would pay an injured person whether or not he was at fault.

But it would eliminate only part of the claims and legal expenses that add to insurance premiums and has its own disadvantages. Some form of no-fault or an arbitration system to accelerate settlements and eliminate some of the legal costs could be useful as part of an overall remedy.

An overall plan also needs to reduce high selling costs; for example, through group purchase and enrollment, such as presently used for medical insurance. Also needed is a requirement that income derived by insurance companies from investing reserves be taken into account in setting rates. But much of the problem of high costs will not be solved until auto manufacturers are required to provide safer and less accident-prone design; for example, bumpers that will better protect against damage, and easier-to-replace fenders, panels and grilles.

Labor unions and central labor councils have become the chief, and often only, public advocate at the state level in fighting rate hikes and wholesale cancellations. Labor groups have also led the way in exploring possibilities of group purchasing and even of establishing their own auto insurance companies.

INDEPENDENT AGENCY NEEDED

Among overall consumer needs on the national level, an independent consumer agency ranks high. If the need for such an agency was ever in doubt, it should be dispelled by the tight leash the Administration has put on the present Consumer Assistant to the President. After the Rules Committee refused to permit a House vote on the bill for an independent agency, Mrs. Knauer called the Administration's more-limited proposal "innovative" and announced her office also would prepare "new consumer measures" for submission to Congress early in the next session.

Meanwhile her office has been emphasizing "consumer education." Consumer education, of course, is the usual fall-back when effective legislative reform is not forthcoming. But even the expensively-printed materials recently produced by Mrs. Knauer's office are of dubious value. One booklet on "Consumer Education," sent free to schools throughout the country, lists such sources for consumer information as the Chamber of Commerce, National Association of Manufacturers, small loan companies, car dealers, supermarket managers, department store credit managers, insurance agents and so on. There is the merest mention of labor unions and co-ops as sources of consumer views and facts. Among "mass media" suggested as "instructional resources for consumer education" are "newspapers, magazines, television, radio."

For a generation of students already stupefied by rock'n roll, Shake'n Bake is no lifeline to consumer knowledge. Nor are aspirin commercials or TV toy ads or the many deceptive "business opportunity" ads in the newspapers.

ADDITIONAL SELECTED BIBLIOGRAPHY

Buyer Dilemmas

Berens, J.S., "Consumer Costs in Product Failure," *MSU Business Topics,* Vol. 19, No. 2 (Spring, 1971), 27-30.

"Consumer Forces Say Packaging Law Fails to Clear up Confusion," *The Wall Street Journal* (November 6, 1969), 16.

Stern, L.L., "Consumer Protection via Increased Information," *Journal of Marketing,* Vol. 31, No. 2 (April, 1967), 48-52.

Questions for Discussion and Review

1. How did inadequate product standards hurt the consumer?

2. How does the "Packaging Law" persist in being confusing?

3. What are the primary consumer needs that haven't changed recently?

4. Why do you feel that it is necessary for consumers to be better informed?

5. How can better-informed buyers hurt small segments of the economy?

PART VI
NEW PRODUCT TRENDS

The aim of product managers and product committees is to commercialize successfully all new products which they are responsible for. It is true that, according to earlier readings, many more new products fail than are successful. What does this failure mean? Can one surmise that the new-product process is obsolete or the marketing research is poorly analyzed? Perhaps there are means and methods to countervail the trend of unsuccessful product launching. The chapters in Part VI encompass this type of thinking.

18

IS THE PRODUCT PROCESS
OBSOLETE?

Perhaps it isn't necessary to follow the new product process as outlined in Part III. If you recall, the process discussed exploration, screening, business analysis, development testing, and commercialization. If those responsible for new product development decide to investigate the purchase of an on-going product that is producing profits for its present owners, all the steps but business analysis can be eliminated. If patents of products can be purchased from financially troubled firms, such purchase will eliminate the time and expense of initiating the step-by-step new product development process. Many firms that have R&D departments or research people fully realized that thousands—or even millions—can be spent on research before a successful new product is launched. Therefore, is it necessary to launch new products only after successful test marketing? Perhaps test markets are no longer needed to identify apparently successful new products or unsuccessful products. Some marketers view test marketing as a "capital budgeting and facility planning device," as mentioned in the Hardin article. Members of the drug industry spend close to 2.5 million dollars and at least 4 years before a drug can be commercialized.[1]

There may be increased growth of and demand for free-lance, product-idea men who develop not only new products but also new marketing ideas for established products. These men develop a complete marketing mix for the products under consideration.

Test marketing catches the eye and ear of competitors and a firm can become entrapped by ingenious and devious devices rigged by competitive rivals, or competitors can come out with duplicate products without having to pay out huge sums for development and testing.

Social criticism (even antibusiness sentiment) has been launched against business firms with increasing frequency during the late sixties and early seventies. This criticism has been based upon the term "planned obsolescence." Superficial design changes that have increased the cost to the consumer of these products with no apparent benefit to the user have been the target of the criticism. It may be, perhaps, that the consumers insist upon these changes or that the criticism is valid and superficial design changes in automobiles, appliances, etc., are on their way out. The following articles discuss some trends in the making concerning the new product process.

SUCCESSFUL NEW PRODUCTS
WITHOUT TEST MARKETING
BY DAVID K. HARDIN

Someone has described a market researcher as a person who has
excellent reasons for being wrong. A more realistic view might be that a
market researcher is someone who has excellent reasons for being either
right or wrong. Since market research involves the examination of attitudes
and behavior, researchers can always have excellent reasons for being right
or wrong. It is the objectivity of the researcher's study design and analytical
interpretation that determines the true effectiveness of marketing research
and of market researchers.

The early 1960's have seen some brilliant and meaningful breakthroughs
in the application of marketing research to new product planning. As a
result, those consumer goods companies that have truly embraced the
marketing concept and, consequently, are oriented toward the development
of new products are making vastly increased use of marketing research data
in their predictions. For example, we estimate that better than half of the
ad hoc marketing research dollars spent today are spent for new product
planning and marketing.

The reasons for this are not surprising. Management, both individually
and collectively, realizes that new product efforts are in the limelight of
failure or success. In no other field of management action are the results
and abilities of management so clearly displayed as in new product

EDITOR'S NOTE: From *New Products: Concepts, Development, and Strategy,* Robert R.
Schrase, ed., Michigan Business Papers No. 43, 1966. Reprinted by permission of the Graduate
School of Business Administration, The University of Michigan, and the author.

launchings. Moreover, in no other area is management faced with so many unknowns and imponderables. Finally, the profits from new product success and the costs of new product failures are increasingly critical to the ultimate profit (or loss) of the company.

Market research has scored some of its most impressive and significant gains in the area of predicting product success prior to test marketing. This increasing reliance on market research technology to determine new product success has come about largely because of fundamental changes in test marketing strategy and theory—changes that to a great extent have been forced on the manufacturer by the dynamics of the market place. In a sense, the test market has become obsolete as an area for the prediction of new product success.

Management's expectations for test marketing results are rapidly changing. No longer are test markets used to identify very successful and very unsuccessful products. Management is no longer willing to risk the cost (up to $500,000) and competitive warning (up to two years) that a traditional test market represents. Instead, the test market is becoming the first phase of national distribution. Management is only test marketing those products for which they already have every expectation of going national. Evidence of this is that leading grocery products companies (e.g., General Foods, General Mills, Pet Milk, Pillsbury) are now going into national distribution with 75 to 85 percent of the products they test market. Obviously, they are selecting the "winners" in advance of test marketing.

What, then, is the new role of the test market? Test marketing is now viewed as a capital budgeting and facility planning device. How large a plant is needed for national sales? What is optimum promotion spending level? How many dollars will produce how many sales? What is the return on investment? A company averaging 20 per cent return may well reject a new product that returns only 8 per cent. Another company might embrace the same product because its average return is 7 per cent. Most companies have budgeted fixed payout perods for new product investment, and the role of the test market is to indicate whether the various levels of marketing spending and support will meet these payout requirements. If these levels do meet requirements, the company must determine which combination of spending level and sales support maximizes profits.

It has been estimated that in the last five years a significant proportion of those major new product entries which "failed" have failed because of overspending or underspending on product introduction—a failure of budgeting, not of acceptance. Truly bad products are no longer test marketed; good products are mismarketed.

Before the test market could undergo such a dynamic change in role, some alternative technology had to be developed to replace the traditional role of the test market, the separation of successful and unsuccessful products. The development of this function of market research, specifically product and concept testing, is my present subject.

During the past decade there has been an evolution of attitude research which developed through a series of major events. Recent changes in attitude research include the following:

1. The obsolescence of the simple attitude and opinion survey as a basis for new product decision making.

2. The rise of experimental design in place of traditional interviewing techniques in marketing research studies.

3. The aforementioned obsolescence of the test market as a technique for basic product evaluation.

Early production planning studies tended to be categorized as general market surveys—the kinds of survey that management used for answering such questions as: "How are we doing, and what does the public want that we are not offering?" Although curiosity was satisfied in this way, management soon discovered that the answers to this kind of question were unrelated to profitability. Management began to doubt the validity of this type of research.

One of two things has happened to most consumer goods managements that deal with marketing research. In some cases, management has abandoned attitude research as a it can go out to our customer." We at CU would add to Mr. Rothschild's remarks decision tool because it simply wasn't producing profit- or decision-oriented results. They may have continued to use it as a device to confirm top level thinking but not as a true decision tool. An antithetical development and the one which is now the mainstream of research growth is the evolution of decision-oriented new product studies. The growth of these studies has been accelerated by the success levels achieved through this type of research.

If the burden of predicting new product success falls on techniques used before test marketing or on marketing research, how are these executed? Basically, the answer is concept and product tests. Today, for example, the major producers of grocery products (e.g., General Foods, General Mills, Pet Milk, Carnation, Pillsbury), the companies doing most frequent experimentation and having the highest rate of innovation, are deeply involved in concept and product testing. We have already seen that this type of research is replacing test marketing as the means of determining the success or failure of new products.

The product concept is a synthesis or a description of the product idea embodied in the proposed new product. It may be a very simple, straightforward, objective statement; it may be a highly subjective simulation of an advertisement:

OBJECTIVE	SUBJECTIVE
Aerosol Barbecue Sauce	Delicious New Barbecue Sauce in a Modern Aerosol Container
Suitable for all barbecue needs. Flavor that is acceptable to the entire family.	This tasty sauce is especially blended for outdoor barbecues by a well-known manufacturer of consumer products. Specially good with hamburgers, chicken, ham, pork, beefsteak, or any barbecue favorite.

Concept testing has been employed in a variety of environments with remarkably good success. More important than the type of concept used is the *consistency* with which management applies concept-testing technology to the alternatives that it is considering. One advantage of a relatively objective approach is that comparability between concepts is more easily maintained. Concept testing, however, has gone even to the extreme of developing print ads for new product concepts—a very interesting idea, but one which is more difficult to maintain owing to lapses or variance in creative attention and input. To limit overstatement of favorable results in a test of product concept acceptance, these precautions may be taken:

1. Reduction of the number of positive attributes mentioned
2. Use of absolute words instead of comparative words (e.g., "good" rather than "better")
3. Use of objective words instead of subjective words (e.g., "acceptable" flavor rather than "good" flavor)

The measurement of concept acceptance can be approached with a number of questioning devices. The highest levels are achieved by merely measuring *interest* in the concept. One can develop a 65 or 70 per cent level of interest in a product and yet still not be able to say with much confidence that it is clearly a candidate for success. Injecting *buying interest* reduces the acceptance levels significantly and, in our opinion, increases their reality. Other steps that we believe are desirable and that will cause a reduction in measured acceptance levels are (1) including a price variable (assuming a price for the product that is not unusually low, such as $500 for a new Mustang), and (2) increasing the number of concepts tested.

When is one restricted to only *concept* tests for the final marketing decision? A question like this is almost redundant in many industries, such as the automobile or appliance industries, where test marketing opportunities simply do not exist. For consumer packaged goods the rule is that the more dramatic the product innovation, the more relevant the concept test. If the idea itself represents the major change (e.g., a sonic dishwasher), then the concept interest is the most relevant single market measurement. If, on the other hand, the product change rather than the idea is most relevant (e.g., a new, stronger, automatic-dishwashing detergent), then a product test will be far more predictive of success than a concept test.

The basic objective is to simulate the marketing strategy itself. Innovated products can be sold with advertising power—advertising aimed at explaining the idea and developing trial usage. Product-change products or "me too" products seem to need actual trial to become successful. An improved formulation, if truly improved in the opinion of the market place, needs to be sampled by the consumer population. The product test is, of course, a forced simulation of consumer trial.

Concept testing, then, is not in itself the answer for the "me too" products. If a proposed product is essentially a variation of a successful brand already on the market, a concept test will tend to have high ratings for attitude and purchase expectations. Yet, if such a "me too" brand actually is introduced to the market where there are well-established brands of equal quality, the "me too" brand probably will not succeed, or it will not be nearly as successful as one might expect from the test of the concept.

As a result, the *product* test is essential. One device that has been quite successful is the multiple product placement approach. This involves placing two or three existing brands and one or two new concepts—all in the same product class—into the household concurrently. This action might well be taken in the case of a cake mix or a dry soup innovation. An adequate amount of each product is supplied to allow the household to try each and to establish somewhat normal usage patterns. From an examination of the attitudes of the users toward each product tested—all of which are presented as unidentified concepts—good forecasts of the success rate of new products can be obtained. In fact, in one product class we have achieved a forecasting precision of about 88 per cent in predicting product success or failure based on ratings achieved in validation tests of this type. This is another reason why the consistency of the testing technology is crucial to the prediction process.

For an accurate simulation of the market place, product and concept tests are often put together in the same configuration. First, the product concept is exposed to the proposed sample of consumers, and the normal concept reactions are obtained. Then the products are left for product testing under normal home use. On the return interview the consumers are asked for their reactions to the product's performance (as executed in the home). One of four possible findings results:

FINDING	SUGGESTED ACTION
High concept acceptance and high product performance	Product should be marketed.
High concept acceptance and low product performance	Product has market potential but more lab work needed for execution
Low concept acceptance and high product performance	Product is limited, but market strategy should be reviewed before idea is shelved.
Low concept acceptance and low product performance	Product should be scrapped.

In tests of this type, it is extremely useful to contrast the *concept* acceptance levels with the *product* acceptance levels after the product has been used in a normal household situation. This helps determine whether the marketing challenge will lie in obtaining trial usage or developing repeat usage. It is also often important to contrast the acceptance of the idea (concept) and the acceptance of the execution (product) to discover whether it is the product or the concept that is lacking. However, one can argue that the ratings of product acceptance are biased by the previous exposure to the concept. The more enthusiastic the promise, the bigger the letdown. In order to eliminate this, it is often necessary to conduct a matched study involving only the product test. Comparing ratings of products obtained in this study with those obtained from persons exposed to the concept provides true product acceptance levels.

Another increasingly important aspect of new product innovation is market segmentation. For many industries, particularly proprietaries and pharmaceuticals, new product opportunities available through market segmentation constitute the major growth area. New ailments are not invented (most of them have now been around for centuries), and technical breakthroughs are hard to come by and legally restricted. Consequently, the market segment has been a key success area. Products such as children's vitamins and medicines and women's headache remedies are examples of this.

Product testing is a particularly valid device for determining market segmentation opportunities. By matching samples of prospective respondents with concept and product tests embodying the current marketing concept in force for a given class of product and with the new proposed market segmentation concept, definitive readings of market potential can be obtained. The food industry, with products such as children's soups and cereals for adults, is also discovering the value of segmentation.

Few managements today are wholly enthusiastic about relying solely on concept research for final product decisions. Yet, as we have seen, they have little choice. There is now a strange anomaly in this research. There are two kinds of users—those who have gone beyond the experiemental stage and are now making concept and product evaluations all the time, and those who have been unable to get past the experimental level and are consequently uncertain about the value of this kind of research and unwilling to undertake the investment. Until some validation has been achieved in the market place, management is understandably concerned. Fortunately, however, the performance of research in this area generally is in excess of management's expectations. Thus, they gradually discover the accuracy of this type of testing, and their confidence increases.

The real stumbling block is the initiation of this type of study. The least valuable concept test a manufacturer can conduct is the *first* one. The comparisions that are provided by an extended exposure to this type of research begin to produce both accurate forecasting and management confidence in these forcasts.

B

AN OUTSIDE JOB FILLS
THE PRODUCT GAP

"As business gets tougher for others," says Philip Nicolaides with a smile, "it gets better for us." The bulky, roundfaced executive is smiling frequently these days. He is president and creative director of The Agora Group, one of a dozen or so youthful companies waxing fat on the consumer market's unappeasable appetite for new products.

Estimates have it that between 6,000 and 10,000 new products are introduced each year through grocery and drug channels. The rate of failure is somewhere between 50% and 80%, says Franklin W. Krum, Jr., a vice-president of N. W. Ayer & Sons, Inc., the advertising agency. With the likelihood of being wrong half the time, or worse, new products managers have been lured by the siren song of the small "outside" companies that promise they can develop items that will beat the odds.

"What we do," says Richard Berger, the slender, bespectacled president of the Center for New Product Development, "is think of an entire package—the product, its name, its packaging, its advertising—all at one time." With a handful of associates and free-lance talent from research firms, ad agencies, and the like, Berger, Nicolaides, and their counterparts at other companies contend that they are creating new products that fit consumer needs.

"Most new ideas at most companies," Berger claims, "are based on past R&D experience." He says that too often a good idea from a new R&D

EDITOR'S NOTE: Reprinted from the May 16, 1970, issue of *Business Week* by special permission. Copyright © 1970 by McGraw-Hill, Inc.

man is voted down "because somebody at the company tried it years ago and it didn't work." When an outside new-products development outfit is called in, it functions without any preconceived ideas of what will or will not go.

One of the things that Berger's outfit thought would go was Silver Cycle, a detergent for automatic dishwashers that would polish silverware. But the product turned out to be too good: It left flat silverware gleaming, but took the patina off more ornate, carved pieces. Undaunted, Berger's group has come up with 14 other projects—all sold to a half-dozen major companies. "If we miss, it is no tremendous loss," Berger notes. "Our fees aren't that great, because we stand to make money on the royalties."

The new product specialists insist they take a systematic approach to their work, even though they might be based in an apartment house (as are Agora and a three-months old company, The First Team) or in a columned, colonial mansion (as is a company called Marketing Innovations, Inc.). "Anybody can dream up a product that doesn't exist," says Jack Springer, a former advertising agency copywriter who is president of The First Team. "The trick is to start with a base of research that tells you whether or not there is a market for it before you create it."

HOW TO START

The First Team uses a computer program to find gaps in the marketplace for specific clients. NEMO—for N-dimensional Evaluation of Market Opportunities—might tell a soft drink maker, for example, that there is no peppermint-flavored, vitamin-rich soft-drink that is served hot; then a series of "concept ads" are roughed out to use in consumer research that indicates the depth of the potential market, "We leave it to the agencies to make finished ads," says Springer.

Some top ad agencies provide "new products workshops" for their clients, and both N. W. Ayer & Son and Batten, Barton, Durstine & Osborn, Inc., have set up costly computer models to predict the chances of success for new brands about to go to market. Emery T. Smyth, managing director of Interpublic's Product Development Workshop (a complete new products service that operates independently of any of the Interpublic agencies) debunks the typical agency service. "Such units," he says, "are not profitable; few top people have time to spend in them, so the efforts usually boil down to "brainstorming" and tossing out ideas for ad campaigns, rather than true conceptual thinking."

In its four years, Symth's firm has done "concept development" on such products as Simba, a lemon drink, and Santiba mixers for Coca-Cola Co., Carnation Slender for Carnation Co., and others for Miles Laboratories, Inc. and Heublein, Inc. Unlike an ad agency's new products advice, which is furnished free to the client, advice from the outside companies comes with a price tag. The companies work on a "project basis"—to come up with a new breakfast cereal or snack item—or on a retainer for three months or longer, during which time they will turn over to the client any number of ideas for a "go—no go" decision. Minimum fees for three months are in the $10,000-to-$25,000 range, and Roy Anthony, who heads Marketing Innovations, gets $60,000 a year from each of eight or ten clients.

Anthony, who pioneered the idea of a new products specialist 10 years ago and whose former employees have started three of the newer companies, notes one problem: "Our costs are still looked on as 'an extra' by many clients. No one ever knows what budget we should be paid from." Nevertheless, his fees have been found in one pocket or another by such companies as Stokely-Van Camp, Inc., Kellogg Co. (for which Marketing Innovations worked on Pop-Tarts), Trans World Airlines, Inc., Bristol-Myers, and others.

WHO TO SEE

Getting to "the critical guy" is another problem. Says Richard Berger: "Some companies are so tightly structured that they cannot cope with an outfit that is not systematized. We went to work for a large cereal company after a single meeting, but a major paper company has had eight meetings with us and different executives still are asking us to explain just what we do."

The new products companies do not bring a client the latest pipe dream of some "baggy pants inventor." Occasionally, consumer need and desire for the product is so strong that the product almost has to be created to meet it. Such is the case with the Center's Color Strokes, an instant-drying nail polish in a felt-tip pen applicator that would permit women to polish nails while riding in an elevator (as one TV commercial idea shows) on the way to work. As yet, Berger points out, the chemical formulation of the polish is not worked out, "but that's a technicality once we were assured of the potential."

"Only six out of 78 product proposals we have come up with have not been technically feasible," says Don Buckley, whose 20-months-old Kahn/Buckley Associates lists General Foods among its numerous clients.

Several of the specialists contend that the lengthening slide of corporate profits is helping them. "After advertising budgets are cut," notes one, "the next step is to slice research-and-development expenditures." At the same time, stockholders have to be told that their company is looking toward the future and working on new products. "Compare our costs," says Nicolaides of Agora, "with the cost of having a single researcher and new products executive on the staff."

Few companies admit that R&D departments are being trimmed, but a number have hired the outside companies to "supplement our own internal efforts," as a Kellogg Co. executive says. At Chemway Corp., which has used new products specialists, Stephan F. Durst, director of research and development, notes that "many companies suffer from the NIH syndrome—Not Invented Here"—and automatically turn away outside help. Phil Nicolaides agrees, but he says that such a reaction is less noticeable every day. "We think our clients, and others using companies like ours, should announce the fact just the way they announce hiring a law firm or an architect."

SUCCESSES

Some do. TWA, Goodyear Tire & Rubber Co., Mead Johnson Laboratories, and Kellogg were among the former clients that furnished Marketing Innovations with "to whom it may concern" letters of praise on its 10th anniversary. "The fact that they were not inhibited by all the reasons that something could not be done was certainly a help in getting many new products and ideas before our top management," writes Goodyear's Lee S. McDonald, manager of consumer market planning.

There are difficulties at times, says an executive at E. R. Squibb & Sons, which goes "outside" for ideas on occasion. "If the protocol isn't written tightly, the companies may go off on a tangent. Their ideas might be new and exciting, but just too far afield for the client to make practical use of. And I worry about confidentiality. You might have a product going through developmental stages three or four years in advance of the market, and there could be a leak from the outside firm to a competitor."

Richard Berger says that his company invests heavily in time and money to develop and test a new product before it goes to the client and has as much to gain from secrecy as the client himself. "That's why," he says, "we can't tell you about the work we're doing right now except to say that four of our products will be in test market by September."

NEW COMPANY INVENTS NEW PRODUCTS AS COMPLETE PACKAGES, INCLUDING ADS

BY FRED DANZIG

Hang in there, new product troops. Help is on the way.

If you're ready to market a new powder that polishes silver in the automatic dishwasher, you're in business. Or how about a new line of non-synthetic convenience breakfast foods? Or a wild new soap for youngsters?

Each of these new items has been developed here at the Center for New Product Development Inc., which opened on Nov. 20 and is now talking with various major companies about a few of the products it has put together.

The silver polish for dishwashers, called Silver Cycle, is an example of the center's operation. The center developed the product, the package, costed the product so that any future marketer knows direct and indirect marketing costs, and has even developed an advertising program. The ad is captioned: "All you guys who make silver polish are out of business." Copy says that women need only to put Silver Cycle in their automatic dish-washer with tarnished silver "and go give themselves a manicure or eat bonbons or something."

Housed in spacious quarters at 572 Madison Ave. that were formerly used by the *Harper's Bazaar* staff, the center is headed by three partners, Richard Berger, president; James H. McLaughlin, technical director; and William Capitman, vp.

EDITOR'S NOTE: From *Advertising Age,* January 9, 1969, pp. 40-41. Reprinted by permission of the publisher and the author. Copyright © 1969 by Crain Communications Inc.

Mr. Berger was recently vp-marketing director at Warren, Muller, Dolobowsky, and before that he was a new product exec at General Foods. He says the center's purpose is to pursue the "simple, direct route" to new products by getting ideas and asking two questions about them: Can people be motivated to buy? Can you make it?

Along with Mr. Berger's marketing expertise, the center team has Mr. McLaughlin's technical know-how to draw upon. In 17 years at Lever Bros., Mr. McLaughlin rose to senior research associate with the Lever New Product Group, and he holds numerous patents on household products and processes. Mr. Capitman is president of the Center for Research in Marketing, a consumer research organization with offices here and in Peekskill, N.Y. The two centers make use of each other's facilities.

The three men are obviously bullish about their prospects, believing that the new center fills a vacuum. "Most companies are organized to sell existing products, not to create new ones," said Mr. Berger. This sort of orientation means product managers "tend to shy away from the effort needed to develop or introduce a new product. They know their careers depend on the profit contributions made by the existing brands."

What happens if a modern company is market-oriented towards the sale of existing products and still supports a new product unit? The center's chiefs believe that, too often, the new product unit has a technical orientation.

"Once a new product idea is passed upon, technical feasibility becomes the major concern," Mr. Berger said. "Testing comes under the laboratory's supervision and the marketing people don't see the product again until a final product is at hand. The fact is that a technically feasible product is more likely to be a marketing failure than a product that has marketing potential is going to prove to be a technical impossibility."

If this broad-stroke analysis of corporate coagulation is on target, the question then becomes: How does the center fit into this picture? And with a "glad-you-asked-that" look, Mr. Berger explained that this company "puts it all together"—marketing, technical development, consumer research and advertising—all into one ready-made package for a waiting client to take over and run with.

In other words, new product managers need only relax and await delivery of the center's packages. Silver Cycle is its current example and the three partners believe it will be on the market before long, to be followed by other products for use in or with dishwashers.

Getting ideas for new products appears to be the simplest part of the center's work. "The first thing to understand in this business is that we live in a promotional world," said Mr. Berger. "The consumer is bombarded with things and promotional material and he buys them, not concept tests. If you ask the consumer for his ideas about a concept and you set up rigid scales of measurement for his answers, you're going wrong. It doesn't make sense to ask the consumer to decide about a product that he will never see again in that form, and without even so much as the conditioning push of an advertising environment."

By adhering to a promotional approach, Mr. Berger went on, "You ask yourself what can the consumer be motivated to buy? We know what can be sold. It's not that we're any smarter than others; it's that we tend to look at things a little bit differently. We look at the life systems around us. They should all be integrated. We follow the woman through her day at home. What does she do as she prepares for company? Polish the silverware? That's a big job. Wash dishes? Do the laundry? We look at the entire life system and look for the link.

"What is the relationship of these jobs? Let's look at the dishwasher? Can it be used for something else or must it remain idle until some dirty dishes go into it? If you have a different soap, you can use the dishwasher for polishing silverware. It's that simple. That's how we got to Silver Cycle.

"But there's more. The dishwasher is a system; it harnesses the ability to put water into a box, to move water around, to pick up items with a stream of water, deliver fresh water rinses, generate heat. We think these capabilities should lead us to all sorts of new products. And the same kind of thinking can be applied to the stove. Even the toaster.

"We develop the concept and the promotional approach and give our technical people the specifications, which they meet, continued Mr. Berger. "We have 1001 families that give us home-use information and, in just one week's time, we can know what we've got. We can finalize the advertising. We bring it to the prospective client company completely ready to go.

"Of course" he said, "they're not going to buy on our say-so. They'll check us out, but they're way ahead to start with and they're not going to be sitting on the product for years because we work on royalties, with the initial fee applied to royalty income.

"If a company wants to spend years fussing with the product after we bring it in, we're protected," Mr. Berger said.

Mr. Berger said he and his associates have calculated that the nation's 500 leading companies are "robbing" the gross national product of about $1.5 billion a year "by not really managing new product development properly. They're getting themselves bogged down in channels and not seeing new products as a promotional field. What we have here in all modestly, is the start of a new industry—a new product development industry."

NOTE

1. John Foster, "Drug Companies Broaden Their Base," *The Exchange*, Vol. XXXI, No. 5, (May, 1970), 3.

ADDITIONAL SELECTED BIBLIOGRAPHY

Is the New Product Process Obsolete?

Foster, John, "Drug Companies Broaden Their Base," *The Exchange*, Vol. 31, No. 5 (May, 1970), 1-8.

Mertes, John E., "Product Planning and Visual Design Policies," *MSU Business Topics*, Vol. 10, No. 3 (Summer, 1962), 61-66.

Weingarten, J., "The Most Dangerous Game in Marketing," *Dun's Review*, Vol. 89, No. 6 (June, 1967), 45, 89-92.

Questions for Discussion and Review

1. Discuss some important trends in the new-product process.

2. What are some of the common dangers firms become ensnared in when test marketing takes place?

3. How can new products be developed today without going through the step-by-step process?

4. Discuss "planned obsolescence," its pros and cons.

5. What steps can be taken to prevent loss in the hazardous world of test marketing?

19

NEW DIRECTIONS WITH
NEW PRODUCTS

A normal practice for evaluating the commercialization of a new product would consist of estimating sales volume, profits, costs, investment, and then determining a rate of return. Many firms attempt to forecast demand for a new product offering based on current data; some firms abandon the idea while others attempt to use some forecasting model. How accurate companies have been in forecasting sales and profits eventually shows up on annual reports. Many companies use statistical analysis where "least squares" and "regression techniques" play an important role. It has been suggested that perhaps the use of probability or Bayesian statistics would help determine more accurately the sales and profits of a firm enhanced from the sale of new products.

Some empirical investigations have been made concerning the growth of a new product through dyadic interactions and by consumer innovators. The power of emulation or word-of-mouth advertising seems to be effective in stimulating growth of new product introductions. If a firm understood the buying habits of the consumer innovator and planned his marketing strategy so that the consumer innovator would be positively responsive toward the new product introduction, new product success would be enhanced. Therefore, by understanding how information concerning new products is diffused to consumers and knowing how to communicate relevant product information to the innovators and users of new products, firms will be able effectively to guide and control to some extent the rate of new product success.

What recent developments are available to ascertain or evaluate the success of a marketing program for a new product can be discussed along the lines of utilizing attitude-change measures. Measuring the rate of change of consumer attitudes toward a new product can suggest that a firm's management make necessary changes in its promotion scheme or package in order to ensure continual success of new product introductions. The following articles discuss the use of a research technique and product diffusion to monitor new product introductions.

THE TRAJECTORY THEORY OF
GOAL SETTING FOR NEW PRODUCTS

BY C. MERLE CRAWFORD

As new products are accepted or rejected faster by the marketplace, it is critical that research techniques be developed to provide early assessment of progress. This article, using an actual case study, proposes one such technique based on the astronautical theory underlying work with guided missiles. Earlier remedial action is the goal.

The value of time has been expressed

by Punch:

"There was a young lady named Bright,
Whose speed was faster than light.
She set out one day,
In a relative way,
And returned home the previous night."

by Dante:

"Consider that this day ne'er dawns again."

by Shakespeare:

"Ah! The clock is always slow:
it is later than you think."

EDITOR'S NOTE: From the *Journal of Marketing Research,* May, 1966, pp. 117-125. Reprinted by permission of the American Marketing Association and the author.

Since few of us can move with the speed of Lady Bright, our fate is more like the sentiments of Dante and Shakespeare. And nowhere is the dollar premium on time greater than in the first few weeks or months of a new product's life. In earlier times, a new product was launched casually, nurtured slowly, and expected eventually to find its proper and prosperous place. There was no hurry, partly because inadequate communication devices precluded any mass effort to inform people about the new item, and partly because competition could be expected to ignore the new product for a long while.

Today opportunity for such a leisurely approach is gone, but many may not realize just how fast a new product's fate is sealed. Nor do marketers always realize the extent to which the rest of a corporation depends on early assessment of a new product's fate.

REASONS FOR QUICKER NEW PRODUCT ASSESSMENT

Specifically, there are six reasons why marketers today must rapidly determine a new product's success or failure probabilities soon after launch:

1. The attention span of consumers in the market-place is short. They will devote little time and energy to deciding whether a new product is worthwhile. Either the initial story makes sense, or some changes had better be made fast.

2. Changes can be made rapidly, thanks to the speed of mass communication. The quicker the action, the greater the chance that the original will be productive.

3. The size of the initial investment grows with each new product to the point where the launch of important new items is backed by dollar budgets which strain the resources of operating units. Knowing that time is of the essence, managements are willing to take budget risks because competitors have never been so anxious to thwart a new enemy entry and protect their current volumes and shares.

4. In any creative, market oriented company, opportunity cost decisions abound. Every time a new product is financed, other worthwhile spending plans must be set aside. Thus, not only is there great incentive to pull back on new product spending if the product appears to be failing, but there is also pressure to move the new product funds to some other project as soon as possible.

5. Nor are top managements known for patience. Partly because of major financial commitments, and partly because of personal involvement, top management personnel usually exert crushing pressure on the marketing team to report progress early.

6. Last, launch of a new product signals the start of many ongoing programs throughout the corporation. R&D is actively at work on product modifications and improvements or perhaps companion products. Manu-

facturing has engineers studying ways to reduce the initial production cost. Other departments such as packaging, traffic and technical service all have (or should have) study or development projects underway. A premium is placed on knowing if a product is going to fail because nonmarketing departments also have standby projects waiting until money or personnel are released from an aborted new product.

For a number of years, marketers have known these pressures were building. As a result, researchers have sought and found new ways to speed the flow of assesment data on new products. New sales auditing techniques and firms now offer inviting alternative often designed to speed up reporting.

Test marketing itself is frequently designed to isolate the critical varia- bles worth close study during the national launch period. Marketing organizations commonly send home-office men into the field at time of launch to speed up feedback of problems, successes, etc. Telephone research (probably the fastest technique in most cases) is on a steeply rising growth curve.

PURPOSE

Motives and practice are rapidly changing the character of today's new product marketing research. Responding to this trend, this paper proposes the following:

1. Describe decision/action ladders to apply to prospects and other variables for the new product.

2. Show how these ladders relate to good research technique.

3. Suggest a system of ladders to frame the research program for a new product launch.

4. Suggest a manner of handling the research data to facilitate analysis and interpretation.

All four of these steps are designed to use a trajectory concept of goal setting, an idea which has been developed to a commercial level in at least one company.

USUAL GOAL SETTING VS. TRAJECTORY THEORY

It seems safe to generalize that customary marketing goals (especially on new products) are of a target character, e.g.;

Sales of $3,000,000 the first year,
Distribution of 45 percent by 60 days,
Brand awareness of 30 percent by three months,
Brand usage of five percent by three months.

These are good goals—logical, meaningful, researchable. Failures are clearly apparent when they occur, and remedial action can be taken. Pressures of time however, no longer permit a marketer to set a goal, establish a research technique to measure achievement and sit back to await results; nor does he want to.

The trajectory concept (as old as the slingshot) can best be explained by comparing it to a guided missile. A missile is aimed (given a target) and fired. But, to earn the adjective "guided", the firing crew has ascertained from past experience a series of intermediate points and speeds the rocket must reach if it is to ultimately hit target, and has built-in control over the rocket's path. If the rocket is heading off target, corrections can be made early enough that a hit will still be made.

Surrounding the basic path trajectory of the rocket itself is a vast network of trajectories—direction, speed, heat, recording, etc. All are plotted in advance, and all are measured at periodic intervals from the time of blast-off. Corrections are made during the time of travel, all designed to keep the rocket "on trajectory." Entering the designated target area is a logical result of these trajectories, measurements, and corrections.

Precisely the same approach can be taken to measure the progress of a new product ... setting up the network of trajectories covering variables acting on the basic variable (sales), measuring progress against the planned trajectories, and taking remedial action when necessary.

One other parallel needs to be drawn, however to complete the concept. Astronautical science has studied space variables to the point where deviation from the trajectory can be analyzed for ultimate effect. If a variable is off two degrees at Time t, scientists know it will be off n degrees at a specified time in the future. The idea is graphically shown in Figure 19-1.

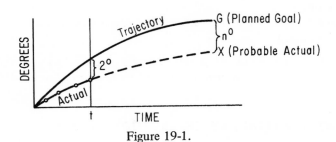

Figure 19-1.

Past study has shown that if the data indicate the error shown on the chart at Time t, a result at X is predictable. If Point X is sufficiently off base, remedial action is indicated. Marketing variables are usually more erratic in behaviour, and predicting the end variance is more risky, but it can be done if sufficient time is spent gathering the necessary data and preparing the trajectories.

NETWORK OF TRAJECTORIES

Using this concept, the next step one takes is to select the variables for which trajectories will be established. This step requires construction of decision/action ladders showing progression of mental or action processes various middlemen and final consumers must complete if marketing goals are to be met. Each step on the ladder must be taken in the proper order. Here is an example.

The prospect must:

1. Have heard of the brand and associated it with the product type or category.
2. Have become aware of at least one of the product's selling points or benefits.
3. Have decided that the product is worth a trial.
4. Have had an opportunity to try it.
5. Have made some effort to assess the product in use.
6. Have reached a favorable conclusion.
7. Have decided to purchase the product again in the future.
8. Have actually made one or more repeat purchases.

(The list can be much more detailed and can go into such matters as using the product in a different way, etc.)

Applied to distribution, the ladder can vary, but might look like this:

1. Wholesalers must stock the product.
2. Retailers must have heard of the product.
3. Retailers must buy the product.
4. Retailers must display the product.
5. Retailers must sell the product.
6. Retailers must achieve a six-week turn on the product.

If possible, all variables expected to have significant effect on ultimate sales or profit objectives should be structured as ladders ready for the setting of trajectories. Theoretically there should be one trajectory for each step on each ladder, although practical economics reduces the number considerably. See Figure 19-2 for an indication of the various shapes trajectories may take.

A CASE HISTORY

An actual case will help clarify these concepts and their use. Product D was developed for holding dentures in place, and for a time was to be promoted to dentists. If the product sold well, the company would undertake consumer promotion, but at first it would rely on recommendations from dentists.[1]

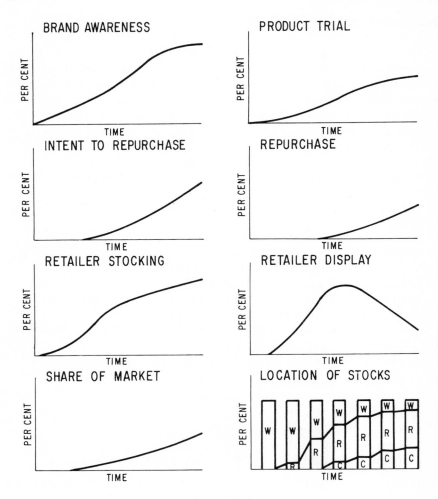

Figure 19-2.

Study of the situation indicated that decision/action ladders would be desirable for the following:

Dentists (by specialty)
Distribution
Sales
Request for a new booklet on care of dentures promoted through package inserts.

Because the usual research budget was restricted, and not all "rungs" on each ladder had been sufficiently researched to permit constructing trajectories, the following were selected for study:

   A. Prospect (dentist):
      Product awareness
      Product trial
      Assessment
      Expected future use
   B. Trade:
      Wholesaler stocking
      Retailer stocking
      Retailer purchases
   C. Factory sales by months
   D. Factory sales by areas
   E. Booklet requests

Since not all of these chartings can be reproduced here, five have been selected to demonstrate the method: dentist awareness, dentist trial, retailer stocking, factory sales by months, and booklet requests. (Figure 19-3 shows the trajectories which were established, and the research data which were gathered.)

Before commenting on the results and looking at how the data were related to the ladders, more explanation is needed regarding how the trajectories were determined and how the data were gathered.

Setting Trajectories for Product D

Because background work that led to the research plan for Product D took several years (and is still going on), any summary here must stress basic concepts and general methods. The specific actions fit a pattern, however, and had a purpose within a framework of marketing management. The keystone, as cited earlier, lay in the theory of projectile movement through space, especially where man has some control over the projectile during flight.

But there are other sources for this line of thought, such as the distance runner. Every miler knows from his past races and his current capabilities what his quarter-mile times should be if he is to finish with any particular time for the mile. Arrangements are made for aides to time each lap and relay information and instructions to the miler. Figure 19-4 shows how one one might chart a miler's run.

If after one minute he has gone farther than he should have, he is in trouble. Either he puts out more effort than usual (and perhaps sets a new record for himself) or he runs down during the last lap and finishes poorly. This appears to fit the concept of measuring intermediate accomplishment as a predictor of ultimate accomplishment, based on known relationships between the two.

Specifically, the concept is that ultimate performance can be influenced

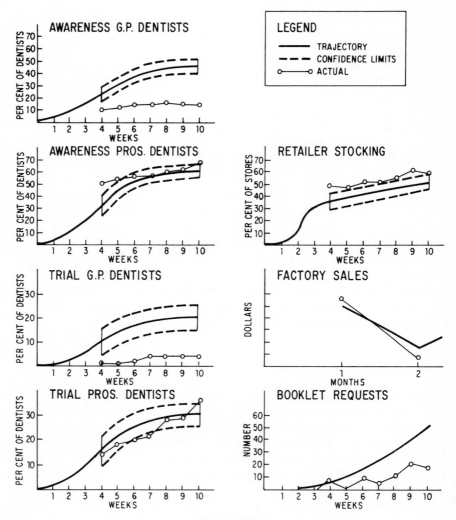

Figure 19-3.

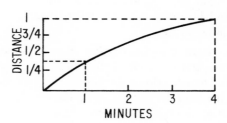

Figure 19-4.

during various stages of input (trajectory), but that some times are more effective than others for doing so. Various input modifications have varying performance effects, and these are quantitatively and economically related to when they are made.

To use this concept, marketers for Product D moved through a six-step procedure to develop the trajectories:

1. *Selecting variables.* Since the purpose of this research was to predict the ultimate outcome of Product D long before actual sales were available and to discover the causes of any sales-retarding problems, the first step was to select a series of sales-determining variables for study. Those variables had to meet a set of rigid criteria. They had to be:

Meaningful—have a significant effect on the ultimate outcome.
Measurable—be quantifiable and researchable.
Actionable—be a variable which the marketer could do something about in case it became a source of trouble.
Graphable—be susceptible to theoretical structure in the form of movement over time.

For Product D, the key potential marketing problems were felt to be:

Overcoming dentists' general lack of interest in this therapeutic area.
Putting enough pressure on the dentist to take time and trouble to specify the product. Even though he briefed himself on the product story, he might not break his long established habit of using some other brand, since the other brand worked well too.
Seeing that the product was available for purchase when specified.
Solidifying the sale (after first purchase) by helping the user understand the natural limitations of all products used to position dentures.

Each of these four potential problems was carefully watched by measuring the movement of a variable which passed these test criteria. These variables (each matching a problem from the list) were dentist awareness, dentist trial, retail stocking, and booklet request.[2]

2. *Selecting the research techniques.* Since researchability was a criterion for selection, the second step essentially completed specifics of the research program: sample size, report dates, data tabulation procedures, etc. Because Product D was only one in a series of new products being studied by the trajectory technique, most of the program details were already decided.

That each new product be studied as nearly like past products as possible is critical to use of this method, since research data have more meaning in their *relative* than *absolute* value. Awareness is a term few would agree on, and absolute awareness may not exist. But if the researcher keeps one definition and one research technique, he can build the body of data necessary for generalization and comparison. The makers of Product D had done this so new data would be consistent with past data, and meaning would come from comparison and deviation, even though one could quibble about absolute awareness, trial, etc.

For Product D, the dentist research plan called for 100 long-distance calls a week, summarized into four-week running totals for plotting and analysis.[3] Each dentist was asked a series of about 10 questions, of which the ones pertinent here were:

Have you heard of a product called D?
Do you recall what kind of a product it is?
Have you had occasion to use this product in your practice?

Retailers were sent double post cards asking them to report their inventory of Product D by package size. This was a weekly sample of 250 drugstores selected at random from a national list. Returns from the drugstores were prompt and generally ran about 150 each week.[4] Again, this technique obviously has chances for various biases, but repeated use over the years and occasional comparisons with Nielsen audits, city-censuses, *etc.*, had identified the amount of usual bias (ten percent) and its character (upward). Since trajectories are set up from past data, it is important that biases be known and consistent.

3. *Compiling past data.* The next step was to search the data bank of past trajectory studies and review past patterns pursuant to setting up trajectories for Product D. Gathering background data is one of the expensive steps in this procedure, and this step cannot be documented extensively here. The general idea however is to review all past data in trajectory form and from these select key plottings pertinent to the new product under study.[5]

4. *Setting trajectory parameters.* From the study just completed, it was possible to establish parameters for Product D's trajectories, but first two terms should be defined.

For each new product there are various ladders for the key variables. For each significant step on each ladder there can be a trajectory. For each trajectory, parameters are needed. The ending parameter (ultimate goal) is called an Accomplished Parameter (AP), and the trajectory points leading to the AP are called Intermediate Accomplishment Parameters (IAP). The general curve shape will locate most IAP's once the curve formula is decided and base points selected. For awareness among GP dentists of Product D, the curve selected was:[6]

$$Y = A + Bx + Cx^2 + Dx^3 + Ex^4.$$

Givens were:

Awareness zero at time zero.
Awareness 45 percent at ten weeks (The AP established for product D).
Week 4 awareness is one-half of Week 10 awareness.
Curve is level at zero time.
Curve is level at Week 10[7]

To determine any IAP on the curve it was merely necessary to substitute the time period in weeks for *x* in the following:[8]

$Y/Y_{10} = .0557x^2 - .0071394x^3 + .00025697x^4.$

One may argue about the proper shape for the trajectories, and this is as it should be, because different variables will have different patterns. Obviously marketing strategy affects curve shape. A good example came a few years ago when one of the leading drug firms introduced a new product to doctors. Its executives wanted immediate awareness so chose to send each appropriate physician a telegram announcing the item. The result would probably have produced a trajectory on awareness more like that shown in Figure 19-5.

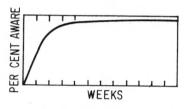

Figure 19-5.

On the other hand, a small firm with a restricted budget might find its curve rising so slowly that it would not level off for six months or more. The point is that enough research should be done to permit the construction of trajectories consistent with the marketing strategy, environment, and goals. Regardless of shape, the purpose of speedy assessment of ultimate goal accomplishment stands as the task of the method.

One other aspect of trajectories needs to be described before analyzing Figure 19-4. Five of the seven curves on this chart are straddled by dotted lines representing "confidence limits" whose purpose is to give a range within which random variation is free to operate. Variations within the "box" are not considered significant.

Since only complex statistical theory tells how to set them mathematically, setting these introduced a problem. (1) Variance around *one* point is inadequate because taking a chance on even one or two cases out of a hundred is not necessary; and (2) variance around a cumulative total is not proper because each point is four weeks, not all weeks to date.

Technically this is a problem of a nonstationary, stochastic, binomial process, with sequential statistical inference based on sample cumulative sums. There are theoretical concepts for testing the significance of data in this setting but they have not been merged and adapted for testing, at least not as reported in the applied journals. No doubt the work could be done, but the question is whether such confidence limits would have a practical value consistent with the cost of preparation.

Instead of this the research process reported here merely substituted an arbitrary 10 percentage-point range within which problems were not actioned, and outside which they were carefully studied using past experience and judgment to determine whether to take action. This approach seemed adequate, as the case of Product D indicated. Modifications would be necessary in some cases, as when the AP was five percent; limits for such situations could be reduced accordingly.

Analyzing the Results for Product D

Referring to Figure 19-3, one can analyze the results. Whereas ten-week goal accomplishment would normally be researched and reported at Week 12 or 13 at the earliest, the trajectory method is expected to yeild an earlier set of answers. To see if it did, assume to be at Week 7 on the chart, and note the following predictions:

1. Both awareness and trial will fall far short of the AP's for G.P. dentists.
2. Awareness will be on target for prosthodontic dentists, but trial appears close to falling out of range.
3. Retailer stocking will be above target.
4. It is too early to predict factory sales from the sales curve alone, as is usually the case.
5. Booklet requests will hit a goal consistent with the poor G.P. dentist product usage but will be well below original goals.

Figure 19-3 shows that all these predictions were correct, with the exception of the concern over trial by prosthodontic dentists. Since these conclusions were available during the eighth week, the marketing team was able to put various remedial programs into action by the time researchers would normally have just been going to the field. The expectation is that a problem can be approached with corrective action even before it becomes a problem.

Further analysis of the data takes one back to the ladder concept from which the trajectory variables were derived. The most important ladder was for the prime prospect group, G.P. dentists. If there had been space to present all the trajectories and the data, eight week analysis would have given an answer to the question; Where are the prospects "falling off" the ladder as they go up?

	Lost on Each Rung	*Cumulative Loss*
Have not become aware	86%	86%
Did not understand any product benefit	6	92
Had no opportunity to try	4	96
Made no assessment	1	97
Made unfavorable assessment	1	98
No reuse	0	98
Satisfied and using	2	100
	100	

This profile immediately tells where a profitable point for action is (awareness) and confirms the earlier analysis. Moreover, the ladder approach puts each of the problems in a status relative to the others. For example, Product D was destined to have another problem because of the 14 percent aware only four percent had tried. Doubling awareness would at best add only another four percent to trial. There were actually two profile problems that remedial action should deal with.

For comparison notice the abbreviated profile of a second product marketed at about the same time as D.

	Lost on Each Rung
Had not become aware	30%
Had not yet tried	50
No assessment, or unfavorable assessment	5
Satisfied and using	15
	100

Here the problem was obviously not awareness (70 percent) but trial. Prospects registered the brand name and its product type, and if they tried the product, they like it. In this particular case, however, several similar products were already available and all were fairly good, so there was little incentive for trial. Obviously a remedial marketing program should be geared to trial, not awareness.

Finally, notice the profile for a third product.

	Lost on Each Rung
Had not become aware	62%
Had not yet tried	5
No assessment, or unfavorable assessment	7
Satisfied and using	26
	100

For this product, of the 38 percent aware, 26 percent had rapidly reached the point of being satisfied users. The problem was almost solely one of awareness, not trial or effectiveness of the product.

CRITICAL PROBLEMS IN THE USE OF THE TRAJECTORY METHOD

There are some significant problems in the use of this method. This is not an easy research technique, and the various problems involved must be understood before use is attempted.

1. *Gathering background data.* There are three aspects to this problem: cost, time, and pertinence. It takes time and money to do enough preparatory research to permit the building of trajectofies. How much cannot be specified because it varies with product type, but no one can

guess what the curve shapes will be without at least some "ball-park" figures as a guide. Moreover, experience with a number of new products with a particular audience is necessary in order to assess research and reporting peculiarities for that audience. Otherwise the data may not be pertinent to the upcoming product.

The question of time and money must always be related to the value of the research. In this instance, considerable investment appears worthwhile. In no other activity in the firm does quick and accurate information bring such a bonus. Even the data bank compilation process yields dividends since it can and should include the study of similar new competitive products. In these cases, competitors' remedial actions can frequently be anticipated well in advance.

2. *Limited research techniques.* While beneficial advances are being made to speed the flow of research data, more remains to be done. Many problems are involved in the techniques available. It is difficult to devise good sampling plans and questionnaire outlines for telephone use, good return incentives for mailed forms and ways to get interviewers into enough homes fast enough for personal interviews. Good field control systems are difficult to maintain when the interview technique is pushed excessively for speed.

Technique problems, however, are solvable when adjusted to the needs of each firm and when innovation, money, *etc.*, is used. Greater latitude is permissible in the trajectory method as long as techniques are not changed too often, because prime value resides in data comparisons, not absolutes.

3. *Confidence limits.* Projecting from the string of plots on the graph is a hazardous task without statistical theory adequate for establishing practical confidence limits. Projecting from around any one point on the plot is possible, but to predict from the last two or three points causes difficulty. Figure 19-6, for example, shows what sometimes happens.

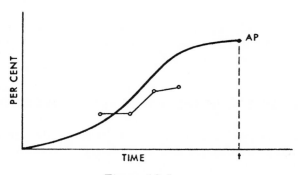

Figure 19-6.

The last point is probably significantly low as a separate point. It is probably not significantly low as a total of all four plots. What is the projection? On target, or off? Since the entire method is geared to making a projection for the ultimate goal or Accomplishment Parameter time period, statistical reliability must be heavily seasoned by judgment.

4. *Establishing confidence in the method.* Marketers are naturally and sensibly reluctant to put faith in a new research concept or method, and the trajectory approach is no exception. In the new product situation, emotional involvement of marketing managers compounds distrust. Months or years of effort go into developing new products and their marketing plans.

With most truly new products, customers usually must be educated, and "everyone knows this takes time." Therefore, the marketing manager is usually reluctant to accept the existence of a problem, or even worse, an abort situation even before the goal period has been reached. Almost without exception his first and natural reaction to a report predicting the eventual development of a key problem is to say, "It's too early for the advertising (or selling) to have taken effect; wait a few weeks and that curve will turn up."

These problems are common ones for the researcher, however, so no special handling is required. If the method produces reliable predictions, it will sell because good information is in the marketing manager's best interest.

5. *Securing the necessary thorough planning.* Not so easily solved, however, is the problem of inadequate planning related to *possible negative* events. In essence, the trajectory variables should cover every answer to the question, "What might happen to cause sales to fall significantly below the goal?"

To properly answer this question, the marketer must assume a negative point of view, a critical and suspicious posture. Since this answer is required at about the time top management is giving final, enthusiastic approval to the advertising, and some time after such items as packaging are locked in, the marketer is naturally reluctant to think of things which might go wrong. Nor can the researcher always prepare even a general list because he may not have known the inner fears or doubts of the marketing manager. The people planning the marketing effort and the product should specify possible problems themselves. To get them to do so will require persuasion and education.

Even after the list is prepared and narrowed to factors thought worthy of the money for trajectory study, a tough planning problem remains. Planned remedial actions and the statistical "triggers" for calling them into use must be specified. For instance, if it is felt that wide distribution is critical to sales success during the early period, what action would (or could) be taken to correct a distribution deficiency? And what distribution level at, say, ten weeks would be low enough to start this special program?

The more a marketing organization knows about the expected results of its efforts, the easier is the trajectory method; the less it knows, the tougher the method. Any group attempting to set trajectory goals will quickly uncover any area where knowledge is inadequate.

FUTURE NEEDS

This list of current problems in applying the trajectory theory of goal setting indicates future needs associated with this technique:

1. More widespread trial on diverse product types and on diverse audience types.

2. Better theories of trajectory shapes.

3. Better statistical tools, particularly to test the significance of variation below a trajectory.

4. Experimentation with mathematical manipulation of the total set of trajectories. Perhaps, if properly selected and weighted, the set could be merged into one summary trajectory whose purpose would be to assess not just one attribute of success, but total success.

5. Better data collecting procedures to reduce preparation and field time.

6. More case histories documenting successful use of the method, if such success is possible.

SUMMARY

This article has stressed the need for new research techniques if marketers are to enhance their skill in introducing new products. More is at stake on new products today, and the fate of each is sealed at an earlier time than before. The research ideal would seem to be to specify in advance the various actions and decisions that must be made by people in the market-place if the product is to succeed, then to devise research to measure these variables, starting at the time of launch. Problems should be identifiable before they happen, permitting planned remedial actions while there is still time to save the product.

The trajectory theory of goal setting embodies some of these ideas and has proved to be of practical value in at least one setting. Perhaps, with proper modification, it can have more widespread value.

THE NEW PRODUCT
DIFFUSION PROCESS
BY THOMAS S. ROBERTSON

THE NEW PRODUCT DIFFUSION PROCESS

Product innovation will be critical to survival and essential to growth for American firms in the decade of the 1970s. The pace of technological advances coupled with the American consumer's receptivity to progress and "newness" will shorten the life cycles of established products and place a premium on new products, although product obsolescence rates will continue to vary among industries and among product groups. In general, the less the commodity nature of the product group, or alternatively, the more the opportunity for product differentiation, then the more rapid is innovation and, concurrently, obsolescence.

WHAT IS A NEW PRODUCT?

The concern of this paper is with consumer acceptance of product innovations (new products). A major difficulty is in defining what is a new product and at least four definitional criteria have frequently been used: (1) newness from existing products, (2) newness in time, (3) newness in terms of sales penetration level, and (4) consumer newness to the product.

EDITOR'S NOTE: From *Marketing in a Changing World,* B. A. Morin, ed., 1969, pp. 80-86. Reprinted by permission of the American Marketing Association and the author.

Newness from Existing Products

Many authors argue that a "new product" must be *very different* from established products, although there is little attempt to make such a definition operational. The Federal Trade Commision has rendered an advisory opinion that a product may properly be called "new" "only when [it] is either entirely new or has been changed in a functionally significant and substantial respect. A product may not be called 'new' when only the package has been altered or some other change made which is functionally insignificant or insubstantial."[1]

E. B. Weiss claims that over 80% of new products are not, in fact, "new" but "simply modifications" of existing products.[2] He does not, however, establish guidelines for distinguishing such modifications from new products. It is possible to extend this point of view to the thesis that all new products are modifications or recombinations of existing items. Barnett, an anthropoligist who has studied innovation and its effects on cultural change, states that "No innovation springs full-blown out of nothing; it must have antecedents. ... "[3] This viewpoint, which is quite prevalent in sociological thinking, looks at innovation as the outcome of an evolutionary sequence. Even an innovation such as the computer can be considered to be a recombination of existing elements coupled with a measure of technological insight.

Newness in Time

Length of time on the market is a second criterion in defining a new product. There has been a pronounced tendency for firms to promote a product as new for as long as two or three years after introduction, under the assumption that the word "new" in advertising or on the package is a positive and desirable sales appeal. The Federal Trade Commission advisory opinion arbitrarily limits the use of the word new to six months after the product enters regular distribution after test marketing.[4]

Newness in Terms of Sales Penetration Level

Another new product definitional criterion is the sales level which the product has achieved. Bell[5] and Robertson,[6] for example, have arbitrarily defined products as innovations when they have not yet secured 10% of their total potential market.

Consumer Newness to the Product

Yet another criterion for defining a new product is that the consumer must *perceive* it to be new. There is, however, invariably some consumer who is "new' to the product and it is not particularly useful to talk in terms of any individual consumer; the aggregate consumer is generally what the marketer has in mind. Perhaps a product could be defined as new when a majority of consumers perceive it in such a way, but this is again arbitrary.

These definitions, unfortunately, need not yield the same determinations as to what products are new. For example, using the consumer perception of newness definition, an item can be new without being substantially different in function from existing products, without being particularly new to the market, and while possessing a significant sales penetration level. There is a further difficulty in the discussion to this point, and that is that a simple dichotomy is being used—a product is either new or not new. More logically a range of "newness" would be the case.

NEWNESS IN TERMS OF CONSUMPTION EFFECTS

The critical factor in defining a new product should be its effects upon established patterns of consumption. It is convenient to think in terms of: (1) continuous innovations, (2) dynamically continuous innovations, and (3) discontinuous innovations.

1. A *continuous* innovation has the least disrupting influence on established consumption patterns. Alteration of a product is almost always involved rather than the creation of a new product. Examples include: fluoride toothpaste, menthol cigarettes, and annual new-model automobile changeovers.

2. A *dynamically continuous* innovation has more disrupting effect than a continuous innovation, although it still does not generally involve new consumption patterns. It may mean the creation of a new product or the alteration of an existing product. Examples include: electric toothbrushes, electric hair curlers, and the Mustang automobile.

3. A *discontinuous* innovation involves the establishment of new consumption patterns and the creation of previously unknown products. Examples include: television, the computer, and the automobile.

This definitional framework, while recognizing that innovations are not all of the same order of newness, does not, unfortunately, distinguish new products from non-new products. It is my opinion that this decision is always arbitrary. It may be possible to agree that new sizes, new flavors, and new packages are not new products. Does, however, the addition of sugar to corn flakes or raisins to bran constitute a new product? Is an instant oatmeal a new product or a variation of the old product? No definition of innovation satisfactorily answers these and similar questions unless we rely on consumer perception and, as suggested, accept majority consumer opinion of what is and what is not an innovation.

MOST INNOVATION IS CONTINUOUS

Most innovation in the American economy is of a continuous nature. Most innovation, especially in the consumer sector, results as an attempt to differentiate products to increase market share. Few and far between are innovations of a discontinuous nature which significantly alter or create new consumption patterns. The image of innovations resulting from the inspiration of the occasional genius does not fit the typical occurrence and even discontinuous innovations are increasingly the result of planned team research. Most innovation today results from programmed, systematic research efforts.

Some Case Examples

If the first detergent on the market represented a fairly discontinuous innovation, then the succeeding proliferation of brands must represent highly continuous innovations. While one brand may be a low sudser, another possess cold water attributes, another contain bleach, and another contain disinfectant for baby clothes, all are essentially minor variations on the basic product. All of these succeeding brands are *programmed innovations.*

The automobile industry is the leading example of programmed, continuous innovations. New products appear on schedule each year and every three years major design changes occur. This planning and programming of innovation occurs across almost all industries. When a major aircraft manufacturer was considering its next venture into the commercial market, it plotted the various offerings then available in terms of such variables as runaway requirements, flying range, seating capacity, and cost of operation and found the gaps in the market. These gaps were in short-range jets and high-seating-capacity jets. The company then planned to innovate in one of these areas and did so.

THE IMPORTANCE OF INNOVATION TO THE FIRM

Innovation, according to a variety of sources, occurs due to: (1) shrinking profit margins for established products, (2) shorter lives for estanlished products, and (3) excess capacity. Schumpeter has attributed innovation to (4) a search for profit.[7] Barnett has emphasized (5) the pressure of competition and the search for product differentiation as factors leading to innovation.[8]

These reasons for occurrence of innovation overlap considerably. Analysis of their content also reveals their all-inclusive nature. Innovation, it would appear, is the solution to all business problems. Perhaps Schumpeter's view of innovation as a search for profit summarizes all of the other reasons; although corporate marketers generally cite growth, or forward momentum, as the most important factor encouraging new product development.

Maintaining Momentum

New products are basic to company growth and to profitability. It is seldom possible in today's economy to maintain momentum or even stability with innovations. Mattel Toymakers, for example, grew rapidly with the acceptance of Barbie Doll, but such growth could not be continued without other new products since Barbie Doll soon reached "maturity" on the product life cycle. It is also difficult to maintain profit margins when a product reaches maturity since competition intensifies and product advantages may be neutralized. The typical pattern in the food industry, for example, has been for profit margins to decline while sales are still increasing so that companies must quickly look to other new products for continued profit performance.[9]

Empirical Data

The contribution of new products to the sales growth of various industries has been researched by Booz, Allen & Hamilton, Inc. Expected growth from new products varies from 46% to as much as 100%, with an average of 75%. Innovating industries are also more likely to be high growth industries.[10]

In another study, Mansfield assessed the value of technological innovation to the growth and profitability of individual firms. His concern was with the acceptance of capital goods' innovations by firms of comparable initial size in the steel and petroleum refining industries. He concludes:

"In every interval and in both industries, the successful innovators grew more rapidly than the others, and in some cases, their average rate of growth was more than twice that of the others."[11]

INNOVATIVE COMPETITION

The importance of successfully marketing product innovations is today being recognized as never before. This is evidenced in the marketing trade magazines and academic journals as well as in the proliferation of consulting agencies devoted to new products and the establishment of new product divisions within existing agencies.

Yet, as more firms become commited to innovation, new product advantages exist for shorter time periods and the "monopoly" power of new products is soon overcome. When General Electric quickly followed Squibb into electric toothbrushes, for example, it added innovation to innovation by marketing a cordless version which was then a new usage concept. The new product marketplace is increasingly becoming more competitive as fairly simultaneous innovations often occur and imitation is indeed rapid. Many firms, such as Mattel Toymakers, prefer to jump from product tests to national marketing since test marketing often speeds imitation.

RISKS IN NEW PRODUCTS

Commitment to new products is not without serious problems and associated risks. Research and development expenditures for 1971 should approach $22.4 billion[12]—most of which will be spent on *unsuccessful* new product ideas. Based on responses from 51 prominent companies, Booz-Allen & Hamilton report that it takes almost 60 *ideas* to result in one commercially successful new product and that three-fourths of new product expense funds go to unsuccessful products.[13] These figures, however, must be treated as estimates only, especially since this is a sample of "prominent" companies and we can probably assume greater sophistication in the research and development process.

Buzzell and Nourse, in an extensive study of product innovation in the food industry, report that of every 1,000 new product ideas:

    810 are rejected at the idea stage
    135 are rejected on the basis of product tests
    12 are discontinued after test marketing
    43 are introduced to the market
    36 remain on the market after introduction[14]

According to these figures, food companies would appear to better the across-industry average reported by Booz-Allen & Hamilton. The Buzzell and Nourse figures suggest that over two successful new food products result from every 58 ideas.

New Product Failures

The greatest risk in new products and the greatest potential monetary loss comes at the market introduction stage. Estimates of new product failures run from 10% to 80%. This wide discrepancy in estimates is due largely to three reasons: (1) *definition* of what constitutes a new product—this is seldom stated; (2) *measurement* of what failure means—while one study may include only product withdrawals from the market, another may include all unprofitable or marginally profitable products. While one study may limit itself to measurement within one or two years of introduction, another may choose a considerably longer time span; and (3) the *sample of companies* chosen—large companies are likely to market fewer failures than small companies and companies in sophisticated consumer-oriented industries are likely to market fewer failures than companies in less sophisticated, production-oriented industries.

While it is difficult, therefore, to provide an average new product failure ratio which will uniformly apply, this failure rate can be quite high. It is probably fair to say that a majority of new products fail, although it would be more meaningful to present figures by *industry* if such figures could be obtained.

Why Do New Products Fail?

New product failures are seldom due to bad products. Analysis of the trade literature provides countless examples of basically sound new products failing after market introduction. General Foods failed with a Birds Eye line of frozen baby foods and rejected a forerunner of Instant Breakfast, Brim, in test markets. Ford Motor Company's Edsel is perhaps the classic example of a new product failure. Campbell proved unsuccessful in marketing fruit soup as well as a Red Kettle line of dry soup mixes. Coca-Cola, despite its strong consumer franchise in cola beverages, was initially unsuccessful in marketing a diet cola.

Reasons for new product failures could be discussed at length, but the foremost problem is in *marketing*. More tightly controlled test market and market experimentation procedures are necessary as well as a greater volume of marketing research in advance of new product introductions. Sophisticated models for predicting new product sales levels should be encouraged. The primary focus here, however, will not be on these concerns. It is the thesis of this paper that the probability of new product success can be increased by understanding the factors governing *diffusion* of new products, that is, acceptance by consumers.

NEW PRODUCT DIFFUSION

Diffusion is the process by which something spreads. Anthropologists have studied the diffusion of language, religion, and ideas among tribes and societies. Sociologists, particularly rural sociologists, have studied the diffusion of new ideas and new practices within societies. Physicists have studied the diffusion of atomic particles within elements. Marketers have implicitly studied diffusion for many years as they have sought to guide and control the spread of new products, but little research or conceptual thinking has been directed toward an understanding of the diffusion process itself.

The diffusion literature, as developed across a number of disciplines, offers for consideration a fairly well-developed theoretical framework which applies to the flow of information, ideas, and products. It is the integration of this framework with the traditional marketing framework which may advance our understanding of how new products disseminate and gain consumer acceptance and which may suggest means of improving new product marketing strategies.

Components of the Diffusion Process

The diffusion process can be conceptualized as: (1) the adoption, (2) of new products and services, (3) over time, (4) by consumers, (5) within social systems, (6) as encouraged by marketing activities.

Adoption refers to the use of a new item. *New products* and services will be considered in the broadest sense from highly continuous to highly discontinuous innovations. The *time* dimension distinguishes early adopters from later adopters. The *consumer adoption unit* may be the individual consumer or a family or buying committee, or even a city of consumers. *Social systems* constitute the boundaries within which diffusion occurs. In a broad sense the market segment as a whole can be viewed as a social system, or more narrowly defined, the consumer's friendship group can be considered his social system. Within these systems, communication will occur—both marketer-initiated and non-marketer-initiated. *Marketing activities* are defined as the mix of product, price, promotion, and distribution plans and strategies.

These several aspects of the diffusion process are interdependent. For example: the attributes of the new product will affect the rate of adoption over time, the types of consumers who will adopt, the kinds of social systems within which diffusion will take place, and the marketing efforts needed to achieve diffusion. Alternatively, successful new product diffusion is critically dependent upon the communication of relevant product information and the matching of new product attributes with social system and individual consumer characteristics. Marketing activities can guide and control, to a considerable extent, the rate and extent of diffusion.

EFFECTS OF MARKETING ACTIVITIES

The opportunities for marketing activities to affect the diffusion process *for a given new product* can be summarized as follows:

Social System

Marketing decisions can select the social systems (market segments) in which diffusion is most likely to be successful.

Promotion, pricing, and distribution strategies can be combined to reach specified social systems.

Marketing activities can, in some cases, chart the diffusion path within a social system to achieve the fastest rate of diffusion. This may be possible by reaching critical individuals first—especially innovators and opinion leaders.

Consumer Adopters

Marketing decisions can establish the consumer profile most likely to adopt the new product.

Promotion, pricing, and distribution strategies can be oriented toward this consumer profile.

Marketing activities can vary by penetration level to specifically reach different kinds of consumers. For example: advertising strategies to reach first adopters should usually be different than strategies to reach later adopters.

Product Meaning

Marketing activities can help define product meaning and can encourage diffusion by emphasizing the most relevant product attributes. For example: should promotion for a new dessert product emphasize taste, convenience, low cost, or low calorie content?

Time

Marketing activities can affect *rate* of diffusion. A low price, penetration strategy, a high level of promotional expenditures, free sampling and deal activity, and intensive distribution will generally all encourage a fast diffusion rate.

These opportunities will now be assessed briefly in turn.

Social System

The characteristics of a social system highly influence diffusion patterns for new products. This can be demonstrated by reference to a study by Graham who researched the diffusion of five innovations—television, canasta, supermarkets, Blue Cross, and medical service insurance—across social class levels. His research revealed that no single social class was consistently innovative in adopting all five innovations. Television, for example, diffused more quickly among low social classes while the card game canasta diffused more quickly among upper social classes.[15]

Graham argues that the critical factor in determining diffusion is the extent to which the attributes of the innovation are compatible with the attributes of the culture of the receiving social system. The "cultural equipment" required for the adoption of television, according to Graham, included an average education, a minimum income, and a desire for passive spectator entertainment. This cultural pattern coincided with a lower social class level.

Other researchers have distinguished between communities exhibiting modern versus traditional norms. The modern-oriented community is receptive to innovations while the tradition—oriented community relies on established ways of doing things. The norms in effect in a social system have a sizeable bearing on diffusion rates. This may vary by region of the country and from rural to urban areas.

Innovations may also diffuse at different rates within particular spheres of a social system. A number of studies shows that an innovation diffuses more quickly among socially integrated social system members than among socially isolated members. For some products, diffusion may be most rapid among older people.

The marketer has at his discretion the choice of social systems in which to market his product or in which to place heaviest support behind his product. This decision must be based on a matching between the attributes of the new product and social system attributes. Should segmentation be on the basis of social class, ethnic group, age, or ecology? Given the selection the most relevant social systems, what are the most appropriate promotional, distribution, and pricing strategies to reach these social systems? Finally, is it possible to initiate strategies to reach the most likely buyers within a social system? While this is frequently possible in industrial selling, it is seldom possible in reaching ultimate consumers.

Consumer Adopters

Ultimately, diffusion is dependent upon the individual consumer. He must decide whether adoption of the new product is the appropriate course of action for him. The adoption process refers to the mental sequence of stages through which the consumer passes in arriving at an acceptance (adoption) or rejection decision. It can be conceptualized as awareness, knowledge, liking, preference, conviction, and adoption, although other conceptualizations are also available.

Considerable research evidence indicates that communication sources are not equally effective at different stages of the adoption process. While *advertising* generally has greatest impact at the earlier stages of awareness, knowledge, and liking, the consumer seeks more objective, evaluative information at the later stages of preference and conviction and *personal influence* (word-of-mouth) often becomes the dominant communication source. This, of course, varies by product and holds most when the consumer perceives a good amount of risk in buying. The important point is that a purchase decision results from the cumulative impact of a number of communication sources and the marketer must attempt to move consumers through an entire sequence of information needs

Not all consumers within a social system have an equal initial propensity toward buying a new product and consumers adopt at different points in time. The earliest buyers, the "innovators," have generally been found to possess different characteristics from later adopters. (A discussion of innovator characteristics is provided by Charles W. King in a paper following this one). An initial goal before marketing a new product should be to establish the profile of the most likely consumer innovators. It may then be possible to design marketing activities in line with this profile. As the innovator level of diffusion is achieved, marketing strategies should then be re-oriented to reach later buyers.

Product Meaning

Extent of a new product's diffusion and its rate of diffusion are, of course, largely a function of the particular attributes of the product. The emphasis given particular attributes and the overall brand image created are critical marketing decision areas.

There are several attribute classification schemes to account for differential diffusion rates. Rogers proposes a set of five characteristics of innovations which he believes are generally relevant. These characteristics are: (1) relative advantage, (2) compatibility, (3) complexity, (4) divisibility, and (5) communicability.[16]

Relative advantage is the degree to which an innovation is superior to the product it supersedes or with which it will compete. While the addition of fluoride to toothpaste was considered to add extra product value, many other ingredients had previously been added to toothpaste without the consumer attaching relative advantage to the resulting "new" product. A dominant marketing management function is product differentiation to encourage the consumer to perceive greater product value.

Compatibility refers to how consistent the new product is with existing ways of doing things. The greater the need for consumers to restructure their thinking and to engage in new forms of behavior, the less quickly the item is likely to diffuse.

Complexity refers to the degree of difficulty in understanding and using the new product. In general, the more complex the item, the slower its rate of diffusion and the narrower its potential market.

Divisibility refers to the extent to which a new product may be tried on a limited scale. In-store sampling of a new food product and marketing of small sizes take account of the divisibility factor.

Communicability is the degree to which word of the new product may readily be communicated to others. Conspicuous products, such as clothes, are highest on communicability.

The important point is how these characteristics are *perceived* by consumers since this is what governs response. In summary form, it can be hypothesized that rate of diffusion is positively related to relative advantage, compatibility, divisibility, and communicability, but negatively related to complexity.

Diffusion rates of technological innovations among firms have been studied by Mansfield, who hypothesizes as follows:

1. Profitability of an innovation relative to others that are available will increase the rate of adoption.

2. The larger the investment required, assuming equally profitable innovations available, the slower the rate of adoption.

3. The type of industry will affect the rate of adoption depending on its aversion to risk, market competitiveness, and financial health.[17]

Considerable work remains to be done relating innovation attributes to diffusion rates and further relating innovation attributes to consumer characteristics. For example, to the extent that a product is high on complexity, this may suggest a slower rate of diffusion, but does this also suggest a certain kind of consumer adopter? Also, when is a product attribute important? Relative advantage may be irrelevant for fashion items and for many fad items since their adoption is largely related to the perception of *newness itself* rather than to better functional performance. Diffusion patterns for fashion and fad products show a much more accelerated growth and an equally accelerated decline phenomenon.

Time

The business firm in general wishes to shorten the diffusion time span consistent with profit maximization objectives. At times it may be desirable to gain maximum short-run penetration, while at other times a more deliberate segmentation strategy, often on the basis of price, may be followed. A strategy of maximum diffusion need not be most profitable. It is probably a fair generalization, however, that maximum diffusion (market share) is the goal for most new products. This is especially true for continuous and dynamically continuous innovations and less true for discontinuous innovations.

In a penetration strategy, maximum diffusion is sought as quickly as possible. Price tends to be set relatively low; promotion will lean heavily toward mass advertising; and intensive distribution will be used. This strategy is most necessary if little product differentiation exists for the new product and, therefore, demand is highly elastic. This strategy is also necessary if competitors are likely to introduce similar new product offerings within a fairly short period of time, despite the continuity or discontinuity of the innovation. Rapid diffusion may discourage competition, although it could also have an encouraging effect when high sales are

noted—especially if the estimated potential market is large. More importantly, however, rapid diffusion will often lead to a large and brand loyal
consumer franchise which is crucial to continuing sales success given the
subsequent entry of competition.

A penetration strategy has implications as to the shape of the diffusion
curve and encourages high acceleration. In fact, in a number of cases for
new convenience *brands,* the diffusion curve is far from S-shaped. In the
pre-sweetened cereal market and in the detergent market, for example, a
new brand (because of concentrated advertising and deal activity at
introduction) may attain its maximum life cycle sales within a matter of a
month and then settle down to a lower "maturity" level of sales. It is critical
to remember that a varying proportion (sometimes very high) of beginning
sales may be for *trial* purposes and need not represent *adoption,* defined in
terms of acceptance and commitment to the brand as reflected in repeat
purchases. A company must quickly determine its trial-adoption ratio or it
can be misled into expanding production for never-to-be-realized repeat
sales.

In a sales staging strategy, the typical progression is from generally high
"skim the cream" pricing to relatively lower prices, from selective distribution to intensive distribution, and from limited promotion to expanded or
mass promotion. Such a strategy is more likely to be successful for specialty
and durable items and is generally dependent upon a differentiated product
and one which competition cannot readily duplicate. The somewhat
discontinuous innovation allows, in effect, a certain degree of monopoly
power.

DuPont's "Corfam" shoe material was marketed using the sales staging
strategy. It was deliberately introduced to manufacturers of quality shoe
products before being made available on a mass basis. Management
apparently felt that maximum long-run diffusion for the product would be
gained if it was not perceived as a cheap substitute for leather but instead
as a quality improvement over leather. DuPont, therefore, by its choice of
manufacturers to whom the product was made available, was governing
intensity of distribution and pricing and extent of manufacturer advertising.

It is interesting to note that the marketer's diffusion strategy very much
influences the shape of the diffusion curve. By the same token, however, the
selection of a strategy is a function of the type of product and the
competitive situation. A penetration or sales staging strategy must be based
on accurate assessment of future market acceptance. Wasson, for example,
argues that color television marketers unsuccessfully followed a penetration
strategy for their products when sales to support such a strategy were not
forthcoming. They misjudged rate of market acceptance and should have
been following a sales staging strategy with selective distribution, relatively
high price, and limited promotion until the growth segment of the diffusion
process was attained.[18] We must also take cognizance of the fact that while
a dichotomy of ideal types makes for expository efficiency, a considerable
range of strategies between staging and penetration is available to the firm.

CONCLUSION

It is essentially an arbitrary decision as to what is and what is not a new product. Most "new products" on the market today, however, involve only minor changes in consumption patterns; they are of a highly *continuous* nature. Such products are the result of programmed product differentiation.

The critical value of innovation to a firm is demonstrated in many industries where over 50% of sales growth is coming from new products. Yet, the risk of new product failures is high and it is probably fair to say that a *majority* of products which are introduced to the market fail. Furthermore, these failures are seldom due to a technically unsound product but instead are largely the result of poor marketing performance.

It is the conclusion of this paper, however, that the probability of new product success can be increased by understanding the diffusion process. Successful new product diffusion is dependent upon the communication of relevant product information and the matching of new product attributes with social system and individual consumer attributes. Marketing strategies can guide and control, to a considerable extent, the rate and extent of new product diffusion.

NOTES

1. This case is developed using modified actual data from the author's experience, but disguised to hide the identify of the real product.

2. Since in the actual situation there were additional potential problems, other variables were also selected for study; these were less critical and are omitted here.

3. This was for each of two groups . . . (1) general practice (G.P.) dentists and (2) specialists in this area of dentistry, prosthodontic dentists. To keep the four-week totals, each week the new 100 calls were added, the oldest 100 calls dropped, and the data plotted as of the most recent date. It would have been more accurate to plot at the midpoint of the four-week period, but it became customary in the firm to speak of the new product's status as of a particular week, so it was more convenient to plot at are end of the period. Since the trajectories suffer the same distortion, comparisons are of like data.

4. In case this seems high, there was an incentive for the retailer to respond, a small merchandise gift.

5. A Philadelphia medical marketing research firm, Lea Associates, has conducted monthly sutdies of physicans for all important new drug products for several years. Each product is on the form for several months. From these studies medical marketers have excellent data for setting trajectories. Perhaps similar research operations are used in other industries. If not, they might be considered.

6. A marketing consultant who helped set up these trajectory curves and methods for their analysis, felt the proper curve for awareness should be a learning curve rather than a growth curve, but there was never enough budget to increase interviews during the first few weeks to find out. Since this early period is not critical from a marketing point of view, the issue was never resolved.

7. For this type of product, repeated study has shown a distinct leveling at about ten weeks. Later, the curve may go up, or down, or just wander around for months.

8. The curve's equation is standard for a growth curve, being a fourth-order polynomial. Substituting the givens into the equation and converting each Y to a percent of the ultimate goal (AP), yields the latter equation which has only one unknown: x (weeks). Thus, for a point at, say, eight weeks, substituting 8 for x yields .96, meaning that the IAP is then 96 percent of what it will be at ten weeks.

9. Federal Trade Commission, "Permissible Period of Time During which New Product May be Described as 'New,' " *Advisory Opinion Digest*, No. 120, April 15, 1967.

10. E. B. Weiss, "That Malarky about 80% of New Products Failing," *Advertising Age*, Vol. 36, August 2, 1965, p. 101.

11. Homer G. Barnett, *Innovation: The Basis of Cultural Change*, New York, McGraw-Hill, 1953, p. 181.

12. Same reference as footnote 9.

13. William E. Bell, "Consumer Innovators: A Unique Market for Newness," in *Proceedings of the American Association Marketing Association*, ed. Stephen A. Greyser, Chicago, 1963, pp. 85-95.

14. Thomas S. Robertson, "Determinants of Innovative Behavior," in *Proceedings of the American Marketing Association*, ed. Reed Moyer, Chicago, 1967, pp. 328-332.

15. Joseph A. Schumpeter, *Business Cycles*, New York, McGraw-Hill Book Company, Inc., 1939, Vol. 1, p. 97.

16. Same reference as footnote 11 at p. 73.

17. Robert D. Buzzell and Robert Nourse, *Product Innovation in Food Processing: 1954-1964*, Boston, Division of Research Harvard Business School, 1967.

18. Booz, Allen & Hamilton, Inc., *Management of New Products*, New York, 1965.

19. Edwin Mansfield, "Entry, Gibrat's Law, Innovation, and the Growth of Firms," *American Economic Review*," Vol. 52, December, 1962, pp. 1023-1051, at p. 1036.

20. "Research: The Cash Pours Out Research and Development," *Business Week*, 2020, May 18, 1968, pp 72-74.

21. Same reference as footnote 18.

22. Same reference as footnote 17 at p. 105 and p. 124.

23. Saxon Graham, "Class and Conservatism in the Adoption of Innovations," *Human Relations*, Vol. 9, 1956, pp. 91-100.

24. Everett M. Rogers, *Diffusion of Innovations*, New York, The Free Press, 1962, Chapter 5.

25. Edwin Mansfield, "Technical Change and the Rate of Imitation," *Econometrica*, Vol. 29, October, 1961, pp. 741-766.

26. Chester R. Wasson, "How Predictable Are Fashion and Other Product Life Cycles?" *Journal of Marketing*, Vol. 32, July, 1968, pp. 36-43.

ADDITIONAL SELECTED BIBLIOGRAPHY

New Directions with New Products

Arndt, J., "Role of Product-Related Conversations in the Diffusion of a New Product," *Journal of Marketing Research*, Vol. 4 No. 3 (August, 1967), 291-295.

Claycamp, H.J., and Liddy, L.E., "Prediction of New Product Performance: An Analytical Approach," *Journal of Marketing Research*, Vol. 6, No. 4 (November, 1970), 474-482.

Day, G.S., "Using Attitude Change Measures to Evaluate New Product Introductions," *Journal of Marketing Research*, Vol. 7, No. 4 (November, 1970), 474-482.

Hamburg, M. and Atkins, R.J., "Computer Model for New Product Demand," *Harvard Business Review*, Vol. 45, No. 2 (March-April, 1967), 107-115.

Heimann, C. S., "Managing New Products in a Changing Market," *Journal of Marketing*, Vol. 26, No. 1 (January, 1962), 23-27.

Lipstein, B., "Modelling and New Product Birth," *Journal of Advertising Research,* Vol. 10, No. 5 (October, 1970), 3-11.

Mills, H.D., "Dynamics of New Product Campaigns," *Journal of Marketing,* Vol. 28, No. 4 (October, 1964), 60-63.

Robertson, T. S., *"Consumer Innovators: The Key to New Product Success,"* *California Management Review,* Vol. 10, No. 2 (Winter, 1967), 23-30.

Tull, D.S., "The Relationship of Actual and Predicted Sales and Profits in New-Product Introductions," *The Journal of Business,* Vol. 40, No. 3 (July, 1967), 233-250.

Urban G.L., "A Mathematical Modeling Approach to Product Line Decisions," *Journal of Marketing Research,* Vol. 16, No. 1 (February, 1969), 40-47.

Questions for Discussion and Review

1. Describe some recent developments in the statistical analysis of attitude panels toward evaluating a new product marketing program.

2. What is a new product diffusion?

3. How do consumer innovators play a role in the successful introduction of a new product?

4. Why are Bayesian statistics important in the successful introduction of a new product?

5. What importance is given the forecasting of sales and profits of new products?

INDEX